Taransay

Key

1 Blackpipe beach
2 Camping beach
3 Sheep base
4 Natural cave
5 Bothy
6 Standing Stone
7 Dunn Loch with children's raft
8 Eagle Golden
9 Campfire by two black houses
10 Wrecked deck and big buoy
11 Black house
12 Deer
13 Dunes overlooking the spit
14 Cave with cormorant's nest
15 Ben Raah
16 Ben Uidha or Inka Ra
17 Paible (the entire living area)
18 Taransay's only trees
19 Buoy Creek
20 Raft
21 Landing craft – carrying supplies,
   sheep, wood, peat and visitors
22 The Rib – belonging to Angus and
   carrying post and light supplies
23 Diving gannet
24 Shags nesting on the rocks
25 The Gorge

Sheila Jowers 9. 2000

CASTAWAY

The Full, Inside Story of the Major TV Series

Mark McCrum

EBURY PRESS

DEDICATION

For the castaways. This is your book, don't shoot messenger.

First published in Great Britain in 2000

1 3 5 7 9 10 8 6 4 2

© Lion Television Limited, 2000

Mark McCrum has asserted his right under the Copyright, Designs and
Patents Act 1988 to be identified as the author of this work.

Castaway 2000 is a Lion Television Scotland production for BBC Scotland

Ebury Press
Random House · 20 Vauxhall Bridge Road · London SW1V 2SA

Random House Australia Pty Limited
20 Alfred Street · Milsons Point · Sydney · New South Wales 2061 · Australia

Random House New Zealand Limited
18 Poland Road · Glenfield · Auckland 10 · New Zealand

Random House (Pty) Limited
Endulini · 5A Jubilee Road · Parktown 2193 · South Africa

The Random House Group Limited Reg. No. 954009

www.randomhouse.co.uk

Papers used by Ebury Press are natural, recyclable products
made from wood grown in sustainable forests.

A CIP catalogue record for this book is available from the British Library.

ISBN 0 09 187500 5

Text illustrations by Sheila Jowers
Designed by Lovelock & Co.
Printed and bound in Great Britain

Contents

Acknowledgements

First of all I must thank the castaways, who from the outset made me welcome on the island and willingly shared their thoughts and, in some cases, letters and diaries with me. I offer special tributes here to Mike Laird, whose comprehensive daily journal of the year was absolutely key to my understanding of what went on; Julie Lowe, whose monthly circulars home provided an always-entertaining overview; Peter Jowers, who generously allowed me to quote from his entertaining and incisive letters to his mother; Roger and Rosemary Stephenson, who gave me their always interesting angle in regular private letters; and Padraig Nallen, who opened up the riches of his secret Irish website. Others offered individual letters, short writings, poems etc – for all of which I was profoundly grateful. I must also thank those who never made it to the island, but agreed to be interviewed about the selection process: Robert Hicks and Jack Holden. And those who left early: Ray Bowyer for yielding up his daily diary and keeping me in touch with his off-island experiences; and Ron Copsey, for spilling the beans in the Harris Hotel.

Next, thanks to the team at Lion TV – Jeremy Mills, Chris Kelly, Shahana Meer, Paul Overton, Elaine Paterson, Becci White, Kate Abernethy and all – who were always free and frank with their interviews, organised my trips back and forth to the island with efficiency, provided prompt answers to numerous tedious questions, supplied me with overnight videotape deliveries, and generally made the author's life much easier than it could have been. Cynthia McVey was more than just a 'tellydemic' introducing me to the Glasgow curry scene and phoning frequently with the latest news. Architect Andy McAvoy was open and helpful, making time for me in the middle of his hectic January whirl. At Random House, editor Hannah MacDonald encouraged and cut with equal skill. Agent Julian Alexander's honey-tongued pitch got me involved in the first place, for which I can barely forgive him. Amanda Baytham's transcripts-on-wheels service saved my bacon. Girlfriend Leonie Edwards-Jones only freaked out occasionally as the flat became ever more buried in videotapes and paper. A big thanks to all.

Author's note

Much of this story is presented in the spoken and written words of the participants in the *Castaway 2000* project. Particularly with material from video diaries and taped interviews, I have edited, often substantially. I have tried always to remain scrupulously true to the original sense, as I understood it, and only hope that I have not misrepresented any of the points of view, observations or attitudes expressed. If I have, I can only apologise.

Prologue

Silent Night

November 3 2000

The sky was clear last night and the stars brilliant above us. Incredibly for the island the air was so still the windmill had stopped turning.

'Remember the Ts on night,' called Roger through the darkness. 'It's four, five, six, T. Silent night. The only other thing is ...'

The Castaway choir, a disparate group of fourteen or so, barely visible against the silhouetted hulk of the schoolhouse, took their orders and tried again. The famous carol rang out across the water. Did the music, I wondered, reach those four glimmering orange lights across the strait in Harris? When the singers finished, the only sound for a second or two was that of the waves lapping into the dark treble crescent of seaweed on the beach below. Then; 'Did you see that shooting star?' cried Philiy, and a more general chatter and laughter began. The light came on in the schoolhouse, songsheets were handed in, many of the group headed back over the frost-covered field towards the steading kitchen for tea and toast. Others returned to their individual pods for something stronger – in my case it was Tanya's rice and raisin wine, which tasted something like saki, considerably nicer than the last lot of Castaway homebrew I'd tried.

They've come a long way since January, the community, they really have. Later, as I lay awake I thought back to the site then, over-run with builders trying to get the project ready, while the national press mocked inaccurately from afar. As for the castaways, fifteen of them were sleeping huggermugga in the schoolhouse, while others refused to come over till their dwellings were habitable. Then, being self-sufficient was just a dream. Now, apart from a few imported solid foods – sugar, flour, oats, etc – it's a reality.

The combination of windmill and hydro gives them all the power they need to heat their showers, light their rooms (even operate their TV cameras). Their waste disappears into compost toilets, while grey water passes through a cleansing reedbed system into the sea. In their polytunnels and the field they've fenced off from the marauding Taransay deer, they've grown enough vegetables not just to feed themselves, but to sell on neighbouring Harris. Last weekend, their Castaway veggie stall, manned by a local, made over £240. Their cows provide daily milk, and their hens eggs. Their chickens and pigs and lambs, born on the island during the year, provide all the meat they need.

And when you wander round the community, sitting in pods (as their little rooms are called) chatting, observing, you realise what a journey they've all been on individually too. They've learnt so much. Painter and decorator Colin is now a trained butcher; management consultant Liz knows how to grow everything from spuds to coriander; city girl Julie can milk a cow. Pensions analyst Toby has 'grasped the basics of Spanish', care assistant Trish has started writing children's stories, insurance analyst Mike is painting watercolours. But more key perhaps than the practical skills are the less obvious life-lessons that have come, *force majeure*, out of the bizarre psychological hothouse they're created for themselves on this island.

'I'm slower to express opinions than I was,' says West Country lecturer Peter Jowers, who has found himself the focus of a good deal of flak during the developing year. 'Now I try and hold off till I can see the more complex picture. I've also realised people are far more sensitive than you'd give them credit for.' 'Psychologically I've been tested,' says castaway camerawoman Tanya Cheadle, who has had a near-impossible role, recording the twists and turns of the story without taking sides or getting involved. 'I've faced a wide range of challenges, met them, and come out stronger.' Almost all of them talk about having become more tolerant of others. As for their attitudes to themselves, the time to reflect and come to terms with their own faults and foibles has reduced two of them to near breakdowns, but for most it has clearly been invaluable.

For many of them this will mean big life changes when they go home. castaway butcher Colin and wife Julia don't see how they could ever go back to their old world of supermarket queues, traffic jams, telephones ringing, 'just the mania of everyday life'. Next year they're taking daughter Natasha travelling, then they'll look for some kind of community or homestead life. Tammy Huff, meanwhile, definitely wants to go back to something more than the secretarial work she was doing before – not sure what, but TV presenting would be a dream. She'll also be moving out of her parents' home and finding a place of her own. Lancashire postal worker Pat and wife Gwyneth Murphy are seriously thinking of settling on adjacent Harris.

It's been, they all agree, an extraordinary year. For many, it wasn't what they signed up for or imagined, but none-the-less, they all say, they wouldn't have missed it. As the community has struggled fairly accurately through Tuckman's famous theory of group formation 'Forming, Storming, Norming, Performing', it has grappled with dilemmas and situations beyond the bizarre.

Some of these have been created by the fact that this was a TV project, observing and documenting itself even as it tried to develop and cohere; others, by the changing nature of that project. Originally planned as a community that was 'cast away' from society, the 'cross-section of society' aroused extraordinary interest in the press, which was then encouraged by the BBC's decision to provide a rolling documentary of the year as it happened. The result being that the Castaways have had to face challenges that had more to do with surviving the excesses of the contemporary media and PR worlds than of the weather – with first journalists, then whisky companies and finally pop bands landing on their beach.

For all the disagreements and upsets that these hurdles have caused the community, there has been a huge amount of camaraderie and fun too, much of it off-camera. The kids' enjoyment of their vast but safe open air playground; the adults growing love for the beautiful island all now unselfconsciously call 'home'. The ready-made social life, from tensely competitive games of Scrabble in the steading to wild parties in the schoolhouse or pods. The endless gossip, which became the most popular pastime of all, as the 'castaways' struggled to come to terms with the increasing weirdness of their reality.

Whenever I've turned up on the island, I've usually wished I could stay longer, am usually envious of some events just passed or just about to come. This last week I just missed Hallowe'en, where the kids, in costumes they've spent the last six weeks making, were led trick or treating round the pods by Tammy and Warren. Jules and Trish dressed up as ghosts, Peter put on his mad Monk outfit, all had gifts or surprises to offer. Later, the community retired to the steading and, surrounded by grinning candlelit pumpkins told ghost stories to each other over a spooky supper. And tonight, it's Ben's birthday and once again the whole community will have crafted hand-made presents – this morning I saw young Jodene's hilarious 'Ben-in-a-bottle', with a model of the tabloids' darling (and his dog) made from matchsticks and plasticine. And in a way I'd much rather be over there, however poisonous the nettle wine is, however smelly and uncomfortable the compost toilet is, however freezing it is at night in Ray's empty pod – than here, alone with a malt in the warm and comfortable bar of the Harris Hotel.

But each time I pull myself away from the mad and magical island, I know I could never have written this book by staying all year. Even in two days you find yourself getting sucked into the latest drama (as I write – whether or not the BBC should install a webcam to produce occasional glimpses of the island on the website in the last few weeks of the project). It's too easy to take sides and get far too involved in the ever-lively local politics, which the Castaways always individually tell you they wish would go away, but somehow just can't seem to help feeding.

On the island they nicknamed me 'the detective', and as I sat in London, poring over my notes and the video diary transcripts, reading letters and diaries, watching as much as I could of the over 500 hours of footage, piecing together the story, I began txo think they were right.

Whatever else, after travels on five continents, it's certainly one of the oddest tales I've ever come across …

Mark McCrum
Harris, Scotland, November 2000

Chapter 1

MM Eve

It was New Year's Eve 1999 and at midnight a new millennium began. On Pitt Island in the South Pacific, the first populated place on earth to greet the new dawn, they danced in a woolshed. In Sydney, Australia, they watched as fireworks illuminated a floating parade of eighteen giant sea-creatures at the centre of an armada of five thousand small boats. On South Africa's Robben Island, Nelson Mandela lit a massive candle. In Giza, Egypt, an enormous laser image of Pharaoh Ramses II was projected onto the Pyramid of Chepren. In Paris, fireworks blazed from the Eiffel Tower as a huge scoreboard counted out *le dernier jour*. In Times Square, New York, they celebrated each of the world's twenty-four millennial hours with lasers, fireworks and performances by a troupe of five hundred dancers and musicians, saving the confetti blizzard and the drop of a big ball made of Waterford Crystal for their own magnificent midnight.

In London, despite queues of disgruntled VIPs held up by security personnel at Stratford tube station, ten thousand joined the Queen and Prime Minister Tony Blair in the Millennium Dome to sing Auld Lang Syne, while outside by the river millions watched 'the world's biggest ever' fireworks display and waited in vain for a much-heralded River of Fire to appear. In Birmingham, the Inner Ring Road was taken over by a funfair as Sir Cliff Richard starred at a concert in the National Indoor Arena. In Cardiff, the City Hall was transformed into an 'intergalactic cocktail lounge'. In Newcastle a 130ft Chinese dragon waddled across the Tyne Bridge. In Edinburgh, the Bay City Rollers led the crowds shangalanging 'Bye, Bye Baby' to the last thousand years.

Meanwhile, on the remote Scottish island of Taransay, an altogether smaller group were partying. Their windy bonfire marked not just the Eve, but the first night of a year-long experiment in community living, which was to be filmed for a television series – *Castaway 2000* – in itself a 'landmark show' for the new millennium. Ironically, despite the presence of the cameras, they had no actual TV to watch all those other celebrations of that magical moment when the BBC's Latin datemark MCMXCIX finally became MM.

Not including the production team from Lion Television (who were making the programmes for the BBC) there were twenty-eight adult 'castaways' present that night, drawn from a wide range of backgrounds and occupations. There was a microbiologist from Hampshire; a retired builder from Manchester; a dinner lady and her postal worker husband from Lancashire; a pupil support assistant from Scarborough; a carpenter and his wife from Birmingham; an art college teacher and her university lecturer husband from Gloucestershire; a doctor and his ex-journalist wife from Devon; a stockbrokers' coordinator from Surrey; a brickie turned driving instructor from Birkenhead; a foster carer from Cheltenham and her painter and decorator husband; a care assistant from the Isle of Man; a pensions analyst from Leeds; a telesales operative from Dublin; a photography graduate from Cheshire; a sculptor and his teacher partner, a management consultant and her sales manager boyfriend, an insurance analyst, a trainee psychotherapist, a journalist and a television director – all from different parts of London. There were also eight children, ranging in age from eleven to two.

The group had been selected, in the words of Jeremy Mills, executive producer of *Castaway 2000*, as 'a microcosm of British society'. From over four thousand applications, he and series producer Chris Kelly, assisted by a team of experts, had chosen a collection of people to be – in the words of the BBC press release that had got the ball rolling a year before – 'cast adrift to fend for themselves for a whole year'. But already, on Night One, things were not going quite according to plan.

Sardines

'This was my fantasy,' says Julia Corrigan, forty-two-year-old foster carer from Cheltenham. 'We were going to jump out of the landing craft and run up the beach going, "Oh, wow! Look at this fantastic island!" Then we were all going to run into our rooms and shout, "Gosh, have you seen the view from the window!" But actually none of that happened at all.'

The central communal area of the castaways' site, the farmstead's renovated cattleshed (in local Hebridean parlance 'the steading'), had been cleared by the volunteers for the celebration of Millennium Eve. Julia had imagined that there would have been time to decorate the place properly and make lots of party food. 'The steading was going to be all glowing with lights and we'd all be dressed up and wearing hats and things. But in reality,' she continues, 'the beginning of the party was so limp it was unbelievable. There just seemed to be one row of chairs radiating out from the stove into this open space, and people were sat around in their huge coats and gloves drinking a can of beer and just looking really down and miserable. Then some food was cooked, but it was a joke, because the stove wasn't getting hot, so they had to cook two chickens separately. Then, when the first was done, everyone came in like savages, ripped it to bits and ran off with it – or one sausage each. We didn't sit down together, and it wasn't until nearly midnight that people had had enough to drink. Then they rallied round and jumped up and down and looked a bit happy, but it was sheer determination, really. "We will bloody well enjoy ourselves," was the attitude.'

At midnight, Paul Overton, the assistant producer from Lion TV, handed out the champagne. 'Shake this up and spray it around,' he told the castaways. 'So we did,' Julia laughs, 'and I was terrified of taking the cork out because I'd shaken it like mad and I thought it would poke somebody's eye out – but it all just stayed in the bottle. Even that didn't behave itself.'

Part of the problem was the crippling flu bug that had spread from a couple of the castaways on the coach journey up to Scotland to affect almost half the group. A somewhat different Julie, Julie Lowe, a thirty-six-year-old redundant stockbrokers' coordinator from Surrey, was one of seven 'laid out like sardines' that night in the front room of the settlement's little farmhouse (known as the MacKay House after the family that owned the island). In a letter home she wrote: 'Everybody, ill or not, needs to be over to the island for New Year's Eve. It's horrible. There's a sick room – seven of us on the floor on thin, narrow, damp, filthy, ex-flophouse-looking mattresses, stained with I don't even want to speculate what. A pathetic fire in the grate, made of grey concrete and coal dust lumps, gives off neither heat nor cheering flame. I shiver and ache and wish I was somewhere else. One by one, we get up, slip outer clothes over our damp sweaty thermals and feel our way across the dark field to the steading for the party. It all looks very pretty in a surreal, feverish kind of way. There are fairy lights. There's a lot of bonhomie. We desperately want all to be well. We put on our party smiles and manners and try and drown the bug with alcohol. Our cameraman, Roy, has made a killer punch. If there is any justice in the world, that bug will have died a heroic death this night! After the bonfire, the fireworks, the bells and the speeches, I slip away back to my bed, but alas not to sleep!'

In all, including a selection of cameramen, producers, researchers and their partners and children, thirty-six were crammed into the little three-up, two-down MacKay House that night. But the overcrowding was the result of a problem more significant than mere flu: the castaways' settlement was not yet fully built. Logistical and planning troubles, exacerbated by the worst winter weather the

Hebrides had seen in thirty years, meant that the castaways' specially designed individual 'pods' were still under construction, a fact that many of them had only fully realised when they'd set foot on the island just hours earlier.

Most upset, undoubtedly, about this state of affairs was Roger Stephenson, 44, the Devon GP who had signed up to act as the project's doctor. He had already turned down the emergency bunkhouse accommodation provided by Lion TV for the castaways on mainland Harris and checked in with his family to the more comfortable surroundings of the Harris Hotel in the little port of Tarbert. 'It had by then become absolutely clear,' he says, 'that everything was not ready. So we were very reluctant to go over at all, because we knew what we were going to see. But we were persuaded to go for the party. And given that that was in the evening, we had to stay overnight. So we choppered across late that morning and mulled around doing not very much – I screwed a kit table together, that sort of thing. But we were brassed off that this wasn't at all what we had envisaged – a community starting that night. That was a complete fantasy. We were already going to be a splintered community, because of differing people's needs.'

Roger's wife, ex Reuters journalist Rosemary, 36, was more specific in her complaint. 'The island just wasn't safe for children,' she recalls. 'It was a building site. There were bits of broken glass everywhere. From the very beginning of this project our bottom line had been that we wanted privacy, a room for our family, access to a toilet, we wanted to be able to wash.'

The couple discussed the situation with the other families. Having spent months winding down their normal lives, packing belongings and treats for a year into a single crate each, travelling several hundred miles north on long and often uncomfortable journeys, this unexpected chaos – on Millennium Eve of all nights – was shocking and unsettling. 'It was patently obvious,' says Roger, 'that this place was completely impossible to live in.' Julia Corrigan agreed. 'I was really desperately upset,' she recalls, 'that what we'd been promised wasn't there.' 'You could see things weren't ready,' says Monica Latore, another mother taking a small child on the project, 'so we were all fighting about where we were going to sleep that night. The cameramen were bagging beds in the MacKay House and we went mad. "Look," we said, "you can't expect us to sleep in a place with kids where there's no loo. If the kids want to go to the loo in the middle of the night what do you do? Go out in the raging wind and walk across to the steading?" In the end we kicked them out and took over the house ourselves, but there were twelve of us in one room.'

The families agreed to stay for the party and decamp the next morning.

Though in the long term this move was to prove hugely significant for the coherence of the community, the decision in itself didn't cause a rift with those castaways, mostly single people, who had decided, illness and living conditions notwithstanding, to remain on Taransay. 'I actually felt sorry for the families,' says Ray Bowyer, the retired Mancunian builder who, at 58, was the oldest man in the group. 'They all kept asking me what I would do and I told them not to fetch the kids to this island in the state it's in, because I wouldn't have fetched mine, it was a death trap.'

Something-or-Other Destiny

By no means all the castaways shared Julia Corrigan's disappointment or Roger and Rosemary's despondent mood. Even Julia's husband Colin, the Cheltenham painter and decorator who had already been on the island for ten days before Christmas, helping with the building in an 'advance party', was still wildly enthusiastic. 'He nearly drove me bonkers,' says Julia. 'I just wanted him to go and fall off a cliff somewhere and let me look round on my own. He was just so excited. He kept saying, "Look at that over there, isn't that *great?*" To him, this was like a bit of paradise that had been slapped in the middle of the sea and given to us. What was it the Puritans used to call America? Something-or-other Destiny? They believed God had put it there for them and they would eventually discover it. Colin was like that.'

Scouser driving instructor Trevor Kearon and Edinburgh-born insurance analyst Mike Laird had not just been up on the advance party, they had stayed on Taransay voluntarily over Christmas. For thirty-year-old Mike, the Millennium Eve was 'fantastic'. 'Balloons, streamers, booze and music,' he wrote in his journal. 'Loads of people, including the camera crews and their families, researchers, producers. We had some dancing, a poem from Ben and first footing done by me and Trish (the Scots).' Thirty-four-year-old Trevor thought the evening 'brilliant': 'It was spot on, everybody was clowning about, balloons were hanging down, everything was looking good, the beer was flowing, loads of smiles, stroke of twelve o'clock came, loads of hugs, loads of laughs, we had a couple of fireworks outside, and a bonfire. It was good.' For Ben Fogle, 26, ex-picture editor of society magazine *Tatler* and another advance party member, it was – in a favourite phrase – 'amazing'. 'Brilliant party, absolutely loved it, everyone got utterly trollied.' Patricia (Trish) Prater, thirty-six-year-old single mother of two and care assistant from the Isle of Man, agreed. 'Nearly everyone was pissed anyway,' she adds.

'It was all a bit chaotic really,' says Liz Cathrine, thirtysomething management consultant with top London firm Arthur Andersen Consulting and live-in partner of 'international jeanswear salesman' Dez Monks. 'But in terms of a great New Year's Eve it was good, because we managed to feed everyone. A lot of alcohol was consumed, too much,' she laughs, 'by Dez, who by 12.30 was throwing up all over the place.'

A Little Sing-Song

One small sub-group of the castaways, however, were not at the party round the bonfire. Being Seventh Day Adventists, Birmingham-resident West Indians Gordon and Cassie Carey didn't drink. Friday night was also the start of their Sabbath. Under the strict religious rules they lived by, food had to be prepared before sunset – even on this extra-special day – because cooking counted as work. 'I was finding it very frustrating,' says Cassie. 'I wanted to cook because sunset was coming up very soon.' She, Gordon, and their two children, Yoneh, four, and Aaron, two, had made a base in the kitchen of the MacKay House. Now she crossed the hundred yards or so of rough, rain-drenched grass to reach the steading. 'I asked somebody for a chicken, but they said, "You can't take that because we have to share between everybody." They were saying, "Ask this person, ask that person, and I got so frustrated that in the end I thought, Well, sunset's soon, and I haven't got anything to cook, and I really and truly don't know where I'm going to find anything. I'm a very emotional person and little things upset me. I went outside to try and get some fresh air to stop the tears coming. But when I went back in they started going over the same thing again and again. They were saying I'd have to wait till after sunset when everybody else was eating. In the end I started crying.'

Somehow, however, a chicken had materialised in the kitchen in the MacKay House. 'Without me knowing,' says Cassie, 'one of the ladies went and put a chicken in the oven up there. They told me it was there. Even then I was upset. I didn't speak for probably an hour after that.' Kindly Lancashire dinner lady Gwyneth Murphy had sorted the problem. But other castaways had a different story. 'They took a chicken,' says Philiy Page. 'I mean, understandably, it was their Sabbath and they can't cook once the Sabbath starts. But there were only two chickens left between everybody. They ate one between them – two adults, two children – and the other was shared between twenty-odd people. Now is that community spirit? I don't think so.'

The Careys spent the rest of the evening on their own. 'We had a little sing-song at the house,' says Cassie, 'like we do at home.' Then they went upstairs to bed.

The television cameras caught the gaiety of the midnight hour and the (generally) well-orchestrated spurting of champagne. Mike Laird was resplendent in his Macdonald Hunting kilt, Ray Bowyer in a feather boa, Leeds pensions analyst Toby Waterman in black tie and purple party hat. Disappointed Dr Roger Stephenson was caught by the cameras blowing a resigned kiss at wife Rosemary. He had a secret which only she knew: it was also his birthday. 'Everybody turned on their joy and ignored the reality around them,' he recalls. 'I felt as if I was an observer,' adds Rosemary, 'almost like I was part of the production team, that I was watching and I didn't belong here and later I was going to get up and go.' Everyone sang Auld Lang Syne. 'Wait till next year!' cried Preston postal worker Patrick Murphy enthusiastically as the music went on and the dancing began.

Sometime after midnight, the families and the sick found beds or mattresses in the overcrowded MacKay House. Trish Prater and Mike Laird stayed up till six in the morning, 'talking about our backgrounds, and how we feel as if something is missing, and we always have to please somebody'. While some bonded over experiences that had perhaps led them to a project such as this in the first place, others danced, while Irish software salesman Padraig Nallen somehow fell and badly hurt his foot. And Ron Copsey, trainee psychotherapist from Hampton and the only openly gay person on the island, who had earlier been, many of the others agreed, 'the life and soul of the party', had a sudden about turn and sank into a depression.

'Earlier,' he recalls, 'everyone had been really negative, so I slipped into my caretaker mode. Roger and Rosemary were particularly down, and I particularly love them people, so I became very cheerful and funny, for the sake of New Year's Eve and a new millennium. But then, come twelve o'clock, I got really depressed. At that time of year you particularly think of friends and family. It made me very pensive, pondering what I'd left behind. What was I doing here?'

Late the following morning the island castaways woke to find that with the exception of Trish Prater and her two kids Jodene (10) and Michael (9), the families had all left for Harris. With them were Ron, Ron's dog Charlie ('I think he thinks he and Charlie are a family,' joked Ben) and two of the iller singles. 'I actually burst into tears on New Year's morning,' says Julie Lowe. 'I just couldn't cope with it any more, hurting and aching and coughing and spluttering. Chris Kelly the producer said, "What are you going to do?" and I said, "I'm going back to the mainland and I'm going to check into the Harris Hotel." I was perfectly prepared to fund it myself.'

'We got up the next day at noon,' says Ben Fogle, 'you know, stonking hangover, and found all the families had gone. Ron had gone. Tammy and Jules had gone, too ill to stay. Padraig had broken his foot, the place was a tip, and you suddenly thought, Oh my God, what's going on? The project's just falling apart. It was a real anti-climax because I had built up in my mind this great January the first, when everybody would leave, and it would just be us thirty-six, castaway for the year. Instead, there's builders walking back and forth smoking cigarettes and driving round on quad bikes and there's arc lights going and the whole house is full of workmen and you had to feed them all. We were missing half our people and half the people still here were sick. There were only about five of us could do any work. It was definitely a real disappointment.'

Auntie's Biggest Bloomer

In less than a week's time, on 6 January, the press were to get hold of at least part of this story. Then, as the BBC trailed and then ran at primetime the first four programmes of the series, describing the selection, over the previous year, of the castaways, the Scottish and national newspapers went wild with stories about what had gone wrong with the 'unique social experiment'. Headlines escalated from BEEB STARS QUIT ISLE and CASTAWAYS WHO FLU TO

Dun Raa

COMFORT to (as skeletons were wrenched from obscure closets) TANTRUM CASTAWAY IN BOOZE BAN SHAME and CASTAWAY STAR'S MUM WAS MOLL FLANDERS. Intrepid tabloid journalists hired boats from Harris fishermen to try to land on the SITE OF AUNTIE'S BIGGEST BLOOMER. Soon, more than one had 'exclusive access' to Taransay, while others printed inaccurate 'quotes' from a conveniently off-contract 'anonymous castaway'. Previous castaways, ranging from original *Castaway* author Lucy Irvine to *Nationwide*'s James Hogg, were consulted. London *Evening Standard* editor Max Hastings remembered his 'castaway father'. 'Former Taransay residents' were discovered and interviewed. Comment writers vied with each other to pontificate inaccurately about the 'soft, sniffling Southerners'. Even leader writers couldn't resist the challenge of discoursing on the accumulated mass of misrepresentation. 'Viewers of *Castaway* have been cheated,' the *Daily Telegraph* began, concluding, preposterously, that the programme was 'accurately reflecting the ethos of the BBC's incoming director general, Greg Dyke'. 'We should be glad they are proving soft,' opined the *Guardian*, whose reporters had not managed to get the true story either ...

So how had 'the ill-fated docusoap' reached this chaotic pass? Was it down, as the Scottish *Sunday Herald* decided, to the 'metro-centric wisdom' of the BBC producers? The misjudgement of the 'experts'? The feebleness of the castaways? The opposition of 'irate locals'? The unexpected wildness of the weather? Or what?

Chapter 2

'I'd Love to See Who Could'

The idea had begun, like so many of the best media wheezes, over lunch. But it wasn't the rambling, boozy affair of myth, merely a modest prawn sandwich in a BBC office. It was autumn 1998 and Jeremy Mills, executive producer of such successful documentary series as *Hotel, Airport* and *Paddington Green*, was thrashing out future programme ideas with Peter Salmon, the Controller of BBC 1.

Though Mills had made his name within the industry as, in agent-speak, 'the king of docusoap', the popular term is one the quietly spoken forty-one-year-old hates. 'It's intensely irritating,' he says. 'We prefer to call it "ongoing, interactive, narrative observational documentary series", which is not,' he admits with a smile, 'quite as catchy.' 'Doc/soap' was, ironically, a term he and fellow BBC producers coined when they were trying to explain to a Controller an idea for a series that would be a documentary, 'but with the structure and attitude of a drama soap'. It was a format that was to project ordinary people such as Eileen the hotel manager and Jeremy the camp Aeroflot manager into the gargoyle gallery of TV celebritydom, and would take Mills and his fellow directors of Lion Television from the drab, Kafkaesque corridors of Television Centre, via a small office in a business centre, to their current premises, the futuristic-looking five-storey Lion House in London's Shepherd's Bush.

Castaway 2000 was the next stage. 'I'd been wanting,' Mills recollects, 'to do something that was looking forwards. I knew a lot of people were making programmes about the end of the millennium and all that stuff. I wanted to do something about the new century. So that's one starting point. The other was that I'd always been intrigued by social experiments, everything from *Lord of the Flies* to psychological tests, like that one for pain where they tell people they're going to be given electric shocks and they don't actually give them. Things like group dynamics had always been fascinating to me. So the two elements came together and the whole concept was born in an hour. For a while I'd been thinking about trying to come up with a television documentary that did more than just follow things, that actually set up a premise.' At the time, he adds, this was a new idea, 'though of course there's loads of them now.

'The BBC,' he continues, 'also wanted something that had some social value. For some time I'd been discussing with friends and family this whole thing about modern life, what are the bits we like, what are the bits we hate, is it possible to divine a way where you can actually have more of one bit and less of the other.'

At the end of the meeting Salmon encouraged Mills to take the idea forward. 'After that conversation,' says Mills, 'we both came out with a number of things that we agreed we needed to do. Firstly we had to work out exactly how we would get a group together that would have some purpose to it, rather than being just a self-selecting group.' Talking things through with his development team, Mills decided that the best way forward was to consult a range of experts. 'So we started looking for a psychologist, an anthropologist, an economist, a survival expert, someone who knew about alternative technology – a whole range of people who could start to give us advice on what we should be thinking about.' The response, Mills recalls, fell into two categories. 'A lot of people said, "This is madness and a waste of time." But then lots were falling over themselves to help us.' Part of what was on offer, of course, for successful experts was TV exposure, and Mills was indeed using his experienced instincts to look for people who would be good on camera.

Talking to others around him about the idea of leaving their everyday life to be on an island for a year, Mills found three reactions. 'Some people said, "I'd love to do that, I can't think of anything better than to get away from what I'm doing and find myself." A second lot said, "Absolutely no way." But actually most of them said, "I wouldn't want to, but I'd love to see who could." So I think there's something within us all that's interested in the idea of returning to the very basic parts of life, whether that means crops, or animals, or just living together as a community. There was also the chance to have time to explore new things. That seems to me one of the biggest problems of today for all of us, lack of time, even though we have all these machines doing things for us. So it's all about that as well, giving people time to think about themselves and their lives and what's important in them, from spirituality to simple survival instincts.'

From all these discussions a central question soon emerged: if they wanted to make this extraordinary experiment work, how many castaways were they looking for? Having consulted the experts, the number thirty was settled on.

This, it seemed, would be a big enough group to have a representative cross-section of British society, but not so big that it would immediately start forming splinter groups.

Meanwhile, the search was on for the place where the volunteers could be stranded. Mills and his team discussed a range of possible places, from islands off the Devon coast to a ring-fenced site in the middle of the Yorkshire moors. 'It had to be near or in Britain,' he says, 'because this was a British project – it's not about going to live on a tropical island.' In the end, one of the more remote of Scotland's five hundred or so islands seemed the most suitable option.

Midges and Wild Sheep

With the more telegenic of the experts retained to advise on selection, Mills and the Lion team now set about looking for volunteers for the experiment. This meant going public. Lion had come to an arrangement with the *Guardian* that an exclusive interview in the New Year in their Monday media section would be the place to launch the project. But, as often happens, the story had already been leaked to the press; on 12 December 1998 the *Independent* ran it on their front page. BBC SEEKS 30 VOLUNTEERS TO BE CASTAWAYS FOR A YEAR. 'With echoes of *Lord of the Flies* and Alex Garland's *The Beach*, the BBC is seeking people who are prepared to spend 12 months completely cut off from the modern world.' Mills was giving blood in Chiswick Town Hall when he saw the spoiler. 'I looked over someone's shoulder and spotted the headline. I remember thinking: Agh, someone's nicked our idea.'

Within a couple of days, the tabloids followed up, pouring scorn on the project right from the outset. SCOTS CASTAWAY SHOW IS 'INSANE' read a headline in the *Sun*, quoting Labour MP Austin Mitchell, of the all-party House of Commons media committee. 'I can't see any purpose in it,' the upbeat representative elaborated. 'It should not be financed with licence-payers' money.'

Nonetheless, reaction from ordinary members of the public was immediate. 'As soon as it was on the front page we started getting enquiries,' Mills remembers. 'It really started taking off then.' Those responding to this early press, and the full official launch a couple of months later, were sent a simple form:

CASTAWAY 2000
An epic living experiment exploring how society could change in the future with 1 January 2000 as 'ground zero'.

Have you ever dreamed of living on an isolated island? Does the prospect of the millennium bug give you an itch to get away from it all? Would you like the power to take decisions about how your life runs and make up the rules as you go along? Would you like to be part of an exciting BBC experiment looking into the way we live in the future?

Below this was a simple form that asked three questions. The answers were many and varied, but Mills's instincts were clearly more on the button than Austen Mitchell's: *Tell us why you want to join the Castaways? What d'you hope to achieve on the island? What experiences or qualifications do you have that make you think you would be suitable to be on* Castaway 2000?

By now the search for an island was on in earnest. Chris Kelly, who was to end up as series producer of *Castaway 2000*, began his involvement with the project sitting opposite one of the development team in the Lion office in London. 'I used to hear him talking to landowners in Scotland,' Kelly recalls, 'trying to persuade them to lease their island to this project, so I kind of had dibs on what was going on. I was fascinated and I used to say, "What's the story?" And it was always clear that this guy was just developing the project, he didn't want to do it, because he didn't want to move to Scotland. And I was thinking, That's going to be a really great project, would it be worth moving to Scotland for? Nothing against Scotland, but I've got a wife and we'd just had a baby and it was all that thing about upheaval.'

The location search was proving harder than expected. A lot of the islands in Scotland are owned or managed by the Scottish Office, who take, says Kelly, a very dim view of television projects. Land ownership in Scotland is a very sensitive issue, and they didn't want to sully their hands with media exploitation. 'I think we lost a lot of time,' adds Colin Cameron, Executive Producer with BBC Scotland, 'looking at islands that didn't really have much potential. We lost about three months in early 1999, which hit us hard later.'

As time went on, the possibilities narrowed down to just a few – all with inherent problems. Shuna had four holiday cottages rented out each summer and one permanent resident in Cath, the shepherd. Torsa was small, not particularly isolated, and with a two-bedroomed holiday home occupied by a headmaster every summer. Remote Swona had wild sheep that might well attack humans. Pabay, off Skye, had boring topography and an evil strain of summer midge. The most likely prospect seemed to be Inchmarnock off the Bute and Argyll coast. It had derelict farm-buildings and one resident who was keen to sell (£800,000 o.n.o.). Jeremy Mills flew up to Scotland and went out to visit on a fishing boat. 'It was absolutely stunning,' he remembers.

But BBC Scotland were unimpressed. 'They laughed Inchmarnock out,' says Kelly. 'If you're sitting in London, Inchmarnock seems remote, but from Glasgow it's not. Colin Cameron said, "I sail round Inchmarnock, that's not *Castaway 2000*."'

'So there's me,' Kelly continues, 'sitting in Jeremy's office one day. He took a phone call from somebody, was crestfallen, I could tell he was miserable. I said, "What's the problem?" He said, "We need someone to go and sort out this *Castaway 2000* thing." I volunteered that moment, even though I hadn't spoken to my wife about moving to Scotland or anything.'

With Kelly now running the newly set up Lion Scotland from a Portakabin in a less than salubrious part of Glasgow, the search for the island was resumed in earnest. Twenty-six-year-old Paul Overton had moved over from BBC Scotland as Assistant Producer on 1 April. 'Was that a suitable date to join the project, I wonder?' he asks, with a characteristic wry smile. Now, armed with 'the bible' – *Scottish Islands* by Hamish Haswell-Smith – he swung into action. 'You'd think that there's any number of uninhabited islands and you'd have your pick, but most of them are being used. If they're that beautiful or suitable to setting up a community or village, it's been done.' Overton also faced the problem of convincing the numerous authorities of the merits of what still seemed on the face of it to be an adventurous, if not downright barmy, idea: not just the Scottish Office, but local planning departments, Scottish National Heritage and Historic Scotland, too.

With Kelly and Overton now 'going for it big style' the focus rapidly narrowed to three: Mingulay, off Barra; Rona, off Skye; and an island in the Outer Hebrides which had been recommended by a friend of Paul's 'just as a joke' – Taransay, off Harris. Though proposals were sent out to owners and contingency plans drawn up for all three, the front runner was Rona. Privately owned by a Danish millionairess and managed by Scottish Woodlands, it had trees, fresh water, and even planning permission to develop an area on the island as holiday homes. It seemed ideal. Producer Chris Kelly threw himself into working with Scottish Woodlands, the Centre for Alternative Technology in Wales, and selected experts to develop a site on the island for the castaways. There were to be state-of-the-art compost toilets, a wind-powered generator and possibly self-build, straw-bale insulated 'post-and-beam' houses. In July 1999 Kelly flew to Denmark to meet the owner and tie up the deal. 'A figure was agreed,' he says. 'She was very 'green' and really into all the alternative technology elements, she was gagging for it to happen. So at that stage I really thought we had the island.'

A Fantastical Long-shot

Meanwhile, press interest in the project hadn't let up. In the tabloids new angles proliferated. In THE PERILS THAT FACE TV CASTAWAYS BY HERMIT WHO LIVED THROUGH THEM the Scottish *Sunday Express* dug up an ex-resident of Pabay, Nigel Smith, who warned that 'the BBC's £2 million plans could end in tragedy'. 'Hypothermia,' he explained, 'could kill them in 30 hours.' The *Sunday Herald* took a different tack. 'Real islanders' found the idea 'patronising', it reported, without quoting one individual who did. Instead: 'I don't see how it can be any kind of microcosm of society,' said Lewis-based writer Joni Buchanan, 'it's just a stunt.' It was 'an excuse for an orgy', added Joan MacCuish, of the community council of Berneray.

Ironically, though, the press pieces only served to intrigue potential volunteers. In London, in the Hanover Square offices of Condé Nast, Ben Fogle, blond and handsome twenty-six-year-old picture editor of society magazine *Tatler*, had been doing his regular job of leafing through the papers 'to see what pics had been taken by who' when his eye fell on the article in the media section of the *Guardian*. WHY DOES THE BBC WANT 30 PEOPLE TO LIVE ON A BIT OF ROCK? asked the headline, before going into detail about the 'determined, extrovert people' Lion TV were seeking.

'There was about three pages in there about this island thing,' says Ben, 'and for me I just thought it was too perfect for words. I was stuck in this hot office, and here was something adventurous, exciting.' Nonetheless, he did nothing about it. It was only a couple of months later, sorting through some papers ('having a bad day, thinking what am I doing here?') that he came across it again and decided, on a whim, to send it off.

In Gloucestershire, fiftysomething art college lecturer Sheila Jowers was depressed by the weather. 'It was February, which is a down part of the year, grey and miserable – leaving home in the dark, returning in the dark – and I'd been doing my job for seventeen years. I saw this article in the *Guardian* and I thought, Oh, that would be so brilliant. So I went home and talked to my husband Peter about it. He'd had a very intensive year as well. He thought it was an interesting possibility but not very real, so we wrote this letter and forgot all about it.'

Big, bearded, softly spoken university lecturer Peter Jowers elaborates. 'It just seemed like such a fantastical long-shot. We're very deeply involved in the local community. The idea of disentangling oneself from all that seemed virtually impossible. So anyway, I typed something out on the computer and Sheila sort of made a humorous addendum. I would never have posted it.'

Some of the candidates took a similarly laid-back attitude to applying. Others, like fifty-eight-year-old retired microbiologist Sandy Colbeck, who'd chased up a piece she'd seen in the *Radio Times*, never dreamed they'd get selected. 'I thought, It's too good to be true, I can't make that,' she says. 'You're having a heart and head conversation with yourself. Your heart wants to do it, but your head is saying, There's other people who are going to be better equipped, somebody else is going to have more to offer than you, it's not going to happen just because you want it so much.'

One surprise for Jeremy Mills was the relative lack of interest among ethnic minorities: 'Proportionally less people from ethnic groups had applied than are physically present in Britain today. There were all sorts of opinions as to why from our various experts. In the end we positively searched out those groups by targeting appropriate newspapers – the *Voice*, the *Caribbean Times*, the various radio stations, community groups, but still the end result was not proportionate. In the end we couldn't actually pressgang people.'

Looking For Personality

Sifting through the gathering mound of application forms (by the end of the process there were to be over four thousand), the Lion team in Scotland – Chris Kelly, Paul Overton, production personnel Penny Loome and Vicki Duffin, researcher Elaine Paterson and Kate Abernethy, a student on part-time work-experience – now started to phone round as many of the would-be castaways as they could.

The main problem for the team was time. Each phone call tended to last a minimum of fifteen minutes. So after a full day trying to get the project going they would need to make all these calls after six o'clock, staying till ten, which was the latest they felt they could call. 'We talked to half to two thirds of the people who applied,' says Chris Kelly. 'Of those we had a grading system: interesting, very interesting, dull, mad. You call the mad ones, of course, just to find out, and there were some total fruitcakes. We got hold of some we were worried might stalk us, people who threatened us on the phone. The girls tend to get it worse, because they get all the lewd come-ons, all that, "Will *you* be there?" "What are you wearing?" kind of thing.'

'Some people you can spend thirty seconds on the phone with,' says researcher Elaine Paterson, 'and know they're not the right person. Others you can spend twenty minutes with before you realise. You're looking for personality. Tone of voice was definitely one thing, and interest another – if they asked questions about it. We didn't want dropouts, people who wanted to go out of sheer desperation. I spoke to people for quite a long time, just to give them the benefit of the doubt.'

'It was like one of those call centres,' Paul Overton recalls. 'All of us just strapped to the phone.' Gradually the heap was reduced to a small pile of about two hundred and fifty. 'At that stage,' says Kelly, 'I got Jeremy involved and he looked at the forms and the biogs we'd done based on phone calls, and he reduced it to about 115.' These were to be interviewed at a series of regional Open Days.

Sheila Jowers had all-but forgotten about her restless idea of February. 'It was now about June,' she remembers, 'and there was this call in the study in the office at school. Normally I wouldn't have answered the phone, but on this occasion I just picked it up and this guy said to me, "So you fancy being a castaway on a deserted island, do you?" I replied, half-laughing, "When can I come?" He told me what I needed to do, and I wasn't sure he was serious. As it sank in, a host of practical problems occurred to me: one very boring one was the reality of covering the mortgage and then there were children's fees for universities. I explained this over the phone and he said, "Oh well, we might be able to sort that out for you."'

'Trying to get that cross-section was a challenge,' says Paul Overton, 'because we found that at least half the applications coming in were from students between the ages of 18 and 25, who had the availability, they could take a year out. Whereas somebody with a family and a nine-to-five job, it's not so easy to give up everything for a year.'

In the Corrigan household in Cheltenham, it had been Colin who had been most enthusiastic about the project. Though currently working as a painter and decorator, he had reckoned that he might stand a chance of getting on the project if he revived his long-unused butchering skills. 'There was an article in the *Daily Mail*,' says Julia, 'where someone said they could look away while a fish died, but couldn't kill a pig, and he kept on thrusting this at me, saying "I want us to go for that." I was reluctant at first, until we got the phone call from Paul Overton. Our house was in chaos when he called, with my daughter and three very noisy kids in the house, all jumping up and down, and he kept saying, "I can call you back if you like," but we stayed on and had this great, long, exciting conversation with him, for ages, an hour and a half maybe, and when I eventually put the phone down, I said to Colin, "I've got a funny feeling about this, I think we're going to go to that island."'

So Sheila and Peter and Colin and Julia and a hundred and eleven others accepted an invitation to go to an Open Day. Before they went, Sheila told her daughters what they were doing. 'Because we don't watch much television I had no idea really what this could all mean. To me it was just about being on a Scottish island and it was to do with survival and environment and sociology and anthropology and all those sorts of things. I didn't really think about the TV angle. My daughters said that if this was going to be a docudrama I had to watch *Paddington Green*. So I did and, God, it was such a farce! I was hoping the new project wouldn't require us to do mad things like changing sex or have some sort of controversial relationship. I didn't fancy that even as a performance. So when we were invited to this interview, I was very undecided but thought at least we'd find out what it was all about.'

Your Real Reason

Roger Stephenson, fortysomething Devon doctor, had answered an advert in *General Practitioner* magazine. He had always had an interest in remote islands, and had spent extended periods working as a resident medic on the tiny Atlantic colonies of Pitcairn and St Helena.

There was a further, atypical motivation. 'When you've got kids,' he says, 'education is a continual anxiety. There's nothing right in education. Whichever direction you go is wrong. Our local state school is very good as a state school, but to see little Felix, aged four and three quarters, as he was when he started, sat in a class of thirty for six hours a day, it just seems completely irrelevant to a child under five. Almost all teacher-pupil interactions are, "Sit down! Be quiet!", that sort of thing, instead of pulling out his creative strand and letting him work from that.'

Roger, encouraged by his wife Rosemary, had become increasingly interested in the idea of Home Education. Indeed, when Roger first showed Rosemary the *Castaway* advert, she had just returned, 'really inspired', from a conference on Home Education in London. 'At that early stage,' she recalls, 'I was the one saying, "Gosh, we could do this, let's find out about it."'

'So we decided,' Roger continues, 'to go to this Open Day to learn a bit more about it. Because it was called an Open Day, it felt as if we were getting more than they were getting, but in fact it was more like a glorified interview.'

Ray Bowyer, bearded and ponytailed fiftysomething ex-builder from Worsley, Manchester, had 'always fancied being dropped off on an island. Shipwrecked or something like that, it appealed to me, how would I survive?' Invited to the Open Day at the Britannia Hotel in Manchester, he found himself being interviewed for over two hours. 'I was acting the goat,' he recalls, 'singing me head off and that. Then they asked me a few questions about the building trade. What kind of work I'd done and how many people I'd run, and in the end it turned into a bit of a joke session. The bloke who was before me was only in for half an hour and as I was coming home on the bus I had an idea that I might get it. I thought to myself, Well at least I look the part.'

The Open Day candidates were given two interviews. First there was a formal interview with Paul Overton which was filmed on broadcast-quality tape. 'That was for us,' says Kelly, 'building the archive, getting material we could use of people irrespective of whether they worked out or not. We asked them stock questions – "Who'd be your worst neighbour?" "What's the best thing in your life?" "Could you kill a sheep?" "What would you miss?" – things that would be revealing in a superficial way, but could be used in the programme as well.'

'It was a bit of a privilege really,' says Paul Overton, 'getting thirty people a day coming in and telling you their entire life history, answering things like, "What's motivating you in this direction?" "Tell me the highs and lows of your life" "If you were stuck in a lift plummeting towards the earth what would you remember?"'

In a second room, in a longer interview, the candidates met Chris Kelly with, depending on the region, either Jeremy Mills or BBC Scotland's Colin Cameron, the executive producer liaising with the production for the BBC. 'For my part,' says Kelly, 'I wanted to know the candidates' real reasons for wanting to do this project. We can all write that thing about wanting to "show an alternative way, at the dawn of a new millennium" and all that stuff. It's just bullshit, really. I had much more respect for people who said, "I want to spend the year writing," or "I want to become a concert pianist."'

With the producers was a woman who was emerging as one of the programme's key experts, Glaswegian psychologist Cynthia McVey. A humorous and personable mother of four, she had worked as everything from a dancer to a legal secretary before she embarked on a psychology career in her mid-forties. She is quite unpretentious about her TV role, describing herself cheerfully as 'media tart' and 'rent-a-mouth'. Paul Overton was impressed: 'She was able to get across fairly academic ideas in an interesting way that you wanted to listen to. It's the balance that you always have to try and find for television, particularly BBC 1, which has to be fairly accessible to the public.' McVey brought with her psychometric tests and a questionnaire, 'about what the candidates liked about themselves, disliked about themselves, why they wanted to do it, what they thought their best talents were, what they weren't good at, what they thought they would gain and lose by going to the island, that kind of thing.' She backed this up with assertiveness questionnaires and a personality inventory, 'to see how extrovert or introvert they were'. 'I also had a wee look,' she adds, 'at their emotions, to see if there was anybody there who was terribly anxious or depressed.'

Some people were clearly marked for the rejection bin before the tests were even completed. 'There was one guy,' McVey recalls, 'who was either trying to attract attention by being completely off the wall or he had some serious problems. What he said on camera was actually unshowable, because he was talking about sheep-shagging and chicken-shagging and all sorts of other strange things as well.'

Another group to be discarded were those who were too blatantly wannabe stars. 'I felt that this year was going to be a huge trial anyway,' continues McVey, 'so if they were going into it for reasons that were related to fame – rather than positive personal reasons that related to learning about themselves, or learning skills, or wanting, for example, to find out about ecology – that this would not be a good idea.'

Then there were those who were too obviously trying to escape from more than just everyday routine. 'I did try and eliminate people I felt were really running away from themselves. You can go to the island as a self-examination procedure, but if you're really running away from yourself you're taking all your emotional and psychological baggage with you. A lot of people think that moving or changing their job or lifestyle is going to cure their personal problems, but it doesn't really work that way.'

They saw one single parent, she remembers, who had four children by different fathers, 'and she had a tiny wee baby as well, and the children were running riot around the place when they were being interviewed. She was clearly trying to get away from her living circumstances, which was abject poverty, really. What she actually needed was somebody to talk to. It might even have helped that she came to the interview, that somebody thought she was worth talking to, but at the end of the day, as far as the programme was concerned, she just had too many problems.'

'There was lots of debate at the end of each day,' says Jeremy Mills. 'We all had pages of notes about whether the various candidates were outgoing, lively, dull, introverted or bolshy. We were looking for a mix. We wanted people who were funny, people who were slightly quieter, people who might be annoying, people who would be quiet and interesting and thoughtful.'

'Much discussion took place regarding the selection of the first short list,' wrote Cynthia McVey in her private report on the Open Days. 'Obviously, there was no way that I, even with assistance from helpful colleagues, could read all the application forms or be present, myself, at all the interviews. I did, however, manage to collect data on most of those attending at interviews and had some idea of measures like assertiveness, extroversion, introversion and mood. I had consulted colleagues, particularly in the forensic side of my department to see if there was such a thing as a "spot the nutter" questionnaire (for want of a better and more academic expression). There wasn't, and short of doing psychopathy testing on every person, a very expensive procedure, there was little I could do about it. It became clear that it would be virtually impossible to identify and screen out every person who might have a serious psychological problem. Lion TV were asking for police checks and references from those eventually selected and it was hoped that this would assist in exposing any serious problems. There was, of course, the question of whether the people who apply for such a project, especially given its public nature, are "ordinary" or representative of the general population.'

There was indeed.

Is This Really Us?

Sheila Jowers was impressed by her Open Day. 'We'd thought, If they don't like us or we don't like them, one way or the other it will be self-selecting, but we came away from the interview feeling that it hadn't been so bad. They seemed like quite serious people. They were interested in all kinds of different angles and it obviously wasn't going to be a farcical programme.'

'We came away from it just more intrigued than anything, really,' says Rosemary Stephenson. 'Then quite soon after we had a phone call asking us to come to a selection week at the Centre of Alternative Technology in Wales. It sounded a bit grim to us, because it was a sort of action-packed week of activities and I just thought, Oh my God, is this really us? But then we decided, Oh well, what the hell, we can just go and do it and then drop out. I suppose we always had that feeling – Let's just go one step further, we can always drop out.' 'We expected everyone to be wallies,' says Roger Stephenson. 'But they weren't, everybody was nice, and it was fascinating.'

The accommodation was something of a shock, however, for a family used to a rambling vicarage in Devon. 'We were staying in this cramped house with four families. It was incredibly hot and we slept very badly, because there was a lot of noise and everybody was very hyper, they were all so desperate to be chosen. You got the feeling that a lot of people were really there to prove themselves, so there was a lot of very intense talking and feelings and emotions.'

'The thing exploded on the first night,' recalls Paul Overton. 'There were drunken arguments till early in the morning and people hitting tables with rolling pins to try and get their point across. It reached a stage where you were allowed to speak only if you had the rolling pin and hammered it on the table. In that first group there were lots of really strong assertive people. It was a huge clash of views and values and beliefs and all the rest of it.'

It had been producer Chris Kelly's idea to turn the selection week into a televised competition with red, yellow and green teams battling it out on 'an orienteering race', over and above the basic instruction about compost toilets, house construction, and livestock management. 'I thought it was just too good an opportunity to miss,' Kelly reflects. 'Originally we were going to just choose thirty people and make programmes about their year on the island. But I thought, Why not make a series about selecting them? And if you're going to do that, clearly the selection has to be competitive, otherwise there's no edge.' For Jeremy Mills this was 'an absolutely brilliant idea – and totally Chris's'. Unbeknownst to most of the participants, it was not the winning that mattered, but the way they took part. Builder Ray Bowyer had sussed this. 'I knew from day one it was a mind game,' he says. 'It wasn't whether you could run up a mountain in twenty seconds. They were playing you off against other people, to see that you're not going to throttle somebody or whatever.' For the time being, however, he kept any such urge well under control.

Televising the selection had some unexpected results. Roger Stephenson was surprised at how addictive he found being in front of the cameras. 'The cameras are probably the most drug-like part of it,' he says. 'For the first time in one's life, well, for an awfully long time, people are asking you what you think about things and filming you and are interested in what ordinary things you're doing. You're used to this little life amongst yourselves and your friends in which people like you and want to know what you say, but then suddenly somebody anonymous is broadcasting your thoughts and you think, God, somebody else might be interested in us. It's all part of the television kick, both horrendous and stimulating. And like heroin, the most horrific side is what happens after your kick, when you see it played back and think, *Oh Christ*.'

Would-be castaway Hilary Freeman, on the other hand, didn't like the cameras at all. Aged 50, she had left behind her carpenter husband, three late-teenage children and a job as a pupil support assistant in Scarborough, to 'come looking for a new challenge'. 'I saw a little bit of how television works that week, and what they see as entertainment, and some of it,' she recalls, 'I didn't like. I just thought what they filmed and how it unfolded was stupid.

'We were in different groups, and one of the things our group had to do was pen a load of sheep in this field. We each had sections of a pen, I think there were seven in all. So we decided as a group where we'd put the pen, and we chose the bottom corner of the field, which is fair enough, but unknown to us, sheep always run uphill, apparently. We fucked up, basically, and it's obvious they're going to film that, because it's going to be funny. But I didn't think it was funny.'

'It was interesting,' Cynthia McVey wrote in her diary, 'that despite the fact that the applicants had received a letter with the information about the weekend telling them that cameras would be present, there were already objections. And the camera was in full view of all. It was clear that the stress of taking part in selection was proving problematic already and some of the applicants wanted to make it clear from the start that they would not be "sitting ducks". This is, in some ways, rather positive, as it would not have been suitable to have had a group of totally compliant people.'

Even as she assessed the castaways both on and off camera, and addressed them with her professional view of the experience they were attempting to let themselves in for, McVey had her private criticisms. 'I was rather surprised,' she wrote, 'at the grumpy behaviour of some, as they were all people who, at least on paper, were very keen to be selected. Of course, they were tired and stressed and anxious, and this is the type of behaviour most often produced in these circumstances.'

Although Rosemary Stephenson found the week at CAT both stressful and 'shambolic', there were, she says, moments that made her glad she'd decided to come. A key one involved her son. 'The biggest highlight was when we went abseiling and Oliver, who was six, suddenly said, "Oh, I'm going to do that." And he got on and just abseiled down this sheer cliff – it was extraordinary. He was being filmed doing it and he was terribly cool, and I just suddenly thought, This is amazing, because it would never have entered my head to take my six-year-old abseiling and here he is doing it. It felt like we were really stretching boundaries. And then I thought, Well if my six-year-old can do it, I can do it. So I did.'

Microbiologist Sandy Colbeck experienced a similar excitement at surprising herself. 'When I saw the itinerary,' she recalls, 'I did note that we had white water rafting one day, and I'm absolutely petrified of lots of water. So I thought, Well, I'm going to do everything else, but I'm not going to do that. But we went along there and I don't know quite how it happened, but I finished up going down this river three times and I still don't know how I did it. I've come to the conclusion that it wasn't me, it might have been my body, but it wasn't me. I had the time of my life that week. I said to myself, If I don't get any further, I really don't care.'

The shared excitement and intimate conditions meant that people got to know each other fast. 'At the start,' says trainee psychotherapist Ron Copsey, 'it was like everybody was on their first date with a new partner. They were all showing the best aspects of themselves.' Soon, however, people were opening up. 'In the car going up to where we were doing our rafting,' jeanswear salesman Dez Monks remembers, 'we were listening to stories from the others. There were six of us there and every single other person apart from Liz and me had a horrific story about their childhood. We were looking at each other in the rear-view mirror as we heard these things about being battered as children and so on, and thinking, Oh my God, we're both from such stable backgrounds.'

Dez was about to discover that this frankness had another side. 'After two days people were coming up to Liz and saying things like, "I don't know how you put up with him, he's really horrible the way he treats you, the things he says to you." One guy actually said, very seriously, to Liz, "You've got to be very careful because if Dez carries on like that and people see it on the telly he's going to be getting hate mail and death threats like that bloke on *Coronation Street*." Liz came back to tell me this, saying, "Maybe we need to look at what we're doing, the way we're interacting, be a little bit careful." And I just said, "Well, Liz, bollocks to that, I'm not going to moderate my behaviour so I can appeal to the masses." I wasn't going to act in a certain way so that people could think, Ooh, Liz and Dez are great because they've got a really lovely relationship. We *have* got a really lovely relationship, but we take the piss out of each other and it's on a completely different wavelength from the majority of people.'

Other, more blushing flowers found their confidence growing. Secretary Tammy (Tamcilla) Huff, who until this time had spent all her twenty-six years, bar holidays, in the little A1-straddling Bedfordshire town of Sandy, had initially been wondering what she was doing on the week at all. 'For the first two days I was blown out, I was meeting all these people, they had skills and characters, and I kind of in my heart hit rock bottom. I thought, Why am I here? I'm not going to be chosen. But as the days went on I was doing everything and achieving everything and having a laugh and saying, "Come on, let's do it!" I realised then that I was perceived as having attributes of humour and determination. So I just took faith in them and thought, Well if they think I'm capable, then they'll choose me.' That Tammy was also both pretty and telegenic was clearly not going to be a disadvantage.

At the end of the selection week the group were taken from CAT to Hereford to spend a night learning survival skills and being assessed by John 'Lofty' Wiseman, the SAS Survival Trainer who had become another of Lion's key experts. For Mike Laird, who had once gone on the selection course for army officer (but having worn ripped jeans and drunk too much, had not been offered a commission) it was 'a complete giggle'. 'I loved it,' he says. 'Outdoor challenges are very much me.'

A Mini-Society

The actions and interactions of the would-be castaways were now scrutinised by both production team and key experts. There were not just varying opinions about the candidates, different relationships had formed. 'Ron, for example,' says Chris Kelly, 'will say things to Paul that he won't say to me. Trish will say things to Elaine that she won't say to Paul and me, because it's a woman thing. So we all got to know these people on different levels and then we sat around in the office in Glasgow and came up with our list. Then I met up with Cynthia and Lofty and said, "This is what we think, what do you think?"'

'The first thing in the remit,' says Cynthia, 'was to produce a cross-section of society, so we weren't looking for exceptional people who were very gifted, very patient, or the sort you might choose for an Antarctic expedition. We were looking for regular, ordinary people who wanted to do this, and within that we wanted the cross-section, which meant that we had to have some assertive people, some quiet people, some humorous people, some people who might be a bit touchy, some who might be a wee bit huffy, people who were very giving, someone to be maybe a grandmother or grandfather figure, or the comedian of the group. You're setting up a mini-society, with warts and all.

'Certainly if I'd said to Lion TV I don't think you should take this person, they wouldn't have, and they didn't. On the other hand, if they had a preference for one person over another and both had the same types of characteristics – assertiveness, for example – I wouldn't object. So they weren't dictating and they weren't setting people up for trouble, as far as I know.'

It was certainly true that some of the most obviously tricky people – like ex-alcoholic bargeman Kim Russell and ex-entrepreneur Jack Holden (who had the charming habit of addressing thirtysomething management consultant Liz Cathrine as 'kid') were not chosen. But the experts' advice was not always heeded by the producers. 'We actually took two people that Lofty said we shouldn't take,' says Kelly. 'Roger and Dez. When he found out who we'd finally got he said to me, "I can't believe you've taken Dez, big mistake, Chris, he's going to wind them up, don't say I didn't warn you."'

Ben Fogle, twenty-five-year-old picture editor of society magazine *Tatler*, had been originally selected, Jeremy Mills admits, for his unusual background. 'He has the poshest voice you could ever imagine. I suppose if we're honest about it, one of the reasons we chose him originally was we thought it would be interesting to see how people reacted to him. I really liked him personally, but we weren't sure how people in that broad group would get on with him. One of the most fantastic things is how he emerged as one of the leaders of the group, in a very consensual, non-domineering way.'

Cynthia was equally impressed with the handsome young picture editor. 'Of all the people in the first group it was Ben who came to the fore. He turned out to have an extraordinarily good leadership style, where he's looking after the vulnerable ones. He's saying, "Right, let's do this" but he's hearing what everybody says, he's allowing it to go up for discussion, he's putting himself out, which is surprising because he's only twenty-five and not used to that kind of orienteering setting. On the face of it he's more used to the high life and champagne.'

As it happened, Ben Fogle hadn't spent his entire life idling in some fantasy toff setting. His father being Canadian, Ben had passed the summer holidays of his childhood living in a cottage on a North American lake, 'fishing every day, swimming every day, repairing boats'. At Bryanston School, a mixed public school in the Dorset countryside, where he had boarded for five years, Ben had got used to shared living arrangements (sleeping in dormitories of up to ten people) as well as hearty outdoor activities like running and horse riding. Finishing school, his adventurous nature had led him to Rio de Janeiro, where he landed with no more than a knapsack and a return ticket from Caracas booked for a year later. 'I remember stepping off the plane,' he says, 'and the hot air hitting me. I just couldn't believe it, there was me on the other side of the world, no parents, no schoolteachers. I could get on a bus and choose to go anywhere – it was that freedom of doing exactly what I wanted that I loved.' What he chose to do was live out his childhood dream of going up the Amazon. 'I headed straight for Belém on the mouth and hitch-hiked onto a boat and went all the way up to Iquitos in Peru.'

At Portsmouth University he went sailing every other weekend and spent a lot of time with the Navy, 'living in this sardine can on water. There would be up to twenty-five of us in it. It was so squashed that we'd have to hotbed it, so people would sleep for x amount of hours and then you'd swap over. We'd be away on deployments for three weeks at a time.' He took another year out in Costa Rica, improving his Spanish, but it didn't match that first fabulous Brazilian adventure. 'I'm always going to be searching for that same feeling,' he says.

Indeed, Ben had only gone to work at *Tatler* magazine 'slightly by mistake'. He had actually been hoping to get an apprenticeship in travel writing on a sister publication in the same firm – *Condé Nast Traveller*. 'I applied to them to do some work experience and whether it was that my spelling was appalling,' he laughs, 'and I missed out an 'r' and put *Tatler* by mistake, or they didn't have any places there, I don't know. Anyway, after three months as a dogsbody, helping out with everything, the editor suddenly said, "Ben, I want you to be my picture editor," and it went from there.' Fogle had no training for or experience of the job at all. 'I know there's people who've studied for years to do something like that,' he says with a characteristic guilty smirk.

Someone else who had fallen for Ben's charms was Tammy Huff, fellow castaway candidate, seen sitting next to him on the grass in a passing shot of Programme One, then clenched in an intimate hug when both discover at the end of Programme Two that they've been selected. 'Island here we come!' she cries, body language giving away more perhaps than she realised as she curls towards him and they clink champagne glasses together. 'We flirted together quite a lot at CAT week,' Ben was to admit much later in the year, when romantic twists had taken an altogether different course. 'I've been asked lots of times by Lion about it and we've both been cagey.' Questioned further by your ever-inquisitive author: 'We got on at CAT week,' he added with a smile. 'And saw each other a couple of times after that.' Tammy, always as beautifully mannered as she is firm, was equally keen to protect her privacy. 'It was Mike, Ben and I who met at CAT,' she told me. 'The three of us sparked off a really good friendship, but Ben and I had more of a spark between us. He came to visit me in Sandy a couple of times, or I went to see him in London, we just sort of met up. It's the beginning stages of getting to know people, and it just felt like there was a good friendship there, who knows, possibly more ...'

'I remember interviewing Tammy on the very last afternoon of CAT about it,' Lion researcher Elaine Paterson told me, 'and it was all very coy, all very "Watch this space", but she did say, "Yes, there is somebody who I'm very keen on here." They wouldn't mention each other's names. Ben was coy too, but he did use the "don't want to burn your bridges" phrase – about being with one person, without having met everybody else who was going to go.'

Besides Cynthia and Lofty, the first group of would-be castaways met Hugh Piggott, expert on alternative power, and Lucy Irvine, who had written the bestseller *Castaway*, about her experience spending a year on the Torres Strait island of Tuin in 1984. Their advice was also added to the mix, as the group of thirty-two men, women and children was reduced to just eighteen adults and four children.

'It was down to me,' wrote Cynthia in her diary, 'to phone the applicants and let them know whether they were going to the island or not. Lion TV asked if I was okay to make the phone calls on camera and so they came up to my office with a crew at tea time on two evenings. Telling those who were going was a pleasure. I held off for a while, teasing them a little, secure in the knowledge that they were getting good news (depending on how you see it) in the end. Those who were not going were told immediately (I was not prepared to beat around the bush with them). In fact, those that Lion and/or I felt might be distressed at the non-selection were told in person. I felt that Lion were very concerned about those that were not being selected.

'This involved, in one case, me flying to London and being taken by taxi to a hotel to stay overnight and then to drive with Paul Overton to tell a non-castaway on film (or off, depending on what she said) that she hadn't made it. Time was short and we were very worried about telling this person that she was not going. There were several calls on Paul's mobile while we were travelling and we were held up by a traffic jam and so were frayed round the edges when we finally arrived. We were made most welcome and met members of her family and had some tea. Finally I told her and she took it rather well, all things considered. But she did not want Lion to use the film of the interview I did with her and was not too happy. She thought we had made a mistake.' (Whether the journey had been organised for filming, psychological or sympathy reasons, this particular piece of rejection footage was never used.)

Self-sufficiency

The chosen eighteen were then invited to a weekend at a hotel in Maidenhead. The purpose, Jeremy Mills explains, was 'To start the process of what they will and won't be allowed to take with them, what sort of allowances they'll get in terms of money, and so on. There were lots of debates about whether they should have radios and personal stereos. If you had radios should batteries come out of the community budget? and so on.' Lion had drawn up a summary document of ground rules for discussion. The castaways were addressed on the subject of Health and Safety by Lion production director Shahana Meer, who also raised the issue of the contract they would eventually have to sign. Last but not least was the key question of which island they were to be stranded on. There were now just two in the frame – Rona and Taransay. The castaways were given copies of maps and planning applications for each island.

Despite the fact that Chris Kelly had spent over four months working on the possibility of Rona, and had now finally tied up a deal with the elusive Danish owner, BBC Scotland was still not entirely sold on the island. 'I used to have weekly meetings with Colin Cameron,' says Kelly, 'and for them the big issue was, "What does 'castaway' mean?" To them Rona wasn't remote.' There were two other problems: a military base at one end of the island and a resident couple who weren't keen to move. Accompanied by Paul Overton, Cameron had now made a site visit with Kelly. 'It was perfect,' says Overton. 'You came in on the boat, you were utterly cut off, and you could see how a community was going to develop there. By lunchtime we were all cock-a-hoop, but then you walk twenty minutes down this dirt track and this farmhouse appears, straight out of *Holiday Homes*.' 'Colin said, "We can't do it, it's not a deserted island." says Kelly. So that's when, at the last minute, everything twisted,'.

Kelly had by now also visited Taransay, which Overton had discovered and had been developing in parallel. 'We went up,' the producer continues, 'and met with the owners. It was a beautiful place, deserted, with sandy beaches, but I couldn't see beyond the fact that there were no trees. I'd fallen in love with Rona.' Nonetheless they shot the footage of Taransay that was eventually to become the programme's title sequence, and presented views of both islands to the newly selected castaways. 'That was the weekend from hell,' Kelly admits, 'when it all started to go wrong. If I'm honest, I was hoping that they'd all watch this footage of Taransay and Rona and say, "We want Rona." Then I could have gone back to Colin Cameron and said, "Well, they all want Rona, so it's got to be Rona."' But the castaways watched the aerial photography of wild deer springing across the green machair, the granite mountains sweeping up from sandy beaches and wave-lashed rocky cliffs and they all said, 'We want Taransay.' 'The whole purpose of *Castaway 2000*,' Kelly concedes, 'is that it's about community decision-making and that was the first decision they took – which home they wanted.'

'I think we, the castaways,' says Roger Stephenson, 'felt that Rona wasn't an isolated island if, two miles down the road, there were two people who weren't us, with a satellite dish and so on. I could have coped with the MOD but this was something different. This wasn't what we were in it for – we wanted self-sufficiency and no messing from outside.'

'So we were going to Taransay,' says Chris Kelly, 'but the problem was we had no planning permission, we hadn't done a deal with the owners, it was August, just going into a Western Isles winter, which starts in September. From that day onward, we were pushing to, and we were constantly reassured that we would, get it finished.'

Chapter 3

'We Never Panicked ...'

'We never panicked,' says Kelly, 'because our view was, whatever work there is to be done, will be a bonus, because all the way along ninety-five per cent of the castaways have said that they don't want to move into some Butlin's camp that's been all done for them.'

That ninety-five per cent undoubtedly included Mike Laird, whose ambition was to live in a cave; Ben Fogle, who was already having 'romantic ideas about the island, about going out, traipsing through the rain and freezing cold, hammering down fences, my dog trundling behind me'; and Hilary Freeman, who had originally answered the advert because 'the challenge to me was the survival, being resourceful and making things out of what we could find naturally.' It probably included Peter Jowers, who was 'very confident in my practical skills', and was later to say that he could have built a habitation in two weeks. But it didn't include Julia Corrigan. 'We were always told,' she says, 'that we were going to have houses, anybody with half a brain cell just had to think, If you're going to bring children into this it can't possibly just be a survival exercise.' Nor Ron Copsey: 'There was never any talk of building the structural buildings. First of all we're not qualified.' Nor, most particularly, did it include the doctor and his wife. 'When we started on this project,' said Rosemary, 'we were told we would have a whole croft for our family, and then the goalposts gradually moved.'

These differing expectations were storing up future problems for Lion TV. For the time being, though, Chris Kelly had a major job on his hands just to get the island basics sorted out. A lease had to be agreed with the owners of Taransay, the MacKay family. Planning permission had to be sought from the Western Isles Council for living structures that hadn't yet been agreed upon, let alone designed or built. (Rejected Rona had not only had existing planning permission, but had, with its trees, been sheltered enough to consider using, at least in part, the 'post-and-beam' houses favoured by CAT.)

'I don't think there was another architect up for the job,' says Andy McAvoy.

'I was questioned by the producer in the car on the way down to Horgabost from the airport on my suitability for the project and experiences to date to do with self-build, quick-erection processes, timber frame structures and so on.'

'The first time I met Andy,' says Chris Kelly, 'was at Stornoway airport. He came recommended, in fact someone had recommended his partner. It was one of those quirks of fate, his partner was ill the day I phoned the office and Andy took the call, and I spent two hours with him on the phone trying to convince him that this was something he should come and look at. At first he said he thought I was crazy, but I told him that it was a great opportunity for him, "a blank backdrop to come up with an architectural gem", a lot of flannel really. I just wanted to get him to the island to see it.'

Driving McAvoy from Stornoway through the increasingly magnificent landscape of Lewis and Harris to the beach opposite Taransay – Horgabost – Kelly went particularly slowly. The journey, normally an hour and a quarter, took almost two hours, Kelly remembers, as he tried to talk the architect into accepting the job. Over and above worries about safety and architectural integrity, McAvoy was worried about the lack of time. He also had existing relationships with Western Isles planners, which he didn't want to put at risk for a one-year project, whatever the exposure it gave his practice.

'We had a great day on the island,' Kelly recalls. 'We walked round the site and at that stage it was like you see on the programme titles – ruins. I kept asking, "What d'you think, what d'you think?" I remember Andy said, "Great. But now I've got to take it all in." We went back to the Harris hotel that night, and he disappeared and had a bath and came back an hour later and he sketched plans, just napkin-type stuff. He said, "Right, this is what we should do. We're pushing it, but the odds are that we can get something ready."'

In his sketches that evening, McAvoy outlined how he would adapt the surviving ruins. The MacKay House had been renovated seven to eight years before and needed little work. The steading had a cheap asbestos roof that needed completely replacing. Of the existing buildings, he was most inspired by the ruined schoolhouse. 'It faced the harbour and by whatever means of transport you come into the island, it's the first thing you see. I thought it was in a state where we could just save it and no more. The client was responsive to an idea of mine not to fully repair the building but freeze it at a moment in time, so that rather than rebuilding the corner wall we leave the hole that was there. It was a tremendous opportunity to put in a large glazed element to make a viewing platform onto the mountain range over the harbour, which on the day I was there had its first dusting of snow on the top of it. I could just imagine these schoolchildren sitting there with a fire at one end gazing out of this corner. Or you could wait there for the boat or the helicopter to come. It would be almost like a lighthouse, a beacon if you like.' As it turned out, this lyrical vision of the preserved ruin was to be seminal in persuading at least one castaway onto the project.

As for the sleeping areas, the architect was going to go away and think about that problem. 'We had this style of post and beam,' says Kelly. 'And at that stage our lot was supposed to be building the accommodation, or at least be involved in building it.' But McAvoy was quick to point out that straw-bale insulated houses were completely inappropriate in those extreme conditions – they would have blown away.

Kelly then gave McAvoy two weeks to come up with some recommendations. The architect's main reservation had to do with the substantial amount of archaeology on site, which would have to be cleared with Scottish National Heritage. As for the planning department in Stornoway, McAvoy 's practice had fortunately been doing other work in the area, and they liked his proposed ideas. If he worked with locally processed material, timber, stone, glass, grass roofs, the application, he was told, might be sympathetically received. 'At that point,' says McAvoy, 'I advised Chris that we had a chance of pulling it off.'

The planning application went in during the first week of October. But preparation had already started as Chris Kelly had ascertained from the planning department that the council would support this ecologically sound project, which was, in part, about whether or not a community could sustain themselves in this economically depressed region. In the meantime, Andy McAvoy pushed ahead with Scottish National Heritage. They had no particular problems with the development plan as long as the archaeology department was happy. So a regional archaeologist was contacted and invited out on site.

Once on the island, the archaeologist asked Andy McAvoy to go through the development plans. 'So,' recalls Andy, 'I said that the majority of the settlement should be on the seaward side of the old village of Paible, to minimise any intrusions in that area. However, over on the other side, I explained, we proposed to put things like polytunnels and drainage. She looked a bit concerned, didn't say very much, but agreed that we were taking the right approach, building in certain areas, like rocky outcrops where the geology was actually the archaeology.'

Having shown her his plans as an architect, Andy was taken back to the start. 'Now I'm going to walk you through it as I see it, as an archaeologist,' she said.

'The dune system here is fairly recent, of the last few hundred years of deposition. Beneath, we don't know what we're going to find. To give us some indication we should walk to the seaward edge.' Andy was taken to a particular sand dune that had been cut in half by the sea. There he was shown clearly layers defined all the way down through six-and-a-half metres. Through shards of pottery, bones and shell deposits, the archaeologist could identify the lowest layer as being Bronze Age. 'Then,' says McAvoy, 'she made a remark to the effect that this could be another Scara Brae, we wouldn't know until a storm came along and removed the whole dune system, or the archaeologists were given the time to pare this all back. "Believe me," she said, "this is a highly developed site with layers of deposition consistently from the Bronze Age, which you could potentially devastate by building in certain areas."'

'No one was interested in Taransay,' Kelly points out, 'before we came. It was a site of scientific beauty but it was uninhabited and no one ever came. When the archaeologist came over I was expecting her to give me chapter and verse about the island, but I knew a certain amount already, because we'd researched it.

'She spent the day there – I'd been off with Andy doing this, that and the other – and at the end of it we had a cup of tea in the MacKay House. "What's the story?" I said. "Well," she said, "I don't know if this is good news or bad news, but I've discovered settlements that I would date as fifth-century BC." Andy and I looked at each other and went, "Oh". For him it was bad news, he was thinking about the development implications. But for me it was good news, because all of a sudden we had fifth-century BC archaeology in *Castaway 2000*, that whole *Time-Team* aspect, and I thought, Great, we're going to have some archaeological digs going on here, while all Andy could think about was, "Where the fuck am I going to put my drainage paths?"'

Negotiator Types

Getting Taransay ready was not the only one of Chris Kelly's headaches. Even as decisions were being made about the island, the Lion production team had been completing the human side of the equation, with another selection week – this time a shorter, four-day affair supervised by Lofty Wiseman at an outdoor centre at Keswick in the Lake District. 'We changed the location,' explains Paul Overton, 'for television reasons. It was going to be a bit same old, same old if we went through indistinguishable activities with a different group.'

New adverts and articles in a fresh range of publications – particularly the ethnic minority press – had brought in a new range of eager candidates for another set of Open Days. 'The initial adverts very much brought in your educated, middle-class people,' says researcher Elaine Paterson, 'and we had to redress the balance, which we did with the *Mirror* article that went out. We got many more builders, and we got a butcher and others with more practical and agricultural skills.'

In Birmingham, carpenter's wife Cassie Carey had seen a piece in the *Caribbean Times*. 'At first it didn't appeal to me, actually,' she recalls. 'I thought, "Who's going to want to go to this Scottish island?" There were some black comedians in there criticising the idea. Some of them wanted to know what shops there would be nearby and things like that. All these people were commenting about it, and, at the end of it, it said, *If you're interested call Chris Kelly.* I kept on reading and reading it, going over it. Then I spoke to my husband Gordon about it. But he said he just couldn't see us getting chosen, that there would be thousands of applicants. I persisted, asking what we had to lose, and pointing out that they could only say no. So I rang up and left my name and number and forgot all about it until one day I was at home and the phone was ringing. "Can I speak to Mrs Carey? This is Chris Kelly from *Castaway 2000.*" And then it clicked, why he was ringing me up. He wanted to know where I saw the ad and he told me what they were planning on doing and invited us for a weekend away.' That there was no Open Day for the Carey family shows how very keen Lion TV were to get their ethnic balance right.

In London, Julie Lowe had just been made redundant. She had spent seven years as a trade-desk co-ordinator at a stockbroker's in the City when one fine day (18 August 1999, to be precise) her bosses had marched into the office. 'Well, boys and girls,' they said, 'as from one o'clock we are no longer in the US Government Treasury market and this office is closed. Sorry about that, but that's just the way it goes.' A week later, adjusting to her new freedom, Julie was having lunch with a friend in town. 'We decided we were going to go to a show that evening, so I bought the *Evening Standard*, picked out our show, and put the paper in my bag. I didn't even look through it till the weekend. But seeing a *Castaway* advert headlined BORED OF THE CITY? TIRED OF MILLENNIAL MADNESS? I thought, Well, I'm not doing anything else, a year on a Scottish island sounds quite good to me.' An Open Day followed shortly afterwards and by the end of September she was thigh-deep in mud in the Lake District.

'Having selected a varied and interesting group of people from the CAT week,' noted Cynthia McVey in her journal, 'we then had to fill some gaps. The first group was, in the main, very assertive and many of those selected were strong rather than silent types. Therefore, I suggested to Lion TV that it was essential to include some quieter, calmer, negotiator types. The second group of interviewees were not all negotiators but in general terms they were less assertive than the first group. They got on exceedingly well together, seemed supportive of each other and were very keen to go to the island.'

This time round the selection was shorter and sharper, with Lofty Wiseman and Cynthia McVey now the only experts advising. Split once again into red, yellow and green teams, the would-be castaways had to face new competitive challenges: constructing a machine to catapult an egg, fishing with a makeshift line, carrying the materials to build a raft through a tough assault course, then racing the raft around a lake.

Like Ray Bowyer on the first course, ex-brickie turned Liverpool driving instructor Trevor Kearon had worked out what the selectors were looking for. 'You basically had to have something to give,' he says, 'but you also had to be able to move about within a group of people and socialise.' He reckoned he might have what it took. 'Being a driving instructor, that's pure socialising constantly. You're dealing with people from the young to the old, there's always a divorce going on, a marriage, an eighteenth birthday, a ruby wedding, there's always something happening with the pupils you're teaching.' ('*Lily Savage on speed* was my phone comment on Trevor,' researcher Elaine Paterson remembers. 'He was very funny, he chatted about all these women he would miss. There was Lusty Linda and Sexy Sadie, he had names for all of them.')

Lancashire dinner lady Gwyneth Murphy had been surprised to be invited at all. 'We never thought we'd get through all the interviewing,' she says. 'If I'd have known what I would end up doing I'd never have gone – but we did it.' Cassie Carey was wondering whether she had made a mistake. 'It was pouring down outside this tent,' she remembers, 'it was really, really cold. I said to Gordon, "D'you mean to tell me this is the condition we'll have to live in when we go on this blessed island?"' Council worker Gordon, however, was now encouraged enough to be hoping for selection. 'I think I can contribute to the project as far as building is concerned,' he told the ever-roving cameras. 'Also, because of my farming background, I know quite a bit about planting stuff and producing stuff.' His reaction to the challenges of the assault course had surprised him. 'I was dreading it,' he said, 'because I don't like getting myself muddy. But, believe it or not, I started to do it, and I actually enjoyed it. I think something's wrong with me,' he joked. 'I must be sick.'

The Most Horrific Weekend

The two groups of castaways were now brought together for the first time; at a weekend in a hotel in the Lake District over 23/4 October. As a scene in

Programme Four was to make clear, there was discord: mostly over the contract that Lion had drawn up, which was not acceptable to some of the castaways. 'It was a completely outrageous contract,' says Rosemary Stephenson. Ron Copsey agreed: 'It was so one-sided. I had done various deals, record contract deals, which are notoriously loaded in favour of the record company. This was a worse contract. So me and Roger – God bless him – fought vehemently.' Shahana Meer, a Lion director, says, 'In fact the contract was nothing like a record contract and contained no real obligations upon the castaways other than the agreement to be filmed – a standard industry practice for television contributors – and in return Lion provided for the castaways for a whole year.'

Much of the disagreement centred around the proposed tie-in *Castaway* book (this very book that you are reading now). 'People were very unhappy about it,' Rosemary continues, 'because we hadn't been told about it – it was suddenly sprung on us, and what we hadn't appreciated was that we were expected to hand over all our private diaries. I was really cross about that, because I keep a diary anyway and I hadn't realised this was part of the deal – that anything you wrote was going to be their property basically.' The contract also expected the castaways to sign away their rights to write or talk about the project in public in perpetuity. 'There was one girl who was a photographer, Ron wanted to write, it sort of meant that people felt they were being gagged – it was totally unacceptable. And on the book issue,' says Rosemary 'we said that we were not prepared to hand over our private diaries, that if we were writing for the book that would be something separate, basically that we would have the right to write a diary that wasn't theirs.' Another issue was accommodation. A pre-fab dormitory block idea was not welcomed by the group – and nicknamed 'Stalag Castaway' by Ron Copsey.

'There were also funny instances,' says assistant producer Paul Overton, 'like when we were suggesting we were going to provide wet weather clothing for them all, jackets and boots. Ron straightaway said, "I've not had anyone buying clothes for me since I was a child. It's just abhorrent the idea of someone else clothing me, just give me the money and I'll go and get them myself." Obviously we were planning to buy in bulk and get a reasonable deal on it.'

For Shahana Meer, the Lion TV production director who had prepared the contract, Windermere was 'the most horrific weekend … it'll stay with me forever.' She had raced to put all the individual contracts together in the short timeframe available. 'What we really wanted to do was try and get the contract sorted out before Windermere, so that Windermere could be a place where the two groups who'd not met could get together and concentrate on the project.

What we wanted them to do was not be sitting there going, "I think point 2:1a is incorrect", but, "Isn't this fantastic!" and "Let's see how this is going to work!"'

Chris Kelly believes that when the castaways got the contract they were slightly blown away by the detail of it. It uses terms like exploitation, but these terms were required to enable Lion to deliver the rights package required by the BBC which, in turn, are terms used in respect of grants of intellectual property rights. It raises the whole issue of merchandising, and I think the white collar workers amongst our lot suddenly saw the revenue potential of *Castaway 2000* and I think mistakenly started to see what they could get out of *Castaway 2000*. Then all it takes is for a couple of people to say, "Listen, we're being taken for a ride."'

According to Jeremy Mills, 'there were two or three people who were basically instrumental in stirring things up. By which I mean Ron and Roger, no question about that. Roger was mostly concerned about the facilities and it not being about survival. Ron was more bothered about the book. He also felt he was being victimised, I think. The finger was being pointed at him because he was the spokesman.'

The problem was further compounded by the difference in attitudes between the first and second groups, something psychologist Cynthia McVey had anticipated. 'Classic social psychology studies,' she wrote in her journal, 'have shown that if one group is formed and introduced to a second group then conflict and rivalry is likely to follow.' As Julie Lowe – of the 'negotiator type' second group – confided to the confessional video diary camera placed in an annexe to the main meeting room; 'It's been one hell of a shock meeting up with the other group. They're in a different place to us completely. They're fairly angry and suspicious at the way the contract things have gone. The second group, my group, I think we were still at the euphoric stage, thinking everything's great, the contract is mainly OK.'

Paul Overton points out another area of divergence: 'This is where the concept of what it was all about really came to a head. The first group were expecting much more of the, "Let's paint a new society, a new future" attitude; whereas the Keswick group had a more traditional romantic view of going back to working the land and traditional methods. It was just completely different outlooks.'

'There was also the inevitable thing,' says Chris Kelly, 'about some people not wanting to go against some of the stronger leaders, because they knew they were going to have to live together for a year. So in public they would put their hands up to agree with something and then come to a member of the production team after the meeting and say, "Look, I don't really agree with this, but I don't want to be seen to go against it."'

'On the Saturday morning,' says Shahana Meer, 'I went round to nearly every single person individually and asked them whether they were happy with their contract. They all said, "Absolutely, we're all fine, it's not a problem." But by the afternoon, when they all got into their meetings, which we weren't allowed to go to, they all voted not to sign. It was amazing.'

In the end it was a brave member of the first group, Ben Fogle, who stood up and made, off camera, what Jeremy Mills describes as 'a calming speech of moderation'. 'Ben got up,' says Chris Kelly, 'and said, "Look, I think we've lost sight of what we're doing this for. There's too much bickering going on and I think we should be looking to see what we're getting out of the island next year." There was a round of applause. Ron stormed out, Roger and Rosemary took it personally, and then Ron went home – which is all in the programmes. Ron's an ex-actor. If you're not saying, "We love you, Ron," he thinks you don't love him. So he did this drama queen bit and came up to me and said, "I'm going, Chris." I think he was fully expecting me to say, "Please don't go, Ron." But I said, "OK, you know, see ya." Then I added: "The door is always open, if you want to come back, give us a call," knowing full well he'd be back.'

In the fourth programme, in front of the video diary camera, Ron makes a dramatic figure in a pale blue tracksuit top. 'I thought the idea of going to the island would be about freedom and choice,' he tells his private primetime audience, 'and living a different way, and it doesn't seem to be about that.' On screen, other castaways then voice their disappointment about his departure. For Sandy Colbeck of (like Ron) the first group, 'he was *the* character, as far as I was concerned. He would have been a wonderful fulcrum, around which a lot of laughter, humour etc, would have centred.' Julia Corrigan, also of the Wales group, tried and failed to persuade Ron to stay.

But Mike Laird wouldn't have missed him. 'It's got nothing to do with his sexuality,' he says, 'I just don't see eye to eye with the guy.' As far as Mike was concerned, the weekend had confirmed that many of the castaways had 'turned slightly soft'. 'They've put in these demands and they're all being met by Lion. They're getting bedframes and mattresses, they're getting wash handbasins, professional builders to assist with the building. At CAT, we had gone on a building programme and we were taught how to make fundamental shelters out of wooden frames. That was my hope: that we would be able to say, "We built this house."'

Despite all the ructions, though, some basic ground rules had been agreed between production company and castaways: 1) that they could receive (and send) letters, but not parcels; 2) that they would allow no visitors onto the island; and 3) that apart from one group radio, the castaways would have no personal radios on their island, nor, obviously, mobile phones (though Harris was still at that time apparently beyond the reach of all networks). For emergencies they would be equipped with both a satellite phone and a VHF radio to contact the local coastguard. Otherwise, apart from the fortnightly visit of a boat bringing essential supplies and mail (subject to the weather), they would be on their own. They would have a fixed budget, which amounted to approximately £30 per person per week, for buying everything from food to necessary tools and equipment; including a suggested £5 'personal allowance', which could be spent on non-essential items, from toothpaste to the occasional bottle of alcohol. Otherwise they were restricted to what they could pack into their single crate (dimensions 1 x 0.6 x 0.6 metres): clothes, bedding, boots, hobbies and so forth. In best *Desert Island Discs* style, they were also allowed one 'luxury item', which could be taken to the island outside their crate if necessary.

We're Going To Do It!

'Are we going to get this finished by Christmas?' Chris Kelly was asking, as he sat, at the start of November, with Andy McAvoy and his sketchpad in the bright, big-windowed front lounge of Tarbert's Harris Hotel. Renovation on the steading and schoolhouse was already going ahead apace, as was construction of the toilet block. But where were the castaways going to live? The pair had decided that the 'Stalag Castaway' block was a non-runner. Quite apart from the castaways' lack of enthusiasm, it wasn't going to look right on camera. Instead the architect had come up with an idea for futuristic looking 'pods' – rounded Scandinavian style wooden buildings that would sit sensitively in the landscape.

'I had effectively two working days to draw it up,' McAvoy recalls. 'I went through various connotations, but eventually came across the idea that to create a rounded form in the landscape we were looking at manufacturing a large rounded piece of timber. It would probably have been easier to do it in steel, but steel in that environment wouldn't be a sensible material to use, because of exposure to the sea, rusting, and also for aesthetic reasons. Timber buildings suit that landscape – it's something that can fall back to earth when it's finished. The quickest way I initially thought of doing it was to take something like a glue-laminated beam, which would form the primary structure of the pod. I'd been given a brief for a minimum of sixteen bedrooms, which meant four per pod, which quickly lent itself to the cruciform plan. Then I came up with a lay-out that would allow the castaways to have direct access via a sheltered porch – where they could cast off their boots and coats – to the door of their rooms. This one door would be their degree of privacy for this year.'

McAvoy returned with drawings that Kelly approved. So the architect immediately got on the phone to find a manufacturer who could put his glue-laminated beams together in a hurry; they were looking at completion by New Year at the latest, he explained. Then he had a bit of luck. A company called Carpenter Oak, with whom McAvoy had worked before, asked if he'd be interested in making his arches from native Scottish oak.

McAvoy was instantly interested, but knew it was quite some undertaking. 'Where do you find twelve bent oak trees, in this time scale, are you sure you can pull this off?' he asked. As it happened, not all of the oak was to come from Scotland. In South Wales, there'd been a lot of storm damage earlier in the winter, and trees that had come down with bent main trunks, so they were able to chainsaw those into a basic form. Then, rather than bring the arches onto site in one piece, the plan was to bring them on in two or four pieces. The Carpenter Oak yard manager assured McAvoy that he could do the job in the time, so there was now a fixed on-site start date of the third week of November. This left just under six weeks for the actual building, not including Christmas.

'When Andy finally clinched Carpenter Oak,' says Paul Overton, 'he was ecstatic. "Right," he said, "We're going to do it!" He'd worked with them before and he was convinced they were going to manage it, because they were some of the best craftsmen in the country and he had assurances from them that they were going to be able to get at least two of the pods ready, if not all four, by the New Year.'

A Spy in the Camp

One castaway who hadn't made it to Windermere now joined the group as a late entry. Tanya Cheadle, 25, was going to be the resident film maker on the island. Already employed by the BBC as a director on *Watchdog*, she had seen an article in the BBC in-house magazine *Ariel*, headlined *Wanted: Film-maker prepared to rough it*. 'As well as having some production experience,' says series producer Chris Kelly, 'our film maker needs to be able to contribute something else to the community – whether it's experience of living on a kibbutz, or of DIY, or growing up on a farm or first aid or whatever. The filming role is secondary. They need to blend in. We don't want them to be perceived as part of the production team or a spy in the camp.'

For Tanya, who had spent time both on a kibbutz and travelling alone, accepting the challenge was not simply a sound career move. That was 'obviously one aspect of it'. But: 'the hook for me is more the observing of the community, on an intellectual level, How is this going to work?' Tanya remembered as a child seeing the famous documentary on the group who tried to live as if they were in an Iron Age community. 'When people talk about the dream of the ideal society, everyone talks about going back to agrarian society, living in small groups, helping each other out, none of this materialism, blah, blah – but this is like putting that to the test. As someone who loves history I can't pass up on the opportunity to be part of that. I mean this is the only time in my life that I can do it, I haven't got any ties.

'If someone asks you to do this,' she continues, 'it weighs you up as a person. I could have said, "No, I'll stay in my nice comfortable BBC job and my nice little flat in Chiswick" but that's not why I got into television.'

Tanya, blonde, attractive, single and 'very self-sufficient', was undoubtedly going to add spice to the experiment. In the series of quick interviews about romance featured in the first programme, she giggles fetchingly as she says, 'What would happen if I slept with a married man on the island? Can you *imagine*?'

You Can't Walk Away From It

Up in Scotland, meanwhile, Andy McAvoy had got the thumbs up from both the Western Isles Planning Department and, crucially, Scottish National Heritage: 'We sent them some 3D sketches of what the pods would look like and they came back and they were ecstatic, saying "Absolutely, if you can pull this off in the time scale that's the kind of approach we would like to be seen taken."'

This gave McAvoy three weeks to start building the foundations and organise the main contractor, who would only come on site at the end of the third week in November if the foundations were ready to drop the oak arches into place. There was one primary concern and that was site access: how on earth were they going to carry pieces of oak weighing just over a ton apiece onto the island? Especially given that at that time they were unable to get any building materials at all over the strait from Harris, because of the bad weather.

'At that point there was a phone call to one of the directors of Lion TV,' says McAvoy. 'We told them that if we were to going to do this, we'd have to rely on being able to helicopter large elements into place. It posed a real big question: we're just about into the twenty-first century, we have the available technology, but is it deemed to be the sensible thing to be seen to be flying in large pieces of twenty-first-century material to an environment like this?'

With just over a month to go to Christmas, it was deemed if not sensible, then essential. 'The helicopters were mad,' says Shahana Meer, who was watching the original budget of £75,000 for the site development spiralling ever upwards, 'but what can you do? You can't walk away from it and you've got a time limit.' So the extra money was found and the helicopter was hired. 'From that moment,' says Andy, 'everything seemed infinitely more possible, and actually the pilots became quite challenged with the idea that they would be dropping into place two and a half tons of oak and helping prop that up on the foundations'. The project had moved quite a way from the days of Build Your Own Post-and-Beam House.

The main contractor had now started pouring the nine necessary concrete footings onto the raw granite of the island. By the time Carpenter Oak arrived on site, two foundations were complete. The contractors worked in parallel, half the foundations being poured as the first oak frames were being erected. 'That ten-day period of overlap was very, very tense,' says McAvoy, 'because we needed forty-eight hours for the concrete to cure before they could load it and the first frosts of winter were coming along. We made it by a matter of hours. And that was it!' Once the frames started going up, the next big challenge was the windows and doors. 'That's when we really started to reinvigorate the local economy,' says McAvoy. 'Every window and door manufacturer in Harris and Lewis was contacted. In the end there was a chap in Stornoway who'd just been made redundant by the biggest building company on the island, and he'd set up his own workshop. We went along with the biggest order he'd ever seen for windows and doors consisting of sixteen full-height glazed fixed screens and sixteen opening doors with full-glazed components on them. And we wanted them in two and a half weeks. He took the bait and said, "That's just what I need before Christmas."'

'Andy's in the programme,' remembers Chris Kelly, 'saying, "We could do it, if we get every day like today." But every day isn't like that in the Western Isles, particularly when you're going from autumn into winter, there are wind speeds that make the builders go off site, down tools. It was a push. They were saying to me since late November, early December, "It's not all going to be ready, what's the priority?" So Andy and I worked on what the priorities were. I talked to Jeremy about the editorial line and it was never a problem for us to have builders on the island, getting it ready. The most important thing symbolically was that all the castaways were on the island to see the New Year in.'

Gelling Quite Well

In addition to the teams of builders already on site, Andy was about to get some extra help – from the castaways themselves. A sixteen-strong Advance Party was now arriving on the island, where they were to stay crammed into the little three-bedroomed MacKay House, along with Assistant Producer Paul Overton and a camera and sound man.

Their first impressions of their new home were encouraging. 'Even more fantastic than I could ever imagine,' Gwyneth Murphy told the video diary that was waiting to record the castaways' intimate thoughts in the smallest of the three upstairs bedrooms. 'It's amazing, absolutely amazing,' enthused picture-editor Ben Fogle. 'Just beautiful, the setting is fantastic,' said management consultant Liz Cathrine. For secretarial assistant Tammy Huff – freshly escaped from Sandy – landing in the helicopter was 'like every Christmas, birthday and dream rolled into one'.

The first of the group to stand out was action-man Mike Laird. Always one of the strongest voices in favour of the survival aspect of *Castaway 2000*, he was determined now that he was on the island that he shouldn't lose sight of his ideals. 'I decided,' he wrote, in the daily journal he had now started keeping, 'that I did not want to set foot in the MacKay House and that I had come to get away from "real houses". These were words I was soon to eat.'

Mike chose to bed down in a tiny builders' Portakabin, which rocked around in the wind. 'I was tired,' he wrote, 'because my sleep had been broken, but I was glad that I'd endured it. I felt proud.' Mike had at least avoided Ray Bowyer's snoring, which troubled not just the castaways who were sharing the ex-builder's room, but architect Andy McAvoy. 'Outrageous,' he told the camera, emerging bleary-eyed in the morning. 'I haven't heard anybody snoring like that since my grandfather.' Ex-stockbrokers' co-ordinator Julie Lowe wasn't too keen on the arrangements either. 'I hated it,' she recalls, 'sleeping with all these strange men I'd never met before. It was very odd going into a room of seven people and not knowing who six of them were.'

In the morning, the weather was, Mike wrote, 'appalling – cold, wet and very, very windy'. Nonetheless the team of castaways set eagerly to work around the site: erecting the temporary greenhouses or 'polytunnels' in which their vegetables would eventually grow; building a bridge over the little stream that ran across the middle of the site; putting up the tank into which drinking water from the loch up the hill would be siphoned; levering into position the windmill that would generate the community's electricity. With time at such a premium the assistance of all these extra pairs of hands was, says Andy McAvoy, 'absolutely crucial. If they hadn't come on and been involved in digging their own drains, helping renovate buildings, stacking and preparing materials, the project wouldn't have been feasible.'

'By the end of the day,' Mike wrote, on 8 December, 'I was totally soaked through. It was partly my fault as I had not worn my waterproofs.' Despite this, he returned stoically to his Portakabin. But, 'whilst asking for some matches to light my Trangia cooker, purely for the heat it would put out, Gwyneth dragged me indoors'. 'I pushed him in,' said the ever-considerate Lancastrian dinner lady, 'and told him to stop being such a silly boy and get in the warm. He was wet through.' 'In many ways,' wrote Mike, 'I was sad, but also glad that I had given up. It would have made socialising tricky.' For Liverpudlian driving instructor Trevor Kearon, Mike was 'trying too hard, a man on a mission'. Ben agreed. 'He tried to do his macho thing and it just made him look like an utter fool.'

Despite breaking his resolution of 'never setting foot in the house', Mike was determined to continue sleeping in the Portakabin, though now on a borrowed lilo rather than the hard floor. But he was happy to join the other castaways as they sat around in the kitchen after their day's hard work cooking, eating, drinking, and having a sing-song – everything from 'Ilkley Moor Ba'Tat' to Irish rebel songs of Padraig Nallen. 'We worked very hard and relaxed in similar fashion,' said the Cavan man. 'We got pissed quite a lot and the mood was really good.'

One castaway who was not joining in with this merriment was black Seventh Day Adventist Gordon Carey, forbidden by the rules of his religion to drink alcohol, eat certain types of fish, and work on Saturday sabbath. 'I can see divisions coming along,' Gordon confided to camera, as he sat alone by the steading, 'but I just hope that they can understand why I have to disassociate myself from some of the activities they are carrying on, because my lifestyle is different to their lifestyle. Most of what they're doing doesn't interest me anyhow. For instance, I don't drink alcohol, so that already put me out on a limb. Also there are certain foods I don't eat, so there has to be a different cooking arrangement for myself.' Gordon had sworn that he would never slag anybody off on the video diary. But off-camera, later, he recalled, 'Because we were all in the MacKay house, we couldn't have our own space, so we had to sleep in the communal area. And they were drinking till one a.m. in the morning and I couldn't get to sleep. This really annoyed me.'

Mike Laird, direct as ever, had another perspective on the Gordon situation: 'He is very religious,' he wrote. 'Also coming from a different cultural background creates ... issues. He spends a lot of time sitting in a separate room on his own. He converses little, rarely shares jokes and never plays cards, even for fun. When he is with us in the same room he often has his radio and headphones on. Some people are getting a bit pissed off with him, saying that he's not really pulling his weight and moans too much.' 'He's ostracised himself,' said Ben Fogle, 'because we've made it our business to say, "Gordon, would you like to come in here, would you like to help out, would you like to play cards, would you like to come and listen to a story?" – whatever. He's definitely apart – when we're in one room, he's in the other. It's almost like he deliberately swaps rooms.'

Musing on camera on his isolation, Gordon was revealing about the extent to which it was self-imposed, or at least expected. 'I've been ostracised for a long time,' he went on, 'in various different things that I've done in my life since I've been in this country, so that doesn't bother me. It's like water off a duck's back, you know. It's like being called names because you're black, it doesn't bother me now at all. At first I just used to want to kill 'em, but now I just realise, as you grow older you get wiser and you think it's just pointless – if they have a problem with it, it's their problem, it's not my problem.'

The group, nonetheless, were forming firm friendships that would surely influence the way things developed over the year to come. On the ferry over from Skye, London journalist Ben Fogle and Gloucestershire decorator Colin Corrigan had been standing out on deck together. 'I was just looking at Colin,' Ben told the video diary, 'and he was saying he's going to bring his daughter Tasha here and that even when he's gone in many years' time and for the rest of her life she's going to have this experience with her, it'll be, like, the highlight. And Colin's eyes started welling up and I just looked at him and my eyes started welling up too, and it was just – oh, I can't really explain the feeling.'

In the kitchen, Gwyneth Murphy and Julie Lowe had been cooking together. 'She's a single woman of thirty-seven,' Gwyneth told me later, 'and we just bonded, she's absolutely lovely, she's like something out of *Jackanory*, gorgeous, and I've never had a sister, so she's like my little sister.' Padraig Nallen and Mike Laird had been for a walk. 'We had a great conversation,' wrote Mike in his diary, 'about the frequency of poos. We discovered that we are both normally once a day chaps and yet I have only been three times since leaving the mainland. Padraig commented further that his have been of average consistency and size and far easier to wipe off as he has not been drinking Guinness.'

As the castaways slowly got to know the human beings beneath the stereotypes there was a certain amount of teasing too. Perhaps inevitably, Ben

Fogle bore much of the brunt of this, laughing off good-natured mockery of his 'posh accent', his habit of describing virtually everything that pleased him as 'amazing' and his lack of familiarity with the ways of the workaday world. But beneath the banter, there were genuine frustrations. 'Preparing lunch,' wrote Mike Laird, who was Ben's cooking partner for a day, 'was totally laughable. I was doing a pasta bake and anything I asked Ben to do had to be explained in detail. Even when I asked him to chop and sauté some onions I needed to explain this.' Mike seemed genuinely shocked, 'It's actually quite staggering what he comes out with and despite his education how little common sense he has.'

'Mike got a bit stressed with me,' Ben confessed to the video diary, 'because I didn't seem to know how to do everything. Most people seem to put up with it and show me, but Mike found it a little bit more annoying, I think, than most people.'

The class issue was highlighted a couple of days later when Ben went for a walk by himself to the top of Taransay's main mountain – Ben Raah. On his return he found a table laid for one, with candles, a vase of flowers and wine, with builder Ray and butcher Colin in attendance as waiters. 'Excuse me, sir, would you like to try it?' teased Colin as he poured the wine. And of the cutlery layout: 'We couldn't get Smithers to put them out correctly.' 'It's to make him feel at home because he comes from a rather grand background,' he added to camera. Ben's loud laughter and cries of, 'I'm embarrassed, I don't want to sit on my own,' demonstrated perhaps the years of training for such tests and teases he'd had at boarding school, where he'd spent his first term away from his nannies and two sisters 'in tears, I hated it'. Or perhaps he was just overflowing with simple good spirits after his climb. 'The island is beautiful,' he told the video diary. 'From the top of the mountain you can see the sand spit going out to where the other, smaller mountain is, and turning round you can see the loch and all the hills in the background, and the clouds coming over and it's just amazing.' 'Colin and Ray laid a table for Ben as he is from a class above us all (yawn)" wrote Mike in his journal. 'It was actually quite funny.'

One thing the group had quickly to get used to was the early darkness and long evenings of the northerly isle. Quite often they dined at four-thirty and were ready for bed at seven. 'I knew this would happen,' said management consultant Liz Cathrine, 'but I'm used to filling my time all the time, going places and seeing different people, so I think I need to think quite carefully about how I'm going to fill my evenings next year. I love talking, but there's only so much talking you can do.' Trevor Kearon fantasised about life back home in Liverpool. 'Usually I'd be out on the town on a Saturday night. I don't know if I fancy sitting round the dinner table playing cards for fifty-two weeks of the year and missing out on me doner kebab and me few beers.'

The arrival of more builders and joiners to work on the pods had now put paid to Mike Laird's survivalist sleeping arrangements. 'Within twenty minutes of being on the island,' he wrote in his journal, 'the fucking pod builders have tried to take over. All my diving gear, which had been laid out to dry in one of the Portakabins, was casually thrown out on the grass. Then they started employing all of Colin's butchery gear. I could hardly believe it. Not happy. To top it all off, they suddenly announced they were taking over the cabins and I had to go and sleep inside. I had two minutes to pack, so stuck all I had into bin liners. I had withstood all the cold and the damp to be turfed out by shitheads.' His first night inside, though warmer, had new hazards. 'With Ray and Colin snoring through the night I did not sleep at all well,' he complained to his diary.

At the end of their ten days of hard infrastructure creation, the castaways had moved things on quite a bit. The polytunnels were up, a bridge had been built over the burn that divided the site, both water tower and windmill were erected and the steading was much closer to completion. They were almost all glad – they told the video diaries – that they had come on the Advance Party. 'Work-wise,' said Tammy Huff, 'we've just all gone out there and got our heads down and worked together as a team, which is really surprising considering how many people we have. So many things have been done since we got here and just looking at what we've created over the time has been absolutely fantastic.' 'I think everyone is gelling quite well,' agreed Colin Corrigan. 'No arguments up to now, touch wood,' said Ray Bowyer.

Management consultant Liz Cathrine had enjoyed, she said, 'doing something really practical'. 'It's weird, though,' she mused, unable entirely to quell her analytical side, 'I mean, obviously we're trying to put something together that's supposedly sustainable and all that sort of thing. But we've now got the paradox of us putting up a wind power system and in due course a hydro system, yet at the same time we've got a helicopter flying in and out, using God knows how much fuel – and the two sitting next to each other are really odd. Spending all this money on putting together our accommodation – we're not really going back to live off the land at all.'

Julie Lowe had eventually got used to her new conditions. 'I thought if anything I'd be having a hard time with the sharing because I live on my own and I've always had plenty of space, but crossed fingers, everything is okay, we're having a great time.' 'It's given us an insight,' said Gwyneth Murphy, practically.

'There are odd things that have cropped up now, so you think, Oh yes, I must bring that.' Ben agreed: 'I know the extra thing I'm going to need to pack – more waterproof trousers.' He also confessed to the video diary earlier reservations. 'I was a little bit wary about coming here, because I thought I might get here and what happens if I hate it and everyone gets on really horribly. But what's amazing is that everyone has got on so well.' Looking to the year ahead, he told the minicam, he thought they were going to 'breeze through it'. Then there were second thoughts: 'Double the number of people that are here now, and add children, and more dogs, and livestock, and less food, and windier weather, wetter weather, colder weather' – he smiled – 'yeah, actually it probably will be quite hard.'

Off Camera

Still relatively reserved with their confessional tool, there were two incidents that nobody mentioned to the as-yet-unfamiliar TV eye. One, surprisingly perhaps, for those used to his ever-reasonable TV persona, involved Ben Fogle. He laughs as he remembers the 'huge sense of humour failure' he had with Lion TV 'over a teeny incident', but at the time he threatened to leave the project. A consignment of booze that architect Andy had picked up in Stornoway for a last-night party was not paid for, as the castaways had expected, by Lion. Ben was furious. 'I just thought they were taking the piss,' he told me later. He had cancelled a party in London and lost a deposit to be on the advance party. He'd driven up to Scotland in his own car. He'd had to pay for his mobile phone to be disconnected. 'Basically I was spending hundreds of pounds to do this for free and I wasn't getting anything back.' For a moment, a mutiny threatened, led by the unlikely alliance of Ben and Ray. 'All hell broke loose,' wrote Mike Laird, 'and Ray and Ben said they would go to Glasgow to sort things out.' The resolution of the dispute was key in its foreshadowing of the terms of a relationship that was to become ever more complex and vexed as the project went on: that between the stranded castaways and their producer overseers. The remoteness of the island meant that moments like this were all too easily blown out of proportion. Once Chris arrived to speak to them direct, the situation was resolved and that evening the hoped-for 'piss-up' took place.

The second incident was to prove more significant, and happened after most of the castaways had left the island, but was still not mentioned on camera by the pair who returned. Gordon Carey, in Padraig's words, 'asked for and received payment' from the builders for work he was doing on the pods. It was only forty pounds, but he was 'shamed by the others' into returning it. Gordon has his own side of the story. 'I was working in the schoolhouse,' he told me in a later interview, 'and the whole place had to be plaster boarded. One day the head builder came up to me. I asked him how much he was paying me an hour. I jokingly said, "I want £30." We were just having a chat and a laugh. He said I was doing a good job and when I was finished he would give me a drink. So when we were leaving on the coach and he was paying the guys I rattled a tin and he called me over and gave me some money. I didn't think I did anything wrong. But that blew up into a huge stink with everyone else on the coach. By this time I was so annoyed, I got off the coach and offered him his money back. He said he wasn't going to take it back. I said he had to take it back, because people were getting the wrong idea. He said to take the money and buy everybody a drink. I said I wasn't going to do that either. So I gave him the money back. The thing that annoyed me was that nobody came to me and asked me what had happened. Instead they are telling you what happened. They were the judges, the jury and the witness. But I don't feel I have to explain myself to anybody.'

Before the project had even started, the community fault lines were already being firmly laid down.

Looking down from windturbine
Graveyard August 21st

Chapter 4

I Go To Taransay

Now in mid-training as a psychotherapist, forty-three-year-old Ron Copsey had led a somewhat chequered life. Born in Hornsey to a father who was a builder and decorator and a mother who was a home help, he was brought up on a big council estate in Tottenham. 'Didn't go to school for the last year,' he told me, as we sat together drinking instant coffee in his quiet flat in Hampton shortly before Christmas. 'Played truant for most of it, left at 15. It was a very violent school, kids throwing desks and chairs at teachers, and knives and beatings-up. Of course I got beaten up a lot because they didn't realise that I was gay, but they knew I was different. And I knew I was different, and somehow that made a difference. I'd be in the canteen at lunchtime and someone would say, "Copsey, we want to fight you." And I'd go, "Oh, no, not *again*." But I learned how to take care of myself, so it was good in a way, but it was quite a tough, sad childhood. Home was a volatile background, there'd be fights and so on.' Ron was the eldest, with a sister five years younger and a brother nine years younger.

As a teenager in the early 1970s, when legal homosexuality was only a few years old, Ron didn't come out as gay. Instead, he wore flamboyant clothes and had 'really long hair when it wasn't fashionable'. 'Before I started drinking and smoking my skin was absolutely clear and everyone thought I was a girl. People used to say to my Mum, "Your daughter's very good looking."'

Leaving school at fifteen he got work as an apprentice to a silk-screen printer, where he lasted three months; then in a factory, 'packing taps and spanners and crap like that'; then he found a job that was to 'change my life', as a messenger boy at the *Daily Mail*. 'The editor's secretary, Ena, took a real shine to me. One day she said, "You know you're smart, and you look great, and you're going to make something of yourself, but you ain't going to make it as a messenger. We've got a job going in here as the office boy."'

The editor of the time was the famous David English, staunch supporter of Mrs Thatcher, later to be knighted. When Ena was in doing dictation, Ron would be manning the outer office. 'I was sixteen and a half,' he recalls. 'I was taking calls from the world and his wife, as you can imagine.'

After a year Ena encouraged Ron to move on. 'You're wasted here,' she told him. Through the good offices of husband Harry – a famous sportswriter – Ena managed to get Ron a job as a trainee reporter with the *Hendon Times*. But after six months Ron was fired. 'Basically, I didn't have the educational clout to do that job properly,' he explains. The newspaper bought Ron everything he needed to go to college and he enrolled at an Adult Education Centre, where he did nine O-levels in a year followed by three A-levels. He was by now dating David English's daughter, Nicky. 'At this point the homosexuality totally suppressed. I knew that my family would take it really bad and my father would probably kill me. And that's exactly what happened, when I did come out, he disowned me.'

Nicky had now moved to Northampton to train as a photographer. She told Ron of a job going on the *Northampton Chronicle and Echo*, which, with a reference from Nicky's dad, he got. But after a couple of years it had all become routine and his laid-back attitude to the job eventually got Ron the sack when he muddled two cases with the same names – a flasher and a parking offence – and the misrepresented party complained.

But Ron had already decided to become an actor. After numerous applications, he eventually got a place at a method acting establishment in the East End, where he did well enough to be awarded a scholarship for his second year. But he didn't make it to the end: 'I got kicked out for fucking a lecturer. They said I wasn't the type of actor they wanted, and I went, "Excuse *me*, you gave me a scholarship."'

Now 'out' as a gay man, Ron formed a cabaret company, which did routines in gay clubs and private functions. Then he got his first professional job, in a nude revue called *Why Not Bangkok?* When that finished, the director gave Ron his first job in panto, as Buttons in *Cinderella* at the Key Theatre in Peterborough. Over eight seasons he worked his way up from bottom of the bill to 'my name above the title, number one dressing room, a grand a week'. During the rest of the year he worked as exclusively as an actor, taking supporting roles in everything from *Inspector Morse* to *Tucker's Luck*. Then, one day, he says, 'the applause stopped giving me a buzz'. Ron couldn't quite bring himself to give up acting entirely, so he borrowed a friend's name and set himself up as a part-time showbiz writer.

But before long Ron got tired of writing. 'I didn't want to freelance any more, and I thought, Well, I've got all these media contacts, so I'll set myself up as a

PR.' He looked after presenters and actors, including, for a while, Lily Savage. 'Then I got bored with that and I'd read this article about Nigel Martin-Smith who'd put Take That together, so I thought I'd have a go at that.' Ron assembled a four-piece band, two girls, two boys, and called it B-yond. They toured Asia, won a song competition for the United Kingdom in Europe and, Ron reckons, 'almost cracked it'. But one by one the girls left. 'At that point, I realised I didn't want to do that any more.'

Fortunately Ron had already found a new direction, training as a psychotherapist. 'There were too many things going on, and I wanted to keep things channelled and put all my energy into one area. I decided it was time to go to college and get a degree.' After a year at psychodynamic school, he switched to a humanistic training. 'Psychodynamics basically believe that people are born destructive and need controlling – and rules and laws to keep them in check. Humanists believe that we're born constructive and, given the right conditions to be able to grow healthily, human beings are basically loving and kind and nurturing.' This tied in with Ron's philosophy. He had been profoundly affected by reading *The Diary of Anne Frank* as a boy. 'It was when she said that despite everything she still believed that human beings were basically good – it just struck somewhere very deep in my heart and I realised I felt the same.'

It was while he was halfway through his first year of humanistic training that Ron saw the piece in the *Guardian* and decided to apply for *Castaway 2000*. 'I think it was something to do with what I'm learning about the mechanics of being human at college,' he told me. 'I just thought, God, this could be really interesting. How would I survive in this group? Who would I *be* in this group?' It would, he felt, help him in his training, perhaps teaching him tolerance and self-trust.

After his Windermere walkout at the end of October, Ron had had serious second thoughts about his dramatic departure. When the weekend was over, Chris Kelly had written him a letter. 'Saying,' says Kelly, 'you know, "I understand the situation but have a think about it." He phoned me four days later and said, "I think I might have made a mistake, but I'm still not sure." It was a kind of halfway house. I said, "Well, think about it, but let me know within the week." Two days later he phoned back and said, "Yes, I'd like to come back."'

It had been the sympathy from fellow castaways that had been one of the key things in persuading Ron to change his mind. Indeed, he told me, one of the reasons he had withdrawn from the project was: 'Who'd be my support when I'm down, when I'm going through a rough time? I wasn't aware that I'd even have support. But the phone calls that came afterwards from the community and the things that were said or written to me in cards made me realise that I would have support systems, and that I had already somehow gained respect from people, there was genuine affection there.'

But having made his decision Ron was still agonising about it, even now, in the middle of December, a fortnight before the project started for real. A couple of nights before, walking his beloved dog Charlie around the block, he'd written a poem, he told me, that expressed (at least some of) his turbulent feelings about giving up his life for a year to go and live on a remote Scottish island with thirty-five strangers. *I go to Taransay to discover my poet,* it began. He was going with the excitement of a child at Christmas, it continued; to add depth and texture and additional colours to his palette; with a special love in his heart for one person; to offer and receive friendship. The fifty-line meditation concluded with a reason that was typical of the romantic, mercurial Ron who was to prove such a key figure in the island community. *I go to Taransay because it calls.*

The Fank and the Tupping

The Lion production team, in the meantime, had been rushed off their feet. 'It was full on,' Elaine Paterson remembers. 'Weekends, social life – forget it. Christmas presents – no, not going to have them this year. It was one of those really intense, dramatic, hellish, but strangely exhilarating and enjoyable periods. Trying to co-ordinate 36 people getting from 17 different locations around the country, with crates, dogs, children and telescopes, at the same time as arranging filming schedules.' Alongside many other more familiar tasks, Paul Overton was helping agricultural researcher Becci Doig finalise choices for appropriate animals for the community. 'You can't just buy two Clydesdale horses and a couple of cows from a farm in Devon. The pigs have to be from Orkney; we got the pony from Muck. Everything had to be right for the conditions of the Western Isles.' The assistant producer was learning on the job. 'I was suddenly finding out what a wedder is – a castrated male sheep. We were going to be supplied with thirty wedders and thirty breeding ewes; the cows were going to have to be staggered so they had calves at different points in the year. It was ludicrous, television people trying to suddenly become farming experts.'

Production director Shahana Meer remembers one particularly confusing meeting. 'There were the owners of the island, two solicitors and myself and Chris and they were talking about "the fank". We had a long conversation about the fank, then I said, "I'm really sorry, what *is* the fank?" So they explained that's where the sheep get dipped. Then they talked about "the tupping", and there were all these boys and me and I said, "I'm sorry, what's the tupping?" They all sort of looked at the ground and at each other and then Norman MacKay said, "The tupping's when the boy sheep meets the girl sheep" and it was like, Oh *right*.'

Still trying to keep control of the budget, Meer was also having a tough time finalising contracts with the more hardline of the *Castaway* participants, in particular Ron Copsey the Latores and the Stephensons. 'It was a series of bitter battles,' says Jeremy Mills, 'really bitterly fought battles between Shahana and certain individuals about what was in the contract.'

'It went on for a long time,' says Meer. 'We had an addendum, then we had an addendum to the addendum. It became very personal. Roger's very good at making things personal. We were trying to make people aware of what the requirements for the programme were, but also that the reason they were enabled to do it was because the BBC had put money into it. A lot of them lost sight of that. We were trying to take on board their concerns, because I could understand that people were giving up a year of their lives to go there, but some got so ridiculous. For instance the satellite phone – we said we'd provide one, then it was, "How's it going to be maintained?" So I said, "Well, I can give you the batteries and we can check the phone, but if someone knocks the phone onto the floor and it breaks I can't do anything about that."

"Well, you have to do something about that – and what if the satellite goes down?" came the reply.

"If the satellite goes down I can give you flares, I can give you marine radio, but if someone steals all the batteries that's beyond what I can do ...' 'Roger" says Jeremy Mills, 'had got it into his head that we were completely out to stitch them up and do them in and it's not true. What seemed to have been forgotten was that the contracts also protected them.'

In the end, Lion set a deadline for the contracts. With some reservations, all the doubters signed.

Meanwhile, up on the island, the race was on to try to get the site ready for New Year's Eve. 'We came to a point just before Christmas,' says Andy McAvoy, 'where we had to admit that all the pods might not be completely finished, but the castaways could come on and occupy three buildings: the existing MacKay House, the schoolhouse that now had its roof off and the steading, which had its new roof on. Everybody was going to have to bed down and get involved in the building process and try and speed it up, with the promise of having the pods ready for some time in January.'

We'll Do It Together

Two of the advance party, Mike Laird and Trevor Kearon, had decided not to return home for farewells and parties like the others, but to stay on the island for Christmas. Without distractions, Trevor had been hoping to get some early work done on the three film scripts he was planning to write as his project for the *Castaway* year. But, as it transpired, Mike and Trev's work was cut out for them just looking after the builders and joiners who were still beavering round the clock on site.

By the following Monday the pair were starting to lose track of time. 'The start of the week is no longer something that affects us,' Mike wrote. But that evening bad news brought them back to reality. Mike's mother called on the emergency satellite phone to tell her son that Noel, an octogenarian retired Edinburgh surgeon who was Mike's much-loved friend and mentor, had died falling down some stairs at a Christmas party. 'Mum had worried about whether or not to break the news to me but I am glad that she did,' he wrote. 'The decision of whether to go home for the funeral only took me a couple of minutes to make.'

Trevor had been listening to the telephone call from the other room. 'Mikey's called to the phone. I think I shouted to him, "Ask Elaine what colour her underwear is" – it's a standard joke with Lion – but Mike just swore slightly and broke down a little bit when he heard his close family relative had died. So he comes into the kitchen, I give him a hug, pass him a hanky, he's quite upset which is understandable. He's been fostered, and this wasn't his dad but a close person to the foster family. We had a little chat for about two or three minutes and I said to Mikey – he doesn't like flying at the best of times – "Well, come on then, mate, I'll go with you. Tell Lion and we'll do it together." So Paul came on and okayed us both to go, then Chris came on saying, "Can we film it, not the actual funeral, but, can we bring a cameraman to the beach tomorrow and have a word with yourself and Trev?" Which I suppose is fair because we've all signed up to this.'

The demands of being part of a television documentary were now truly felt for the first time. 'Chris had mentioned to me last night,' Mike wrote in his diary, 'that he wanted me to speak on camera about Noel's death, but that he was concerned from a sensitivity point of view. I said that it was OK and that they could ask me stuff on camera. A chap called Jed came over from Harris and interviewed me. More tears. Then he interviewed Trevor. Then he shot the pair of us walking down the beach. I felt like I was doing a shoot for a gay travel programme! Then we were filmed getting into the helicopter to start the trip home to Edinburgh for Noel's funeral.' At Glasgow airport the pair were met by Cynthia McVey. In his diary Mike described Trevor's reaction: 'He said, "First it's helicopter, then hire car, then aeroplane, now shrink." A bit cruel, I thought. We all love Cynth.' The psychologist provided supper and dissuaded the pair from crashing the Lion Christmas party. The next morning they caught the train to Mike's mother in Edinburgh.

It had meant a lot to Mike that Trevor had agreed to accompany him home for this sad farewell. The father who had adopted Mike and his twin sister at birth had died some years before. An Edinburgh solicitor, he was 'very serious, his head in books, two degrees from Oxford, one degree from Paris', a complete contrast to adventure-loving Mike who had jacked in his degree at nineteen to get a job. Though Mike admits they 'loved each other to death' they had always been 'chalk and cheese'. Surgeon Noel, though never officially a foster father, was 'a lifelong friend who was a great influence in my upbringing'.

Funeral over, Mike was eager to return immediately to the island, without even attending Noel's wake. 'The temptation,' Mike says, 'was there to stay for Christmas because this was now 22 December. Lion told me I could stay for four days and go back on Boxing Day, but I wanted to get back to the island and get on with it. Otherwise, I'd settle down at home and be too comfortable, get upset, whatever, and I wouldn't be able to get off my backside and go back there.'

Mike and Trevor arrived at Horgabost beach just in time to catch the last helicopter flight over to the island. 'The crew had no idea that we were to be travelling to the island,' Mike wrote. 'If we had missed that flight we would have had to stay in a hotel for the next four nights.' But they were in luck, whisked over the stormy Taransay sound. Andy, the pod-squad, and all the other builders and joiners had now left and they were alone in charge of the island for Christmas.

300 Earl Grey Teabags

Back in their various homes on the mainland, the other castaways were closing down their old lives and attempting to pack their new one into their year's allowance of a single crate.

Colin and Julia Corrigan packed 'loads of fleeces and jumpers, went completely over the top. Every time we went into a shop and we saw a different fleece we bought it. Then loads of thermal socks and four scatter cushions. Everyone laughed about that, but I thought that as our bed was going to be a sofa in the daytime, I might want to lie on it and read a book and I'd want to feel I wasn't in bed.'

Ben Fogle's mother helped him with his packing. 'There was about 300 Earl Grey teabags, some champagne, some wine, some Pimms for the summer, zillions of candles, a teapot, pillows, a carpet, various games, lots of paper, pens – the idea is to write a book.'

Having finally made his mind up to go, Ron Copsey wanted to make sure he was challenged and stimulated by the year. He was taking watercolours, oils, pastels, a Linguaphone course to learn Spanish and French, writing material, pens and paper, and last but not least, pornography. 'There are times,' he said frankly, 'when, as Cynthia Payne says, "If the balls are full the mind's empty." It's why one of my concerns is that I have my own room.'

Tammy Huff had perfume, a 2kg bar of chocolate and an 'emergency kit' of lacy bra and pants. Padraig had foot odour destroyer; Ray, brewing equipment and a Rod Stewart wig; Gordon, a hot water bottle; Toby, a snorkel. They all had plans and ambitions for the year. Tammy Huff was going to learn to juggle, find out about photography, write and 'hopefully relearn French'. Sheila Jowers, the art teacher who as a student had sworn she would never teach, was now going to paint again, for herself. This was an intention thoroughly approved of by husband Peter: 'She's very talented, I said to her when we had children, "Don't go to work"; but we didn't have any money, she felt the need to, which has stymied her creativity, she's always giving her creativity to other people.'

Dr Roger Stephenson was going to teach himself 'particular piano pieces' and 'tackle my carnivore status', while wife Rosemary put into action her experiments in Home Education. Management consultant Liz Cathrine's primary objective was to 'learn different things and go back rounded'; Irishman Padraig Nallen hoped to 'learn a lot' ('even if it's just a little bit of a lot') and leave his cynicism behind; Toby Waterman might 'try a bit of sculpture, maybe flirt with a little poetry, play games, teach kids, everything'; Hilary Freeman had packed a Hedna fretsaw, and had all sorts of ideas about making 'things like jigsaws of the island, puzzles, I don't know'; artist Warren Latore had a plan to make a giant conceptual sculpture involving four enormous horns, one for each of the four winds, to be mounted on top of Ben Raah; Sandy Colbeck had bought a sewing machine and yards and yards of beautiful white cotton lace, with which she intended to make 'beautiful Victorian-type christening robes'.

The couples had each other and the singles – who knew? Ron Copsey *definitely* wasn't going to the island looking for love. 'If I wanted that I'd stand a much better chance here; but I'm actually going through a period in my life where I'm choosing not to date and not to have relationships.' The only person he found attractive anyway was, 'someone on the production team – OK, it's Paul Overton, we've developed quite an intimate relationship, he's straight, and he laughs about it and says, "This will never happen" and I say, "Well, you wouldn't be the first person to say that – which is the truth." '(Overton chuckles as he puts his view of the situation: 'Ron's suggested that to me quite often and has had to be told, pretty matter-of-factly, that it's not going to happen, Ron. Wake up and smell the coffee, mate. It would take a million years and I would still never be attracted to you, I cannot put it much more bluntly than that.')

Toby Waterman wasn't seeking romance either: 'It could be disastrous, spoil your friendship for the rest of the year. Nothing worse than to rush in and have to back out again.' He was philosophical about his prospects. 'Of all the women you meet so few are a match, why on earth should there be a good match on this island?' After her time on the advanced party, Julie Lowe was clear on her position: 'As regards the men on this island,' she told me, 'I'm very firmly ensconced in a relationship – it makes life an awful lot easier, because I really do not like being hunted as prey.' Trevor was equally forthright: 'I've come out here to do a job, if I wanted to be knocking around with women, or getting me head busted up with, Does she fancy me? Am I on for a hump? then I might as well have stayed home. I'm going celibate for the year. I'll live on me memories – all two of them.' Little did the driving instructor realise the lessons about love he would actually learn over the coming twelve months.

With who knows how many similar private hopes and fears about their year ahead, the castaways said their farewells to home and family, some at parties filmed by Lion TV. In Manchester, Ray's wife and daughter got him a strippogram, yielding a memorable shot of his grey, ponytailed head being clamped between the artiste's voluminous breasts. In Farington Leyland, Lancashire, Patrick Murphy was pictured grinning and jogging up and down with delight as he was serenaded by an Irish singer. In Cheltenham, Colin and Julia Corrigan got married on camera, with other castaways in attendance. And Ben Fogle, who had been one of those invited to the Corrigan wedding, was seen kissing goodbye to a sequence of beautiful young women at the trendy Market Bar in London's Notting Hill. His party had been 'just the best, everyone came, about two hundred and fifty, and that's when it suddenly sunk in, Wow, this is for a whole year.'

Though Ron Copsey was present at this event, Tammy Huff wasn't. The close friendship between picture editor and secretary had, according to Ben 'just cooled off'. 'We realised,' he told me much later in the year, 'that we were probably just too different. Perhaps it was more one-sided on my part. That is possible. But I thought really that I was coming on this as me, Ben Fogle, a single spirit, and I didn't want to come on this as a couple. That is what it felt like it would have been if we'd continued on.'

'We're two very different people,' agreed Tammy, in a separate interview. '*Too* very different,' she explained, 'too much very different. It wasn't right for us. His way of life, his way of thinking and his background are totally different from mine. He's a lovely guy, but there's a näiveté, he's a bit insensitive in areas, our viewpoints are different.' In a hotel the night before the Corrigans' wedding Ben, had made Ron his confidant. It was a confidence he was later to regret, 'Basically,' said Ron, some months later, 'he told me that he was going to dump Tammy. But he didn't dump Tammy until he was on to the project. He strung the girl along for a couple of months.'

Bad News

Christmas over, the castaways were finally on the move. In London, Ben, Ron, Tanya, Monica and Warren and their daughter Ciara all boarded the coach. It was, said Ben Fogle, 'a horrible journey, we were on that bus for ages, it was really cold then really hot. I think that's one of the reasons everybody became ill.' Tammy Huff joined at Sandy, and Sandy Colbeck at Woodall Services on the M1. 'We were all rather tired,' she says, 'particularly those people who'd come from London, they'd been on the coach since half-past five in the morning. But it was a good trip, we ate and drank and had music.'

Two other coaches picked up castaways from the West of England and Glasgow. All were headed for a hotel in the Kyle of Lochalsh. 'Two of the coaches got stuck in the snow in the middle of the Glencoe pass,' remembers researcher Elaine Paterson. 'We were all on our mobiles. "Where are you now?" "Oh, you're lost." We were trying to stick to the schedule. Paul and Ray were dying with the flu. Everybody was panicking and upset, except Ciara, who'd never seen snow before. She was poking her nose out the window and saying to Monica, "Look, Mummy, the stars are falling from the sky."'

Ex-stockbroker Julie Lowe had avoided joining 'the poor beggars' on the 'coach nightmare' by flying direct from Luton. As hand luggage she brought with her her luxury item – a tin bath. 'I decided that I couldn't be going for a year without a bath,' she says, 'so I found a tin bath in Covent Garden big enough for me to sit in with my legs straight. I walked with it on my head from Covent Garden, through Leicester Square down Piccadilly and up to the Ritz, where I was meeting friends for tea. The doorman told me they actually had their own baths, I didn't need to bring one in, so he took it off me. It was hysterical. It was so big and people were going, "Forgotten your umbrella, luv?" or "I'll scratch your back, darlin'" and crazy things like that.'

Trish Prater had also flown in, bringing her beloved dogs, Fran and Clare, who had to travel in a crate in the hold and ended up by accident on the conveyor belt in Baggage Reclaim.

Owing to the terrible weather conditions, the London coach didn't meet up with the other groups from Glasgow and Bristol at the hotel in the Kyle of Lochalsh until after ten at night. 'They chucked us into this room to eat,' says Ron, 'they didn't even want us to go and check into our rooms and change our clothes, everything was rush, rush, rush.' All the castaways were then up at 6.30 to catch the ferry to Harris, where they were driven to a bunkhouse outside Tarbert. 'That was really chaotic,' says Ben. 'All the children were there, the dogs, it was seriously hectic.' At this stage most of the castaways were still in the dark about the unfinished state of the island.

'We're in a bunkhouse,' says Ron, 'everyone's falling down like flies, with flu, chest infections, everything you can think of, and although there are a lot of clear days on which we could have gone over to the island we didn't go – so I smelt a rat.' 'They kept on putting us off,' says Warren Latore. '"Oh, we're waiting to talk to Andy," they'd say, and then it got to a point where Chris had to come over and talk to us.'

Producer Kelly was now on the island, finally coming to terms with the fact that he was going to have to explain to the castaways that their home wasn't yet fully ready to occupy. 'Between Christmas and New Year,' says architect Andy McAvoy, 'there was a forecast for even more severe weather and at that point some of the contractors decided they didn't want to build in that weather, and that they would rather come back later to complete. So there was a period of consolidation and re-planning. We spoke to the castaways, letting them know that the weather had been the deciding factor in it and that it had beaten us, but that it wasn't the end of the project, it was only a case of re-strengthening ourselves and all coming back in January and having a big push to get it finished.'

As well as major problems with the weather, because it was the Millennium a lot of the builders started getting a thirst for home. Naturally, they'd made arrangements for parties and big family gatherings and most of them were very worried about transport.

'Until I reached Tarbert on that bus,' says Paul Overton, 'I was still fully hopeful that there was going to be enough accommodation for everyone on the island. We'd explained to them that they were going to have to share for the first month, and we were looking at ideally two, but definitely one pod being ready, with room in the MacKay House, the steading and, if need be, the schoolhouse.'

On 30 December a meeting was called on the mainland. Chris Kelly rose to address the castaways: 'I'd like you all to go over today and look at the island and those of you that want to stay today, stay, and those of you that don't, can come back. All I'm asking is that you come for New Year's Eve, so that we can see the New Year in on the island.'

The problem of the unfinished site was now compounded by illness, which had spread rapidly through the bunkhouse. Philiy Page reckoned the bug had started with Ray, who had arrived at the Kyle of Lochalsh ill, 'coughing and hacking. The rest of us were fine, then everybody got it. In the bunkhouse, Ray was right by the door, and we were all sleeping around him, so I assumed it was Ray because he was the most ill when he arrived.'

Unbeknownst to the castaways another disaster had hit the project. On 27 December Elaine Paterson took a phone call in the Lion Glasgow office. It was Andy. 'Are you sitting down?' he asked.

'Er ... yes.'

'You'll never guess what I've been doing all morning.'

'What?'

'Picking up personal belongings from the beach at Horgabost.'

The helicopter carrying the crates of possessions over to Taransay had dropped, from 150 feet, a pallet of four, scattering belongings over a wide area. Elaine remembers thinking 'This is not happening,' then looking round the room going, 'Whose? Whose?' because some of the castaways were in the room, waiting for the coach. The unfortunate castaways were Dez Monks and Liz Cathrine, the Latore family, Julie Lowe and Ron Copsey.

The news was indeed shocking. 'For Miss "My-home-is-my-castle" Lowe,' wrote Julie in her circular letter home, 'this really is not fun. Going to retrieve my belongings from the trailer that everything has been chucked into is a miserable experience. I had had (among other things) five wine boxes, hot chocolate powder and a mirror in my crate, which in addition to sand, mud and salt water, makes for a right old mess. Lots of things are smashed out of existence and I am very upset.'

The whole thing had been made worse because of the destruction of a secret item that Julie dared not even tell the other castaways about – an old Vodaphone analogue mobile phone, that would work, she had discovered after extensive research on the phone to Harris, from the top of Ben Raah. Now Julie's lifeline to family and close friends lay smashed and covered in cocoa. (In floods of tears she confided in Ron, a man with whom she had never seen eye to eye, whom she later described as 'a constant source of irritation from Day One'. 'He asked me what the matter was and I told him. He was very sweet and supportive.')

For Ron Copsey the situation was made worse by the fact that the production team had decided to hold back the bad news. 'They chose not to tell us for three days,' he says. 'We just found that patronising. They treated us like children. They judge when we can handle news and when we can't.' 'It was held off for a day,' says Paul Overton. 'There was a big party, a karaoke night in the hotel, and I didn't go out that night, partly because I was ill, but partly because I felt bad about not telling them.' Lion – increasingly viewed as an authority figure – was once again taking the blame.

Over on the island the news had evoked a different response. 'Trevor and I,' wrote Mike in his journal, 'had been discussing the possibility of this happening earlier in the day.' Having discovered that he wasn't one of the victims, 'we did have a laugh at other people's expense and felt more sorry for some than others, which is, I think a measure of what is thought of the person themselves. Great hilarity erupted when we heard that Ron's gay pornographic magazines had been blowing about up and down the beach in full view of the assembled contractors and journalists.'

Chris Kelly meantime was learning just how sceptical some of his castaways were. 'One of them said to me, "How did you decide that it would be Ron and Julie's crates that should be dropped?" I said, "What d'you mean? You really seriously think we primed a helicopter to drop crates, just to get a reaction?"' 'As if!' cries Shahana Meer. 'As *if* I'd want to add any more stress into my life at that time!'

In the bunkhouse, meanwhile, the flu was spreading, and not just among the castaways. 'It was the first time in my life,' says Paul Overton, 'I've seen a virus just spread through a group of people within days – a couple of days. It just wiped out eighteen to twenty of the entire bunch.'

The fortunate ones who were still well were now heading over to their new home by helicopter. 'We had the most beautiful glorious weather,' says fifty-eight-year-old Sandy Colbeck, who had been waiting for an adventure like this all her life. 'I'd never been in a helicopter before, either, it was something I've always wanted to do. And there was the whole picture from the air, the sky was blue, the sun was beating, I don't think we could have had a better day to see the place for the first time.'

Last to arrive on the scene was – unfortunately in the circumstances – Dr Roger Stephenson. He had been working until Christmas Eve and had then had two sets of family to say goodbye to, in London and the Isle of Man. 'So we arrived late on 30 December, at Harris. We were supposed to stay in this bunkhouse place, but everybody had flu, so we said, "No way!" We were healthy, we weren't going to catch these bugs sleeping in this cramped accommodation, so we just repaired to the Harris Hotel and grabbed a room of our own, the four of us, and stayed there. Very interesting discussions with Chris the producer that night, because it became absolutely clear that everything was not ready. Still they were giving us the positive spin of, "Don't worry, one pod's finished," so we were very reluctant even to go, because we knew what we were going to see. But we were persuaded to go basically for the party.'

Psychologist Cynthia McVey summarises how the doctor's unwillingness to stay was seen by many of the sick castaways in the bunkhouse. 'There was a lot of resentment built up, with people saying, "Where is he? He's supposed to be,"' – Cynthia's voice drops to a discreet whisper – '"the bloody doctor!"'

On the evening before Millennium Eve, the conflicts of January were shaping up nicely.

Taransay Starlings

Chapter 5

The Doctor and the Press

'My hangover isn't actually too bad,' Mike Laird wrote in his journal on New Year's morning. 'Certainly not as bad as yesterday. Many people returned to Harris, including Padraig, who had to get his leg treated. Vegging out took up quite a lot of today, but there was also a fair bit of work done on the steading. Many are still ill.'

Trevor Kearon, laid out on the floor of the front room of the MacKay House ('as ill as a dog, it was the illest I've been in my whole life')' was nonetheless looking on the bright side. 'I was on a mat down there, couldn't move and was being looked after fantastically by the ladies. The only problem you have is wondering who's going to come in next with some fluids for you. You couldn't think of a better place to be. There was about six others there, so when you're waking up to a woman either side of you most mornings it's not a bad result, even though you've got so many clothes on by the time you'd have got to them you'd be exhausted.' 'Trevor was on top form in that sick room,' says Sandy Colbeck, who had no sooner arrived on the island than she'd fallen ill herself. 'He had us in absolute fits of laughter. We were wetting ourselves with some of the stories he came out with.'

Padraig Nallen had not at first realised that his ankle was broken. 'He didn't know he'd done it,' says Mike Laird, 'and poor old Gwyneth tried to help. She's not a doctor, but she's a very caring person. "Oh, you've probably twisted it or something," she said. "Go and have a walk and it'll be fine."' In fact, Padraig had broken one of the main bones in his leg. Fortunately, a professional opinion was still (just) on hand. 'I was on the beach with the kids,' says Roger Stephenson, and I saw him limping across from one house to the other. He couldn't put any weight on his leg, and I thought, That's funny, is he pissed or lost his boot or something? Then I thought, Hold on, there's something a bit more to all this, so I started following him and he'd a very swollen tender bone in his ankle, so

I said, "Look, you've got to get this X-rayed."' The Irishman was put on a helicopter to the mainland.

Among the others who returned to Tarbert that morning, the staunch spirit of the island sickroom was not evident. Ron Copsey had choppered back ('the only chopper I'm likely to see this year') to find that the holiday cottage Lion had booked him into didn't accept dogs. 'So me and Charlie had to get out,' he recalls, 'and they book us in to a B & B which will accept Charlie, but that's not ideal, as I have to go to the hotel for my lunch and dinner, or to one of the families in the other cottages.'

When the castaways began to set off for Taransay , Lion had still been optimistic that there would be enough accomodation. Nevertheless, Warren Latore was annoyed. 'The effort we'd had to make in order to meet the 27 December deadline to collect us was huge. Then to be dragged all the way to the Outer Hebrides to be told we couldn't go and live on the island yet was ridiculous.' 'We could have stayed at home,' adds Monica, 'a week or two longer. There's so much to do when you leave your life for a year. Another week would have made a big difference. But they just wanted us over there for that New Year's Eve party. I think they should have said, "It's not ready, you've got another week or two." Then we could have staged a party when we get over there and they could have pretended it was a New Year's Eve party.'

When this suggestion is put to him in the Lion offices in London, executive producer Jeremy Mills is horrified. 'We would never do that!' he cries. 'That's outrageous! We would never have faked it. Stand back a little,' he continues. 'It had taken our team here at Lion in London weeks to organise the collection of the crates, the coaches up, the passage across. It was a big tanker of practicalities going along. Also a lot of the castaways had given up their jobs, their lives – they didn't want to be at home, they wanted to be up there. I think it was the right thing to get them up there.'

With hindsight, Mills continued, there were a lot of things Lion might have done differently. But, he points out: 'Nobody's ever done anything like this before. Nobody's made a programme like this, nobody's actually built a community on an island, against this time scale, and then thrown in all the odd factors like the people you've got who you don't really know that well, the sudden illness, the extreme weather, and then, for example, four crates being dropped, which means the production team are running around trying to cope with that as well.'

'It was a really difficult time,' says Elaine Paterson. 'Not just for us, they had a tough time too, not wanting to be where they were, wanting instead to be across the water on the island. People – particularly Gordon – were feeling incredibly frustrated. Colin was just a lost man really. Dreadful. I personally felt incredibly responsible and guilty about the whole thing. Not being a builder of pods, I shouldn't have really had that feeling, but I felt very upset for these people who'd planned a year of their life to be whatever they wanted it to be, and it hadn't started.'

A Diplomatic Mission

The castaways were now divided between island, Taransay, and 'mainland' Harris. In the comfortable surroundings of the Harris Hotel were Tammy Huff and Julie Lowe; Julie so sick with the flu that she would break a rib coughing. Also resident in the pretty whitewashed, blue-timbered building, set back behind a double sun lounge from its neatly bordered walled front garden, were Roger and Rosemary Stephenson, and their two children Oliver and Felix. After one night roughing it on the island, they were not, they had made clear to the Lion team, going to join the Careys in the dormitory surroundings of the bunkhouse.

The other families had been found accommodation up the hill in a row of self-catering cottages at the top of the little town. As holidaying Hogmanayers moved out, the castaways moved in. Warren and Monica Latore, with their blonde, four-year-old daughter Ciara; then Colin and Julia Corrigan, with dark-haired, six-year-old Natasha; in due course the doctor and his family; finally the Careys, Gordon and Cassie, with daughter Yoneh, four, and son Aaron, two, who were the last to leave the bunkhouse. Ron and Charlie were now in a B&B that accepted dogs, traipsing down to the Harris Hotel to spend the days in bar or sun or TV lounge.

Tarbert is not a big place. The one-sided main street winds down the hill to the little port below, from where a regular car ferry sails out through East Loch and over the sea to Skye. There's A.D. Munro's grocery-cum-butcher's, Morrison's newsagent-cum-grocer's, a couple of little shops selling Harris tweeds and jumpers, a craft emporium, and one astonishing cornucopia of clothes, hardware and souvenirs run by the town's long-resident Pakistani, Mr Akram. In summer, there are a scattering of tourists, hikers, bikers and Americans and Antipodeans checking out their roots. In winter, once Hogmanay is over, visitors stand out. The presence of the black Carey family, exotically long-haired, mixed-race Warren Latore, tall blonde wife Monica, the Corrigans, Stephensons and flamboyant Ron Copsey plus dog, hardly went unnoticed.

Remaining on the island was the majority of the castaways: the twentysomething 'youngsters': posh Ben Fogle and soft-spoken Yorkshireman Toby Waterman; fetching blonde filmmaker Tanya Cheadle and dreadlocked New Age traveller Philiy Page. The thirtysomethings: macho man Mike Laird; chirpy Scouser Trevor Kearon; Glasgow-born single mum Trish Prater, with kids Jodene (12) and Michael (10); ever-practical management consultant Liz Cathrine and go-getting partner Dez Monks. Then the more mature of the party: bearded and bulky, hippyish-seeming university lecturer Peter Jowers with skinny artist wife Sheila; gruff, ponytailed, white-haired and bearded ex-builder Ray Bowyer, 58; good-looking mum on sabbatical from her family in Scarborough, Hilary Freeman, 50; laid-back Lancastrian postal worker Pat Murphy, 56, and pretty second wife, dinner lady Gwyneth, 51. Finally the granny of the group, serious-minded, grey-haired Portsmouth microbiologist Sandy Colbeck, 58.

After supper on New Year's Day, this disparate group gathered round the glowing coals of the cast-iron stove in the steading and had a meeting. 'We sat down as a group,' says Liz Cathrine, 'and tried to think about how it was all going to work, what jobs we should be doing. The main point we sorted out was kitchen duties, because there were certain individuals spending all their time in the kitchen, while the boys were spending all their time building. I'm glad to say I made sure that evening that the women weren't going to spend all their time in the kitchen.'

That night the weather started to deteriorate again. By the following evening – Sunday 2 January – it was blowing a gale. 'Weather atrocious,' wrote Ray, in his always-succinct diary. 'Rain non-stop.' Over half of the castaways had now moved from the MacKay House and steading to sleep in the schoolhouse. Liz and Dez were up on a pair of mattresses on a platform in the roof, but abandoned their perch half-way through the night. 'I was so scared I thought I was going to die,' Liz confided to the video diary. 'The winds were just incredible and you could hear the whole of the top of the house creaking. So we thought, if the roof's going, we're going with it, so we moved downstairs.' 'We heard reports,' wrote Mike the next day, 'that the wind was between 110 and 140 mph.'

Sheila was downstairs next to Peter, huddled in an arctic sleeping bag on one of the fifteen metal-framed camp beds that crammed the room. 'It was quite funny,' she told the video diary, 'because the wind in the rafters, and in the boards on the roof, was just howling and rattling, like some sort of monstrous creature calling out, and it only echoed the sound of Ray, who in his sleep seems to belch, fart and rumble continually through the night, and call for help.'

In the morning damage to the site was extensive. The roofing felt had been torn off the top of all of the pods. Half the toilet block roof had been ripped off and hurled over a hundred yards. One of the pigsties had flown twenty metres. A wheelbarrow had landed on top of one of the builders' Portakabins. 'There's sheet ply flying around,' wrote Mike. 'Cement mixer's blown over. People – particularly children – can't move outside. We spent a lot of time clearing up the carnage.'

Despite the wind and the fact that it was Bank Holiday Monday, the helicopter was flying, starting to bringing back builders after the Hogmanay break and taking any castaways who needed to go over to 'the mainland'. Ben Fogle and Sandy Colbeck were on one of the first flights. At a second after-supper meeting the evening before, the castaways had agreed that they should go over and speak to the families in the Harris Hotel, and try persuade at least some of them to return to Taransay to assist with the work. 'At the moment,' Philiy Page told the video diary, 'we need manpower and we're kind of hoping that the mothers will stay behind with the kids while the fathers come over and help us.'

But no sooner had Ben departed than the families' worries about their kids proved founded. Ben's six-month-old puppy Inca was discovered, with a gash in her leg, 'shaking and a wee bit shocked', said Mike. 'It could have been anything,' he continued. 'A piece of broken wood, iron, barbed wire, something natural or builders' materials.' Animal-loving Philiy volunteered to accompany the wounded whelp to the mainland. It would be better, the castaways agreed, to get her over to where Ben was. Roger the doctor might be able to do something. Furthermore, Liz had found out from one of the builders that there was a vet in Stornoway.

In the warm coffee-lounge of the Harris Hotel, meanwhile, despite (or perhaps because of) the presence of the TV cameras, Ben and Sandy weren't making much headway with the families. 'I went over to the mainland,' Ben was to tell the video diary, 'as a sort of ambassador for all of us, because the community's completely split between the families and Ron and the two sick people over there – and us. So I volunteered to go over and tell them what's been going on, ask them a few questions about how they wanted things organised, because they can't be in on our meetings here.

'I felt like I needed a bit of a lie down afterwards, but I'm glad I did it. I was a bit frustrated with Roger and Ron. Some of their demands and the things they were saying weren't completely – what's the word I'm looking for? – legitimate, maybe. Roger seems to be on a bit of a mission. I don't think it's the project for them. He's come here as the doctor and he keeps saying to us that he can't do this and he can't do that.'

However intransigent it was starting to seem to others, Roger and Rosemary's position was, they thought, entirely fair. As far as they were concerned, Lion TV had promised to provide them with finished living quarters and they had failed to deliver on their side of the bargain.

Ron supported the doctor and his wife, though for somewhat different reasons. 'If I'd wanted to be a labourer or a builder,' he says, 'I'd have left school at fifteen.'

Not A Racist Issue

On the island, meanwhile, another of the male castaways had been getting fitted up as a new bogeyman for the group. 'Gordon came over in the helicopter,' said Philiy Page. 'I don't know why he came over because he decided that in twenty minutes from landing he was going back again. He only came over to get his sleeping bag and stuff, which he could have asked the production crew to do anyway. He then walked into the MacKay House kitchen and started to take food that the pod people had brought for themselves. We stopped him on that one and pointed out that it wasn't even ours. So then he tried to take the food that had just been delivered for us, and we said, "No, that's for the community here." Next he came down to the steading kitchen and took some food right out of Sandy's hands. She grabbed a couple of things back and he bolted for the helicopter.'

Sandy Colbeck was so outraged that she ran after the Caribbean carpenter and tried to follow him onto the helicopter, pleading with the pilot. 'I stopped him taking off. I said, "Hold on, I need to speak to Gordon." So I had a word with him and he did surrender two tins, a tin of fruit and a tin of rice, but what else was in the bags he had, I'm not sure. But I just can't believe he did it.'

'Let me tell you what happened,' says Gordon. 'We had a certain amount of food in the bunkhouse. The researchers came and took it over to the island. I have two young children to feed. I came over to the island to do some work. I took a tin of peaches. I was getting on the helicopter to return and somebody asked for it back. I didn't argue. I thought it was pretty mean, but I gave it back. The following day the researchers came over and gave us some money, because they realised we had no money or no food at all.'

'He was told,' Philiy Page told the video diary, 'he could go to the hotel and eat. Have a fucking three-course meal! That man is just so arrogant.' Mike Laird was equally outspoken. 'I've never met a more selfish individual, who seems less committed to the whole project.'

At the castaways' third consecutive after-supper meeting, on that evening of Monday 3 January, Gordon's behaviour was, after the debacle of Ben and

Sandy's Harris Hotel diplomatic initiative, the second main topic of discussion. Management consultant Liz Cathrine wanted 'the food incident to be addressed'. She had witnessed the scene in the steading, and found Gordon's manner 'aggressive'.

The debate widened. Padraig brought up the occasion on the advance party when Gordon had demanded to be paid by the builders for his work. 'If it hadn't been for people shaming him into returning it, it would never have crossed his mind,' he said. There was a short debate about Gordon's religion (did he believe in Jesus Christ or the God of the Old Testament?) before Padraig agreed that this was irrelevant and Sandy got to the heart of the problem. 'What we're looking at is the behaviour of an individual within what is supposed to be a cohesive group trying to form a community.' But rather than being the last word, this only provoked more argument. Peter now wanted to make the interesting observation that the castaways might not actually end up as one cohesive group but 'a series of grouplets'. He then ignited the most fervent dispute of the evening by remarking that Ray's behaviour in cooking a private fry-up for himself when he didn't like the food prepared by the community was 'not far off from Gordon going in and helping himself, is it?'

'There was a great big discussion at night time,' wrote Mike Laird in his diary, 'and Ray was really losing his cool. He was swearing left, right and centre. He even threatened to leave the island.'

As the island group began to settle down into routines and form structures that would enable them to live together, Ray's uncompromising preference for old-fashioned over more contemporary foods was undoubtedly proving a problem. 'We've been living like bleedin' paupers for the last few days,' he told the group. When quizzed by the ever-efficient Liz, who was trying in vain to tie the meeting down to practicalities (and keeping rudimentary minutes for the first time), he explained what he meant by 'a good meal of a night' – one that enabled you to work hard in the day and that stopped you falling ill. 'I'm talking about meat and two veg,' he explained. He didn't want the flan that Gwyneth thought was 'sufficient'; he didn't want one of Philiy's vegetarian curries; he certainly didn't want ravioli or spaghetti. 'See, for me,' returned Liz, 'the last thing in the world I would want is meat and two veg every night.'

The argument raged on, now bringing extra considerations: of the castaways' set food budget of £30 per head per week as well as the fresh meat they could expect once the farm animals (and Colin the butcher) were on Taransay and the island community was properly up and running. This was confused by yet another issue, as Dez pointed out, 'If everyone here was in the same boat, fine, but when there are people only ten miles away having a gin and tonic, it's a different story altogether.' Peter put it more succinctly. 'I don't give a monkey's about the budget as long as people are sitting in hotels and helicopters are flying in – it's bullshit, complete bullshit.'

The fractious scene hardly augured well for the eventual goal of a peaceful and productive community. But then many of them had barely slept during the wild winds of the night before. And outside the settlement was chaotic: a huge building site where, under the supervision of Andy McAvoy, who was now acting more as site manager than architect, teams of boiler-suited professional builders and joiners were hammering and sawing and drilling furiously as they raced to get the pods roofed and divided and glazed. They were sleeping five to a room in the MacKay House or in the rash of Portakabins up on the slope behind, fed by a separate cooking team led by Trish Prater, who had installed herself firmly in the MacKay house kitchen and was 'loving every second of it', preparing fry-ups for the podmen's breakfast, big soups for lunch and a hearty meal for their tea. After which they would put their boots back on and head out to work on into the arc-lit, arctic night.

The next day another of the island castaways returned to the warmth of the Harris Hotel. During the stormy evening meeting, fifty-eight-year-old Sandy Colbeck's voice had degenerated to a barely audible croak. 'That night on the Monday,' she recalls, 'I went to bed and tried to lie down and I couldn't breathe. I felt as if I was drowning in lung congestion, it was the most awful sensation I've ever experienced. I thought I was going to die. The following morning my voice had completely gone and three people said, "You cannot stay here. Go ashore." So I did.'

As Sandy flew one way, yet more returning builders flew another. With them was a man whose ears must have been burning, so much had he been discussed on Taransay. 'Gordon came on the island again today,' wrote Mike in his journal on Tuesday 4 January, 'and loafed around all day ending up in the steading. He sat in the kitchen while I was peeling veg and I heard him talk shite to various people giving different stories to different people. Gwyneth was discussing something and he kept shouting her down. She asked my opinion about something to bring me in to support her and it was like lighting blue touch paper. I lost my temper and gave him something to chew on. He tried to counter me and then I hit him with the story of him accepting money from the builders and then being shamed into giving it back. That shut him up. I was absolutely livid. Some people came in because they were worried it might get physical. I was later told that I called him a "lying, stealing, lazy bastard". Some people said my language may have been a touch strong but every single person was behind what I did. Someone had to say it. It just happened to be me.'

Toby Waterman had a somewhat gentler perspective: 'Mike is a great guy, but the way he approached it there, it's too much, too soon. So I sat down with Gordon, had a friendly chat and just sort of said, "You do understand about the food thing, don't you, Gordon?" I explained our point of view, it's the community's food – he and his family can get it on the mainland. He seems to hear, but I'm not sure he listens as yet. But it needs more calm explanation, and reasoning with one another. Shouting is not constructive. So I hope it doesn't go that way too often.'

Concerned about Mike's attack on Gordon, Chris Kelly had suggested he apologise. 'I went to the group with this,' Mike wrote in his journal, 'and I said, "Guys, was I out of order?" Everyone had heard the exchange from up the other end of the steading. I said, "Lion have asked me to make an apology." They fell about laughing and Trevor actually stood up and said, "Mike, if you're forced to make an apology I will leave the project." Lion had also said, "What about the likelihood of a racist accusation?" I said, "Well, I'll phone up my last coloured girlfriend and you can ask her how racist I am." It's not a racist issue with me at all. I've been out with black girls in the past, so he's got no foundation there whatsoever.'

Gordon's stoic response, when asked about this incident, echoed his pre-emptive words of the advance party. 'There are no names,' he said now, 'that these people can call me that I haven't been called before. There is no racism they can do to me that hasn't been done to me before.' For him, was there already an assumption of racism? For Mike there was most definitely not; despite his unfashionable use of the word 'coloured' he was dealing, extra-fairly if anything, with a difficult man.

Unaware of all this strife, Ben Fogle had spent the past twenty-four hours with his puppy, taking Inca to the vet in Stornoway and having her leg sewn up. He had been given a lift across Harris and Lewis by some of the production team on their way back to Glasgow. Returning to Taransay by helicopter on the Tuesday afternoon, he regaled the now-regular after-supper meeting with his view of the scene on the mainland.

'Tell us about the food in the Harris Hotel,' teased Dez. 'Tell us how warm it was. Did you have warm toes in the Harris Hotel?'

Ben was no longer entirely loyal to those he'd been so diplomatic with at the previous day's meeting. 'Ron kept saying about how he was enjoying his twenty-two pound buffet,' he said, 'and then he told me to stop whingeing about food!'

Encouraged by the noisy – if largely good-humoured – outrage of the islanders, Ben continued in this vein. The mainland castaways were getting themselves in a vicious circle, he said. The Harris Hotel was 'a very unhealthy place'.

CASTAFLOPS!

Two days later this burgeoning split between two groups of a small community temporarily divided between two remote Scottish islands threatened to escalate into something of altogether greater significance. The first representatives of the press arrived on Taransay. Not the local *Stornoway Gazette*, but the nationals: the *Mail on Sunday*, no less, in the form of a short reporter with a cheeky smile and big glasses, a tall, cocky, gum-chewing photographer and an altogether maturer freelance from Inverness, whose face was almost as crimson as his smart top-to-toe waterproofs.

Until this point, press interest had been largely as Lion and the BBC Scotland press office had orchestrated. Pre-arranged interviews, matching individual castaways with appropriate newspapers, had been appearing over the New Year, gradually preparing the nation for the screening of the first two programmes – featuring the selection process – on 18 January. Peter and Sheila Jowers had been allocated to the 'Real Lives' section of the *Guardian*, who reported that 'the TV production team thinks Jowers could become the father figure in the community, pivotal to its survival'; intrepid Sandy Colbeck to the *Telegraph* ('I think there will be quite a few young free and single people on Taransay,' observes Mrs Colbeck drily 'It doesn't take an Einstein to work out what's going to happen there.') Trish Prater, born in Larkhall, Glasgow, had been assigned to the Scottish tabloid *Daily Record*; while 'action man' Mike Laird and 'game for anything' secretary Tammy Huff had been profiled by the *News of the World*, who quoted Tammy (interviewed in November) as saying, 'There is someone I'm attracted to already, but we will have to wait and see'; while Mike had 'his eye on a fellow inhabitant and is hoping for a bit of shared bodily warmth during the year'.

Of the scandal-hungry pack, the *Sunday Times* had come up with the juiciest angle. BBC GIVES ITS CASTAWAYS A CUSHY BILLET it reported on 2 January. 'They expected to forage for food, build their own shelters and wash in icy water,' wrote Stephen McGinty, describing the wilder aspirations of, say, Mike Laird or Ben Fogle fairly accurately. 'But the 36 castaways marooned last week on a remote Scottish island ... have central heating, a washing machine and deliveries of shopping. The 21st-century Robinson Crusoes are living in five wooden huts with double-glazing constructed by a team of professional builders ... Critics say the castaways have it too easy.' There were, in fact, four pods, with stoves not central heating, not yet installed, into which the castaways had not yet moved. The 'washing machine' was a primitive, cold-water 1960s-type twin tub, which half the castaways weren't using anyway, and the only 'critic' the newspaper could find to quote was 'ex-islander John Ferguson, 79', who opined knowledgeably, 'They seem to have everything they want, all the modern conveniences ... no wonder our television licence fees are so high.'

The trio of *Mail on Sunday* journalists who landed on the island on Thursday 6 January were given, as the first invaders often are by the natives, a friendly enough welcome. Finding their way to the steading they were offered a warming cup of coffee by Philiy Page and Toby Waterman, who were hard at work preparing an all-veggy meal for the evening. They looked a trifle disconcerted to find the TV cameras turned on them by ever-ready Tanya Cheadle, but reacted gamely enough. 'I raise a toast in good cockney to the success of the *Castaway 2000* project,' said the young reporter called Andy. The gum-chewing photographer admitted cheerfully that their visit was unauthorised. 'Have you got clearance from the BBC Press Office?' asked Tanya. 'Absolutely not,' he replied, drowning out his colleague's prevarications, 'because if we did, they'd say, "You can't come."'

Meanwhile the crimson-faced Scottish freelance was demonstrating the guile of experience. 'How are you coping with the elements?' he asked the group sympathetically. 'You've had a pretty harsh baptism,' he continued, before assuring them with a warm if somewhat unconvincing laugh that they weren't intending to do 'a knocking piece or anything like that'.

Ex-*Watchdog* director Tanya Cheadle, however, was not to be fooled. 'I think it's "no comment" to everything,' she replied curtly to their questions. 'Arseholes,' whispered Toby Waterman, genially enough, as they left. Out by the pods the newshounds were confronted by Andy McAvoy, who wanted them off site 'for Health and Safety reasons'. 'Someone might get hurt. There's a sheet of plywood took off from over there the other day and hit the helicopter pilot for instance.'

Of the other castaways, Ray Bowyer seemed to be the only one who seriously minded the intrusion. 'Invaded by the press,' he wrote in his diary, 'so I slipped off for a walk.' On his return he gave Tanya's camera his reasons. 'I don't want them here. Don't think they should be here. It's defeating the whole point of why we're here. I mean, if I want a madhouse I'll go and sit in the middle of Manchester.' 'Well, Ray has run off in a huff,' said Ben. 'He grabbed his walking stick and we thought he was going to have a showdown with them. He keeps threatening to put his Rod Stewart wig on and run up and down the beach if journalists appear, which he didn't do today. Maybe next time.'

For Ben, the arrival of the journos was not as much of an intrusion as it could have been. 'I don't feel we're completely castaway yet,' he told the video diary. He was, however, a bit concerned what they might write. 'They'll definitely write about the fact that there are builders still on the site, helping with the building. I imagine that they're going to be curious about the eighteen missing people. We were told by Andy to tell them they were all ill with the flu. My worry is they're going to go back and this Sunday there's going to be this big thing of – I don't know – CASTAFLOPS! – they'll come up with something, and it's just a bit worrying, because we're doing so well. Hopefully they'll go and write that we're all having an amazing time, we've got these useful buildings and our wind turbine is up, but I suspect they'll write something' – the ex-*Tatler* editor scrunched up his face knowingly – 'newsworthy. If they just go back and say what a lovely project, it's not going to sell lots of papers. Whereas if they say, *The biggest documentary the BBC have done in x number of years isn't even ready and it's running late* ... but that's what newspapers do.'

As for the idea of actually being in the papers: 'I don't think they took any pictures of me personally,' mused the unwitting future heart-throb, 'but that would be extraordinary, the thought that, you know, they would come up here and next Sunday my parents, who I'm not going to be able to speak to, or anything, for the next year, might see a photograph of me, I don't know, picking my nose or whatever – it's strange.'

Peter Jowers, who had had previous dealings with 'the press', organising music festivals near his home in the Forest of Dean, was more succinct: 'My experience with running a festival is don't trust them further than you can spit,' he said, generalising in a manner he would surely never have allowed his students.

Even as the intrepid trio were trying without success to get the islanders to spill the beans, a new angle had at last been found on the mainland. Other journalists had been interviewing Tarbert locals who 'had noticed the strangers in weatherproofed jackets staying in the privately owned flats'. 'One housewife said: "I saw these smart people at the shops and realised they must be the castaways who were supposed to be on Taransay. I don't know why they are here. Maybe everything has been blown away in the storm we've had."'

It was a story that made all the next day's papers, from the *Independent*'s sedate TV CASTAWAYS RECOVER FROM ILLNESS IN HOMES WITH CENTRAL HEATING through the *Scotsman*'s wry CASTAWAYS WHO FLU TO COMFORT to the *Mirror*'s absurd DESERT ISLE DESERTERS.

'It started off,' recalls Julia Corrigan, 'when we heard that some people had come up and booked into the Harris hotel and that they were journalists, so we were warned not to go up to the hotel. Ron still carried on going up, but we stayed in the cottage, and then one evening there was a knock on the door and two chaps were stood on the doorstep. "Oh hello," they said, "we're not sure if we've got the right cottage. Are you from Taransay?" I said, "I'm certainly not from Taransay," but I didn't know what to do then, because they were quite friendly, they weren't savage bastards wanting to take pictures the minute I opened the door. But they missed their chance, because Colin was in the bathroom and he just jumped out into the hallway and said, "Go away, we're not allowed to talk to you" and slammed the door. So they headed off to the Stephensons. I said to Colin, "Quick, get your boots on and go and warn Roger and Rosemary!" But when he got there, Roger had let them in. We were horrified. They didn't say much to them, but everything they said was printed.'

'Under our contract,' says Rosemary, 'we are not allowed to speak to the press at all, so when we had journalists at our door we said, "Can't talk to you, sorry." Well, inevitably they started inventing stories, because they could see there must have been about fifteen of us wandering about Tarbert looking very obviously not local and not many of us still had flu.'

To be fair, the representatives of the press, though guilty of exaggeration, inaccuracy, misrepresentation and repetition, had not yet resorted to invention. 'Yesterday,' said the *Daily Express*, in a typical report, 'at the block of four modern flats ... the various occupants refused to answer questions about who they were or why they were there. One young boy, who said he was seven years old, shouted: "Go away! We're not to speak to reporters." A man, apparently accompanied by his wife and several young children, said: "Look, you probably know who we are and why we are here. But we're not allowed to talk to the media. We don't want to be rude but we have signed a contract." ' (Roger, a stickler for one side of his contract, could hardly be seen to break the other.)

Faced with this sudden barrage of interest, Lion were faced with what producer Chris Kelly describes as 'a news management issue'. They decided to admit to what had been discovered, but major on the flu side of the story in the hope that the real reason for the families' presence in Tarbert would not emerge. 'We never lied about it,' says Jeremy Mills, 'although we didn't always tell the full story.' Quite apart from anything else, he adds, he was trying to keep his storylines for the TV programmes. 'Mr Mills,' the *Express* continued, 'said yesterday at his London office: "Yes, it's true. Some of the castaways are in the flats. The virus which has affected so many others in Scotland has badly affected the fly-on-the-wall documentary project. Nearly all the castaways and the production crew too have been suffering from this bug over the past week." According to Mr Mills, many of them were battling on and trying to keep warm on the island and taking the usual medicines. However, as a precaution, the youngsters, their parents and the worst-affected adults were being put up temporarily in the comfortable flats in Tarbert until they get better. Mr Mills added: "It may be that we can get them all back to Taransay tomorrow."'

By Thursday evening Lion was worried about the effect the press invasion was having on certain castaways and decided it would be wisest to get the families out of Tarbert. 'The production team,' says Rosemary Stephenson, 'said to all the families, "You either have to leave Harris or go to Taransay. We can't have you in Tarbert for any longer." They were saying it was to protect us from the press harassment, which they felt was going to get much worse, but also, obviously, they didn't want the story to come out that the island wasn't ready.

'Our instant reaction was, "Well, we'll leave." But we didn't want to go onto the island. We knew it wasn't ready, and felt once we got there, that's it, we've got no bargaining power, we'd be stuck in these intolerable conditions. We weren't going be pressured into going there. At the same time, we didn't want to go home to Devon, because that would break the spell for us, having put so much energy into leaving.'

The Stephensons did, however, have the option of returning to London and borrowing a friend's flat. Within an hour of telling the production team this, says Rosemary, they had booked the family flights for the next morning. 'It was all terribly dramatic. And I suddenly said, "D'you think we're over-reacting here?" Because actually we didn't really want to leave. We felt it was better to be there. Roger was able to medically look after the community, because he could go over to the island and also look after the people in the hotel who were actually quite sick. I said, "Hang on, let's just check this is really necessary." So I rang Chris Kelly in Glasgow and I said, "What are you frightened of? Why are you so desperate to get us out?" And his line was, "It's to protect you and we're really worried about the press interest getting out of hand." I said to him, "I predict that if we leave it will be badly perceived on the island. The community will not understand it, they will resent it." He said, "Don't worry, Rosemary, we'll make sure they understand." So then there was an evening of panic as Roger had to then go to the local GP, Dr Finlayson, and explain that he was leaving and that basically the whole community was landed on this poor chap's plate, which was not really very fair.'

The couple left the next morning and flew to London. As they were the only ones who had let the press into their cottage, their faces were now on the front pages of several of the newspapers – Rosemary in a thick padded jacket, grinning, captioned, *A suffering castaway*. Roger likewise, emerging from the 'plush' flats, captioned, *In the lap of luxury*.

Meanwhile, the other mainland castaways, despite being offered the option of hotel accommodation in Glasgow, had decided to stay put. 'We were all devastated,' says Julia Corrigan. 'We thought, We're on the bloody doorstep of the island and now they're going to try and take us away again. Roger and Rosemary were pushed into it, they took them at their word and packed, but I was ill that day, I thought I was about to go down with massive flu. I can remember sitting down on the sofa and everyone milling around and saying, "What are we going to do?" and I suddenly said, "Well, I'm not going anywhere. I don't feel very well and I'm not going to Glasgow." Then Warren said, "I'm not going either." Then Monica said it. Then we all said, "That's it, we're staying," and we refused to go. But by then Roger and Rosemary had started packing. They were already in motion really.'

Despite their early departure, the doctor's flight was discovered by the press. On the morning of Saturday 8 January, the Scottish *Daily Record* had CASTAWAYS READY TO DESERT THEIR ISLAND. 'A family of four yesterday fled the BBC's £2.4 million Castaway 2000 project ... yesterday locals in the Hebrides said they thought BBC bosses had bitten off more than they could chew with the scheme to strand 36 volunteers on remote Taransay for a year. They believe that the whole project, due to start transmission on January 18, could soon fold ... critics of the most ambitious documentary ever attempted claim it is a waste of licence payers' money.' No critics were named. 'It is understood,' the *Record* report continued, 'fewer than eight castaways remain on Taransay.'

The Pulse of the Waves

For the eighteen castaways remaining on the island, the press furore on the mainland didn't make a lot of difference. For most, the main preoccupations were recovering from their illness, clearing up the damage from the weekend's storm, then getting on with helping the builders and joiners with the roofing and dividing of the pods, installing door and window frames, glazing and insulating. Others worked on the steading and schoolhouse, all in the hope that very soon the two halves of the community could be joined. 'Frustrations remain the same,' Padraig told the video diary, 'regarding the group being split in two, and I suppose some resentments are beginning to grow, which is a bad thing. The sooner we are all together, the sooner we can begin to deal with them, because until we are, hearsay is gonna play too large a part.'

Otherwise, the island castaways were, in the main, extremely content with their new life. 'For now,' Toby reported to his video diary, 'it's absolutely fantastic for me – perfect. The work is still hard. I've been up with Philiy on the pods today, shifting timber around. But what I like about the whole way of life here that's beginning to show itself is the routine where you wake up around half eight, crawl in for breakfast, groggy-eyed, you have your porridge, second bowl of porridge, cup of tea, and then it's out to work. The time just flies. You work away until lunch, and when you come in there's a big steaming bowl of soup waiting for you. You have a quick smoke, then it's back to work all afternoon, then in the evening, a nice big evening meal. What's been happening most days after that is a discussion and it seems like a good time, 'cos everyone's together and relaxed, no more work to do, and we've had some quite constructive ones.'

Quondam New Age traveller Philiy was in a similar frame of mind. 'We're feeding enthusiasm off each other over here,' she told the video diary. 'As

Tanya filming

Patrick said to me today, "You're the happiest I've seen you." And I said, "Yeah, it's 'cos I'm working, I'm doing something, I'm feeling useful."'

For Lancashire dinner lady Gwyneth Murphy, it was the beauty of the treeless island that was the novelty. 'Last night was wonderful,' she reported. 'I've never ever seen stars or a sky like that. You could actually see the Milky Way, the band going out across. And I saw a shooting star, that's the first time I've ever seen a shooting star, and oh, it was wonderful, it really was.'

Artist Sheila Jowers was similarly impressed. 'I just went off on a walk alone and I was so in love with it I was wondering how I'm going to cope with the end of the year – being nostalgic about it before I even start. From a distance everything appears quite stark and lacking in detail. Then you start to see closer up and things come into focus and just everywhere's a myriad range of detail. The lichens are something I'm really fascinated by. I counted about twelve different shades.' Her mind was already racing ahead to the idea of making felt from discarded sheep fleeces, which she could then dye. Each lichen shade, she reckoned, would produce a different hue. 'I suppose that's where Harris Tweeds get all their different colours,' she concluded. Husband Peter had been off in the hinterland too, birdwatching, and seen an oystercatcher, terns, sandpipers and flocks of starlings.

It wasn't until Sunday 9 January that any of the newspaper reports actually made their way onto the island. 'There were some newspaper articles available to us,' Mike wrote in his journal that day. 'The Press is giving us a hard time and in my opinion it's quite justified as the project has become somewhat more farcical than I would have hoped.' Ben found the whole thing amusing but extraordinary. Never in a million years had he thought that the story of sixteen people getting the flu would make the front pages of a newspaper. Liz felt likewise: 'It's a bit weird really, being a topic of interest in the papers, I haven't quite got my head round it, to be honest.' Toby was defensive: 'If you try and build a village on the mainland in calm weather conditions it'll take nine to twelve months. We've got to do it on an Outer Hebridean island in incredible weather in three months, so of course the project's going to run over a little bit.' Trish was furious: 'Saying that as soon as we have a sniffle we're off, which isn't true because most of us were ill before we came on the island anyway. We're not eating champagne and caviar like everyone thinks.'

The Top Man

It was ironic that of all the castaways, it was Roger Stephenson who was now back in London. Islands had always been an inexplicable passion for him. 'I can never answer this,' he said. 'I simply can't find within me, the reasons for my fascination with remote cut-off island communities.'

This was not to a video diary, but to me, the book's author, as I sat beside him in the bedroom of the Paddington flat he'd borrowed from a friend, the shrieks of his children coming through the wall from the living room next door.

Though born in Devon, he told me, he had spent his earliest years abroad; his father had been a civil engineer in Iraq. 'He built a lot of the bridges,' he said with his characteristically inclusive smile, 'that were exploded in the Gulf War, so he watched those missiles exploding his work.' Back in England, as a boy Roger had passed a voice trial to become a chorister at Canterbury Cathedral Choir School, which was 'a wonderful experience, you're doing a wonderful thing singing and making great music and people are listening to it'. On to Marlborough College, the famous Wiltshire public school, with a music scholarship. Here he continued to sing, played the piano and took 'A' levels in science subjects. Thence to Corpus Christi College, Cambridge, to read medicine. For a while music took a back seat as he became 'a bit sporty and boozy', got his degree and moved on to University College Hospital, London, for his clinical training. It was during the following year, doing house jobs on the Isle of Man, that his 'musical fantasy', that of becoming a concert pianist, made him decide to pursue music seriously. He studied privately at the Royal College of Music in London, supporting himself with medical jobs. 'It was bloody hard work,' he remembered now 'I was practising the piano all day then doing overnight jobs to make the money.' Then he started on the 'competition ramp', but 'As soon as I hit a big competition I realised I was nowhere.' At that crucial contest in Hastings, he had found himself outclassed by younger and better would-be professionals.

It was a galling moment. 'That was when I decided medicine had to be my money earner, although I'd never be doing it as hard as everyone else did.' He took the rest of the year off and accompanied a heart patient to Everest Base Camp, moving from there to the remote Atlantic island of Pitcairn, where he stayed for several months acting as the settlement's doctor, 'until eventually the boat came and took me off'.

Returning to Devon he trained as a GP for another three years, during which time he met Rosemary (the daughter of two North London doctors) who was at the time working in London as a journalist for Reuters. She, too, had been at Cambridge, reading history. In 1990 they married and promptly headed off to another remote Atlantic island, St Helena, where Roger worked in the hospital, while Rosemary improved her radio skills with Radio St Helena. 'It was a tough year,' she recalled, when it was her turn for an interview, 'because Roger had a very difficult job and it was so isolated, you just couldn't get off.'

Back home the pair settled down to a quiet life in Devon. They lived in a village and Roger was one of two GPs in a small country practice. Rosemary freelanced as a journalist, for Reuters, the BBC World Service and local radio. 'Then I had a baby, then I went back to work, as a researcher for Radio Devon, then I had a second child and gave up work.' Five years passed: 'a comfortable life' in a house with six bedrooms and a huge garden. It was ten years since they'd been on St Helena. 'I was at a turning point,' said Rosemary. 'Very much thinking, What am I going to do? In the past I've been a journalist, I've been a teacher, I've never stuck at anything for long enough to feel I have a natural career to go back into.'

Roger was in no way restless. 'You can ask my medical partner about that,' he said. 'He said to me, "If you want a sabbatical, now's the time, because your kids are this age," and I said, "No thanks, I'm comfortable, I've got a decent income, wife's content, kids are content, local school's OK. So this comes not out of restlessness, but out of educational issues, because Felix was coming of age to go to school.'

'I've been with my children since they were born,' said Rosemary, elaborating on her interest in the idea of Home Education. 'I've watched how they learn and I think when you put them into school you suddenly make a decision to start doing it in a different way that is very artificial. I think children want to learn, and they have this innate capacity to learn, and they do it anyway. If you put them in school you start to introduce all these structures. "You will do this now." "You will stop doing it now." "You can't finish those sums now because you've got to go out and play." It's incredibly artificial and the cynicism sets in. My seven-year-old is already going, "Oh, I'm not going to school it's so boring."'

Home education wasn't just Rosemary's dream. 'It's mine too,' said Roger. 'I've helped out at the local school and I get a lot of joy out of that interaction with kids.' On a visit to Taransay with the producer at the end of November, 'as yet undecided on our commitment to this project, we were finally sold by a look at the school building.' Andy McAvoy's vision had found its first fan, whose enthusiasm was expressed in words that touchingly echoed those of the architect. 'It's a little old stone building,' Roger told me, 'which has tumbled down. It's just four walls, in fact one corner had fallen out, right onto the beautiful sandy beach. And that's the corner that looks out over the sea and the mountains of Harris. And they've replaced that corner, not with stone, but with glass, so you've got this wonderful stone school building with a wood burner at one end, open fire at the other end, small, cosy, and this corner as a glass, with this fantastic view, and the children can tumble out of the front door onto the beach – so there's that fantasy of the children having the most wonderful year.'

Now, with the London traffic rattling and beeping outside, the doctor and his wife were seriously wondering what to do. Should they abandon the project altogether? 'The problem is,' Rosemary told me, 'we're so deeply involved. We've made bonds with people. And as Roger says, it's addictive, we still have this vision of what is possible.' 'The only thing that would stop us going back,' said Roger, 'is the community saying, "Well actually, we don't like you any more, because you pissed off."'

Before they'd left Tarbert, the couple had written a hurried letter to the community, which they had given to Ron. 'We said, "Can you read this out explaining our actions, this is why we've left, because we feel we have no choice but to leave. We've been put in a position where we've either got to go to the island, or go away."'

Dear Castaways,

We have been very excited about Castaway 2000 for many months. We can see enormous potential in the project and are sure it will be a great success when it gets properly under way. We feel we have a lot to offer the community (and indeed already have behind the scenes) but not at any price. We would be happy sharing a room with our children for the year, and if we are to occupy the MacKay House, as suggested, sharing the house with one other family. We believe the schoolhouse should be a space where the children and adults can play and learn freely. This rules out using it for accommodation. Overcrowding is an intolerable burden to impose on us as we attempt to create a community in such a hostile environment. Sadly, we feel that our only option is to leave until what was promised at Windermere has been delivered.

We send you all our very best wishes,

Rosemary and Roger

'So,' Rosemary continued, 'Ron read this out to the community and he reported back to us that the feeling was actually quite negative. He didn't name names, but there were quite a few people who felt they didn't understand. I think it's because throughout this whole project we've been quite vocal and quite cynical, really, saying, "What about this? What about that?" We've always been pointing out the loopholes. Roger has fought to get the contract changed, he had the whole thing rewritten – now suddenly these are the people who hop on the first plane out.'

As this was an observational documentary, covering all aspects of the developing situation, Ron had of course been filmed reading the letter to the island castaways gathered in the steading; and on the Harris Hotel phone to Roger and Rosemary in London. 'Roger freaked out,' said Rosemary, 'when he knew they were filming Ron talking to us, because he felt the whole thing had got so out of hand it was ridiculous.'

After the phone call from Ron, the pair felt very unhappy. 'Because it hadn't been understood,' she continued passionately, 'that the reason we're here is not because we've cut and run, but because we felt pushed out. So we rang Chris and I said, "Well, look, you assured me this wouldn't happen, this is exactly what I predicted would happen, what are we going to do about it, because I'm not going back to that community if I feel they think we're just a bunch of skivers." He said, "No, we'll explain to them" and so on. Then we rang Jeremy because we thought this was unfair to put this on Chris, because poor Chris is right in the middle and he's busy at the same time editing the four initial programmes. We wrote Jeremy a statement we wanted him to sign, going right back to the beginning of our involvement in this project and explaining how right from the beginning we never said we were in a survivalist project. We were given the impression and reassured that we would arrive and have somewhere to live, that gave us a certain amount of privacy ...'

At a meeting in Lion House, Jeremy Mills declined to sign the Stephensons' long statement. Instead he wrote them a short letter, outlining Lion's position and apologising for the fact that 'our decision to take you off Harris seems to have caused problems with the rest of the community'. It was agreed that Roger should fly back up to the island the next day and put his case to the community direct. 'He was terrified about it,' says Production Director Shahana Meer, who was with him on the flight from London. 'I was really worried about him, I thought he was going to have a heart attack, he thought the castaways were going to give him a really hard time.'

Meer had decided to fly up and inspect the site for herself. While Roger's drama had been unfolding in London, things had not been going well for the exhausted Lion production team in Harris. As well as being besieged by journalists, two hire cars had been involved in accidents on the narrow island roads, both on the same day. One car had had Warren Latore at the wheel, taking Padraig into Stornoway hospital for a check-up on his injured foot, accompanied by camerawoman Tanya. Though this looked like a lighthearted enough incident in the clip shown in the programmes, it had been potentially very serious. 'If Warren hadn't done an advanced driving course,' says Paul Overton, 'and he hadn't handled the skid as well as he did, steering it into the mountain, it would have gone off the other side, which was a 50ft drop. It was pretty close.' Overton had actually arrived at the scene of the second crash, when researcher Elaine Paterson had come off the road between Tarbert and Horgabost. 'The production team were just falling apart by then,' he says, 'it was all the culmination of people going through a very stressful time. You couldn't have written it, put it that way.'

The 'negative feeling' that Ron had reported as the reaction to Roger's letter had not been just about their sudden departure to London. Since before the New Year, many of the castaways had felt that Roger had not been pulling his weight as a doctor. 'The thing that gets me,' Trevor Kearon was to tell me, when I arrived on Taransay the following week, 'is I'm a brickie and Ray's a brickie, and if I hadn't come out on the advance party, people'd say to me, "Why didn't you go, Trev? You're a bricklayer, this is your trade, this is where you supply your wares." Now his job is a doctor. He could have sent his wife and kids home and stayed up here roughing it with us, and he could have got the brownie points.'

But, as always in this complex little community, things were never entirely clear-cut. What people said in public meetings, or when the cameras were on them, was a very different thing from those private thoughts they would share with the video diary. 'I know there's a lot of ill-feeling about Roger and Rosemary not being here,' Sheila Jowers confessed to the ever-sympathetic minicam. 'But in a way perhaps they're doing us all some good by holding fast on certain conditions being reached, because it would be good to see the pods really sorted out, so that we can all start to find our own places and sort our accommodation out.'

Now, on the afternoon of Thursday 13 January, Roger choppered into the island and made his case. Trevor remained unimpressed. 'I said to him, at the meeting, "I was calling you everything under the sun when I was on that floor, Rog."' Philiy was more forgiving. 'Roger the doctor came over to talk to us and dispel some rumours that had been flying around, and it really has been like Chinese whispers, a lot of what we've heard has been second-hand, exaggerated. So it was good to see him, but I still feel that he should come over with the families and muck in and we could have found a room for him and his kids.'

Chapter 6

Moving in

The future of the doctor and his wife wasn't, of course, the only thing on the castaways' minds, as they worked all day alongside the team of professional builders who were still, at the end of this second week of January, very much a part of the island scene, hammering and sawing and drilling away on the pods from before dawn till well after dusk. Though surrounded by piles of timber and plastic-sheeting-covered materials, the four rounded, modernistic structures were now looking almost finished, with divisions to the rooms established, doors and windows glazed, and curved roofs covered with thick black waterproof material.

Trish Prater was still Queen Bee in the kitchen of the MacKay House, keeping the podmen going with breakfasts, teabreaks, lunches and suppers, often joining them at the end of the long working day for whisky or beer round the glowing anthracite fire in the cluttered front room. Down in the kitchen at the steading, meanwhile, a cooking rota had been established, and the castaways were taking it in turns to prepare a communal lunch and supper for their group of eighteen. Breakfast was still a help yourself affair – toast or cereal, a teabag dunked in a cup, a scoop of instant coffee from the big tin.

Otherwise they were doing what they could to get their new home finished. Ray Bowyer was building a verandah along the front of the schoolhouse. Liz Cathrine was 'just happy having got stuck in and set tasks for myself – I never cook and I baked my first bread this morning'; she and Dez had been tiling the shower block, another new experience. Pete and Sheila Jowers had been working on the polytunnels and fencing. And Mike Laird was furious with Andy the architect because he had criticised a dry stone wall he, Ray, Ben and postman Patrick Murphy had been building.

Andy McAvoy had been having his own problems. As well as acting as architect, site manager, Lion liaison man, and archaeological policeman, he had seen a ghost. 'This is a story he told us one night,' Toby Waterman told the video diary, 'and I think it's true. He was walking along the beach and he saw this rotund figure with loads of clothes on and a flat cap. He approached him, "Hello, hello." The figure didn't answer. He got a bit closer and then he realised it was some sort of ghost. Straightaway he ran back and up to the pod area and told people what he'd seen. So ever since then I've been walking around thinking about this ghost, because it's completely dark here at times. Last night I felt I had to get this out of my system, so I went to the old Paible graveyard. I was feeling very calm and happy and relaxed, it was a beautiful night with a moon out and you could see everything. I just stood at the graveyard and sorted my head out basically, saying to myself, "What is there to be scared of? If there is a ghost, it's a ghost, it won't hurt you, so don't worry." It's really nice to have a ghost as your major worry, rather than, say, being concerned about being stabbed in the middle of the city centre late at night or being in a fight or being raped or all these horrible ugly things which I hope won't rear their ugly heads on this island. I'm sure they won't.'

An Interesting Divergence

Peter Jowers had been reflecting on the progress of the developing community. 'Quite interesting,' he told the video diary, in the mellow, reflective tones of a detached observer, 'how efficient rotas for work have emerged, particularly around the cooking front. Two people do a long day, which starts one evening and finishes the next, and they're expected to cook, provide three meals, clean and keep the fires going. That's quite a long stint, but it's also a chance to be with a friend or a partner, so it's quite a social occasion. It's a chance to play one's CDs, so that each group creates a different atmosphere in the kitchen, and that's a really interesting process, watching how different people handle that – and the different types of food. I've got to say we're eating very well. I've never eaten more in my life, but simultaneously I think I'm losing weight because it's such a strenuous sort of life, whizzing about doing physical and manual work.' All too soon Peter was forced to rest from the work when he fell off a ladder and banged a hip. It was nothing serious, but it was a bit stiff.

'I think what's going to crop up in the next week,' he pondered now, 'is who goes in which pod.' Peter had noticed that an interesting divergence had started to appear between the 'youngsters' and the older castaways. The youngsters were more convivial, socialising a lot longer and later, whereas the more mature tended to seek more privacy, and also smaller conversational groups. Another trend he'd spotted he was sure would intensify. 'Also there's beginning to emerge reflection on the notion of fairness and pulling one's weight,' he told the minicam. 'In the context of thirty to thirty-six people, fairness will become absolutely central.' Having lived for years in a shared house in Gloucestershire with three other families, Peter had, he felt, good experience of this issue. 'I know how differently one can define this elusive word,' he elaborated, 'and I'm not sure that any resolution of it will ever occur, especially within one year. There are all sorts of different kinds of work, it's hard to assess what counts. I think there's going to be a tension between those who see the need to grow things and do the jobs that are necessary – get the coal in, wood, basics – and those that are wanting to use this year to express themselves.' How right he was! If only he could have foreseen how much tension – and how it was to involve him – Peter might have packed his bags then and there, and left.

Ben and the other twenty somethings had, in their rapidly-evolving group, been discussing many of the same issues. 'There's certainly a – well, it's not a division – but a difference between the young and the old. We were all saying, God, if it was just us here, what we'd do all day is like have a big sleep-in, go for a big walk, get completely trollied in the evening and we'd just get by, we'd just make beans on toast or something. I certainly wouldn't have the guilty feelings that we have with everyone else around and kind of looking at us.'

This difference in attitudes was reiterated by Ray. 'I look at these young ones sometimes,' he grumbled, 'and there's just no work in them. I don't know what it is. I've started work every morning with four people and I've been on my own by twelve o'clock. I don't expect the likes of somebody from an office to shovel one of the spades with me, but I do expect a trier. But you see it on their faces. They'll be with you an hour and then it's an excuse.' 'I'm bloody glad we're friends with the Russians HA HA!' he wrote in his diary.

Thirtysomething Trevor, as he saw it stuck in the middle, had observed the same thing. 'There seems to be a bit of – not aggro – but contention between the young element and the elder element. So far the twenty-four-year-olds aren't getting on well with the forty-fours and fifty-fours basically.'

There was another, rather different criticism the other way, by the young of the old. 'They love gossiping,' said Ben, 'that's the thing I've noticed, especially Peter, he's the gossip monster of the island.'

Entwined

And there was now more to gossip about than just whether the youngsters could do a good day's work or not. 'Romance,' said Toby, the unlikely spiller-of-the-beans on the video diary. 'There's been some romance already, I'm not saying with who, but I think it's very early, to start relationships in a fortnight. Personally I'd rather stand back and see how it goes and if nothing comes, nothing comes – if it does, fine.'

Mike Laird's diary revealed all. 'I'd had enough of work today,' he wrote on Wednesday 12 January. 'There are plenty of other people around doing very little. Many who had been drinking until the small hours did not get up till noon. Philiy and Padraig were entwined in each other's arms. This is the latest romance after Tammy and Ben. The next guess is on Toby and Tanya.'

As Philiy and Padraig's beds had been for a while squashed up against each other at one end of the schoolhouse, the affair had been an open secret off-camera among the castaways. On camera this was to lead to some rather cryptic video diary entries. 'There's been a lot of gossip,' Philiy complained to the minicam a couple of days later. 'I've felt quite upset by it and I've tried to confront the people who have been gossiping. I'm not going to name names, but we came to an understanding that I wasn't happy with what they were doing. I felt good that I dealt with it there and then, and didn't let it drag on. It's still going on, but not to the extent it was. I feel a bit calmer about it. I mean there was one day when I was just really, really upset and I went and sat on the beach and you know, I really love this island, I feel so at home here, but for a moment I was thinking, Oh my God I can't live with these people.'

'I told Ron,' says Peter, 'when he came from Harris one day, that Philiy had a relationship with Padraig. She flipped her lid. She is prone to do that from time to time. But I don't really understand why it has to be secret. I think Padraig emotionally needs the relationship more than she does.' 'I came here not wanting a relationship,' Philiy was to confide to the video diary much later, 'I even said to people, "No, I don't want that." Even when we got together I was thinking, "No, I really don't want this. Not him, but I didn't want a relationship.' In that he'd hit on some, at least, of the truth, it was hardly surprising that Peter's assumptions and insights (and how many of these had he passed on to that master of stirring, Ron?) had got to Philiy so deeply.

Unacceptable Behaviour

Philiy wasn't the only one to find herself at odds with Peter. With Roger and Gordon safely on the mainland the bearded lecturer, once tipped as a possible 'father figure' for the community, suddenly found himself in the bogeyman frame. 'He's picked on Jodene,' wrote Mike, 'who's eleven, and she was very upset about that. He's called Philiy to her face a hypochondriac, and yet she's had real flu. He's also suggested that certain sheep dogs, which he considers out of control, should be shot – and I've never seen two lovelier sheep dogs than

Trish's. He's taken a pop at Gwyneth. He's had a go at many of the women and the youngsters – and I just think it's totally out of order.'

It was a relatively trivial incident that ignited this gathering bonfire of resentments against Peter, but it brought into focus issues that were at the heart of the developing community. The trouble began on the night of Saturday 15 January, at the changeover between cooking shifts. Mike and Tanya had been cooking all day. Now, after supper, it was Peter and Sheila's turn to take over. 'The food went down well, as it does most evenings,' wrote Mike in his diary, 'and I sat down in the snug having washed the main course dishes. Shortly afterwards Gwyneth asked me to go up to the kitchen. This I did and found Tanya in tears speaking to Peter. He said (in his words) that the state of the kitchen was unacceptable and that we should have washed up the pots. Tanya had had a very tiring and stressful day as she had to pop out to film things, the lights went off, the generator failed etc. I really felt for her.

'As soon as I entered the kitchen she bolted out of the door as I spoke to Peter and told him he was out of order. He told me I was too! I pursued Tanya and gave her a hug, but she said she would prefer to be on her own and headed off towards the MacKay House.'

For a moment, Mike debated whether to enter the steading via the kitchen and confront Peter or whether to bypass the conflict and simply go to the snug. He decided to go for the former. 'On entering the kitchen,' Mike wrote, 'a discussion ensued and I headed for the sink. After lengthy chat and washing everything in sight I left and went to sit in the snug, comfortable in the knowledge that whisky was once again on the menu.'

A somewhat different account of these events was given by Sheila, in an anguished video diary two days later. 'When we walked in on Saturday night the place was an unbelievable tip. All the dishes were filthy, the floor was disgusting, there were vegetables, bits of burnt paper all over the floor – it was just a terrible mess. It was dark because the wind was right down, so it was difficult to see, but even so, we just had to set about tidying up. Of course certain feelings of resentment start building up when you feel that you've put every effort into making it an orderly, tidy place.

'So when Tanya came in, because she was one of the people who had been cooking that day, Peter said to her that he felt that it was just not on. He said it was a delicious meal, which it was, but it was an unacceptable mess. He was very straightforward, he didn't perhaps phrase it in delicate terms, he just said things had to be tidied up. And Tanya, who for all sorts of reasons, like the fact that it was dark and she has to do the filming, was very sensitive and couldn't cope with being spoken to like that. She walked out of the room, as did Mike. But a few minutes later Mike came back in – he must have thought about the situation – and said, "What can I do, how can I make it better?" So he helped tidy up and it was all sorted out. Well, Tanya was obviously really upset so I tried to persuade her to come back and she said that she just couldn't accept that Peter should talk to her like that at this stage, that he should have talked to the whole group. I thought, in Peter's defence, that to have talked in front of everybody would have been perhaps humiliating. And for Peter it was a spur of the moment thing – that was the way that he felt about the room. I'm sure I would have said it in a very different way, but Peter was just really straightforward. And so this erupted into a lot of upset. Peter in turn was upset about what had happened and obviously this was something that had to be discussed.'

Peter and Sheila didn't join the young castaways that evening, gathered round the fire in the snug with the whisky. In the morning, he and Sheila were on duty early, ready with breakfast in the steading. 'Now I'm *persona non grata*,' he muttered mournfully. 'All I said was the state of the kitchen was unacceptable. We had an agreement ...' But none of the youngsters joined them; they took Sunday breakfast in Trish's kitchen in the MacKay House. 'It was a bit naughty,' said Ben. 'It just happened unofficially. We didn't cook, we just had some toast and coffee up here, it was an unintentional little strike.'

A Castaway Myself

These last comments were not to the video diary, but to me, as I sat with Peter in the steading or Ben in the front room of the MacKay House, sipping endless cups of tea and weak instant coffee as I did the rounds doing interviews.

I had arrived on the morning of Friday 14th, swooping in low over the blue-black sea in the little propeller-engined BA plane to land by the drab pebbledashed bungalows of Stornoway. Then it was onwards in a hire car through the spectacular landscape of Lewis: that gets better and better as you head south, as the tufted grassy flatness of the north island gives way to ever steeper and more magnificent mountains, reflected that sunny morning in perfect detail in glassily still lochs. The small town of Tarbert marked the start of Harris, then it was a twenty-minute drive down a mainly single-track road to the dunes at Horgabost, where oil drums lined the summer car park that had become the temporary helicopter landing site. All seemed cheerfully chaotic. The chopper had just taken off for Taransay as I drove in. The lanky, blond Scotsman on the ground explained that the pilot had taken the ground crew with him, so he'd probably be gone a wee while. If I was the author of the book, that was OK, he was going over on the boat in an hour or so and I could go with him. He was Angus MacKay, it transpired, from the family that owned the island, the official castaway boatman for the year.

From the far end of the beach, across the surprisingly narrow strait, you could clearly see the castaway settlement, tiny against the bulk of the island behind: the schoolhouse central, the steading and frames of the four pods away by the futuristic windmill to the left. Though it was mid-January, the sea was almost as flat as the proverbial glass, partially reflecting the sunny ochre-green of the mountains in its gorgeous pale blue.

Before I knew it, the helicopter had reappeared, and I was whisked across in a minute and a half to a field within twenty yards of the grey little three-up, two-down I was soon to be calling 'the MacKay House'. I had met a small group of the castaways before, when they were doing interviews with the press in the lobby of a London hotel. So Mike Laird was ready with a friendly handshake and helpful introductions.

Here in the downstairs kitchen was blonde Trish, stirring away at the huge vat of soup that was the builders' lunch. This bright-eyed, reddish-brown-haired lady was Gwyneth, who was also sleeping in the house, and this rather shy,

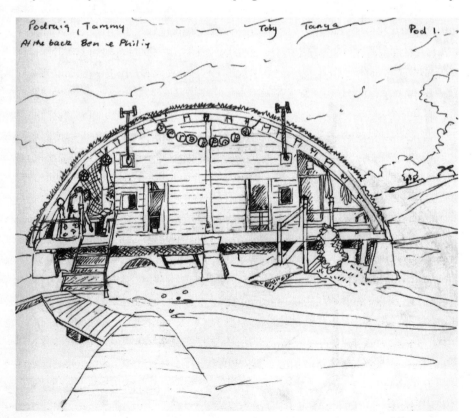

good-looking woman who didn't meet my eye was Hilary. Up across the top of the field, where the grass sheared off suddenly into a low sandy cliff, was the schoolhouse, where clothes and books and sleeping bags were strewn haphazardly over the fifteen or so metal-framed camp beds. Out the front in the sunshine was pony-tailed Ray, working on his wooden verandah, 'so that the schoolkids don't break their legs falling off onto the beach,' he told me now, in the thick, syrupy, rather breathless Manchester accent that the youngsters, I would discover later, had off to a tee.

Walking along the seaweed-strewn shore, Mike was enthusiastic about the wildlife he'd already seen. Fourteen seals, several sea otters, four whales. Then about the wealth of archaeology. Where this dune was sliced away by the sea you could see the layers of deposition. Some of the stones here were probably gravestones. There was an old graveyard over there, and the ruins of three churches.

Five more castaways now appeared. Blond Ben Fogle, as genial and genuine as when I'd met him in London. Ginger-curled Irish Padraig, pretty Tanya Cheadle and tall, dreadlocked, nose-ringed Philiy Page, who had a question. 'Could we see some of your other work?' 'Sure, sure,' I replied, heart sinking, in case they hated it and refused to co-operate.

Back across the empty field was the steading, the kitchen at one end, the central section piled up with as yet unopened crates, a thick green plastic curtain dividing off the 'snug' end by the cast-iron coal fire, around which was a circle of tatty looking armchairs, a couple of makeshift drying lines above hung with trousers, T-shirts, towels.

I headed round doing my interviews, constantly being interrupted and having to move. There was no such thing as a quiet warm indoor space on the island. The MacKay House was at risk from builders with cups of tea; the steading snug from castaways coming in to slump down in front of the fire; even the schoolhouse was regularly invaded, and in the evening it seemed to be Ray's private haunt. I took my chances, talking to Trevor, for example, on the floor of the MacKay House upstairs bedroom where seven of them were sleeping.

On the Friday evening I ended up with Mike, Ray and five electricians in their tiny Portakabin, making merry in the condensation-dripping warmth, working our way through a rich variety of alcoholic drinks. Their singing Hebridean accents seemed almost more Welsh than Scottish. At one point big old Ray, grey-bearded and saturnine, drinking whisky from the tiny sharp-edged capful of Mike's private bottle, leant forward and suggested a night on the town with the leccies in Stornoway; Danny, the 'lad' who'd invited us in, told him to much laughter what he could do with that suggestion. Back at the MacKay House the insulating team who'd been on the floor of the front room had returned to Lewis for the weekend, leaving me alone with their mattresses and old beercans on the red carpet by the glowing fire, a luxurious bit of privacy I kept extremely quiet about.

By the Saturday I felt like a castaway myself, sitting by the steading stove as the Tanya/Peter/Mike row developed at the other end of the building, and people ran in and out like characters in a Chekhov play: Tanya in tears, then Ben departing to console her, then a furious Mike (did both he *and* Ben fancy her?); a Gwyneth seething with quiet fury at the attitude of 'that man'. Later I shared more whisky with 'the youngsters' and listened to their complaints about being told what to do by the older folk. It was the first time since they'd lived with parents they'd had to take it, they said. But they all seemed to love Ray as a colourful eccentric, and Toby's imitations of him were particularly fine. They also bantered a lot about being on TV. They joked that a haircut that Ben had would soon be known as 'a Ben' (little did they realise the sudden stardom that was about to envelop their young pal).

On the Sunday I walked off my hangover with an exploration of the rest of the island, striding up over the rock-strewn, sodden tundra that I soon learned to call the 'machair'. In the pale sunshine it was more tan and burnt sienna than green. The gently sloping central valley led after half an hour or so to a narrow pool, the still water thick with long grass. Fifteen minutes more walking brought me to a proper loch, with deep, dark water, and a row of stepping stones out to a little circular island, built up round its circumference with a seven-foot-high granite boulder wall – surely, I thought, some kind of ancient fort? It was, I later discovered, the intact remains of a two-thousand-year-old Celtic 'dun'. All around were the low, jagged-outlined mountains of grey granite: grey from a distance, but stopping to sit on a rock and look at it closely you see that it was a wonderful mixture of colours, veined with pink and white marble, scuffed over with lichen in a pale, almost plasticky green. Likewise the turf under the long brown grass was a mass of vivid hues over the black, peaty soil.

Climbing up leftwards from the loch, I reached the ridge and saw the bothy directly below, smoke issuing from its chimney. I dropped down the steep slope and found a little one-roomed stone house, perhaps forty foot long by fifteen foot wide, with a corrugated iron roof. The wooden door was open. I pushed into the gloom, half-expecting to find Dez and Liz, who'd escaped there for the weekend, only to be joined by master of sensitivity Ray and his mate Hilary. But it was empty.

There were big fireplaces at both ends; in one a fire still smoked. From the girders that marked off the roof area hung some hammocks made of blue/green fisherman's netting. By the fire was a swinging chair in the same material. On the mantelpiece stood a half-empty bottle of Glenmorangie and some Fairy Liquid. A scattering of picnic type plates and cutlery lay on a table under the window.

There is no law of trespass in Scotland, and the idea of the bothy is a heart-warming one. You pitch up, you stay as long as you like, then you leave it as you'd like to find it, perhaps with a little food or drink or fuel for the next comer. A book on the window ledge revealed the sort of use this remote little place had got before Lion had picked Taransay for TV stardom. *30th August–3rd September. Spent a few stormbound days here. Today is fine and calm – sunny and warm. Paddling back to Horgabost. A. MacPhail.* Or: *Alone together for 7 days, no visitors yet, many thanks to the weather. Anna.* Then, in November the first castaways: *What an amazing place for weary wanderers to rest. Just a little piece of heaven awaiting to be seen. Rest well and travel safely. Tammy. X.* Then the first journalists, on 6 December. *Arrived by helicopter, explored a bit of the island before starting fire and drinking our Beaujolais from Glasgow airport! Good luck to all the BBC volunteers.* On 7 January, Mike and Toby had written, *We came, we saw nothing, we left. What, no journalists!* A day later: *The island is too beautiful for intruders, bye, Jodene.*

Beyond the little dwelling the island is divided in two by a narrow isthmus, with a lovely sweep of sandy beach on each side. Beyond, to the south, is another smaller peninsula, complete with its own mountain and valleys. I decided to walk right round it, but gave up after an hour, worried about getting back before darkness closed in at four. Even up at this end, the slopes were corrugated with lazybeds, the grassed-over little cultivation trenches and ditches that I'd first seen in the west of Ireland, where they had been abandoned in famine times. Here they had been used for growing potatoes until the early part of this century; the very last inhabitants leaving the island in the late 1970s.

A drizzly mist had blown in now, and striding back through it, I nearly ended my participation in the *Castaway* project, pausing just in time before I walked over the edge of a sheer cliff round a huge blowhole, which had been already named by the castaways, 'the Natural Arch'. Thanks for warning me, guys.

Back at the bothy I found Dez and Liz loading up their knapsacks and bedrolls for the forty-minute walk back to Paible. Liz was also carrying a large red buoy, with which she planned to decorate her pod. I walked ahead with Dez, who gave me a useful impromptu geology lesson, pointing out, amongst other things, the difference between that coarse-grained igneous crystalline rock called granite and the foliated metamorphic rock called gneiss.

A Very Healing Process Really

That evening, after supper, the bubbling anti-Peter tension finally overflowed into open conflict. A meeting had been called to resolve a key issue – what to do with the families when they arrived, as expected, from the mainland the following morning. Half the castaways sitting around the fire in the steading snug felt that the builders, who had been staying in the MacKay House, should sleep in the half-finished pods, and the families should move into the MacKay House. Half thought that the site wasn't yet ready for the families, and they should be encouraged to remain on the mainland. The builders' needs, they argued, were paramount if the building was ever going to get finished.

After an opening ten minutes in which I spoke to the gathering on the subject of the book (how alarming it was having a camera poked in your face!) it was the turn of Graham, the tall, balding insulator who was representing the contractors. He was adamant that the builders needed to stay in the MacKay House to get the job finished as quickly as possible. He told us they were threatening to down tools if they were moved. Some of the gathered castaways thought that this was the only thing that made sense; others, though, were desperate to get the families over and get the community 'up and running'.

Personally, I thought it was total madness to bring the families over before there was anywhere for them to go. I sat silent for a good twenty minutes as the debate raged, then couldn't help putting my point of view. Did it sway things? I hope not, because I immediately regretted having intruded into something I was supposed to be observing. Before too long, though, it seemed to be generally agreed that the builders should stay in the house until they had finished the job.

Just how absurd all this was only dawned on me the next day, when I flew back to the mainland to find Warren, Colin and Gordon waiting with their bags at the helicopter landing site. Lion had already made the sensible compromise decision to send the men over to work and leave the women and children in Tarbert. A good forty minutes of fervent castaway discussion had been entirely wasted. (Not for the last time.)

As the meeting moved on to discuss the previous night's fight between Peter and Tanya, the film-maker became so involved she had to put down her camera while she fought her corner with Peter. 'This is all about me, isn't it?' she said angrily as she passed the equipment to soundwoman Philiy and sat down next to Peter. 'I'm sorry,' she protested, when Peter reiterated his complaints about the untidy kitchen. 'But I really think you were rude to me.'

Peter disagreed. 'I said I think this kitchen is not up to the required standard in a very – in my terms – neutral tone. What happens is, I'm a very big person,

I'm an old person, a bearded person and people project onto me all sorts of their own thoughts.' Peter was sticking firmly to the principles developed from experience. 'I think in the beginning of a community – I've lived in one for twenty-five years – if you don't establish the rules and stick to them other conventions begin to develop and it's a very dangerous precedent.'

Viewers were to see this argument as a highlight of Programme Five, ending in frank group discussion and a reflective video diary by Tanya and Philiy ('I thought we were coming here to build some sort of Utopia, and yet we're all bringing our prejudices with us ...'). In reality, though, the anti-Peter eruption continued and escalated, as Trish joined the fray, answering Peter's criticism that her dogs were sheep worriers.

'You don't have dogs! You don't have sheep!' a furious Trish shouted at one point, as Peter cried 'Let me finish!' The real issue, however, was saved until the end. 'You should raise your points here,' Trish continued, across Peter's protests. 'We have meetings every night here. Instead of bitching behind all our backs.'

'We had a meeting all together in the evening,' Sheila told her video diary the next day, 'and there were all these cross currents, these feelings that were hidden and criticisms lying amongst us all, and so it all was brought to a head and I think it was a very healing process, really. Perhaps it needs somebody like Peter who seems abrupt. It's painful, it's like lancing a boil, but when you lance it the pressures are released. Anyway lots of things came out into the open, like Trish's feelings that she was being criticised from the people in the steading, I don't know how personal that was, whether it was directed at Peter – I mean as far as I'm concerned Peter's never criticised Trish. And I,' she concluded unhappily, 'who have felt very calm, very positive about it all, I'm beginning to get anxious. Anyway, I'll go out into the fresh air, whether it's wet, windy, stormy, calm, or beautiful. It has a pace of its own and when you enter that, then you can cope with these turbulent emotions.'

'Yesterday's meeting was very important,' said Dez, 'because that's when the barriers came down. Liz and I talked before the meeting and we both decided that it was important that people did express their views so that everybody heard them. I tried to make sure that two issues were discussed, and had they not filtered through, I would have brought them up: one, the dogs, and two the kitchen fracas that happened on Saturday. The most important thing, though, is that at the end of last night, after all these heated discussions, people made up, people hugged each other and a few tears were spilled.'

'The most wonderful thing,' Ben told the video diary the next day, 'was that Trish and Gwyneth suddenly appeared down in the snug – we were just sitting there – and they basically said they could not stand going to sleep feeling the way they were, so they wanted to make up. And Peter's got a bit of a gammy leg, but he went over and they had a massive hug and tears kind of welled in Liz's eyes, so I was set off as well. We had a really lovely hug. You could feel the atmosphere being sucked through the keyhole of the door, and it was all light and breezy.'

Wriggly Worms

Ron had been supposed to accompany the other men to Taransay, but had developed a chest infection, he told me, when I caught up with him the next day in the Harris Hotel. He was keen to point out that it wasn't that he didn't want to go to Taransay. They were all bored in Tarbert, as well as worried about what the island community was really thinking of them. 'They tell us to our face that there's no animosity, no resentment, that they want us to be where we want to be. But then people like the architect say that when he's working with people individually they're going, "Fucking lazy bastards, they're not here" and that there *is* resentment.'

But he was, unfortunately, ill. He had been to see Dr Finlayson that very morning, who had told him he wasn't fit to go. The thing that had really enraged the would-be castaway was the attitude of Lion TV. 'I called Chris Kelly and he said, "I hear there's a hitch." I go, "Yeah" and told him the story about the chest infection. Chris says, "I'll phone the doctor and I'll phone you back." I'm really insulted that he has to phone the doctor to check my story is true. It's that lack of trust. For me, the pair of them, Jeremy Mills and Chris Kelly, are wriggly worms. They want me out of the way because they think that once episodes one and two are screened the press are going to be here again and they obviously don't want anyone around.'

Lion were naturally keen to avoid a repeat of the tabloid frenzy of a fortnight before. But there was another issue, too. 'Frankly they should be working to get the island ready,' said Chris Kelly, as, mobile phone ringing several times an hour, he worked round the clock getting the fourth programme finished in the edit suite in Glasgow. 'The original plan that they all signed up for was that they're building their own homes. And now we've got builders in and people are coming to me and saying, "What – we've got to cut the turf for our pods?"'

'I think a huge dependency culture built up on Harris in this first three or four weeks,' says Jeremy Mills. 'Our lot were being made to run around after endless requests: "Can you get this for us?", "Can you do that for us?"'

Plenty of the island castaways would have agreed with this analysis. But Ron's mistrust of the programme makers certainly found echoes elsewhere. Warren Latore felt that he and Monica and the rest of the families were being continually misled about how prepared the pods were for occupation. 'It didn't matter to me,' he says, 'but it did seem like there were loads of lies being told. I can't quite see why, because it was not a big enough thing to tell a lie about. Why tell us the buildings were ready when they weren't? I'm not particularly saying it was Lion who were lying, but somebody was, and I can't see why they did. It was really frustrating for that whole period.'

Having signed their release forms and given away a year of their lives (for who really knew what individual motives) others of the castaways were now wondering just how cynical an operation the whole documentary was. 'I've said this to Jeremy several times,' said Rosemary. 'If you set us up to fail, you may get a very interesting television programme, but I'm not accepting to be part of something with built-in disasters.' At the same time, Liz, observing from a professional view the 'chaos' that she saw on the island had been led to wonder if, 'they may have wanted it like that, because it maybe makes good TV'.

So Surreal

On Tuesday 18 and Wednesday 19 January the first two programmes went out primetime on BBC 1 and the nation was introduced to the first group of castaways, as they battled against each other on the first selection course in Wales. The reviewers were quick to agree that one or two stars were already emerging. 'The third team was led,' said Robert Hanks of the *Independent*, 'by Ben, a blond, muscular public schoolboy, for whom the psychologist has clearly developed something of a soft spot, describing him as "superman" and "ideal leader". The lesson here appeared to be that the upper-classes have natural leadership qualities and democracy is a hollow sham.' The *Daily Telegraph* found 'two obvious stars: Ben, the picture editor of *Tatler*, who put in a fine performance as The Posh One, and Ron who played (or possibly overplayed) the Camp One with gusto'. Similar mileage was made out of Cynthia McVey's brief burst of praise for Fogle: 'Indeed, his ability to combine being "task-centred" and "people-centred" (and the tendency to remove his shirt a lot) seemed at several points to reduce her to psychological jelly.' 'A star was born in the handsome shape of Ben Fogle, a posh 25-year-old,' agreed the *Guardian*.

On the island itself, the real-life participants of the project remained gloriously oblivious to all this. On the evening of 18 January, Mike Laird finally took a much-needed shower, which was 'fantastic'. 'When I took my clothes off it was amazing how much grit fell out. The other thing that never ceases to amaze me is just how bad my body can smell.' Unsuspecting Ben Fogle, meanwhile, looked after the newly arrived sheep and made bread and cement and cleared away rubbish and built a dam, 'which was taken down the next day – that was really annoying'.

It was only on Friday, when the families flew over for a discussion about who was to go in which pod, that the reaction of the outside world impinged. 'All the families arrived yesterday,' Ben told the video diary, 'and went, "God, Ben, you won't believe the publicity. It's in all the newspapers, and your name's been written in lots of different articles and the *Evening Standard* called up all the *Tatler* girls." And it's all,' he stuttered, 'I don't – I never know what to believe because for me sitting here, as far as I'm concerned, it's just like a normal day-to-day sort of thing. I can't believe that there are slightly more people now that know who I am … if that makes any sense. It's so surreal. I haven't seen any of it yet, and I'm sure it's been slightly Chinese-whispered along. I imagine they'll write, "Posh boy Ben was silly with the sheep", some little review thing like that, and it's been built up.'

The young picture-editor was genuinely bemused. 'It's still strange to hear – it's a factor I'd never really thought about. Obviously once these programmes properly went out I thought, yeah, maybe. But not now. Not while we were on the island. I never knew that friends of mine were going to be talking about me more than they might if I was just away in South America for a year or something. I don't know, it's all very confusing.'

He missed his friends, he went on; and the staff at *Tatler*, and sometimes he wondered what was going on in his absence in the *Tatler* office. He had, in fact, named some of the newly arrived flock of sheep after them – those *Tatler* girls. 'Which I think is a compliment,' he laughed nervously. 'I mean someone did point out actually that the sheep are all boys, that had been castrated, but I think that sort of counts as a girl.' So, as he rounded them up, each morning, he called out their names, George, Hilary, Wendy. 'And they come straightaway.' The only exception was Shalla, who was not a posh London magazine chick but one of Philiy's favourite Hebridean builders.

Steered and Engineered

As for the crucial accommodation meeting, people were surprised how easily it went. 'I thought it was going to be an absolute nightmare,' said Philiy, 'because we were all really hungover when the families arrived and they interpreted this as us being depressed and fed up, which we weren't at all. We just wanted to get stuff down, and we knew the families were going to have to get back over to the mainland. So Liz had all these little post-it notes and stuck them all over the place and we all roughly got the rooms we wanted, so I'm really pleased. I'm in Pod One and I look out on the back where there's some rocks. Me and Tanya are going to have it as a kind of open plan room, because her bedroom's quite small, so we'll use both of them.'

'We had the families over,' Mike reported, 'to see the progress on the pods, and I think generally they were fairly impressed. At least we've now sorted out where people are going to go. I'm in Pod Three with Trev and Liz and Dez, they're my next door neighbours, so I'm pretty happy with that. I've got the small room on the left hand side, so I've got a view of the sea.'

'We got the room we wanted,' said Dez, remembering the allocation process sometime later with a grin. 'With the best view of the sea. The whole thing was completely steered and engineered.' 'Suddenly we were all thrown together,' says Liz, 'and we had about an hour and a half to sort it out. We knew that no one else would do it. So I just thought, Well, in the interests of getting it done, and in the interests of getting the room we wanted, it did make sense to do it myself. And I would quite happily admit that that was me in a work-type mode manipulating.'

The meetings were now being minuted, more or less properly. Earlier lists headed *Talked About*, *Decisions*, and *Actions*, which had barely filled a single page of the chunky hardback 'minutes book', were now replaced with numbered subject heads, basic details of the discussion and the proposed action. *Wood supply* read one such *Haulage from Inverness costs more than the wood. Action – seek alternative supplier.* Gradually, the castaways were getting sorted.

Taransay Blues

After twenty days on the trot cooking for the builders in the MacKay House, Trish had decided she needed a break. Taking her children Jodene and Michael with her she headed off up the island towards the bothy, intending to spend the night away. No sooner had she set off than there was a very bad turn in the weather, and the ever-solicitous Gwyneth Murphy suggested to Mike and Trevor that they should go up and check that she and the children were OK.

'So I grabbed Trev,' said Mike, 'and the pair of us kitted ourselves out and went up there. We're glad we did, because in our opinion they didn't have everything they needed. Our arrival made things a lot more comfortable for them. We lit a fire, put some candles up, fed the dogs – they'd forgotten the tin opener.' They had a few warming drinks around the fire and then, while Trevor decided to stay over, Mike headed off back to base.

'After about a third of a bottle of whisky,' Mike wrote in his journal, 'I set off back despite the weather. I had given an estimated time of return and so had to get back so they would not worry. The wind carried me up the hill and it seemed nearly effortless. This may also have a lot to do with the fact I was quite pissed. Nevertheless, I was happy when I could see the lights of Paible. But about 400 metres from the steading I slipped on a rock and hurt my right ankle. I sat for a minute cursing myself, but I knew I had to make it back so I limped. The pain was pretty bad but lessened by the alcohol. The most direct route home was straight across the bogs and the deepest parts of the river. When I got back I stuck my head in at the steading to see if Gwyneth was there. She was at the house, so I hobbled up there and she put a bandage on it for me.'

Not that a mere minor injury was going to stop the Action Man enjoying himself. 'Then it was back down to the steading,' he wrote, 'where a great big party was going on. It was the last night for some of the builders and there was also a twenty-first and a twenty-fifth birthday. Graham was playing the guitar and people were singing made-up verses. It was called Taransay Blues and had us all in hysterics. The booze was flowing freely. My last recollection of the night was at about 5.30 a.m. when a few of us staggered back to the Portakabins.'

'It was kind of a goodbye party for the builders,' said Philiy, 'and there was a full moon as well, so it was a full moon party. It was just wonderful. There was a lot of whisky drunk, not by me, though, I was sober. I was quite happy just watching everybody. Murdo, one of the builders, came in before they'd really started drinking and he said, "I have to sing to you this evening." And he got Graham, one of the other guys, to play guitar, and he sang me Eric Clapton's "You Look Wonderful Tonight", which was quite funny, but it touched me as well. I've not been serenaded before, and it was lovely. They're a really lovely bunch of guys and it's going to be so strange when they go. It's going to be a totally different atmosphere, because they've really been part of this place. They're smiling all the time, they're laughing, and they work so hard. I'm going to miss them a lot.'

The merriment continued until six in the morning, when Mike 'threw up all over the place' and crashed out. In the bothy meanwhile, Trevor had passed a less happy night with Trish and her kids. One of Trish's dogs had pissed on Jodene's sleeping bag; kind-hearted Trevor had lent her his, 'and I must admit I froze all night. Put all me trousers on, all me jumpers, me Berghaus, everything, I was sitting in a chair, round a couple of candles, freezing me nuts off.'

Mike came to at about three in the afternoon with a very sore head and an even sorer leg. Such was his state by Monday morning that he had abandoned his former antipathy and 'was really glad' to see Roger (now back from London and over on a day visit) and have his ankle professionally checked over. The doctor's diagnosis was a possible crack in the lower part of one of Mike's leg bones. 'I was very grateful indeed for his diagnosis, and even more so for his compassion,' Mike wrote. There was no alternative but to leave the island for a check-up in the hospital in Stornoway. The ligaments, it transpired, were damaged, so a second of the young male castaways was now reduced to crutches.

Wonderful Material

It wasn't just the doctor who was making site inspections of the nearly-completed island settlement. When Mike returned to Horgabost beach the next morning he found producer Chris Kelly, accompanied by the man who had dreamed the whole thing up in the first place, Jeremy Mills. The executive producer was impressed by the realisation of his idea. 'When I actually went on the island,' he says, 'I thought it was brilliant. I thought, What's all the fuss about? I slept in one of the pods and it was great. I really thought, I do not understand what's going on here. I expected to go up and find a building site, a complete mess, in fact I found four places almost ready to move in to.' Mills was impressed by the castaways on the island, who were 'great, doing a fantastic job' but less so by those who were still off. 'I got the sense that probably all some of them did was whinge and sit in the bar of the Harris Hotel.'

From the steading, Liz Cathrine had watched the Executive Producer arrive. 'He came up to the fence and paused for a good minute or so. He was looking as if to say, "Oh God, this is so fantastic. I've created all of this." It was just his body language. It was superb and very very funny.'

Accompanying the producers were a journalist and photographer from the one newspaper that Lion TV had cannily favoured above all others – the local *Stornoway Gazette*, who were to write a thoroughly upbeat article on the situation on Taransay. Far from 'blasting' *Castaway 2000*, this writer found it 'a unique, considered and well-managed project that may well turn out to be a landmark series in television history ... worth the modest sums the BBC have invested in it ... we should be pleased rather than cynical that this unique experiment is taking place on our doorstep, bringing much needed work to a host of local trades and people and giving a little boost to the off-season tourism trade in Harris.' After praising the 'frontiers men and women', who were 'much more like pioneers than castaways', and the pods ('everywhere is Scottish oak

... the design is a credit to architect Andy McAvoy'); the article went on to describe Mills as 'an active Christian, a Methodist from Manchester', whose 'talent has been to realise that the soul searching that is popular with the well-to-do professionals that make up the British middle classes just might contain a few questions of genuine and universal interest'. ('I'm not from Manchester,' laughs Mills, 'I'm from Cornwall.' But he is a Methodist and he was pleased with the piece.)

It was all quite a contrast to the reports filed by the unauthorised press, who, encouraged by the continuing TV programmes, were now back in force in the Harris Hotel. 'It was very much two camps,' says young, personable dark-bobbed manageress Sarah Morrison. 'The castaways were in the residents' lounge and the journalists were in the sun lounge, and they weren't talking to each other at all. We had guests coming in for lunch, people from Tarbert and other locals, just for the entertainment value – they thought it was really funny.'

'The hotel phone kiosk was our office basically,' says researcher Elaine Paterson. 'You'd be standing there and you'd suddenly look outside and you'd realise there was a presence and of course it would be some journalist listening to you. You'd feel like saying, "Clear off! I'm speaking to my mate." But of course they got information. It was just the sheer fact that they could see who was there and who wasn't.'

The flu story had now been supplanted by the 'softies in luxury' angle. THEY'RE AIRLIFTED OVER FOR PUB GRUB, the News of the World had reported. Viewers who had seen the castaways learning how to kill animals had been misled. 'The only chickens they encounter are already dead – served up with potatoes and vegetables in local bars.' It was NOTHING BUT A SHAM, concluded the newspaper's TV correspondent.

Meanwhile events on the island itself were taking a more dramatic turn than the most excited tabloid hack could have imagined. A Burns Night party was taking place, which began with the castaways sitting down with the producers and psychologist Cynthia McVey to watch episodes two, three and four of the programme on a specially imported portable TV. It then progressed to a celebratory meal where a haggis was serenaded by a stuttering Mike ('What a balls up I made of this,' he wrote later. 'It was totally embarrassing. I had to read the poem out of a book, half pissed and without glasses because I'd lost them ... the absolute worst part was when I accidentally said the word "gusset" instead of "gushing".') But the party ended in a noisy fight, in which Ray called Padraig 'a lazy bastard' and Padraig responded that Ray was 'a fat Northern pig' amid a hail of richer expletives. Interestingly, it was Cynthia McVey, not strictly a castaway, who was at the centre of breaking things up, calming the drunken ex-builder and telling him not to get over-excited. Observant viewers of the scene eventually aired as the climax to the fifth programme would also see producer Chris Kelly in the background, and at the end it is Chris who leads Ray off with the suggestion that he come for a walk outside.

'I had an interesting night,' reported Padraig the next day. 'As you do at Burns Night we drank quite a bit of whisky. Late in the evening, certainly post-midnight, I was at the bottom of the steading in the snug with one of the builders and Dez. Well, Ray walked in and he and Dez had already had a bit of a barney that morning about the kitchen rota, so things were resolved and they gave each other a hug. Then we started talking and Ray said something about only being here to do thirteen jobs and then he was on the next boat out. All I asked him was, why, if he'd signed up in the first place, he wasn't prepared to do the full year. He avoided answering it, and I kept pressing him, in an increasingly loud voice, and I suppose an intractable tone, to answer the question I'd originally asked. It got to the stage where Ray was shouting abuse at me. I was sitting on a chair with my leg up and he was standing above me, spitting practically, with his fists either side. Dez was trying to calm him down. Then eventually more people ran in from the top of the steading and I said a few things that I suppose I shouldn't have, taking advantage of the number of people in the room. The second one actually inspired him to make an effort to get me with a punch. But there were enough people around to stop that. So he went out, shouting abuse at other people as he went.'

'Ray got louder and louder,' said Dez, 'even more aggressive than he'd been with me earlier, to the point where it was a struggle and people were having to restrain him. Even Hilary, who's probably Ray's closest ally on the island, was knocked over by Ray.'

'It was an odd statement to make,' said Hilary, 'you know, "I've got a certain amount of jobs to do by a given date in March." It didn't seem to signify. So anyway he got really annoyed. I said, "Come on, Ray." But he pushed me out of the way. Then he stormed off and was quite insulting to Ben and repeated, "All these young 'uns are lazy and not doing any work."'

'He's not a vicious man,' says Padraig, 'it was just an argument that got out of hand. I wasn't prepared to concede a point. We'd all had a fair bit of drink and when Ray gets a bit in him, he gets unreasonable sometimes. He's from a different generation. And being almost rudely challenged repeatedly by somebody less than half his age would be upsetting for him.'

Ray was as succinct as ever in his description of the same event. 'We had a bit too much to drink last night and I'm afraid I lost my temper with Padraig. All through the whisky. But we made it up this morning.'

'This morning,' Padraig continued, 'I was in bed and I heard footsteps outside and suddenly the door opened and in came Ray. I thought he was going to beat me up. But Tanya came in after him with the camera. He knelt at the bed and he said, "Padraig, I'm sorry, forgive me." So we shook hands and I apologised and it was a very surreal wake-up call. I've no hard feelings against Ray – I like him a lot – but he can be a bit unreasonable and aggressive sometimes.'

The fight, taken with the earlier argument that Ray had had with Dez over the kitchen rota he'd drawn up, provoked some thought in the others about the builder's role in the developing community. 'I know we're a cross-section of society,' mused Trevor to the video diary, 'but none of us would normally meet. Even though we all want the same objective, of getting it right and it going well, people are so different in so many ways. It's really tense a lot of the time. I don't feel it is for me, but you can see it on people's faces. It's getting tougher as we go along.'

Hilary had been in the steading when Ray appeared in the morning: 'He walked into the kitchen and sort of looked at us and said, "Oh, I didn't do anything wrong last night, did I?" So I said, "Oh, Ray, I think you did and I think you ought to apologise," and he said, "Oh God, I'll have to stop drinking." So we said – Peter and myself – in a jokey way, "We'll have just to make sure you don't overstep the mark."'

On the video diary Ray had his own final thoughts (or was it merely a justification?): 'The reason I probably had the slanging match is, I've got me feelings it's not going to come together. I've been having a word with Peter and Hilary and they're under the same conclusion as I am.'

Back on the mainland Jeremy Mills found the Harris Hotel packed with journalists; MUTINY ON CASTAWAY ISLAND was on the front of the *Record*; and the *Scotsman* was quoting once-trusted expert Lofty Wiseman as saying that, 'the flu-struck islanders should have stayed and coped if the programme was to be authentic. I am not saying the BBC are conning people but they are certainly letting them down.'

Mills decided to hold a press conference there and then in the public bar of the Harris Hotel. He admitted to the gathered journalists that the community had become split between those on the island and those in the hotel, but, with several mainland castaways beside him to back him up, he denied any 'mutiny'. Although none of this had been planned, he told them, 'from my point of view it's fantastic material. The pressure that it's put them all under as two groups of people has brought out some utterly fascinating insights into human nature and human relationships from a TV point of view. That's the key thing.' Meanwhile, Cynthia McVey, keeping very quiet about the events of the night before, gave the press some revelations due out that evening in the fourth programme – in particular the smashed crates. Finally, Mills revealed that he'd just spent the night on the island. 'It was a magical experience,' he said. 'And we are getting wonderful material.'

As indeed they were. But the press, far from showing a suitable gratitude by softening their line on the project, just took Lion's latest revelations as grist to their ever-critical mill. WE'VE CASTAWAY YOUR BELONGINGS was the headline in the next day's *Daily Mirror*, while the *Daily Mail* had an alarmingly realistic-sounding portrait of life at the Harris Hotel. 'Yesterday one rebel – gay psychotherapist Ron Copsey – imperiously sent his eggs back to the kitchen. Astonished staff were told he wanted them sunny side up. "They are overcooked and I will be sick if I eat them," he whined.'

Unfortunately, though the journos' eyewitness accounts had the smack of authenticity, the complex truth of the triangular relationship between Taransay, Tarbert and Lion TV was still eluding them. 'Those left on Taransay are furious with the rebels,' the *Mail* report continued. 'Yesterday, feelings were running so high that Dr Stephenson had to address the group and see if they would accept his family's eventual return.' Somehow, clearly, a garbled version of the previous week's events had reached the ears of journalists. In fact, the previous day, Friday 28 January, *had* seen the doctor on Taransay – clearing out the MacKay House prior to his final arrival.

For at last the island castaways were leaving the cramped conditions of farmhouse and schoolhouse and colonising the pods. Ray was first in. 'I'm pretty comfortable,' he reported to the video diary. 'I've got all me duvets and things here, which is a change, and a room of me own. So I can quietly get on with the brewing – I'll have to keep off this whisky, you see. Get back to the old beer.'

'Mine is going to be the bee's knees,' said Toby of his new home. 'I've been working hard on it late into the night. I've dragged up huge logs from the beach, four hundred metres with a rope, it's been a nightmare, but I've got a good solid platform up there, which shakes a little bit in the high winds – it's quite weird.'

'There was a mass exodus from the MacKay House today,' Mike Laird wrote on the Wednesday, 'as people moved into their pods. The house has totally lost its atmosphere, which was created by its lively, although transient, inhabitants.

Now it is just me and there is certainly a feeling of being alone, although no sense of being lonely.' Being on one leg, he wrote the next day, was 'certainly an impairment. Very, very frustrating when there is so much to do and you see others doing it.' 'The group have agreed,' he wrote on Friday, 'that we are allowed the next three days to do our own thing, which is also aimed at letting today's new arrivals settle in on the island.'

A Seventeenth-Century Pioneer

For the families were at last on Taransay. Ron – bronchitis notwithstanding – was on Taransay. Roger and Rosemary were on Taransay, trying to sort out a room for themselves and their children in the abandoned MacKay House. Having spent the week still deliberating about whether they were in or out of the project, they had that morning on the mainland received an ultimatum, from Colin Cameron of BBC Scotland. 'We were breakfasting early,' Roger wrote in a letter to me, 'in order to get the first helicopter across to remove the stale urine, beer bottles and cigarette butts, the detritus of two months of grossly over-crowded living in the one room of the MacKay House in which we were to sleep. The ultimatum was that we were to pack our belongings and leave for Taransay in the full expectation that we were to stay – or else go home.' 'He was, by that stage, playing power games, frankly,' says Colin Cameron. 'We were having our tails tweaked. He'd been on and off and on and off and he was now going to go back over to tidy up and decide whether he was going to stay or go. I discussed the situation with Jeremy and rang Roger from Heathrow on the Friday morning. I said if he didn't go on the project that day, then he was off the project. I got the usual line back, "Are you trying to bully me?" and I said, "Absolutely not, but this is a project we've got to make work and either you're with it, completely, or you're out of it, completely.' 'For my family,' says Roger, 'I had to ensure a bed, a mattress, a sleeping bag and one small room was actually habitable before making the final move. We stuck, as ever, to our side of the deal, and returned that night alone to Tarbert.'

Even as the doctor and his wife stuck determinedly to their principles, they had managed to leave behind resentment, not just from their BBC overlords, but more important, among their fellow castaways. Mike Laird had been – with difficulty on his crutches – trying to organise his new pod and was still sleeping in the MacKay House. Meanwhile: 'Roger and Rosemary had totally emptied my belongings from one room to another, so that they could sort it for themselves. I identified for them what was mine so that they could lay it to one side. However, on returning to my room it was nothing short of a fucking disgrace and all of my stuff was buried under all manner of furniture. God knows how they thought I would ever find it.'

'It was a storm in a teacup,' said Rosemary, when asked about the incident later. 'The room we were moving into had had ten people sleeping in it. Most people had moved their stuff out, but Mike hadn't. So we said, "Anything that obviously belongs to people we'll put in a pile over here." But what happened was other people came to help us and those things that we'd put carefully in a pile got other things piled on top of them. Then Mike came over to find his sleeping bag and couldn't find it, so he flipped and got really angry and that led to him and Trevor talking about it on camera.'

As Roger and Rosemary headed back – BBC ultimatum notwithstanding – for a final weekend alone in the Harris Hotel, the newly installed pod occupants were greeted by a force ten gale. 'It was so scary,' Liz told the video diary, 'I thought the pod was going to take off. It was like being in a plane with really bad turbulence and you hear all these creaks and groans and, 'cos it's a new building and it hasn't gone through these winds before, you wonder what's going to happen. But we survived.' 'The bed was just rocking,' said Toby. 'It's a really strange way to wake up, I didn't know where I was. But it was quite nice after a while, I just lay in bed for an hour with it rocking – it's the only rocking bed I'll get this year anyway.' (Was this modesty true or false? Certainly the pensions analyst's prediction of his romantic future on the island was false.)

Roger Stephenson was, he felt, 'richly rewarded' for ignoring the BBC's ultimatum. 'For the following Monday,' his letter continued, 'we became the only Castaways to arrive on Taransay the proper way – by boat. It was a magical experience – not matching my previous maritime adventures to Pitcairn and St Helena, but still very much more real than the helicopter, which had become rather passé. You will know the feeling – you're on a level with your destination, the distance is clearer, the inaccessibility more measurable. The arrival is more gradual and your new home widens its arms so gently and so gradually to embrace you. People flock down to the beach and you look up to them, not down on them. And that seventeenth-century pioneer in me found irresistible the need to jump ankle-deep into the water as we hit the beach.'

After all the hullabaloo, the project was starting – for all of them – exactly a month late.

Chapter 7

Snow and Valentines

Showing the castaways the first four programmes had never been the producers' original plan. But because of the delayed move to the island the Harris group had seen themselves on TV. 'So then we had to show the rest of the programmes to the ones still on the island,' says Colin Cameron. 'I'm sure that that had an impact on the dynamics of the group and on people's self-perception. Dez, for one, was really shocked by how he'd come over. It's bound to have had an effect – but in the end that just becomes part of the dynamic of the project.'

Certainly, during the week that followed the group viewing of the selection programmes, the ex-sales manager went into a visible depression. 'A couple of people have been feeling down about the way they're portrayed,' Trevor said to Toby in a joint video diary. 'Yeah,' Toby agreed. 'Of all the footage that's been taken, only certain bits have been selected to show them in a certain way. With one person in particular, it seems that way.'

'Yeah, Dez.'

'You see him to be a bit of an arse, but he's a really nice, sound bloke, he's got a side to him you don't see.'

Girlfriend Liz was more vocal about it. 'Dez has been pretty down in the dumps,' she told the video diary. 'Primarily because he's had all the castaways coming up to him and saying, "Oh, you've been portrayed really horribly, and my friends and relations have written to me saying how sorry they are that I have to spend a year with that guy."' Gwyneth, for example, had had lots of letters from the children at the school in Farington Leyland where she was a dinner lady, saying, 'Sorry you've got to be on the island with that horrible man'; and she had 'actually asked Dez to write a letter back to them saying, "I'm not a horrible man". I think that's really upset him, quite understandably.

'And I would just like to say what I think,' Liz went on, addressing the minicam more directly. 'You say that as programme makers you balance the broadcasts. Well, I haven't seen a balance in the way you've portrayed Dez. You've only shown his nasty side and I know for a fact you've got loads of footage of him being the joker, messing around, being caring and things. So I haven't been very impressed about your integrity in terms of showing a balanced view of people. For example, I remember, Chris, you saying to me that if an incident occurs you'll always then go and interview that person afterwards and hear what they have to say. Well, I didn't see any of that in the programmes, so I look forward to you addressing that in the programmes to come. Certainly knowing that loads and loads of people think you're an absolute arse because of the way you've been portrayed is a bit hurtful. So I hope you can do something about it,' the management consultant concluded combatively.

Other complaints were less serious, and not necessarily focused at the programme makers. 'I was not totally happy with how I was portrayed in Programme Four,' wrote Mike, 'but there is nothing I can do about it now.' 'I'm a bit pissed off,' Philiy confided, 'not with anyone, just with me. After we watched the programmes I felt I was seen to be really quiet. Paul did point out that I was probably quiet at the time, but it's really frustrating me that I'm being perceived as something I'm not.' 'Colin likewise,' Dez told the video diary, 'has been a bit concerned that the bits he's seen on TV are not portraying him in the light he feels is acceptable.' 'I just haven't been on the programme very much,' said Colin.

Little Old Me

A reaction of a more complex kind lay in wait for someone to whom the programmes had been kinder. 'I still don't understand the huge interest in this project or me,' newly crowned tabloid darling Ben reported. 'I'd never in a million years have thought that me, Ben Fogle, little old me that worked at *Tatler* anonymously, likes going around London by myself, doing a bit of shopping, just being me – why people are interested in me. Suddenly the post arrived yesterday and I had probably about thirty or forty letters from strangers. One from Mummy, one from friends and family, and literally thirty-five letters from people that watched the programme and they were so lovely. All of them start, *You probably think I'm really strange doing this* and *I'm not a complete weirdo, I just watched the programme and felt so strongly about it I can't stop thinking about all of you – that I have to write a letter.* And then they tell you all these things, they give you a secret, so I've got thirty secrets that I've been told by people I've never met. It's incredible. I just lay in bed last night reading them, just going, Oh ah. And I'm building up this whole picture about all these people that have written to me and it's just a whole new element to this project. I suddenly know thirty new people. On a deserted island. And that's really strange, because I'm supposed to be just with the thirty-six of us here. Some people have sent books, some photographs. It's really lovely, so heart-warming that I can't get my head around it, I really can't.'

That he could be so concerned about thirty total strangers perhaps indicated at least part of the heart-throb's appeal. Handsome hunks are two a penny on television, and the 'posh' not currently idolised. But Ben's essential good-natured decency was a rarer quality, and one that the viewing public, fed an endless diet of the cynical, self-obsessed and worldly wise, the hard-eyed autocuties and the pudgy meeja lads, perhaps hungered for. A man with the enthusiasm to swim to the middle of a lake! And the sensitivity to be visibly upset about strangling a chicken! Yes please! That his qualities were more genuine than most, had already been tested by close proximity to his fellow castaways. Builder Ray was not the most obvious fan for such a Woosterish fellow, yet of all the youngsters, he rated Ben the most. Dinner lady Gwyneth had rhapsodised to me on my visit about how 'unspoilt' he was. Postman Pat had a project to try and get him to swear – 'at least once' – during the year.

'It goes back to this interest specifically in me,' Fogle continued. 'There's two parts to that, well, three parts. One is I can't really understand *why*, because there's lots of other really lovely people here. Not that I'm necessarily really lovely, but that's what I'm reading about myself. So I can't understand why it's happened. The second is I'm flattered, and I really like it. But you know when someone says to you, "God, you've got a really funny laugh" or "When you sneeze you do this funny thing with your nose", you become really conscious of how you laugh, or how your nose goes. So when I get these letters, and see some of these newspaper pieces, and they all say, *Ben Fogle has proved to be the star of the programme, with his ease in front of the camera*, I start thinking: OK, well *how* am I being easy? Then you start thinking, Oh my God, everyone's obviously got expectations of me, what happens if I don't keep up with them? All the reviews said: *Ben is such a lovely, helpful, thoughtful person* and I can't help but think, Oh my God I've got twelve months, what happens if I break at any stage, it's going to be so embarrassing, because I'm going to break everyone's expectations of how I should be reacting. So the second part is I suddenly feel a pressure I didn't think I was going to have.

'Then the third part, which for me is building up and building up and I can't wait for it to stop, is that I never asked anyone to be so nice about me. Now certain people here are starting to feel that it's not fair, that they should have a turn and be allowed to have stories and pictures done about them. It's quite hard because people will now start thinking the camera is going to be focusing on me.

I'm just here for this year to have a wonderful time, to bring my dog up on this wonderful island, to learn how to make bread and build and live with thirty-six other people and grow crops and learn how to fish – I mean everything. But there are other people for whom the cameras are the main reason for being here and it's coming out, it's slowly coming out. You can see people vying for the camera more. It even came up at a meeting: Why are some people being filmed and other people being ignored? I myself don't see that happening, but that's the way people are starting to see it.

'When the first newspaper reports came out about me everyone had a real giggle. Liz was reading them out and it was funny, because it was just so strange. But now, suddenly, when a new report comes in and there's a picture and a little story it's deathly silence. They read it and it's just passed on. But I can't help that, which is why I'm looking forward to us going out of the limelight. No more newspaper reports. I want to get on with everyone again. This is supposed to be a documentary about following what happens when thirty-six people are put in a different environment and now suddenly we've got this whole new element cast upon us. There's a new name for the programme: *Castupon*. What happens to thirty-six people when suddenly the country's eyes are cast upon them. It's extraordinary.'

Though to be later derided both by some viewers and a sprinkling of his fellow castaways as short on brainpower, Ben's albeit rambling ruminations had seized on a truth that had been picked up so far by only one of the professional critics of the programmes. 'The genius of the project,' wrote Muriel Grey in the *Sunday Herald*, 'is that it's not about creating a new society. It's not even about how the bunch of handless, wilderness rookies cope. It's about television itself.'

For other castaways there were more mundane preoccupations. Having resolved her difference with Mike, Rosemary Stephenson was settling her family into the upstairs room of the MacKay House, and at last getting started on her reason for coming in the first place – the school. For the previous month the children's lessons had been impromptu efforts in the sun lounge of the Harris Hotel; for the pair on the island, Trish's kids Jodene and Michael, there had been no lessons at all. Now at last they all had a space. 'We spent a day,' Rosemary told the video diary, 'with several people, just cleaning up. Gwyneth and Sandy were brilliant, they helped scrub down the kitchen. It was just disgusting, like everything in this house. It's a bit like moving into a squat – I don't think it's been cleaned for years and years. The things we're finding are just incredible. I must have picked up a hundred empty beer cans in the last week. So at last we've got a space that's useable. Haven't really got enough chairs or tables or things like that, so using the floor quite a lot. We've set up a system, the kids come up in the morning: the older ones go in the kitchen, the others in the living room. The kids are brilliant. They don't quite realise the degree of chaos all around them. They're mucking in really well. I'm very proud of them. It's been hardest for Oliver. He's been very homesick. He really, really wants to go home and I don't blame him. We've given him a tough time and I just hope we can make it up to him and make this all worthwhile.'

For the other new arrivals from Harris, the impact of the weather and landscape was enough. 'I've never known weather like it,' said Ron Copsey. 'It's wet and it's cold and it rains and when the sun does come out all of a sudden, there'll be a shower of hail that will hit your face at twenty miles an hour and just sting sting. But it's a challenge and it's incredibly beautiful and I've never lived anywhere like it. Although England is surrounded by sea, it sometimes feels here as if the sea will just have its way with us, creep up and cover the island. From any window that I look out of I can see the waves smashing up against the rocks. There's that element of danger. People have fallen down and broken their legs and sprained themselves and the first day I fell over and pulled the muscles in my arm.' 'I just look out of the window at the mountains,' said Tammy Huff, 'or I walk along the sea shore and everything goes back into perspective.' 'The views are breathtaking,' said Julia Corrigan. 'That's such a cliché – but you could cry looking at the mountains in the distance with the snow on top.'

Slowly everyone was finding their feet in their new homes. 'The arrival of the families,' observed Sheila, 'has coincided with the pods being ready and poor weather and it's had two totally different effects on the whole group. Before they arrived we were all living together in the schoolhouse and eating together and all felt very much of a group, but now we're all going off to our own pods. In one way it's made people much more creative. They're improvising and gathering and hoarding together all sorts of materials and creating all sorts of wonderful individual spaces.'

'Quite a lot of things,' added Peter, 'like fruit juices and food and stuff is disappearing into individual pods and I think that's an issue that we're going to have to address. There's a new word we've come up with on this island – scurraging, which is sort of half way between rummaging, scrounging, scavenging. Not pilfering – it's just taking anything that's lying about – bolts, bits of fruit juice. It's not in order to get something from somebody else, just to create something for themselves in their own little group.'

'My beautiful pod room is my lifesaver, my sanctuary,' Julie Lowe wrote in her monthly letter home. 'It's very similar to my house, only smaller. I wonder if everyone's is? Wouldn't it be fascinating to find out?! I've sanded (by hand!) the floor and varnished it with two coats of Sadolin's "Antique Pine", which is a shame as it's oak, but that's all the varnish that was there!' Furthermore, she was delighted to report, two of the 'supremely capable' builders had made her a platform bed, giving her a two-storey condominium! 'Add to that, shelves covered by Japanese style screens of white scrim and wood, a thick rust coloured rug and tablecloth and a large mirror and I'm very comfortable thank you very much!! There's something very bizarre about this rather sophisticated nest building, out here in the wilds, that really appeals to my sense of the ridiculous. Mind you, there's a lot that's bizarre about this whole "Castaway" thing – this laptop computer for starters!'

Even the doctor seemed finally content. 'I am lying,' he wrote, 'propped up on one elbow on my bed which fills nearly a quarter of our room. Oliver and Felix's beds fill another quarter and crates, now used as cupboards, fill much of the rest of the available space. Outside there is a storm-force 10 blowing from the northwest. However, the close conditions in this room, together with the warm glow from our wood-burner, give a feeling far cosier than our five-bedroom Old Vicarage in Devon ever gives. Or is it simply that we are feeling again, now that we have dragged ourselves out of the featherbed existence an Old Vicarage represents?'

On Monday 31st January, the full quorum of castaways had met together on the island, proper members of one community at last. They immediately agreed on two key steps towards building their future. First, they had set up kitchen rotas: four people per rota, to be responsible for cooking and washing-up two meals on a single complete day (thereby avoiding the fuss that had arisen between Tanya, Mike and Peter in the previous month); these meals to include options for both vegetarians and carnivores; the rota to apply to weekdays only, with weekends being a 'do your own thing' arrangement. Second, they had drawn up working groups for key specific areas. Catering, Animals, Buildings, Education, Health and Safety, Sewage, Power, Filming, Arts and Entertainment and so on. Priorities had been worked out: for the time being, building animal enclosures, constructing fencing and windbreaks, sorting out the schoolhouse, and turfing the roofs of their pods.

Island Mysteries

Trish had had a strange experience. Waking up beside her two children in the middle of the night, 'I could have sworn there was somebody else in the pod. So eventually I got Michael awake and asked him to turn the light on so I could come down from the bunk. So I get down, get into Michael's bed and pull the blankets over my head – a spook was in the bedroom. I don't care what anybody says, I know what I saw. It was something white, I won't get into details. It came through the door and it passed right through me and out the other side of the pod. I lay there awake all night trying unsuccessfully to convince myself that I'd never seen anything, but when it went through me I was freezing like I've never experienced before in my life – and it's really warm in my pod, we have a gas fire to dry it out.'

It wasn't just Andy and Trish who had had supernatural encounters on Taransay. Philiy Page had been experiencing strange things, too. 'Walking across from the schoolhouse at night – I know it sounds gibberish to say it – but I've felt people running past me up the hill, and felt scared by it, but carried on walking, then my torch went out, even though the batteries were fine. It was only after people were talking about the history of the island, and talked about the massacre that happened here that I connected it with that. That made sense, then. Those people must have been running away from the beach and going up into the hills, because the houses were down there.'

Round about the time of the Burns Night party the ex-traveller had done a video diary wearing goggles and fairy wings over her red T-shirt and holding up a placard. MISSING, it read. LUCY THE SHEEP. REWARD IF NOT PUT IN STEW POT AND RETURNED TO PHILIY AND BEN. 'I've lost my sheep,' she explained. 'I'm quite sad actually 'cos I had seventeen and now I've got sixteen and nobody's eaten her yet, so – missing Lucy come home. We think she's drowned at sea, but we're going to go and find her today.'

But by the start of February, not only had Lucy not reappeared, Philiy had lost five more. 'I don't think Angus was very happy today,' she reported to the video diary, 'when he heard I'd lost six sheep, but they seem to be coming back one a day, so by the end of the week we might have them all back. But some of them have got – liver fluke is it? Some of the ones that belong to him, they've been dying, so we've asked him to come over and look at ours, so they will be all right. Anyway, I'm learning.'

TRUE CASTERWAYS

The older men in the party, Peter, Ray and Gordon, still working hard, had been building a chicken run at the back of the steading. 'Lots and lots of enthusiasm,' reported Peter. 'Fences were going up really fast. We were having a whale of a time. Things were nearly finished, then on Thursday Andy the architect came across and said we couldn't do it – and he'd walked past us all week. We couldn't do it for archaeological reasons, apparently. So after amazing enthusiasm and total fun and gorgeous light and a wonderful place to work, and a very, very good spot for the chickens because it's got shelter and everything, I was told it had all been futile. This wasn't the first time something like this had happened. I didn't have a row with Andy, but Ray and others did. I was deeply upset. I said, "Sod it! I'm having a day off."'

'Before Peter and I finished the chicken runs,' wrote Ray in his diary, 'Andy the architect came over and said we can't have the chickens here I nearly blew my top that's 3 JOBS he has changed his mind if I wanted to work all day for fuck all I might as well go home and do it so I grabbed the helicopter pilot and asked him to drop us off in Inverness Andy came running over and gave me a bullshit excuse that it was archaeological but there was already a mile of fencing well I'm not doing a bloody thing till everyone's off this island and then we can start being castaways its like piccadilly circus and I'm not the only one who's pissed off we had a meeting tonight I don't go to them and Andy walked in so Peter walked out.'

The following morning, Friday 4 February, Mike, newly appointed Community Fire Officer, decided, on Andy's instructions, to test the alarm. It was clearly an important priority in these wooden dwellings with individual stoves. Keen for it to be a surprise, Mike had told only two castaways: Trevor, who was helping him activate the system; and Tanya, so she could film the event. 'As soon as I heard the alarm from Trev,' Mike wrote in his journal, 'I set off to the polytunnels, which was the muster point. It was 7.21 am. After having sounded the alarms for 12 minutes, only 14 out of the 36 people here had been accounted for. It had been a dismal failure, but we had learnt a lot.'

But the new Community Fire Officer was about to get it in the neck. 'About an hour later,' Mike wrote, 'Ron came to the kitchen and hurled a torrent of abuse at me. Many other people were hugely upset, too. Then there were those who gave me their support and were glad it had been done. I was rather disheartened and so returned to my room to catch up on some sleep. Minutes later Ray stormed through my door and was about to give me loads of abuse, so I told him to go and see Andy. This turned out to be bad news all round.'

'We are in bed,' wrote Ray in his diary, 'and some arsehole let the fire alarm off without prior warning it could have caused someone to fall and have a accident we have 3 people on crutches and Stornoway Hospital are running out of them if that's what some will do to get filmed they must be crackers well it's Friday and I want all the people off the island it's becoming a sham its 7 weeks now for the ones who have been here roughing the newcomers don't realise what we have been through I think they think we're incapable of doing the jobs but after what I have seen my grandson could have done better I am doing nothing till everybody's off this island it's been a fucking comedy programme I have been here since 29th DEC 1999 and have never I mean NEVER been off.'

'I was not present,' Mike's journal continued, 'when Ray's wrath was set free but it must have been pretty bad. Andy instructed all of the remaining workmen to finish up as they were now all leaving the island. They had been due to stay another 3-4 days. Ray's temper had once again cost us dearly and thankfully no blame was directed at me as I was acting under instruction. It was very sad to see Andy, Murdo, Angus, Roddy, Donny, Ken, Iain and Ivor and the others leave under such circumstances. Dez gave Andy the mini-pod which we had all signed. Padraig gave him a bottle of Scotch and I gave him one of the plugs of granite from when the wind turbine was erected. The rest of the day there was a very different atmosphere and we were all saddened.'

'We had what I call an island day,' said Ben Fogle, 'which is when a small thing happens and it spirals out of control and you start building it up to be slightly worse than it probably is.' 'I am feeling great now that everyone is off the island,' wrote Ray. 'Some of them are walking around with sore faces but these are the whingers what are they here for now we will see if playtime is over WE ARE NOW TRUE CASTERWAYS.'

'I felt sick to my bones,' wrote Julie Lowe. 'After all the hard work that the builders had done for us – for them to leave on such a sour note, without any kind of thanks and completion party send off – exactly the opposite in fact – was horrible. As the helicopter dwindled into a speck in the sky and we were left with just us castaways on the island, I felt totally abandoned and isolated. Our last contact with regular life had just disappeared – suddenly, and before I was ready – and it felt wrong and dangerous. Emotions were mixed among the other castaways. Some were pleased to be "just us" at last and some like me were very upset. For me, I think it felt dangerous because of my instinct that while the outside world was still involved with us there was still a measure of normality – of normal social constraint. Without that there is a distinct possibility of anarchy, which although fascinating to a TV audience makes me a little nervous for my personal security and well being. Haven't I got a vivid imagination!!'

Despite Julie's fears, scenes of licentious misrule didn't immediately ensue. The next day the community agreed that, it being a Saturday, there would be no formalised meals. 'Everybody's in a pretty good mood,' Ray told the video diary. 'We've all been cooking separate, and having a few drinks in each others' pods tonight.' 'In the evening,' wrote Mike, 'I lit candles as Toby and Tanya were coming for dinner. Trevor was invited but was asleep. When they came in I gave them each a can of Guinness and some peanuts, both of which are now increasing in scarcity. They came armed with grated cheese, milk and fruitcake from the steading. The Trangia cooker was out and so I started cooking tortillas with garlic, coriander and melted cheese. They tasted heavenly compared to the boiled swede, which seems to accompany most meals lately. Philiy and Tammy dropped in and were fed too, and it was all rather pleasant.' (Unbeknownst to the gathered women, Mike's feelings for one of them had spilled over from mere friendship into something more. Earlier that week he had given one of the builders a Valentine's card for posting on Harris.)

The Doctor's Dilemma

Barely was the weekend over when the next crisis hit. 'It's Monday 7 February,' reported Julia Corrigan, 'the sky's completely overcast and it's raining and we had a really fierce storm last night. People were struggling to get back to their pods it was so bad. And on top of that I have a horrible feeling mayhem and panic may be about to break out because there's been a meningitis scare on the Isle of Harris. This is really so worrying. I have to think of Natasha, she's already a bit poorly because she's got this bad eye, it's all swollen up and quite sort of crinkled – it looks like a wrinkled prune, poor thing. But the thought of meningitis is just so frightening for us all.' 'They could in effect close us down if they felt it was necessary,' said Mike. 'So fingers crossed for tomorrow, we're all sitting on tenterhooks here.'

'No sooner had I finally emptied my crate,' wrote Roger Stephenson, 'than I received a call from James Finlayson, the GP in Tarbert, whose locum I am for Taransay. I was told of four cases of meningitis that had occurred in Lewis in the last few weeks. The next day it had increased to six and this constituted a massive attack for such a small population. Three of the cases were directly connected with the builders on Taransay.

'As you know, it is a funny disease. There are two bacteria involved, but the most serious one, the quickest killer – the meningococcus, is harboured by up to ten per cent of the population. It is often under specific circumstances that it causes an outbreak – principally first-year students at universities: i.e. a new community.

'So the next day, a huge praying-mantis like beast of a coastguard helicopter landed and disgorged public health, environmental health, James Finlayson and nurse in order to take throat swabs and to give us Rifampicin.'

This put the doctor in a 'fascinating, unique and desperate' position. 'I come from a practice in Devon which prescribes sixty per cent fewer antibiotics than the national average – the lowest in the county. My partner and I do so because we believe they are not a panacea, and indeed have very significant dangers. Here on Taransay we were told we should take them immediately rather than waiting for our swab results which, we were told, might take up to five days. Professionally, of course, I agreed that this was the safest course of action. But I have never given my children antibiotics, and we were only being asked to do so "because of the conditions we were living in" – conditions I had spent months fighting to prevent.'

So the doctor now questioned the director of public health's advice at a full meeting of the community. A lively debate followed about whether everyone should take the drugs straightaway or wait for the swab results then only treat the carriers. Professionally, Roger's advice was for the first option, but his personal advice was to wait. Both cases were made in public to the assembled castaways. Eventually it became clear that the debate hinged on whether Roger himself would give his own kids the Rifampicin. 'I left the debate to discuss it with Rosemary,' says Roger. 'With a very heavy heart we took the official line and gave drugs to our kids.'

Julie Lowe couldn't understand the doctor's dilemma at all. 'I think messing with a bug this serious is stupid and irresponsible,' she wrote. 'However, there were many people, the Doctor's family included, who didn't want to take the antibiotic. I was amazed at this. Couldn't believe it. As far as I can make out, their reasons were as follows: 1) They didn't like pills on principle; 2) Perhaps we weren't the carriers and it would be unnecessary; 3) Why the hurry to take the antibiotics – couldn't we wait for the swab results to come back?; 4) Would non-takers reinfect the takers? The arguments went round and round for hours and hours. Eventually it was decided by all but one that we would take the antibiotics. The non-taker agreed to quarantine himself over at the bothy until the swab results returned.'

The 'non-taker' was – perhaps unsurprisingly – the egregious Ray. 'I'm being sent to Coventry for not taking the pills,' he wrote in his diary. 'So I've got 5 days fishing at the BOFFY I'll have a great time SEE YOU MONDAY.'

'Well there's not much fishing being done,' was his next day's entry, 'this is my second day at the boffy and last night was a force ten gale with horizontal hailstone and rain I'll never call the weather we have in Manchester bad again. Yesterday I arrived at 9 o'clock and lo and behold faithful BEN showed up with my food to last me out I wish they were all like him. Well I packed some lunch and not forgetting my rum flask I set off to the south of the island, past the arch and headed east to Leopold's cave but having gone ½ mile the sky which was blue suddenly turned black as if someone turned a light off so I decided to run for cover I sheltered under a overhanging ledge seeing I was down wind I saw two deer one was a stag with massive antlers it stood staring for a couple of minutes. I bet it thought what's that daft bugger doing out in weather like this.'

Later that afternoon the builder returned from a second walk to find some visitors. 'Trevor and Toby opened the door wearing shit overalls and dust masks trying to convince me I was the carrier when I saw them I thought they had come to do some cleaning so I gave them the usual bollocking and we made our way back to camp.'

The lads had been up to other comic pranks as well. Trevor did a video diary in which he peed in a glass to show off the alarming pink colour the antibiotic had given everyone's urine. Toby and Padraig took it a step further, pretending, with a sample flask full of Ribena, to drink their piss on camera, a skit that was to make it into Programme Six. The following scene, however, in which they pretended to eat their own shit, did not.

Valentines' Surprises

Health scare over, the community was back at work, getting on with the crucial job of turfing the curved roofs of their futuristic dwellings. Once the heavy turfs were on, the pods would be weighted against the ever-unpredictable gales. 'At the moment, when the wind blows hard,' wrote Julie Lowe, 'the pods shift and sway. The first time I experienced this was in the middle of the night and I felt just like a small boat that was being tossed on a wild sea. Apparently March is the worst month for gales, so we're really going to have to get our skates on. The weather has been so foul lately, it's been too dangerous to go up onto the roof and we're close to running out of time. It's such an exhausting, dirty, heavy job. First the turfs have to be cut with a spade and turned over. Then they have to be wheel barrowed to the pod being done (the cutting area is quite a hike from the pods and wheelbarrowing through the mud is a really tedious repetitive task). The turfs are then handed up to waiting hands on the scaffolding towers and thrown up to the people harnessed on to the roof for patchworking on. A large hairnet thing goes over the top to keep them down, which is secured all around the base. Dez worked out that each pod takes around two thousand turfs. When you think that we can only barrow a maximum of six turfs at a time, because they are so wet and heavy, you can see what a mammoth task this is.'

'I was wheelbarrowing most of the time,' Sheila Jowers reported, 'which was really heavy work, but to be outside in the elements watching the sea while you're working was just wonderful, the ever-changing sky, and also working in the soil, getting to know what the earth was like and how the lazybeds were formed and how deep the earth was and imagining how this had been going on for centuries was just a wonderful feeling of immediacy and of being part of the past and working for something in the future.' Tammy had more practical concerns. 'We're doing so much manual work, the weight's just dropping off me. I love this diet, I think I'll put it in a book.'

She was in a fine mood for the main event of the following weekend – 12 February, her twenty-seventh birthday. Mike and Toby had spent part of the day collecting mussels for a special dinner. In the evening Mike got Tanya and Tammy 'to put my hair in tiny bunches'. 'The table,' he continued, 'was laid (not by me) with candles and wine and it really looked quite nice. Tanya, Tammy and Philiy all dressed up and put make-up on and looked gorgeous.' In the schoolhouse there were cakes and chocolate and the old personal conflicts of January already seemed like ancient history. 'Me and Peter have got a little Booze,' wrote Ray, 'so with Rodger the dodger on the piano, Gordon and Peter on guitars, it should be a good night out also we will have Ron the drama queen strutting his stuff I'll tell you about it in the morning.' 'We sang songs round the piano,' Mike wrote, 'as Roger played, and had a fantastic time.' 'Tammy enjoyed the attention she got,' Ray concluded, 'it only lasted two hours.'

The party was, of course, filmed and in Programme Six, several of the castaways are seen joking about the alcohol running low; but though this was indeed the case in general, thanks to careful stockpiling that night there was no serious shortage for the youngsters. 'Then it was off to Tammy's for some more to drink,' wrote Mike, 'and a rather revealing question and answer game. Questions such as, "When did you lose your virginity?" and "What is the oddest place you have ever had sex?" It transpired that Trevor and Tanya were the slappers (only joking) having lost theirs earliest.'

The passion glass was undoubtedly rising; and on Monday it was Valentine's Day. Mike received two cards. 'One was immediately recognisable as having come from my Mother. The other was also postmarked Edinburgh and I suspect it came from A—- D—-, an old friend of the family. Despite the fact that neither came from a nubile female admirer they were both very welcome and cheered me up.' There was only the question of the card he had sent anonymously to the woman he referred to in his diary as 'T', who only a few nights before had been sitting in his pod drinking Bacardi and Coke and 'posing some surprising questions to us, such as, "Do you miss the opposite sex?" I say surprising because she is normally very reserved.'

'The way I had written it,' he explained to his diary, 'she would know it was either from myself or Toby. As yet she has made no mention of it and perhaps she never will. The slightly sad thing is I shall never know how it was received. You can't exactly ask and then, of course, there is the very real chance it may not have been received well. I do not intend to do anything more about it, but she is the only single girl here that I am attracted to now that I have started to get to know them all.'

Ben Fogle, by contrast, received over fifty cards. 'I could count on probably one, no two hands how many Valentine's cards I received before this year,' he told the video diary. 'I don't know how many of these hundred letters are Valentines but probably about half. I am really flattered, it's really nice, but really, really strange.' In an interview that Tanya filmed privately in his pod he showed her some of them. 'Lots of unsigned ones,' he told her. ' *"To the cutest boy on the island." "I am thinking naughty, don't be dirty, don't be shy, I know I will be thinking of you tonight, all my love." "Just because I am sending you a Valentine card doesn't mean I am going to leap into bed with you, oh all right yes it does, God you are a sweet talker." "You can't imagine how my mind constantly thinks about ripping off all your clothes and giving you a right good seeing to, just a shame you're not here, isn't it?"* There's another pile of them downstairs.'

'So all your Valentines were from people off the island?' Tanya asked.

'Yes. I didn't get any from anyone on the island,' Ben replied.

'Did you want to get any from anyone on the island?' she teased.

'Did I want to? Well it is nice to get a Valentine's card of course. I don't think anyone brought any with them.'

'They could have made one. Anyone you would have wanted to get a Valentine's card from?'

'Well, there are some really nice people here. So it would have been quite sweet to get Valentine's cards from anyone really.'

'Be more specific.'

'That is being quite specific. Didn't get any Valentine's cards but would have been very happy to get some.'

'But no one special?'

'No.'

Even as the young humans played at romance, serious animal procreation was under way. 'We didn't know,' Julie Lowe told the video diary excitedly, 'that Trish's elder dog, Fran, was expecting puppies. Then just about a week, ten days ago, we thought, Hmm, either she's eating from the slops pail all the time, or she's full of sand, or she's going to have puppies. The vet came over and said, "Yes, she is" and we were all thinking, Wow! Especially me, because I had wanted to have a dog so badly as my luxury item. I thought it would be lovely to have a puppy here of my own to train up, because we don't normally get the time to train dogs when we are working, back in real life.'

At about 6.20, on Valentine's morning, 14 February, Trish came and banged on Julie's door, crying 'Puppy!' Julie rushed out straightaway: 'I saw the other puppies being born. One had just popped out. The last one came out at ten to nine. It was absolutely wonderful. I've never seen anything being born so for me it's quite a magical experience. I stayed with Fran and the puppies and the others went off to get some lunch and just on twelve o'clock, I noticed Fran turning towards her back end again and trying to pull. This is what she had been doing with the others, she was pulling the sack with the puppy out of herself. But, poor thing, she was really, really tired and then sort of went 'aw', and gave up. I had a look and I could see a little tongue and a little kind of wriggle, just at the entrance there, and realised that Fran had given up on the pushing and pulling business. So I pulled very, very gently and then Fran gave another push and this little puppy just plopped into my hands, which was just amazing. I can't describe how emotional it was. People having babies and things is a much bigger deal, but for me this is probably going to be the closest I'm going to get.'

Having been at the births, Julie was smitten with the new arrivals. 'They're pure bred collies and they're absolutely beautiful. I really, really want one. Of course we have everybody else to consider, and the mutterings are that not everybody wants more dogs on the island, we've got four already. But these are special, they're proper castaway puppies. There's going to be a big meeting this coming Thursday and we shall see. So keep your fingers crossed!'

Sheer Laziness

Mike had heard nothing from 'T', so after lunch on Valentine's Day he went to join the team turfing the pods. 'As my leg is still causing me a few difficulties,' he wrote, 'I stacked all the turfs as they were dropped off by those pushing wheelbarrows. Dez steers the group when we are turfing. Normally he is so motivated and focused and can pass that on to others, but today he was despondent. Other peoples' lack of enthusiasm and reluctance to help on this job had really eaten away at him.'

'Bearing in mind,' Dez told the video diary, 'that the turfing is probably the biggest project we have got this year – to me at the moment there's nothing more important than covering our roofs with turf so they don't blow away – it's just not fair really that some people are not turning up.'

'It's really, really hard,' Liz reported, 'when you're watching four or five individuals getting up very early, working come rain, come shine, wind, snow or hail – busting a gut on a job and then there's one or two other individuals sitting there and doing absolutely nothing. Ron is an example and to me it shows arrogance beyond belief. I guess it's thinking you're superior to others so you don't have to do it and it's really bugging me.'

Ron, naturally, had his own angle on all this. 'People are running around trying to do every job possible,' he said. 'Then other people like me go off and do things on their own like, I don't know, I started whitewashing the steading yesterday and then I was filling in holes that have been dug for piping. I just find jobs to do and get on with it... We don't have to be charging around. I take things a bit more laid back than that. I like to have a fag and a joke.'

'I think now the weather is starting to have an adverse effect on a great number of us,' wrote Mike. 'It is increasing people's reluctance to get out of bed and go and work. People are not all affected and some never seem to be at all. Dez, Liz, Ray, Hilary, Toby and Trevor are among those that go out to work in all but the very worst of weathers.'

Julie Lowe had related frustrations. 'At one of our interminable meetings, we agreed that our working day would be ten to four, with an hour's break for lunch between one and two. Hardly arduous. However even this seems to be too much for some people.'

Lovely White Snow

'I find I am spending a lot of time here writing and thinking,' Mike wrote as he sat alone in his pod again after supper on the evening of Tuesday 15 February. 'In spring and summer I hope that I shall spend far less time in my room. At the moment though it's dark, wet and windy most evenings, so the most sensible place to be is inside. I cannot spend too much time in the steading with all of the children as I find it very stressful. Some of them are so unruly and yet others are angelic. One has been nicknamed Satan!

'At 10.30 I went to do my teeth, have a wee and fill my waterbottle. There was a light covering of snow and the temperature had dropped dramatically. No one was in the steading, most people's lights were out and for the first time since I had been here Trevor had not popped in for a chat. It all seemed rather odd to me.'

Ron was unable to sleep for the cold. 'So I got up and took some photographs of the snow in the moonlight – it was really beautiful. By morning the kids had built this huge snowman and everything was covered in a couple of inches of snow.'

For Tanya Cheadle, *Castaway* filmmaker, the dazzling morning crystallised the complexity of her dual role. 'I came down from my pod room,' she told the video diary, 'and it had snowed – the most beautiful, beautiful day, everything covered in lovely white snow – and my first reaction was, Oh that means I've got to be working all this morning, because I've got to film. It's almost as if I've got to work first and then I can appreciate what we have here after I've done that work. It's not to say the filming wasn't enjoyable, it was – but it's not me experiencing it, it's filming so that the experience can be translated for others. I don't want the level of filming here for me to become so great that I'm no longer a castaway, because at the moment that's what's happening, the only job I do here at the moment is kitchen duty.

'As a filmmaker you're meant to be objective, or at least as objective as any individual can be, but the problem is at six or seven o'clock I don't go home from work, I go and socialise with these people – so how can I spend a year not forming friendships with people, not becoming involved? Then the problem is if people know you personally how can they accept you as an objective filmmaker? It certainly makes it harder.'

Tanya was also learning that the decisions she made about what and what not to film had become very political. 'There are people in the community,' she went on, 'who feel that I'm not covering certain aspects. So when I filmed the children playing in the snow – because it was beautiful and should be filmed and it might not snow here again – I got a complaint the next day: why was I not filming people putting up fence posts?'

There was also the problem of the degree to which Tanya's role was considered serious work. At this point, she had about twenty tapes, which she had yet to view and log, because she had been spending so much time filming. 'So I've got to sit down for two or three days solid, and just view all the tapes so they can be sent off and made into a programme. Initially I was doing this in my room, which was possibly not a good move. I've now moved into the steading, where I do it openly.' This was to avoid criticism that had been made of her at one of the evening meetings – why wasn't she out turfing the roofs? 'Turfing is a much more important community activity than logging tapes,' she was told. Tanya didn't agree: 'I feel the community is here because of the television programme, therefore if these tapes don't get off to Lion, no television programme, no community.'

This led on to another thorny issue: the whole problem of her perceived close relationship with Lion, something that had intensified since the arrival of the new group from Harris. 'It was all triggered off,' she continued, 'by an incident where I was filming a difficult issue surrounding one of the children, which several of the community felt I shouldn't have been filming.' By all accounts Trish's son, Wee Mike, had been taking things out of adults' pods, hiding them, then going to the person concerned and saying he knew where the vanished item was. When Ron finally broke the community's embarrassed silence on the subject, Trish was furious, more with the community than her son: 'If somebody had told me,' she explained to me later, 'I could have knocked it on the head.' When she found out, she had 'gone berserk' with her son and grounded him for a week, an effective treatment.

'This then seemed to spark off a big debate within the community,' Tanya continued, 'about my relationship with the production company. I had made a phone call to Lion that evening to discuss the whole issue of filming and children and the law. And they had seen this, I think, as an illustration of basically how I was in one sense spying on the community. So I had a day of people not talking to me, gossiping about me. I was hearing second-hand all sorts of things.'

It seemed that having volunteered to take part in a television programme, some of the community members were in denial that they were in one: and sensitive, conscientious Tanya was bearing the brunt of that denial. Since, as she had pointed out, the whole justification for the community was the television programme, this wasn't a problem that was going to go away.

Tanya wasn't the only one to be the focus of unwanted gossip. It was the main thing that was upsetting Philiy (was it just a coincidence that she was another young attractive female?). 'The thing that's on my mind,' she reported to the video diary, 'is the gossiping that's still going on and it's really affecting me. I'm trying to put on a thick skin every morning and go out and do some work or whatever, but it's really getting me down and I'm kind of losing my *oomph* to do anything and my heart's just not in stuff anymore because of it. I'm just sick of people being nice on camera and really bitchy behind the camera. So you get two sides of a person and the public will only see one side.'

'Someone said last night,' said Tanya, 'that gossip can kill a community. I think that if anything is going to destroy this community it's going to be that.' 'Apparently communities thrive on gossip,' Ben reported, 'so Peter tells me anyway, and he is our community expert. There's been a lot of gossip and backbiting and rumour-mongering here and little snide remarks by a handful of people. It's often about the fact that Tanya is here with a specific agenda to film certain people. Ron said the other day, "Why is it that certain people only have to fart or burp and they get the camera straight on them, whereas other people don't get filmed at all?"'

Who could the trainee psychotherapist have been thinking of? Still, the green-eyed monster hadn't totally taken over his soul. By early afternoon the snow was melting, 'By evening,' Ron told the video diary, 'the whole landscape had totally changed again. There was just this golden, golden light over the field in front of the steading and Padraig and Philiy were walking towards me and I suppose that's the type of light that people making films want to recreate when they want something to look really romantic. And as they were walking towards me I told them about this light that they were walking through and they pointed out what they could see behind the steading, which was just this most amazing sunset. And that was all in one day, from the night time when it snowed, through to the sunset of the same day.'

It was paradoxical that the psychotherapist had seen the island's newest couple in this dreamy fashion, because they had just split up. 'On Valentine's Day of all days,' Padraig told me, much later in the year, when they were both (individually) finally happy to talk about their relationship on the record. 'It was when Tanya mentioned the likelihood of us being asked to do an interview about each other at some point. It was so early in the day that Philiy didn't want to countenance anything like that, which was fair as far as I was concerned. So we parted, but only for a few days. We got back together again when I came back from Stornoway after having my cast off.'

Mike, meanwhile, had discovered why Trevor had failed to call on him on the previous evening. 'It transpires that Ben had a gathering in his room and they were all drinking absinthe. I must confess that I am pretty pissed off that no one came to get me after the number of times they have all been over to mine to drink. Never mind, eh?' The Action Man had gone 'for a bit of a wander, leaving bootprints in the virgin snow'. Then, after a day's hard turfing, 'I got to the steading for a coffee and Jodene pounced on me with a question. "If there was a nuclear holocaust now and I had to pick a woman to repopulate the world who on Taransay would it be?" The answer quite plainly is Tanya.'

Still there had been no response from 'T'. The filmmaker, unfortunately, had other things on her mind.

Problems with Animals

Philiy Page had learned more about the problems faced by the *Tatler* girls and their wilder peers. 'I'd like a word with Angus, really,' she told the video diary.

'He's the guy who owns the sheep. He gets headage, which is the percentage you get given by the Government for keeping sheep. So sheep eat any trees, any plants that grow here and they've all got liver fluke. They're just dying like flies, there's dead sheep everywhere. Me and Ben even discovered one behind the wood pile. I'm glad we found it because we took it out and luckily the vet came the next day and he was able to open it up and check what was wrong with it and it was liver fluke. I'd spoken to Angus earlier and said, you know, "The sheep are ill – are you gonna give them something?" and he said, "Oh yeah, I'll bring them round the bay." But it's stormy weather and the boat hasn't come for weeks and weeks.'

But as the snow melted, there was contact with the mainland again. On Thursday 17th, a helicopter appeared full of production personnel from Lion TV, accompanied by a Health and Safety officer, project psychologist Cynthia McVey, and architect Andy McAvoy. 'It was particularly nice to see Andy again after the sad circumstances under which he left the island,' wrote Mike. 'He did look a good deal less stressed, which is a blessing. How he did not have a breakdown whilst on site is a miracle. I may have said before that he was architect, engineer, site manager, wage negotiator, agony aunt and wet nurse to castaway and builder alike.' But Ray's view of his ex-overseer had not changed. 'Well, the architect's arrived so I'm off for the day,' he wrote.

While Ray walked right round the northern half of the island and saw two golden eagles, exciting things were happening down on the beach. More important perhaps than the temporary extra humans, the rest of the castaways' animals had finally arrived: three cows, a pony and an assortment of chickens and cockerels.

Ben, ever-enthusiastic, was on hand. 'I just jumped up on the front to lead them off – it was the most wonderful thing. Ironically, we had started to have lots of debates and meetings about the fact that we were getting three cows and we didn't have a full dairy for them, so a lot of the milk we got from them would go to waste until we got the pigs. People were concerned that we didn't have all the equipment, and the pony wasn't going to be trained. All the time the sheep were dying. To tell you the truth I think it was just that people were a bit twitchy about getting animals, because that was suddenly a huge responsibility. Up till now we'd been getting our bacon and eggs and sausages and lamb and chicken from the mainland; now it came to the crucial date where these animals were going to be arriving.'

Mike arrived late on the scene: 'I am somewhat wary of large animals,' he reported. 'And the strength that they have, so I am very cautious, even frightened, to approach them. This is something I hope to get over in the next ten months here. True to form Ron decided to steal other people's thunder. When the camera went to the pony he was there attempting to lead it around the field when it really should have been Trish and Jodene as they will be the ones looking after it. When the camera turned its focus to the cows he was there again, when it should have been Philiy and Tammy. Finally he was to be found in front of the camera down at the chicken sheds. Originally he was to be assisting with the cows but has decided he doesn't fancy getting up each morning to help with milking. Let's wait and see whether his interest with the chickens remains steadfast throughout the year.'

'I've got a half share in a cow,' Padraig reported enthusiastically. 'I'm going to be milking her morning and night and I'm really looking forward to it. The smell of the cow on my hands and my clothes is already making me think of my childhood and being around animals in Mayo on my parents' farms. So yeah, I'm going to be milking, and I'll be singing *Cullen Does Crouch on the Moor* every morning, which is an Irish song about a guy who falls in love with a milkmaid.'

It was not, however, the recent arrivals that caused the next castaway crisis, rather those animals the island had produced itself. That night's now regularly established Thursday meeting, when the six new-born puppies were to be discussed, did not go well. Once again the doctor was the centre of the objections. 'Poor Roger,' wrote Julie Lowe, 'it never rains … His concern is this: in this part of the world, there is a worm to be found in infected sheep offal, which, if eaten by a dog, can be passed on to a human via licks on the face. If a human does pick this worm larvae up, there will be no symptoms of infection for up to ten years, after which time surgery could be needed to remove what could by that time be a big parasite.' But according to Julie, Roger's fears were unfounded. The vet, Hector Lowe, had handed out the appropriate worm pills for the dogs, which they had taken and would continue to take every six weeks while they are here. The pills, the vet promised, were a hundred per cent effective. Among all the families on Harris and Lewis that Hector had been involved with over the last ten years, he told the castaways, he had known of only two cases, and these were where dogs were not wormed and had daily access to sheep carcasses.

'Not an animal lover anyway, poor Rog appears not to have heard, believed, or assimilated what the vet has said and is convinced that the dogs are a serious and unnecessary health hazard, and is unhappier than ever,' sighed Julie. 'He is also unhappy with our levels of hygiene in the kitchen and with the compost toilets not being proper compost toilets, as well as being unhappy about the schoolhouse not being ready. He looks like he's heading for a nervous breakdown, which as well as being terribly distressing for him, is distressing for us witnessing his unhappiness as we all like him very much.'

'I have come as near as I've ever been to quitting this project in the last couple of days,' wrote Roger. 'It's down to the combination of our sheep (whose shit comes right up to our kitchen door) dying with hydatid disease, continuing poor sanitary conditions (no towels to dry hands, people washing mud off hands into kitchen sink because no alternative facilities etc) and a new litter of six puppies (which are the main vector of hyatid disease in transmission to humans).' He had already had to come to terms, he continued crossly, with four dogs in the community. Suddenly to increase that to ten was unacceptable.

'I want one of these puppies,' Julie Lowe continued. 'So does Ron. Trish is happy for this to happen and for the other four puppies to be sold and to leave the island. There was a big debate at our last Thursday meeting and a show of hands was called for, to ascertain how many castaways were opposed to keeping two puppies and wanted them all to go. Four out of twenty-eight adults wanted them all off, and the rest were happy for them to stay. At this Roger and Rosemary left the meeting and went back to their room, Roger saying that this was the last straw and that he was going to leave.

'I like Roger, and Rosemary in particular,' Julie continued, 'but I'm getting to the stage where I think, For heaven's sake, why come and be a castaway if you don't like animals, or communal kitchens or making do. If you don't like it, stop being miserable and unhappy and trying to change everything, and go home.'

'So health, dogs and yes,' Roger's letter continued, 'the continuing saga of the schoolhouse. Our *raison d'être* on Taransay is that stunning building – "the most potent setting for creative learning", I think I have previously described it as. It remains a damp, cold shell with a bare concrete floor, half of which is a puddle every time the rain comes from the southwest or south.'

But amongst all complaints, at least Roger was still enjoying the spectacular scenery of the island. 'I took Oliver out of "school" yesterday, my lowest day – took him hiking to the dun on the loch,' his letter continued. 'It was a dazzling day and life felt normal for a few hours. We intensely loved our surroundings and each other, and all our struggles were briefly forgotten. Returning was difficult – I obviously looked rather glum and several people asked "How are you?" rather than the "Do you really want to leave?" that I would have preferred.

'Today was another glistening Taransay day and we went *en famille* to the sand spit at Roa. It is the physical representation of a classic castaway emotion. A finger of sand points towards Harris and beckons you out to sea. Oliver and I couldn't resist the call and found some good solid hours of castle-building fun. We were nearly off the island, surrounded by sea, with waves grabbing from all directions. At low tide the distant phalanx of this sandy finger was curled, coiled, ready to be sprung, to flick us off the island. I was in the mood to leave, and this finger could do it for me. Reality returned, of course, and we returned home to chop firewood for the school (still inadequately in the MacKay House) and to plan our next move in the canine campaign.'

'I think on Saturday,' Dez reported, 'they were very, very determinedly talking of leaving. Roger looked very, very pale and troubled and it was distressing for a lot of the community: Liz got upset, Ben got upset, a number of people got upset and it was really, really horrible. Liz and I wrote them a little note and just explained that we didn't want them to leave, it was just important that they were here and they'd made a valued contribution.'

'I was speaking to Roger last night,' Ben reported, 'and he said the thing he would find hardest if he does leave, which I really hope he doesn't, was the thought that someone was replacing him, and that they were going to have all the best parts of the island for themselves – the summertime, the swimming and stuff. .And I thought that was really interesting, 'cos I've thought about that and I know I wouldn't want anyone to replace me.'

'I found out,' Toby told the video diary, 'that Roger and Rosemary might be leaving and it surprised me really how saddened I am at that. When they were over in Harris I didn't know Roger and Rosemary and I didn't really care whether they came or not, but now they're here and I've got to know them a little bit, I really, really do not want them to leave – it's sad and I've said that to him. So I hope he rethinks. Roger, please stay.'

'I think if anyone leaves this community,' said Liz, 'we've all failed, really. Because if we can't, as human beings, all pull together and support one another then I think that's a real shame.'

Chapter 8

One Down...

'Sat night,' wrote Ray in his diary that same weekend of 19/20 February, 'me and Peter drank two bottles of whisky we did some laughing then about 2.30 there was a full moon Peter put on his monk's habit with a big hood and went on a walk I have been winding people up about a Mad Monk in 1546 butchered all the people in Taransay because they were pagans anyway Peter walked over to the schoolhouse there was no electric as the windmill had stopped it was an eerie night on the way back Sandy and Tammy saw the monk in the moonlight about 30ft away Tammy said Who's that at which Peter just stopped and turned round on not seeing his face they asked again at which he started to walk towards them they nearly wet their pants and ran and woke Warren up Warren came out with an axe but when he asked Who's there Peter turned said nothing and shuffled away Warren was scared an all so he did not follow I couldn't stop laughing when he got back I had tears in my eyes also I was legless the glum faces in the morning told us it didn't go down very well.'

Ray's drunken prank with Pete marked perhaps the high point of the relationship between the northern ex-builder and the southern university lecturer. Drawn together by age and perception of a shared work ethic, if not background or experience, the two fiftysomethings had encouraged each other in taking a dim view of the idleness of the young ones, both on camera and off. Ray's diary summary of his fellow castaways, which had Julie Lowe down as 'the Jolly Hockeysticks Brigade', Ron as 'a right drama queen', and Dez as 'one of these blokes what thinks Rome was built in a day', had an especially warm entry for Peter and Sheila: 'the Professor and his wife Sheila these are lovely people very knowledgeable.' Since moving into the adjacent pod, Ray had been a frequent late-evening guest of the Jowers (whose wing of their shared Gloucestershire court house had always welcomed interesting visitors, from local CND activists to African musicians taking part in the regular summer festivals Pete helped organise).

If Peter was 'knowledgeable', Ray had a fund of stories to tell, about his many years as a builder and builder's agent, not just in England, but in Europe, the Middle East and Africa, too. 'You've got to travel,' he says. 'If you're going to wait for building work to happen in your own town, well, it gradually runs out.' He was, he adds, into the whole *Auf Wiedersehen Pet* thing long before the TV series. He'd been taking English bricklayers over to the Continent for years. 'We're the best. The fastest and the best. And they did everything for us, all new equipment, they couldn't have done more for us. When the job in Holland finished me and four of the lads decided to go over the border into Germany. I'm one of these ones, you know, that if I get to a town I seem to land on my feet. I've done it all my life. Good digs or a good job.'

Ray had had many colourful adventures in the days when he could lay three square metres in twenty minutes and his bosses 'could never believe' the amount of work he'd done. But then he'd started having trouble with his back and found he had a disc 'what had popped out of me neck, about a quarter of an inch and it was trapping a nerve, so I went to hospital and they said, "Well, your bricklaying days are over."' Had he seen *Castaway 2000* as another such lark? When he'd spotted the advert in the *Mirror* he'd thought (he'd told me, on my January visit) 'What an opportunity, I could go and supervise, teach people how to do things.' After a glass of whisky, he had confided: 'I think they probably picked me as some sort of leader. I am very straightforward. If somebody steps out of line they get told. I'm very up front and I won't stand no nonsense. I may be a little bit too hard and bit too outspoken. Probably these people have never come across somebody like me before. I wouldn't like to start any violence, but I have been in a world of violence, in the building trade. You get twenty-seven English bricklayers drunk as arseholes in Germany and you're trying to keep a bit of order. It takes some doing.'

But the reality of *Castaway 2000* hadn't turned out quite like that. Those he had hoped to supervise had proved, by his standards, feckless. The food had been 'slop, prison food as I call it, I could get myself arrested if I wanted to eat as these do'. The community had been run, not by a dominating hard man, but endless meetings, with agendas and votes carried by the majority, which Ray had found so dull he'd retreated, in the early days of January, to the schoolhouse, then to his pod, where his nose had recently been stuck in a novel called *Duane's Depressed*. 'It's about a guy who has a breakdown,' Peter told me later. 'Ray was just obsessed with it.'

'Ray is sort of really disappearing into the background,' his old Advance Party pal and helper Ben observed as February drew to a close: 'I haven't spoken to him for literally weeks. He just comes in and sits down and doesn't really say much. He doesn't do any building any more. It's really sad. I know he had a lot of setbacks with the building, being told to tear things down, so he's had a hard time, but I don't know why he's so completely not himself.'

Towards the end of February Ray's diary came to an abrupt stop. 'THE END,' he wrote, after a free-associating passage that included: 'I still say it the people who lived on this island must have been remarkable the work involved in just collecting fuel and carrying it back where your feet are sinking in the sand and bog tells heavily on your legs and being damp all the time I thought I had roughed it but being here taxes all your strength.'

A poem followed. ('Mark, my first try it will get better I hope.')

Taransay

The wind blows and delivers ice to your bones
you will never find shelter and warmth
why call, shout, scream you will only hear
stillness and quiet
the rain falls sidewards hitting your face
in your heart you know Taransay
is not your place
every day looking at the sky
your life passes by you do not notice
there is only me to try
try try what more can i do
to make my life become easy
there was work, work, rest no play
here alas on old Taransay

On 1 March Ray had a row with his best ally Peter, whose kitchen team he was on. 'We had a team of four,' Peter told Tanya's ever-roving camera. 'Me, Hilary, Sheila and Ray. Then Ray announced yesterday he wasn't giving up and Cassie was going to do it instead. There was quite a lot of feeling that everyone should have an equal share of the kitchen rota, because it's quite an onerous one. It goes on for twelve hours, and there's lots and lots of washing up. I just felt, Well, I don't think it's fair – so it upset me a bit. Fairness is something I feel very strongly about.' 'Peter's one of these guys,' said Ray, 'who wants to have a finger in every pie. And because somebody says something to him he jumps down their throat. But when he tries it with me, it doesn't work.' 'He'd been really obnoxious for about a week,' Peter told me later. 'The evening before we were due to cook, he said, "I'm not cooking." I just said, "Well, you're a monumental arsehole, Ray." I walked out and didn't speak to him again.'

'Then there have been the bigger issues to do with his building work,' Julia Corrigan told the video diary. 'He's had to face the architect telling him, "It's not right, it's got to come down." This has happened time and again, so it's very soul destroying.' 'His identity was as a builder,' said Peter. 'So when somebody comes along and says, "Tear that down" it is a bit of a blow.' 'I have decided not to have any part in the building side,' Ray had written on 17 February, 'it will just be the growing side from now on.' 'Both Colin and I,' Julia went on, 'have noticed that Ray hasn't been himself at all. We've tried to have conversations with him, and he's been just not there in the conversation, it's as if his mind's a thousand miles away. He isn't the man I first met at CAT, who came to my wedding reception. The island has had an effect on him and it's not a good effect. It might not be Taransay itself – it's just all the stuff, the angst that's gone with it.'

'He gradually seemed to fall apart,' Peter told me. 'We started working on the windbreak and he was increasingly aggressive and rude. We would say, "Perhaps you shouldn't put the nail there" and he would just flip his lid. He used to go, "Watch my lips! Watch my lips!" being really violent and aggressive, particularly to Sheila and Hilary. Then one night he declared his undying love to Hilary, yet he wouldn't give her a glass of whisky.' 'He was saying,' Sheila added, '"Hilary, I adore you." And she was saying, "Can I have a glass of whisky?" He wouldn't give her any.'

'Was he hoping something would happen?' I asked.

'I think he was,' said Sheila. 'Yes,' agreed Peter. 'When he realised it wasn't going to happen he definitely changed. There was suddenly real aggression when we were out working.'

'When he finally fell out with the three people that had taken him under their wing – Peter, Sheila and Hilary,' Dez told me in a separate interview, 'he had nowhere else to go. Except to his new friends in Pod Two, who had just arrived: Warren, Monica, Julia, Colin and Ron.'

A Real Pianissimo

Despite Ray's decline, for the rest of the community island life went on, with, for a change, surprisingly few major dramas. On Sunday 20 February Colin Corrigan had slaughtered one of the castaways' sheep, not for eating, but to see how healthy it was. 'The purpose of this slaughter,' wrote Mike Laird, 'was to see what extent of carnage has been caused by liver fluke. The sheep had already been chosen and separated in one of the stables. It was Shalla and he knew his fate. You could see it in his eyes.'

Mike was glad he didn't have much time to dwell on what was going on. As there was no specific area yet in place for the slaughtering of animals there was loads to do. Hands and boots had to be sterilised; knives were readied. Aprons were put on, a bucket for blood lined up, the humane killer gun and spare shell collected and a wheelbarrow was arranged for the guts.

'It was time,' Mike wrote. 'To Shalla it was probably like death row. Colin was great with the animal and went into the stable to calm it down. At first it was leaping all over the place and head-butting the door. Moments later, Colin had pacified it in the corner and dropped it with one perfect merciful shot to the middle of the head. I then went in and put a rope around its back leg and hoisted it up on a beam. There were still muscle spasms but it was definitely dead. We put the bucket under its head and started to bleed it. At this point Tanya could do the sound no more and broke down sobbing. Warren continued to film.

'I was not at all sure how I was going to react but thus far I was fine. Colin was a great teacher and his calmness passed itself over to me. I felt odd as this was the first time I had ever done anything like this. I thought I might have felt sick but I did not. We laid the beast down into a skinning cradle and Colin then made the initial incisions whilst I held the skin taut. He showed me how to punch under the skin to separate it from the pelt. It felt very odd to put your hand inside the skin of a warm animal, which had so recently been killed. After the skin, hooves and head were off we strung it back up. It was time to open it up from end to end and let its guts spill into the wheelbarrow. This was moderately unpleasant as was the smell but it certainly could have been a whole lot worse. I kept on having weird thoughts about being an executioner three hundred years ago and doing all this to a live human!'

'Really shocking,' Tanya confessed to the video diary. 'It wasn't so much the initial bolt gun going through the head, I could cope with that, it was when it was strung up and there was the sound of the blood running in to the bucket. There's something about blood, isn't there, the life force of a being … and just to hear it draining away. But I'm glad that I saw it, on a personal as well as a professional level. I think everyone should see that, especially if they're going to eat meat. And as a filmmaker I thought, I've got to do this. I think it almost made it harder doing sound. I've filmed an operation before with a camera and it's fine because you're getting the images through the viewfinder in two dimensions. It's harder to ignore in three. Anyway, it's not a question of popping into Sainsbury's to get your pre-packed leg of lamb. I saw the leg being cut off. Living in a rural community is all about things like being closer to death, and I think it's going to teach us an awful lot of useful lessons. It's almost like it's some sort of right of passage to eating meat.'

'The guts slopped unceremoniously into the barrow,' Mike concluded, 'and Colin picked out the heart, lungs, liver, spleen, kidneys one at a time to cut open and look at. There was a touch of liver fluke but nothing else. The remainder of the carcass is healthy to eat.'

Roger the doctor, meanwhile, had recovered from his depression and was starting at last to relax. 'Firstly, the dog issue was settled,' he wrote, 'a true British compromise: one puppy will stay, and various dog-related rules have been agreed. Secondly, we did have a couple of glorious moments in school. Because we have not been able to access the schoolhouse, we haven't got any meaningful music going. Until one morning I put on a tape of the accompaniment to a song written by a friend of mine – "The Wreck of the Amphitrite". It was an instant, wild success: seven children from such wildly different backgrounds, united by a single, previously unknown song.

'The other redeeming moment was after a slightly rowdy music session this afternoon. I have a little leitmotif that runs through my childhood music sessions. "All music begins with silence." So we listen for that silence. There are giggles and scuffles and words to begin with, but gradually all seven listen out for it. All the sounds fade out until breathing is the only sound available to our ears. And it is a beautiful sound. Seven young pairs of eyes meet yours, amazed at the sound of their own life. Then we started singing, ever so quietly, a real pianissimo. It was a magical moment, in such contrast to the thundering winds and waves we persistently hear outside.'

Julie Lowe, meanwhile, had been getting to grips with the primitive sanitary arrangements. 'In each of the corrugated plastic roofed cowsheds that they call toilets, there are two loo seats on top of a large platform. There is a white loo seat and a brown loo seat. Whoever built the steps up to the platform must have been of peculiar proportions, as when sitting on either "throne" my feet hardly touch the step and I am not a small person! Inside the white loo, there is what looks like a metal mixing bowl with a few holes in the bottom. This is for wee only, and you have to fill an old tin can with water to swill the basin round after you've "been". If you position it right, you can fill the tin can up with the drips from the leaking roof! Unfortunately the platform around the seat is continually wet which is most unpleasant.

'If you want to poo, you have to shift over to the brown seat. Eco-friendly loo paper can go down, and then finally a sprinkling of sawdust to cover the evidence! At some point, this will need emptying. We have also been advised to put worms in it. Bags not me for either duty! Please! The other thing is (and nobody warns you) the cold wind that blasts your undercarriage, which results in an outbreak of goose pimples over the affected area. It discourages a long stay, that's for sure. I do like a nice warm loo and it's one thing I'm really missing.'

Though Tammy wasn't telling the video diary about it, she was observably depressed. Back in Sandy, her mother's long term illness had taken a turn for the worse. Allowed to speak to her on the emergency satellite phone, Tammy had been reduced to tears. 'She has been particularly low for a few days,' Mike wrote. 'It seems to be a mixture of Ben, Tanya, her Mum being in hospital and general stuff thrown in for good.' Besides Tammy, the Action Man was still one of the few people in the United Kingdom not to be a fan of the handsome ex-*Tatler* picture editor. 'Trish commented on the fact that Ben had once again stolen the camera's attention by reading out a lengthy fan letter and people were becoming rather disenchanted by it. Further that Ben is anything but a leader and the only thing he leads is Inca. He has been built up by Lion and the Press far too much and I doubt he can remain on his pedestal for the next ten months.'

On Monday 21st February, the first Ethics (or Community Principles) meeting was held. It had been agreed at the regular meeting the previous Thursday that it was important that the Community try to work out some common goals and principles to live by. Sandy, Peter, Liz, Ben, Toby, Ron, Cassie, Philiy, Padraig, Pat, Hilary and Dez were the volunteers. Mike, amongst others, was not much bothered with the meetings any more. 'Generally,' he wrote, ' they just seem to churn over the same old topics and it bores the pants off me.' He and Trev had retired to his pod where they had managed to record another two Channel 69s, plan an intended 'survival outing' and drink Mike's penultimate bottle of Scotch. 'I went to bed,' concluded the Action Man, 'happy and stress free (i.e. pissed).'

Hot Headz

In 'the mother of all video diaries' Liz, whose hair had for some unknown reason turned green (resulting in her being saddled with the nickname Turfhead), developed her ideas about work and community. She had eventually spoken to 'that person' who had been arrogantly not doing their bit, managing even in her anger not to name Ron. 'I got very wound up about it,' she told the minicam, 'and ended up exploding at someone who I didn't feel was really pulling their weight. We had a chat about it and their argument was that their definition of work is different to my definition of work – and I don't buy it, really.'

The other thing, she went on, that was driving her mad, was the 'blame, blame, blame thing.' She had been brought up to take responsibility for herself and her life; on Taransay, it seemed, if something wasn't going right, you blamed somebody else. Take the deer fence as an example, soon to be erected round a field where the crops would in due course be planted. Instead of getting together and all agreeing where it should go, half the castaways were waiting to be *told* where to put it. And as for the schoolhouse, the amount of moaning she'd heard about that ... OK, so it wasn't entirely watertight, but the school could still operate there. 'I mean, fifteen of us *lived* in it for a month or so!' she exclaimed.

A central problem was, Liz felt, clear: 'If you take any group of people normally, they have a goal or an objective they're working to. But here, I don't feel we are. There are different people here for different reasons. We've started having these ethics-stroke-principles meetings on Monday to try and thrash out a common aim or goal. I think a lot of the problems we're having are because there isn't one. For example, there are lots of people, myself included, who want to try and be as self-sufficient as possible and lead quite a frugal life this year. To me that's very important, that's what the project's about. But there's others who are more concerned with just the social side and still want all their luxuries here. And that's causing a problem.

'When I get to the end of this year,' she concluded, 'I'm going to ask myself, Did I really get on well with all those people? Did we really work together? If I can't say yes, I think that'll be really sad and we will have missed a real opportunity.'

Toby had been worrying about an issue that also had to do with individuals putting themselves above, or at least apart from, the community – parcels. Receiving these was of course breaking one of the three rules agreed between Lion and the castaways back at Windermere: no parcels, visitors or electronic goods. 'There's a big, big storm brewing,' he told the video diary perceptively, 'and it's to do with how castaway we actually are. I think we should stick to our original agreement and receive only letters, but there have been parcels coming through.'

'Meeting last night about parcels,' Padraig reported on Friday 3 March. 'I'm against them, I don't think it's playing fair. It's undermining the level playing field upon which we are all supposed to start. It's allowing people with financial clout and more resources back home to resupply themselves and keep themselves living in a relative luxury others can't afford. This is really not the idea of a community of equals, which is what I hoped, I thought, we were meant to be. So we're going to talk about it on Monday at the ethics meeting we're having. And yeah, it promises to be another shit storm, but I'm looking forward to it all the same, I think we have a chance to actually achieve something moral, almost. Lay down the principle on which we should base part of our lives for this year. A bit of self-denial, which is far less than the self-denial I imagined, wouldn't hurt, not in my opinion.'

Somewhat surprisingly, survival-enthusiast Mike Laird disagreed. 'It was funny,' he wrote, describing the ethics meeting of the following Monday, 'to see people's reactions to the parcel issue. Part of the problem we have with many of the issues we discuss is to do with the actual name "castaway". As Julia said, how many castaways have a hydroelectric system and wind turbine? I did not come here to live anyone else's dream. I came here to live mine and if I do not get it then my year has been wasted. I shall go out and do the survival bit with far less than most people here could ever have envisaged and at a far tougher time of year. After that, though, I am quite happy to get in whatever I want from the outside and enjoy it to the full. The long and the short of the meeting was that we can get small gifts from outside so long as we do not specifically request and pay for them and we must not solicit companies for freebies. This made me wince as I already have, and everyone at the meeting gladly ate the proceeds.'

Mike's on-the-quiet solicitation was perhaps worthy of a bigger wince than he'd realised. CASTAWAY TURNS TO SAUCE TO SPICE UP HIS LIFE, a headline in the *Stornoway Gazette* was to read later that month. 'The limited food available on Taransay has prompted one of the Castaways to write to a sauce company in England to help out. Scotsman Mike Laird, sent a letter to Hot-Headz Sauces, based in Gloucester, begging them to send something to spice up their cuisine. Mike has been using the mail order service for the last three years. The company has duly responded by posting Mike a selection of hot sauces, salsas, mustards and marinades ...'

'We are allowed smuggling,' Mike's diary continued, 'as this is "more fun" and "takes initiative". I must say that I fail to see the difference. The whole thing is farcical. As soon as anyone we know visits the island they will certainly bring loads of stuff to whomever they visit. The more visitors you have the better supplied you will be.'

To say that smuggling took initiative was perhaps overstating the case. From January onwards, Angus MacKay had obligingly been bringing the castaways beer and whisky, ordered and paid for when one fortnightly supply boat arrived, delivered along with the food and mail on the next one. Though slow, for those with the money, it required about as much personal effort as internet shopping.

'People were also saying,' Mike went on, 'that we should all be equal. If this were to be the case then the crates should have been searched. Radios were to have been a luxury item only and yet loads of people have bought them. I have not. In any event it tends to be the less well-off in the community who are saying we should not be allowed to send off £15 and get a bottle of whisky. It was Philiy who said this and yet she was happy enough for me to send off for replacement films for her camera. I still find this a double standard. People are not equal in the outside world and I was never told we had to be equal here. The only thing we can be equal in here is having a voice. Even in that, we are not equal as some people choose not to be heard by not attending meetings. We cannot be equal in intellect, sex, amount of work done or physical strength. It's all nonsense.'

In the area of romance, at least, Mike was clearly right. 'T' had given him no signal, nor had anyone else. In a group video diary Ron filmed with the youngsters, the subject of snogging was central. 'Does Mike want to snog Tanya, though?' the psychotherapist asked, to laughter. 'No!' replied Mike firmly. 'Dearie, tell me about the men I'm going to meet in the next year,' asked Tammy of Trish in a video diary where they were both got up as gypsies. 'I don't think there's any worth having,' Trish replied. 'Maybe a few helicopter pilots, but that's it.'

'What d'you think the boys are missing?' Philiy asked Tammy over a glass of wine in her pod, filmed again by Ron.

'It's obvious,' Tammy giggled.

'They are gagging for a shag!' Philiy laughed.

Ben, still buried under fan mail, had been thinking about how the second of the Windermere rules was actually going to work out in practice. 'I think we've all realised,' he told the video diary, 'that come the summer there's going to be a lot of people coming who come anyway. If you go down to the bothy and have a look in the book there's about fifty people that have signed a little entry in there, so without question there's going to be probably hundreds of people who are going to come over here, whether it be for a day, to stay at the bothy, in canoes or yachts or whatever. We've accepted that, but we haven't decided how we're going to tackle it or what we're going to do.' Soon, he mused, the project would end up as *Castaway 2000 and Friends*.

Trevor had similar feelings, prompted by the surprise arrival on the island of two of the ex-podmen, Ruiri and Neal, for the weekend of 4/5 February. Having beached their boat, they had gone straight to Pod One, where they'd been let in. 'A real no-no,' the Scouser told the video diary. 'My personal view is that it makes a mockery, so really nobody should be invited on. Maybe Lion should come down and work out a set of tighter rules for us.'

A Pig Mystery

In contrast to the podmen, Saturday 4 February saw some universally welcome arrivals – the pigs. Sow Molly and numerous piglets arrived to complete the developing community farm. So far there was Angel, Lady and Misty the cows, looked after and milked in turns by Philiy, Padraig, Tammy, Julie Lowe, Ben and Sheila; Aillie the pony, fed and watered by Trish and Jodene; the hens, fed and relieved of eggs by Ron, Gordon and – on occasion – Cassie; and those ever-dwindling woolly darlings, the Tatler girls, who were primarily Ben and Philiy's responsibility.

Padraig had foreseen problems with the porkers. 'It's going to be a nightmare just to get them across the beach,' he had speculated, 'especially if they land on the same beach as the cattle did because it's further from the field we're hoping to herd them into. If they run we're just going to let them run, there's no point trying to stop pigs running. So I don't think we're going to oblige Lion TV with the comedy value that they're hoping to get out of us chasing helter-skelter around after thirteen angry, distressed and frightened pigs.' 'We've come up with all these plans,' said Ben, 'of how we're going to get them from the beach to their pig enclosure. It's quite exciting, it's a bit like a battle plan, because basically Patrick has said that if they go, there's no point in trying to chase after them, because we'll never get them.'

'We had been discussing for weeks,' wrote Julie Lowe, 'various methods of transporting these pigs. They had to be brought along the beach, up the hillside, across the field, through the gate, past the polytunnels and into their own fenced enclosure. In the light of our previous rather disastrous attempt to herd sheep, that everyone enjoyed in Programme One, we needed to prove ourselves and regain some credibility!'

Happily 'Pig Master' Pat had come up with the winning design – a 'walking pen'. This was a large, rectangular enclosure made out of corrugated metal roofing sheets, with wooden lifting poles stretching across the whole frame, sticking out each side, front, middle and back, enough for two 'lifters' on each side of each pole. 'It worked brilliantly,' wrote Julie. 'We didn't lose a single one. You should have seen them jumping for joy when they eventually reached "home". It was an absolute delight. I had previously thought that only lambs gambolled. They started investigating their sties, whiffling through the straw, turning the earth with their snouts, rolling, bucking, squealing, grunting, running around like mad things. They're very endearing, pigs. Hopefully we won't get too fond of them, though. We do have to remember where bacon sandwiches come from.'

A more masculine perspective on the epic landing was provided by Mike. 'In the early afternoon a boat was sighted down at Horgabost, so many of us congregated down at the schoolhouse or on the beach. Ray was there and his intention was to leave if he could. After about two hours we could see that the boat was finally coming. It was similar in design to a military landing craft. Once all the hay, straw and animal feed had been taken off by human conveyor belt the boat manoeuvred onto the beach and the ramp went down. Pat had built a type of mobile holding pen and the pigs were herded on to it. Colin and Ron got in to ensure the pigs kept moving along. Ron decided to beat them on their backsides with a stick of seaweed and got rather stressed out when I told him not to use too much force. He seemed to be enjoying it too much.

'I was very glad to go and get a shower to remove all of the sand, straw, hay, animal fodder and sweat which had built up on me during the afternoon. Many of us were annoyed by those who did not come to help. My mood rapidly improved by finding some leftovers to eat and washing it down with some of Ray's home brew.'

If Mike was annoyed, others felt more strongly; and not just at those who hadn't helped with the first part of the operation. 'I've come up here,' complained Tammy to the video diary that evening, 'because I'm really angry. We had our pigs delivered today, all went well, we got them into the pens, and there were so many people around and we unloaded everything, the straw and the feed and everything onto the beach. Everybody was all jolly, jolly, jolly and off we went, got the pigs in the pen, brilliant, fantastic. Got to go down and pick up everything else off the beach and what happens? All the lazy fat people off they go again. And the usual group of people that work – we've been doing it again. Liz has hurt her back. I've strained myself carrying those bags and a lot of people have really pushed themselves and there's another group of people in the steading cooking their tea, cause, oh dear, it's five o'clock. I'm not going to eat tonight because now I've got to go out and do the cows. It's just not right, I mean where do they get off, who the hell do they think they are? And if you started to say something to them, it would be, "Well, we've got kids, we've got to feed them, we're this, we're that." Even Sandy was out there helping as much as she can – and little Michael and Jodene. It's just damn right bloody laziness and they've got a cheek.'

As the next day dawned the work party's mortification was immediately superseded by a new outrage. 'Early the following morning,' wrote Julie Lowe, 'it was discovered that someone had deliberately opened both the front and back gates to the pig enclosure. The front gate leads to the polytunnels and the back gate to the hills. Fortunately, it was raining, and the pigs (not stupid animals) had decided to stay in bed, so the attempted sabotage backfired with no harm done, thank goodness. It upset everyone. Also, later that day it was found that someone had smashed a hammer with considerable force through a large plastic tub of emulsion. It's only petty vandalism, but I found it disconcerting to think that someone was running around with all that anger and vindictiveness in them.'

Who had done these things? The two visiting podmen, Ruari and Neil? Ray? A proactively disgruntled vegetarian? Or someone else? Asked point blank on camera, Ray denied any part of it, but misgivings remained. 'The main topic of conversation was Ray,' wrote Mike. 'People have their suspicions that he is responsible for the pig gate and paint pot incidents. The lack of trust is now so great that no one will give him their mail to post.'

Gross Misconduct

'Despite it apparently not being a snap decision,' wrote Julie Lowe in her circular letter home, 'Ray appeared to be very unhappy and confused towards the end of his time here. Because of various violent episodes back in January that he was ashamed of, and that he apologised for continually, he had shut himself away and turned himself into a virtual recluse. He would never socialise in the steading in the evenings, but would eat his supper and retreat straight back into his lair with his booze, not to be seen until early next mealtime, although the neighbours in his pod would hear him. After all this self-imposed isolation, to find himself the centre of attention, the chief topic of conversation, and in the midst of a whipped-up frenzy of hullabaloo must have been bewildering for him.

'The actual manner of his going was very unfortunate,' the ex-stockbroker continued. 'We are meant to give eight weeks' notice if we want to go, after which time, Lion TV will arrange our passage home. Ray, not a man noted for patience, wanted to go NOW. When Lion wouldn't jump when he wanted, he contacted the *Mirror* and arranged for them to come and get him, thereby smashing his contract into smithereens and making life far more difficult for himself than it ever needed to be. Silly man. He had at least three other options that I can think of. He could have put in his notice eight weeks previously when he first started talking about this 6 March leaving date; he could have got a "sick note" from Roger – he was clearly desperately needing to leave; or he could have quietly gone off with Angus on the next supply boat. Instead the media circus was turned on.'

Ray had given his notice in to Chris Kelly on Friday 3 March, when the producer was over on the island on the fortnightly Lion visit. 'I hadn't spoken to him the previous day,' says Kelly. 'He just came up to me outside the steading and said, "Let's go to the schoolhouse." We walked up there and I asked how he was. He said, "I'm down and miserable. These bunch of idle ..." This, that and the other, the same old stuff. We got to the schoolhouse and he just said, "I'm leaving. I want to give my notice in." I was surprised. Irrespective of how down he was I thought he'd always be there. But he said, "I know we're supposed to serve notice but I'd like to go next week, on the next boat." I said, "I'll have to talk to somebody about that. We'll get you off as soon as possible, Ray." I tried to persuade him to stay. "You're down," I said, "Can't we try and see if we can get you back up again?" But he didn't want to know. Then I got a call from him on Saturday from the satellite phone, just saying, "What's the news on the boat?" I said it wouldn't happen till Monday. Then on Monday we were getting calls at the Lion offices.'

'The first I knew about it was quite casually over the weekend or on the Monday,' says Jeremy Mills, 'when I was having to go up to Glasgow for a meeting anyway. But then that suddenly escalated by the end of the day to being a list of demands, which we see on the programme.'

'I phoned Chris up on this particular day, 6 March,' Ray says. 'I said to Chris, "I'm leaving for breach of contract." He came over the phone to me and said, "D'you know I can portray you as a violent man?" Well, when he said that, and I know I'm not, that was it.'

'I think the thing that really angered him,' says Ron, 'was their threat to portray him in a certain light. That incited him.'

'On the Friday,' says Chris, giving his side of the story, 'after he'd said he wanted to go, he said, "Just because I'm leaving, you'll make me out to be the demon in all this." All I said to him was, "Ray, you leaving will have no bearing on what material is used in the programme. If we've got material that we were going to use, we'll use it whether you left or not." Which he then interpreted as a threat. I basically said we'd be using the Burns Night material, if that's what he was talking about.'

Tanya Cheadle, trying to do her job and film the recalcitrant builder's departure, now found herself in a more critical version of the compromising position she had complained of back in February. 'The morning started,' she reported to the video diary at lunchtime on Monday 6 March, 'with Ray issuing me a threat basically, that he had three tapes with filming on them, and that he didn't want me to film him leaving the island. If I did film him leaving the island he would not return the three tapes. At first I thought he might have stolen the tapes from my room or the film cupboard or from the camera, and he assures me he hasn't done this, but we just don't know. He stole a tape from a camera yesterday, which I managed to get back.'

Over the next twenty-four hours their relationship deteriorated. 'Basically,' the film maker reported the next day, 'I've become enemy number one. I epitomise to him Lion television and all of his grievances against them and it's not nice. The island feels very small when you've got one person who obviously dislikes you so much. This place doesn't feel safe for me any more. I lock my door every morning, I lock myself in at night. I hate to take the tapes out of the camera as every time I've filmed Ray he glares at me, every time we're in the same room, he refers to me as "the spy in the camp". And it's hard not to let it affect me personally because a couple of days ago I went for a walk with Ray and Hilary and I spent ages trying to persuade him to stay, because for me he's been a friend here. I spent two months with him and he was like a grandfather figure to me and I really do care about him. And within a day he seems to have forgotten about that.

'It's strange,' Tanya continued sadly, 'because we've had a great filming relationship up until now, I've filmed lots of things with him. And now, although he's happy to let Ron film him, he just has an issue with me that's become more and more exacerbated, to the point where I do feel threatened.'

'Ron,' Julie Lowe explained (reaching, in her distaste for the trainee psychotherapist, almost prize-winning heights of irony), 'who seemed to have intuitively sensed that during this time of intense attention, interest, activity, chaos, upheaval and disruption, Ray would need support, gallantly zoomed in to become his friend and confidant. As their friendship grew in trust, and as poor old Ray developed an aversion to being filmed by Tanya, our official camera person, Ron even took over the filming. Ray's negotiations with the *Mirror* and Lion TV were filmed, in the interest of truthful and accurate reporting rather than any prurient curiosity, you understand – and may be shown in evidence, M'Lud.'

'Peter and Hilary,' says Chris Kelly, 'who were Ray's peer group on the island, really, said repeatedly that Ron showed no interest in Ray until the last few days.'

'Ron filled that vacuum,' Ben agreed, in a later video diary, 'and whether he meant to have an influence over Ray or not, he did.

'Ray has told me,' Mike wrote in his diary that Monday evening, 'that he has no intention of saying anything to the papers about anyone here, but that he will speak about Lion if he does not get his £2500 plus a compensatory payment for wasting his time. Not surprisingly Lion have not bowed to this and in a later telephone conversation Ray told Lion he had spoken to an advisor (he did not use the word lawyer).' Padraig, however, had reported back on 3 March, 'it seems from what he's said, and what others have inferred, that he's basically been gearing up to sell his story from Day One'.

The identity of Ray's mystery advisor/lawyer was never actually stated by the builder. However, whoever it was seemed to have a sound working knowledge of the complaints of the less-survival-minded of the castaways. 'I've spoke to somebody,' Ray said on the satellite phone to Paul Overton in Glasgow on the Monday afternoon (captured on camera by crisis reserve cameraman Ron) 'and they gave me a list of what to say to you, right ... No, no, the doctor's in the other place ... Right, well number one is I want to be off the island as soon as possible by boat or 'copter. Two, I want travel arrangements here to home. Three, I want my end of the project fee plus for the time wasted, we'll come to some agreement over that. Number four, the BBC can only hold me to a contract if there is a contract. Five, I believe there is no contract ... No hang on, Paul, let me finish, there is no contract as the island was not ready, there was no schoolhouse, no adequate heating, no medical cover for the first month. And Chris told half the members of the community that the contract was out of the window because the project was in chaos because of the time. Number eight, if you agree to my conditions, I will not talk to the press, and I will give Lion all material, films, diaries, journals what I have for the book on the mainland. Right, that's all Paul ... Pardon? ... I can't give you that, it's somebody I called ... You know I have people on my behalf.'

'They clearly weren't Ray's personal demands,' says Jeremy Mills. 'The tone and the words and everything else were not his. Anyway, it's not clear how he would have been able to get hold of a lawyer and talk to them. No lawyer has since appeared anywhere.'

'The doctor,' Ray told me later, 'and Ron Copsey had the camera in the MacKay House while I was on the phone to Lion. We all kept calm and everything. At the end of it, Paul Overton says to me, "You're not talking like you did before. You're talking legal things now. How d'you know about these –

breached contract, no medical care, no torches, this and that?" Roger clicked his fingers on camera, you know, as if he wasn't there – because I was going to mention his name. After we'd finished, Ron Copsey said, "This is our insurance." Then we went to Ron's pod, me and the doctor and him. Ron says, "Roger, you shouldn't have clicked your fingers, because you're part of it. We've got to scrub your clicking of fingers off the film."'

'Paul,' says Chris, 'asked, "Who else is in the room with you?" Ray was about to tell him and I think Roger didn't want himself identified. So they went back and wiped it over basically. There's an abrupt cut in the tape that looks very suspicious even if you didn't know about it.'

'It was wiped off at Ray's request,' Ron told me (when I asked him, two months later, point blank, whether he had tampered with the film or not). 'So he stopped the film,' Ray's account continued, 'and then he came back to my pod in the night time and did an interview with me about why I was leaving. So the film would be continuous.' 'What happened,' Ron explained (in that same later interview), 'was that most of this island had turned their back on him. I had never been in Ray's camp. I was never one of his closest friends. But the man was falling apart and I felt very sorry for him. I spoke to Roger and we thought if Ray wanted to leave it was very important that he didn't get into a state or get into a situation where Lion could accuse him of gross misconduct. The truth is we did advise him and we did help him and we told him not to lose his cool, we told him not to swear on the phone, not to hang up on anyone. He showed us a whole list of papers of crazy thoughts and things he was going to do and we said, "If you really want to do this, go home, get advice, then do it." He said, "I don't want Tanya to film me because she's a spy in the camp, she tells them everything." So I said, "Well, how about I film you then?" He said, "Why?" I said, "Ray, it's very important you have it documented how you left the island, because if anything ever happens, you've got that on camera and a court could subpoena that material. And if you're being polite and not effing and blinding and you have your integrity that's going to look good for you."'

'I had hoped,' Roger explained in a letter to me dated 7 March, 'to be no part of Ray's departure – I would be sad to see any of us leave. But the BBC's chickens really are coming home to roost. The continued absence of a school building means that school continues to share space in the MacKay House with the "emergency" satellite phone. The continued lack of a real bar to this (I have warned Lion of this on many occasions) means that anyone here can phone anyone over there. Thus Ray, angered beyond anyone's reasonable tolerance, asked for me to act as messenger to Lion/BBC. He wanted them to know that he was desperate to leave, and that unless Lion arranged it today, he would organise for a newspaper to evacuate him. He had been begging Lion to evacuate him for 48 hours.'

Ray had asked, Lion explains, for 'about £9,500' to stop him going to the paper he had read for forty years – the *Daily Mirror*. 'It was three or four different things,' says Mills, 'the end of term thing, getting home, project fee, resettlement. He wanted recompense for time wasted, this, that. Of course it was blackmail. "Do this, or I'll go to the papers." What else d'you call it? But we were still at that stage trying to talk things round and get him to stay. We wanted him to stay. Even on the Tuesday we were saying, "Come on Ray, just calm down, think about it and then let's talk about it."'

'I spoke to him on Tuesday morning,' says Chris Kelly, 'and he said, "I'm off. If you don't get me off I know I can phone a journalist and they can get me off." I asked him to give us till four that day, because we had to get hold of Colin Cameron from BBC Scotland.'

'I've been accused,' says Ron, 'of giving him the *Mirror*'s number. 'The truth is he had a piece of paper in his wallet, with the number on torn from the back of the *Mirror*. He gave it to me and said, "I need to phone this number."'

'At first he got the *Mirror*'s accounts department or something,' says Roger, laughing at the memory, 'something completely inappropriate, and said, "Can I speak to a journalist please?" in his sort of Ray way. They told him it was the wrong department, so he had to ring another number, he was shunted around until he got through to a reporter in London and was told to go to the Glasgow office. So there were several phone calls, in between all of which there was one to Lion saying, "I've spoken to the papers, now what are you going to do?"'

'We had the printouts from the satellite phone,' said Mills. 'So we could see what numbers had been called. We knew he had already called the *Mirror*. We could see the time, the minutes, everything.'

'Around lunchtime I went on the phone,' says Roger, 'and said to Chris, "Look, Ray is about to phone the *Mirror* if you don't get him off the island. He really is.

'Colin Cameron came round,' says Chris Kelly, 'and Ray phoned us back and wanted an answer. The phone was passed from me to Jeremy, and from Jeremy to Colin and it ended up with Ray saying, "If you don't say you're going to get me off now, I'm going to call the papers." Colin said, "Well, if you do that Ray, that will be inappropriate use of the satellite system and we'd have to act on gross misconduct." Ray said, "Fine." Then he went to the papers.'

'What came out of that phone call between Ray and Colin,' says Roger, 'is that he was sacked. Even though Ray had already expressed a desire to leave, Colin said he was sacked, removed from the project.' 'He had not "expressed a desire to leave",' comments Colin Cameron, when told this version of events. 'He had expressed the desire to have a sum of money in order to buy his silence. And that was enough for me to say, "You're off the project."'

Accused of gross misconduct, Ray phoned the *Mirror* in Glasgow.

'We spoke to him after that,' says Chris Kelly, 'and he said, "The boat's on the way." We said, "There's no need. We're sending a boat tomorrow anyway." He said, "You can send your boat, but I won't get on it." Then we got the weather forecast. The boat couldn't get over. Ironically, nor could the *Mirror*'s. So we sent Paul in a helicopter to get him.'

That Tuesday evening, knowing they had failed to stop Ray handing himself and all the island secrets over to the *Mirror*, the BBC decided to issue a press release. TARANSAY LOSES CASTAWAY, it read. Executive Producer Colin Cameron was quoted as saying, 'After a number of documented incidents involving Ray culminating in an ultimatum which was inappropriate to meet, we have had to invoke part of our agreement with him. This means that, in consultation with the Castaway community, we have removed him from the project.' The release ended with a quote from 'a spokesperson for the Castaways'. 'It is in the best interest of both Ray and the community for him to leave the project,' it read.

'Chris spoke to three people, I think it was,' says Jeremy Mills, 'and asked the question, "D'you want him to go or not?" The quote they came up with was, "It's better for Ray and for the project if he leaves." We were doing it against a deadline of about ten minutes.'

'I wanted to be on the front foot in terms of getting the information out,' says Colin Cameron. 'We discussed whether it would be helpful to have some kind of statement from the castaways themselves that would indicate their position. Chris talked to a number of them, and felt we had enough to draw up a reasonably ambiguous line, in terms of it being – not, This is invoked by the Castaways to chuck him off – but an indication of the trouble there had been with Ray and the tensions that had been aroused by him. All I was looking for was something that indicated that there was support in the community for Ray's departure – it was never intended to imply that they had voted for his removal.'

The press release hit the Press Association wires at 17.43 on the evening of Tuesday 7 March, under the headline BBC CASTAWAY TO BE REMOVED FROM ISLAND. By the following morning the ex-builder was national front page news: THE CASTAWAY CAST OUT – TV ISLANDER BEGS MIRROR TO RESCUE HIM, the 'exclusive' in the *Mirror* was headlined. 'A star of real-life TV drama has been kicked off the programme,' the report continued. 'Ray Bowyer is being booted off the Hebridean island of Taransay after a series of incidents. A spokesman last night claimed the decision was taken after "an ultimatum which was inappropriate for us to meet". But the *Mirror*,' the report continued, 'can reveal that Ray begged us to "rescue" him from the island in a series of phone calls yesterday. He said, "I can't stay on any longer. The BBC have treated us so badly. The food is awful and they've bullied families with young children to stay when they wanted to leave. I have told them that I am desperate to leave but they've said, 'no way'. They even warned the doctor that they'd cut the phone line if they found out we were phoning out for help."'

Other newspapers, not having been the first refuge of the errant castaway, stuck more closely to the BBC line. The *Mail* (THE MAN WHO BECAME AN OUTCAST ON CASTAWAY ISLAND) quoted the press release and then Colin Cameron in person. 'Ray is a very physical, domineering person who is used to getting his way ... this has caused increasing problems with the others ... he began getting increasingly aggressive and started picking on several castaways. He would bully them about anything he could.' After quotes from Jeremy Mills about the £10,000 'blackmail', the report concluded with a considerable elaboration: 'It is understood one of the other castaways told Mr Mills: "Ray is being really stroppy with all of us and is refusing to take part in communal activities. At one stage he even was threatening to build his own house so he would not have to talk to us. He's got to go. Please take him off."' The *Express* went even further. Ray had been 'kicked off ... after an uprising by other cast members ... after a series of spats, the others taking part in the project were preparing to ask him to leave under the community's "three-strikes-and-you're-out" rule.' ('Well, that was true,' says Mills, who remembers having such a conversation with the castaways on the violent Burns Night evening after Ray had gone to bed. 'There were big discussions about it, till about two o'clock in the morning, "If he does it again, he should go," they said. Then they talked about whether they should have a "three strikes and you're out policy".') In the *Express* article, A '*Castaway 2000* insider' was quoted as saying: 'The man was just a menace.' The *Sun* had: 'A show insider said: "Ray was a pain in the neck." Producer Jeremy Mills added: "We have some interesting footage of what happened."'

At this stage, with no journalists on the island, the only actual castaway any of the press could have canvassed was Ray; and he had spoken exclusively to the *Mirror*. However, the Lion offices in Glasgow had been besieged with calls. 'As soon as the Press Release went out the calls came,' says Jeremy Mills. 'Hundreds.

Masses and masses and masses of calls. Colin, myself, and Mandy and Mairead from the Press Office were giving them briefings. "Is it true the reports of fights? Is it true the reports of him hitting a woman?" – those were the sort of questions being asked. One can only assume the genesis of it was largely something they had got from somebody up there. We think there were journalists who'd been hanging around the Harris Hotel and, after all, there were other people who'd been on the island like the last of the builders. I was briefing quite straight. "Yes, he was involved in a fight. Yes, he was drunk." But the general briefing we were giving was, "He's no saint and he's no sinner." We were saying that because that's how we felt about him. But equally, of course, we couldn't deny the fact that he'd been involved in an argument, because it was coming up in the programme. I'd been there for goodness sake! But it's amazing what gets into the papers – how far away it is from what you actually say.'

On Taransay, meanwhile, the weather was deteriorating. On the Wednesday morning assistant producer Paul Overton headed straight from the Glasgow office to a helicopter at Cumbernauld airport. 'We ended up having this nightmare helicopter journey, dropping like a stone out of the air twenty, thirty foot at a time, with the windscreen wipers going constantly, couldn't see five foot in front of us, and the pilot's telling me, "I don't get paid to shit myself,"' Paul laughs nervously at the memory. 'In the end we had to ditch down in a place called Arisaig on the West Coast and stay there for the night. There was some concern that we had died, because we were supposed to be on the island by then.'

Trapped on the island he was desperate to leave, Ray used the satellite phone again, to call home. 'I phoned the wife,' he said, and she says to me, "Have you seen what they said about you in the paper?" She read him the *Mirror* report quoted above, which included both material from the BBC press release and his own statement about the BBC bullying families to stay. 'The BBC,' the confused builder concluded, 'were trying to set me up. They said I was intimidating families. So what I did, I had myself photographed with Trisha. I thought: I've picked a family who's got no husband. Because if somebody intimidated my family he'd have me to deal with. So on the Thursday I photographed Trisha at half-past seven in the morning with a big placard across her chest saying *March 9th*.'

Roger Stephenson was not happy with the BBC's news-management, either. 'The gist of the press release,' he says, 'is that they claimed to have consulted the community and the community had rejected him. But that wasn't the case. They had asked one or two people in the community under different circumstances, "What is Ray feeling like?" Certain people may have said, "I think he should leave." But that doesn't mean that they want to get rid of him. That means he feels he wants to leave, therefore he should leave. They twisted this in their press release into something else.' The concluding statement, says the doctor, which quoted the 'spokesperson for the Castaways', was based on something Julia Corrigan had told Chris Kelly, 'not realising she was making a statement for a press release. She was just chatting informally about Ray being unhappy. They wanted a quote. School was still here. I was in with the little ones next door, so I took the call. Chris asked me if I wanted to make a statement. I said I didn't. Chris asked if somebody else would. Jules and Monica didn't want to, but Julia was through here. I asked her if she wanted to make a statement to Chris about Ray. Julia said she would do it, not realising that this was going into a press release and she was going to be the spokesperson of the community. We felt that was very badly managed by Lion.'

'I spoke to Roger first,' says Chris, putting his side of the story, 'who said "Speak to Julia about it." I explained exactly what we wanted – a quote for the press release. I said, "D'you want to do it?" She said, "I'm quite happy to do it."'

'I was very sad when Ray went,' says Julia Corrigan. 'I had tried to talk to him about leaving but he really had made his mind up. I was very upset about the press release that went out, which I felt strongly implied that the community was behind some version of sacking Ray. But Ray wanted to leave of his own accord. I made a statement – I think comment is the nearer description – that we felt that because Ray wanted to go it was in his best interests and it was in our interest, too, because if somebody's here who doesn't want to be, then it makes it difficult for all of us, it leads to a lack of motivation. We were all hanging around with him waiting for a helicopter or a boat to arrive to take him off, and it made us all feel a bit strange and down and made us aware of the big wide world outside.'

'When it came back in the press release,' Ben reported, 'and this statement had been used slightly out of context, there was this furore: "How dare Lion do this, how dare they con me into giving that statement." And a lot of people thought, Gosh, that's a bit rich, why didn't you come down and find a group of people and come up with a general community statement?'

'Contrary to the implication of the BBC press release that we voted him off the island,' wrote Julie Lowe, 'we didn't. We all knew that he needed to go, for his own sanity and peace of mind, and we supported him in his decision. There's a difference.'

'Of course,' says Jeremy Mills, 'we had to make sure it was clear that we had thrown him off the project and it was also the case that we genuinely thought they wanted to see him go. If that has then been extrapolated to become a general thing that they were pleased for him to go, it was because of the context. What we were talking about was now, six o'clock on Tuesday evening: "Are they pleased to see him go?" "Yes." It was the quote we had been given.'

But, for all the protestations about the BBC's handling of the situation that were to follow, as always on the Island of Chinese Whispers, nothing was ever totally clear-cut.

'I do worry slightly that me spending time with Ray could alienate me from the others,' wrote Mike on the evening of Wednesday 8 March. 'He is now viewed as an outsider. On the outside he appears to be OK but he is getting a very cold shoulder from many people here. It must be so hurtful to think that only seven days ago he was part of the community, albeit a slightly distant one, and today people are not giving him their mail and yet they are hugging him goodbye to appear compassionate in front of the camera. I think that it all sucks and it shows how shallow some people here really are.

'Ron said some really nice things today and was supportive whilst others turned away. We were talking about the lies and negative press and most people said nothing, which may have meant they thought he deserves it. Ron on the other hand said it was dreadful and hurtful and that Lion should not get away with it. Where though did the *Mirror* get their story from?'

Mad As Olly

The morning of Thursday 9 March brought better weather. Mike was up early for kitchen duty. 'Ray came in not long after I had got up. He brought me about fifty stamps, a blanket and a duvet. He has been giving away a whole load of his stuff to those that he gets on well with, so I was very flattered. It's funny how things, which mean so little in "normal life" mean so much out here.' Ray then asked Mike if he could borrow his camera, to take some photos with Trish. A little later Mike and Ray were standing in front of the MacKay House looking down towards the sea. 'Suddenly we spotted two unknown figures in lifejackets,' wrote Mike. 'This was it. The *Mirror* journalists had arrived.

'We grabbed his bags, which had coincidentally been leaning against a nearby fence. As we walked to the beach the photographer was busily snapping away. Rucksack on, rucksack off, sunglasses on, sunglasses off. Word was meanwhile spreading around our encampment. Those who were up were running frantically around like worker ants. Many people were still in bed as it had not yet turned 8.30 a.m.

'Following more photos it was time for Ray to get into the dinghy on the sand. It was a tiny grey and yellow affair. This would take him to a larger orange and black Delta Rib with a single large Yamaha outboard. The chap in the drysuit had great difficulty in dragging Ray and his bags off the beach and onto the water. In the end he waited for a wave to come up the beach to ease his task. The small craft with Ray in it was led out to the larger boat. By now there was myself and Trish on the beach with her two dogs and both journalists. A little way away on the grassy bank stood Trevor, Toby, Ben, Padraig, Tammy, Roger, Rosemary and Tanya with her camera. There may well have been others but both my eyes and thoughts were focused on the boat a little way out to sea. We watched as he cautiously moved from the smaller boat into the larger one. He sat perched up on the seat with his sheepskin coat and sunglasses on giving us an occasional wave. The majority of us felt sorry for him and the fact that he was going like a lamb to the slaughter. They took yet more photos of him as he

9. 3. 2000

Ray waiting to leave, 9 March 2000

sat on the boat like a prize catch on a fishing trip. Another boat went whizzing past. Perhaps they were other journalists. We shall never know. I waved as the boat disappeared, not knowing whether Ray was looking back at us as he left the island. I was deeply sad and plodded off towards the showers.'

'When the long awaited boat actually arrived,' wrote Julie Lowe, 'early one cold, damp, misty, grey morning, and he was sat in the back in solitary state, wearing his bulky sheepskin jacket, his toque hat and John Lennon dark glasses, it was spookily reminiscent of the funeral boat scene in the Donald Sutherland and Julie Christie film set in Venice – is it *Don't Look Now*? Surreal.'

'One down. How many more to go ...'

'It was strange seeing him taken away by these journalists,' Toby told the video diary. 'Since then, we've heard the headlines in the papers, and one of the things they reported was that Ray was actually drunk when he was picked up and it's quite scary because it wasn't true. And he wouldn't be used to that kind of rough treatment from the Press.'

But Ray, as it turned out, was more than a match for the hacks. 'We were coming across the sound,' he told me later, 'and three speedboats come from nowhere, the *News of the World* and some others, it was like James Bond. I cracked on that I was a bit tipsy, drunk. But I hadn't had a drink. I'd been up all night planning what I was going to do to the *Daily Mirror*. Because I knew the day before they had printed lies about me, So what I done, when I got off at Harris, I got in the *Daily Mirror* car and he did about 140 mph to Stornoway.'

The Ealing comedy-style fiasco that now took place was to make all the next day's nationals. 'Mr Bowyer arrived on the island of Harris,' reported the *Daily Telegraph*, 'aboard a fast craft hired by the *Mirror*. A car waited to whisk him away but there was a delay after rival journalists noticed the arrival of the castaway's launch. A series of big money deals were shouted at the burly builder, and at one stage, the single track road to the beautiful Amhuinnsuidhe Castle was blocked by journalists battling for the first exclusive interview. Mr Bowyer jumped into the *Mirror*'s car and raced, with a blanket over his head, to Stornoway.'

'When we got there,' Ray continued, 'suddenly a car come in the back following us. So this *Mirror* reporter, Steve, shot off into this bungalow estate. When we parked up, he turned round to me and said, "That's the way to lose them, Ray." I thought to myself, Yeah, and in about five minutes you're going to lose me.

'Then he parked the car in the supermarket car park. I saw a woman and a man passing in front of the car, and jumped out. Steve said, "Where are you going?" I never said anything. I just walked between the couple into the supermarket and into the toilet. I was thinking: What am I going to do to get away from them? So what I did, I came out and I had got a packet of BIC razor blades – 95p. Then I went back to the car with him and I sat in the back of the car and I was shaving my beard off dry. Then suddenly I cut myself. This was all done intentionally, so I could get out of the car again. I'm thinking they think I'm playing ball with them, but I wasn't. I was two steps ahead of them. So I went back into the supermarket and into the toilet. Shaves me beard off. I just wanted time to think, you see. They thought I was drunk. So I came out of the toilet and these two *Mirror* men were standing there, so I picked up the *Daily Mirror* off the news stand. I said, "That's a lie." Then I did a beeline, ran through the supermarket, through the warehouse and got to the roller shutter doors. There was a young lad there, and with me having blood on my face, I said, "Open the doors! Only me wagon's outside." He must have thought I was a wagon driver. So he rolled the doors up and let me out. The *Mirror* men were still trying to find me, running all over the place. There were about ten of them. I jumped over this wall and ran through this garden. This fellow stopped me. "What are you doing?" he said. I said, "I'm sorry, I'm just trying to find the main road." So then I turned left and found a butcher's shop. I went in and explained who I was and that I was being chased by journalists. This butcher gave me a jaffa orange and his good wife phoned a taxi for me and took me to the *Stornoway Gazette*. It's only a small paper. I said, "I'm the one what's just escaped from Taransay."'

MADDER THAN OLLY was the *Mirror*'s headline the next day, with pictures of Ray alongside movie castaway Oliver Reed. 'Boozed-up Castaway Ray Bowyer ran amok yesterday,' the front page exclusive reported, 'after the *Mirror* rescued him from his island hell. In scenes reminiscent of the Ollie Reed movie *Castaway*, barking mad Bowyer stumbled around an island on a drink-fuelled rampage. Stinking of liquor and screaming abuse at locals he caused a near-riot in a Stornoway supermarket before hiding in a bush. He then disappeared for an hour while he hacked off his straggly beard with a dry disposable razor, badly cutting his face in the process.' In the full story inside, the foiled hacks went to town. 'To the unrelieved joy of 35 other castaways he left behind,' they reported, 'he declared: "I don't care if they won't miss me. I'll certainly not be going back." … His dirty face framed by straggling hair and smelling as if he had not washed for a week Bowyer admitted he had been up all night drinking.' HALF-CUT screamed the *Daily Record*. ISLAND REJECT GOES ON DRUNKEN RAMPAGE, HACKS OFF BEARD, SLAGS OFF CASTAWAYS … AND HE WONDERS

WHY THEY KICKED HIM OUT. The *Sun*, meanwhile, had CAST ORDERS! 'Boozy castaway Ray Bowyer finally quit his island hell yesterday – and made straight for the pub. Beer-bellied Bowyer escaped from remote Taransay after blagging a free ride on a fishing boat. As soon as he was on dry land he hailed a cab which sped him to the nearest boozer an hour and a half away in Stornoway ... he bolted from the pub just thirty minutes later with his mouth bleeding.'

Meanwhile, back in the world of non-fiction, Ray had arrived at the *Stornoway Gazette*: 'A dishevelled figure walked into the offices of the *Stornoway Gazette* last Thursday,' the weekly was to report a snappy seven days later, 'and declared: "I'm the one that escaped." "Escaped from where?" asked our bemused receptionist. And so began a week of farce as the escapee turned out to be the infamous castaway Ray Bowyer whose arrival gave us a scoop, leaving the tabloids reeling in our wake.' If truth and sympathy were to be respected more than hard cash, Ray had chosen wisely. 'The canny castaway,' enthused the local paper, 'hid from the pursuing pack.' Once at the *Gazette* 'reporters Katie Smith and Iain MacSween, alert to the opportunity that presented itself, paid his taxi fare and took him into hiding. Then the *Mirror* reporters arrived, as did those of a quality broadsheet. The intrepid Smith and MacSween managed to keep all our guests blissfully unaware that their quarry was sitting next door, completing his interview. The *Mirror* had apparently offered Bowyer £5000 for an exclusive. The same exclusive cost the *Gazette* a fiver, if you count the costs of a taxi ride, a ham roll and a lift to the ferry terminal ... the *Gazette* is the only paper in Scotland to have given the BBC's *Castaway 2000* project a positive write up, so maybe karma plays a bigger part in securing a scoop than the chequebook journalists would like to admit.'

'Maybe,' commented the *Scotsman*, quoting this last line in its diary. 'Then again, maybe not. Adept as ever at turning muck into brass, the canny islanders have been lapping up the publicity surrounding the ill-fated series. At a quiet time of year, hotel rooms are fully booked and the pubs bulging with drouthy hacks.'

Down at the ferry terminal Ray found those same thirsty pressmen waiting for him. 'They were all there – *Island Post*, the *Mirror*, the *People*, the dailies.' Spurning the lot of them, Ray enlisted the help of a kind lady who worked on the ferry to buy him his ticket. She lent him £10, which he made a firm promise to return, then persuaded the ship's purser to make the *Mirror* journalists release his rucksack and luggage from their car boot. Meanwhile, a thousand times more was being waved in the ex-castaway's face. 'They kept saying £10,000, £20,000 and all this,' Ray told me. 'But I never spoke one word to them from leaving the island. The only words I said, were, "Manchester United, 3 – Derby, 1." I just kept repeating that. They printed a load of lies over me and I wanted to just stuff it right up 'em.'

'Despite the smell of money being thick in the air,' reported the *Scotsman*, 'the erstwhile islander insisted loudly that he would talk to none of the assembled media pack, except to say that he was on his way home to Lancashire. "I will tell the world in May what happened to me. You will have some story then," he said, before adding the fond farewell, "Now get lost the lot of you."'

Two and a half hours later, as the ferry arrived at Ullapool, a new press pack closed in. 'They were threatening me,' Ray continued. 'They were flashing the cameras, all coming up to me and saying, "We'll give you this, we'll double that." Then the inspector at the bus depot came up. "Are these people annoying you?" he said. I said, "Not really. I'm not saying anything to them." So they were all taking photos of me outside the window. Then the half-six coach came to take me to Glasgow. I got on the coach and had a word with the driver. He knew what was going on. He said, "You're being hounded by the Press, aren't you?" He said, "When we get to Pitlochry we'll stretch our feet." I said, "I'm going to stretch mine a bit further."

'At Pitlochry he said, "Your rucksack's at the back wheel on the offside of the road." I said: "When we stretch our feet, I'll hang back." It worked to a tee. When they got on the coach I nipped round the back, grabbed my rucksack and the coach was off, doors slammed, to Glasgow. But then I could hear cars screeching around looking for me. So I went to ground for four hours. I sat under a plastic sheet at the back of a caravan in a pub car park. It was absolutely throwing it down. About a quarter to twelve at night when the pubs had emptied I walked to the police station. I told them I wanted to borrow money. They said I could phone my family. I said, "Hang on a minute, it's too late to phone my family." I walked out of the police station and they did exactly what I knew they were going to do and followed me down the road in a transit van. They pulled me up and asked me who I was. I told them I'd just come off Taransay and everything. They put my name through the computer. No bother. Because I've never been in a court in my life. So they let me go.'

The valiant builder now walked the nineteen miles to Ballygallard, arriving at three in the morning. A lorry driver from the Co-op in Stornoway – the very supermarket Ray had 'run amok' in – picked him up and took him to Perth, where he dropped him off, at Ray's request, at the police station, where another kind woman lent him £10. He caught the 5.45 train to Glasgow. 'But I had no money. The idea was to walk across Glasgow to the motorway and get a lift home. But because people were sending me in different directions, I was walking all over the place.'

What kind of a state must the bewildered ex-castaway have been in to then return to the arms of the very production company he had been so critical of, was apparently so keen to escape? Lost in Glasgow, he first phoned Paul Overton and got an answering machine. At two in the afternoon he tried Chris Kelly. 'I was at Hampden Park football ground by then. Chris says, "Stay where you are and I'll come and get you."'

'He was in an Asda car park,' says Chris. 'I went over there in a cab. He was bending down between the cars on his haunches. For the first five minutes he was acting like he was in some spy film. Literally. I know it sounds funny in its way, but he was whispering and looking around like he was being followed. I took him to the police station to get a bag he'd left there and it was a bit better. I remember standing in the foyer and he stank. He smelt of the island. That unclean thing.'

Kelly took Ray back to his flat, gave him 'a huge brunch' and a bath. Then he was going to take him to Glasgow airport, to fly him back home to Manchester, where waited Pam (THE DESERTED WIFE WHO IS THE REAL VICTIM OF CASTAWAY ISLE, in the words of the *Daily Mail*).

But Ray had yet more surprises up his sleeve. 'As we're getting near the airport, I'm thinking, All the Press are going to be at Manchester airport. So as we get there, I say, "Sorry Chris, I can't fly." I said, "The last two planes I got in, one of them nearly crashed and something happened to the other." I said, "Hire a car."' Despite using Kelly to help him home, Ray was convinced that Lion were trying to set him up. 'I knew what was happening all the way,' he told me. 'They were making me out to be the bad guy for publicity for the show.'

Kelly drove Bowyer to Manchester. 'We phoned up his house and there were still journalists outside. I said, "D'you want to go home? There'll be a scrum if you do." He went, "No, I've got a mate who'll put me up." I said, "I've got a better idea. We'll check you into a hotel."' Kelly registered him at the Britannia under the name Paul Overton.

'We gets in,' Ray continued, 'and he says to me, "You've not got to get out of your room." What it was, he was giving himself time to do his Press thing, with Colin Cameron in Scotland – how they were going to make me go home and look like the bad guy to save the show. So I'm in the hotel all night, I ordered room service and everything. Then in the morning he tells me they're going to have a Press conference and what did I want? I said: that when I left the island I was of sane mind. I was not drunk. I also wanted a retraction and an apology from the *Daily Mirror*. Chris said, "I don't think you'll get an apology."

'Then he went away and came back and asked me, did I know a safe house where he could drop me off, as all the journalists was in our street waiting for me? So I mentioned Alan, who is the treasurer of our local club. We get to his house. Chris says to me, "I'd rather you meet Pam, not at your house, but what about the Labour Club?" I thought to myself, Oh wouldn't that be good headlines. Ray comes 800 miles from the Hebrides and his first port of call is the Labour Club. I thought, You're not on. So as we're leaving Alan's house, we pull up at some traffic lights and there's a telephone box there. So I jump out and phone Pam up. I said to her, "Walk to the Labour Club. Don't drive. Walk." I timed it that would have taken her about seven or eight minutes to walk up to the Labour Club and it would take us four minutes to get to the Labour Club. It was perfect timing. As Chris turns into the Labour Club, I jumped out of a moving car. I opened the door and he says, "What are you doing?" I said, "I'm out." I jumped over this wall and met me wife half way down the road. I flung me arms around her. We walked to our house and lo and behold there was just one photographer there. Where were the forty journalists? Waiting for me at the Labour Club. Chris thought he was being clever, but he picked on the wrong one. I tell you, he's a bastard, he's the one been issuing the lies about me.'

'I took him to his mate's house,' says Kelly, 'then I dropped him home. But on the way he said, "I've got to make a call." He jumped out of the car when it was moving, made a phone call, got back in the car. I was going to drop him at the Labour Club, where he was going to meet his wife, but he jumped out of the car again in the car park, while it was moving again, and ran off. I ran round the corner and there was Pam, his wife, and they were hugging. The Labour Club was deserted. There was just one guy mopping the floor.'

Back in London, executive producer Jeremy Mills had been in constant contact with Kelly. 'We were trying to get him home with the minimum of extra attention,' he told me later. 'We were concerned that photographers didn't get a picture of him holding a drink in his hand as the first thing he did on his return home. And we'd been told there were photographers outside the house, so we were just trying to find a way of him keeping out of their way.'

'Ray is an ordinary chap,' was the quote Mills gave newspapers, 'who has his good moments and bad moments like any of us. We are very sad to see him go. We will continue to do our best to ensure that he is all right.'

Chapter 9

Civil War!

As Ray was sitting under a tarpaulin in Pitlochry's pouring rain, back on Taransay the castaways were doing what they did best: having a meeting. 'We were read,' wrote Mike Laird, 'amongst other things, the Press Release and today's *Daily Mirror* article. It did not go down well and a letter will be sent to Lion to protest about the twisting and implications. It will only be signed by those who choose to sign in but it really is a self-preservation exercise in case the rest of us leave. We have no wish to be crucified. Another letter will be sent to Ray stating that it was his choice to leave.'

As always, this meeting was filmed, but half-way through it was agreed that the camera should be turned off while the full implications of the Lion/BBC handling of the press release were discussed. 'I wanted to point out,' says Julia Corrigan, 'that I felt my words had been used out of context. And I was frightened of repercussions from Lion if I spoke my mind. We've always had to worry about this. Because if we say or do something and it's on camera, instead of Lion standing back and being objective and watching it all, they come in and take action. I've called it putting your finger in the Petri dish. And it wasn't just us. Lots of voices shouted out, "Yeah, turn the camera off." Then Peter said, "If you turn it off, I'm going. So we said, "Go then." He didn't go. So I said, "Well, I'm not happy talking about these things on camera, so let's talk about something else." So anyway the camera went off.' Had Julia realised what repercussions were to flow from switching off the camera she might have preferred to leave it on. The Petri dish was not just to be dipped into, but well and truly rocked.

Never a keen attendee of community decision sessions, what would the ex-builder have made of his post-mortem? As he had stood on the beach waiting to go, rookie filmmaker Ron had asked him a leading question about the islanders he was leaving behind. 'Who have been your mates, Ray?'

'Well, there's Colin, he's genuine, I've nicknamed him Toughslaughter, good lad, nice family, Julia and Natasha and all. There's dragon lady Sandy and bag lady Hilary, I mean she's really cleared this job up untold with her bags, you want to see her room it's like Steptoe's yard. Then there's the Chicken Slayer, I've nicknamed him the Control Freak, Peter, I'm making him a crown for the island because you'll all be dancing round him by the time October comes. Sheila, his wife, very nice woman. Then you've got the Road-runner Dez and Mrs All-Right, Liz. Trevor Catch-Me-If-You-Can and Rambo Mike, or Miss Mike, you know, all the stunts he's pulled. Then there's Gordon, Dr No as I've nicknamed him and Cassie, Mrs Havealot. There's Roger, Dr Who and Tinkerbell, his wife Rosemary. We've got Tammy the Actress and Tanya Mrs Stoic. Going through the pods now we've got Jules, Henrietta Hockeysticks I've called her, and Mr Elusive, Pat and Miss Hygiene Gwyneth and of course there's Ronnie, you can't get him out of bed of a morning, he's doing a night shift at the bakery, I think. I'll miss 'em all, it's just a pity Lion fucked it up from the start.'

After lunch the next day the castaways held another, as Mike put it, 'Ray-related meeting'. 'This was to prepare the contents of the letters being sent to Lion and Ray. I made a brief appearance, but did not feel like discussing it all over again.'

'So Ray left,' summarised Ben, in a later diary. 'We had a week of journalists arriving by boat again, various photographers of course, all snooping around trying to get stories. Of course we're still bound with our "Can't talk", you know, going up to them, "Hi, hi, hi, sorry we're not allowed to talk, we'd really like to," 'cos it's quite nice when you're living with thirty-six people, when a new face suddenly arrives. You think, oh wow, that's nice, it would be quite nice to have a nice natter about what's going in the world, how's the publishing world, tell me all about *Tatler*, I want to know about all the gossip that you've heard. But you can't, so it's all very superficial and they leave in a huff because they haven't got the story they wanted. Then they go back and we get sent in the post various clippings that have got misquotes by all of us, which puts us off more. And now we've got this reputation in the press that we're all terribly hostile, which is not really true, it's just the way our contracts work.'

Some continued to discuss the whys and wherefores of this first departure from the group, but most seemed to feel that this was the story of a man who had needed to leave, and had gone. His full reasons were hard to fathom and it was just a shame. It wasn't particularly a community failure.

Otherwise life moved on. Julie Lowe was enjoying spending quality time with 'the newest member of the Lowe family'. 'Meet Floozie,' she wrote in her circular letter home. 'Small, sleek and a glossy, jet black, she sports four dazzlingly bright white ankle socks and a very delicate white "opera scarf" round her neck. Someone must have used the tip of her tail as a paintbrush, dipping it into a paint pot, and then drawing a very fine line with it down her face.'

Toby was sorely disappointed with Ben, who had bottled out of the lads beard-growing contest and shaved. 'Could see it coming,' he reported, 'he just didn't have what it took to actually grow a beard, never mind keep one.' He himself had started smoking again. 'I've been weak, only gave up for four days. What can I say? The most addictive drug on the planet.' Otherwise he'd been getting up every morning at seven-thirty with Pat and Gwyn to feed the pigs. 'They're just so funny, great to look after, and yeah I love them. Will I eat bacon, will I eat pork? Course I will, it's absolutely beautiful.'

Padraig was equally happy with his new agricultural routine. 'As far as work goes,' he wrote on 10 March to his Mam and Dad in Cavan, 'things are good. I'm one of the milkers, now. We've had the cows three weeks. One is pregnant, one gave birth last Sunday (Fantastic – a beautiful shorthorn bull calf we've called Taran) and the third is milking. There are six milkers (two teams of three) and we work one week of earlies (7 am) and one week of lates (7 pm). It's great getting up so early and having the whole length of the day. When you're on earlies you work till 1 pm and then the day is yours. I'm teaching Michael one morning a week and Jodene the same. He can be hard work because he's got a short attention span. He's a good kid, though.'

Sheila Jowers had been finding time to draw and paint more, filling up a ring-bound sketchbook with vivid watercolours of landscape, weather and sunset; studies of 'deer on the horizon', 'all the hues of a Harris tweed', shells, periwinkles and dog whelks, husband Peter playing the guitar, Ray leaving, the buoys that littered the shores of the island.

Trish had found time for creativity, too. She had written three children's books, featuring characters based on her island neighbours: Mighty Mikey, Dynamic Dez, Trickie Trevor, Level Lizzie, Jolly Jules, Philosophy Philli and of course, heroine Jodene. After a long post-builder hiatus when she hadn't really known what her role was and 'felt useless', she had finally 'found a space that was vacant – and it's the space of being pooper-scooper. I go round picking up all the poos from the cows, the horses, the dogs, and I have a place here. I am now the Poo Officer of Taransay and I'll wear that with pride.'

Rosemary Stephenson had been getting to grips with trying to realise the dream that had propelled her onto the island in the first place. 'We, as a family,' she wrote, 'are faced with a difficult dilemma. We basically entered this project with the idea of exploring the possibilities of Home Education, to find out how our children developed when freed from the constraints of the "education system". We, of course, recognised that we would not be educating our kids entirely on our own. Indeed the presence of at least eight kids, in total, was essential for us. But I don't think we realised how difficult it would be working with four other families, all with such different ideas on education and expectations for their children.'

Still feeling they were unable to use the schoolhouse because of the regular flooding from the leaky door in the front left corner, Rosemary and teachers Monica, Julia and Julie had been based for the time being in the two downstairs rooms of the MacKay House. Trish's children, Jodene (11) and Michael (9), had joined the other 'big ones', Colin and Julia's daughter Natasha (7) and Roger and Rosemary's Oliver (7), around the big table in the kitchen; while the "little ones", the doctor's other son, Felix (5), and the Careys' little girl Yoneh (4) and the Latore's daughter Ciara (4) were on the floor by the fire in the front room (at two years old, the Careys' other child Aaron was too small for school, and was left with his mother Cassie in her pod). 'We've found,' wrote Rosemary, 'we need three adults: one to supervise each group and a third person to help with the older kids, keep the fires going, make drinks etc. Seems crazy to have such a huge range in ages, but behaviour and ability made this necessary.'

The routine established was that 'structured school' (i.e. sitting down with pen and paper) ran from eleven in the morning till one and then the afternoons tended to be for freer activities. 'So far,' wrote Rosemary, 'we've attempted music and art, as well as environmental studies (i.e. a walk on the beach, planting seeds in the polytunnel, a talk about wind power). Of course once we get a proper space for indoor activities we have plans to involve lots of community members by sharing their skills with the kids – woodwork, drama, dance – the possibilities are very exciting.'

Although for the moment the main teachers were still Julia, Monica, Julie, Roger and Rosemary, gradually more members of the community were getting involved. 'This afternoon,' Rosemary continued in her diary, 'Colin and Warren took them all for art and got them painting their own thing on the walls of our new schoolhouse – a wonderful sight! Yesterday Dez and Patrick took all of them (including Aaron) for a walk along the coast, collecting shells etc and discussing the geography and geology of the island. So they are getting an amazingly varied timetable, given that they are stuck on an island in the middle of nowhere. They have access here to most of the skills they could possibly need and enough new experiences to feed their curiosity and fire their imaginations for many, many months.

'So despite our deep frustration and disappointment about not having a proper space to work in,' she concluded, 'good things are starting to happen. This first month has felt very chaotic, as we have tried out different systems and strategies. We realised after about three weeks that teaching the older children together was not working. While Natasha and Oliver are similar in age and ability and seem to function well together, Jodene and Michael were clearly getting bored working alongside two seven-year-olds. We attempted giving Jodene lessons one to one, which she much preferred. We then had offers from various people (Philiy, Padraig, Mike) to help us give Michael individual tuition. So, for the last week Jodene and Michael have had two hours of one-to-one each morning, which means we have four adults tied up with seven kids. It seems quite excessive (given 1:30 is the normal ratio in state primary school) but it works much better. The older kids get a different adult every day. We have roughly drawn up a timetable, but in reality we tend to follow the children's interests. It means they can write about what interests them and if they want to do sums all morning (as Oliver does!) that's just fine. So we do seem to be creating something workable out of the chaos. I'm really proud of that.'

The Person Inside

As they worked and lived together, the castaways' initial impressions of each other, formed on selection weeks, at Maidenhead or Windermere, on the Advance Party, or over the troubled arrival month, were changing. 'Take Gordon,' observed Tammy in a video diary. 'On the advance party he must have found it very hard because people were drinking and joking, using foul language, whatever, and that's not his scene and his reaction to it came across as very rude, and to be honest, up himself. I thought, My God, how am I going to get on with this man? But since coming here and actually taking time out with Gordon and working with him, I think he's brilliant, I really do. He has such a sense of humour, we banter all the time. And through this friendship that's developed, whereas before I couldn't find out about his religion or why he hates certain things, now he's beginning to open up to me. I suppose it's a form of respect. He's telling me about his religion or his beliefs and everything else.'

Philiy agreed. 'I think people are being a lot more considerate and coming out of their shells as well, we're finding out what people are like. Like Gordon and Cassie, they make me laugh so much. They're lovely, lovely people. Cassie has a wicked sense of humour.'

'I think everybody's finding their feet,' said Ron. 'There's some very positive things going on. I have a good growing friendship with Gordon Carey, who admits to being homophobic because his religion and his church tell him that homosexuality's wrong and I think I'm the first person that he's had a friendship with that is gay.' With buoyant optimism Ron went further, 'And through him I'm getting to know Cassie a bit better, she's quite difficult to get to know, she stands by her man, what her man says is what is right.'

Trevor, meanwhile, had revised his opinion of the doctor and his wife. 'They are definitely mucking in an awful lot which I personally didn't think they would, even though they said, "Oh yeah, as soon as we get here we will be a hundred per cent, blah, blah, blah." I took that with a pinch of salt, but all credit to them, Roger is on the barrow giving it loads and Rosemary was out there doing the pig fence with me and prepared to get her hands dirty, not the middle-class approach that I thought I would be seeing.' 'It's extraordinary,' Ben observed, 'the whole Roger and Rosemary situation. When they were over in Harris there was a lot of Roger and Rosemary bashing – I wasn't immune to it, I mean, I wasn't not guilty of it – and now they're both here, everyone is going, "Oh Roger and Rosemary are the most wonderful people."'

It wasn't all good news, though. Ben, still coming to terms with his sudden star status, had been forced by events to alter his opinion for the worse of one in particular of his fellow castaways. 'I still don't understand,' he confessed to the video diary, 'why anyone would be jealous of me. I'm doing something that I really like and he's jealous of me being here. But you can have different ways of showing it, can't you? You can be openly jealous and just go, "God, Ben, you're quite jammy, that's so good they portrayed you quite well in those first programmes, lucky you getting fan mail." But instead I've had what I call the Chinese water torture over the last few weeks. Drip, drip, little rumour here, little rumour there, a little blatantly in front of me. It can be something as small as, "Oh Ben, I hear you were using the satellite phone," which wasn't true. Or it can be as blatant as someone on the other side of the camera saying, "Tell me, Ben, it's not true you're gay." I can laugh about that because I'm comfortable in myself that I'm not. Obviously if I had a real paranoia about it then I'd be very twitchy. But then it goes on and on and on and other people start saying, "What's this rumour I've heard about you?" It all adds up and it does start to affect you, really. I went through a couple of days of being really low. Jules came up to me the other day while we were milking and said, "Gosh, Ben, there are some people really out to shoot you down here, aren't there?" Then she said, "Well, I suppose if you've been billed as the golden boy, that's what you've got to expect." I can see that, but I don't think it's fair, because I didn't ask to be portrayed that way.

'And when I tried to source it back, it came to the same person every time. But I've never made a big deal about that. I've never spoken in front of the camera about it, the only person I ever spoke to about it was Toby and maybe Dez, and that was a simple – I mean how would it be if you couldn't go to somebody and say, "I'm really, really upset because so-and-so did this." So they can go, "Don't worry Ben, we can see it happening as well, just forget about it, it'll die over." And then you think, OK, I'm not going mad, phew. Peter put it down to psychological bullying. And I've never experienced that before, so perhaps I was weak in coping with it. But when you're stuck on this isolated island and there's only thirty-six of you, it is more affecting because it's there in your face happening every day. So I just – stiff upper lip and all that – keep it to myself. There've been times when I've thought to myself I'd like to go home now. For a couple of days.'

'Ben was threatening to leave,' says Ron, whose behaviour towards the tabloids' darling was, of course, the subject of this troubled soliloquy. 'He was feeling very paranoid about things. He had heard that rumours had started and I had started them, which is rubbish – I don't do that sort of thing. But it was fuelled by the fact that Ben, before we came here, told me certain things. We went down to Colin and Julia's wedding together and stayed the night in a hotel.

'Now when he came here, certain things happened, and he thought because those things happened, that I had betrayed him. Basically, he told me before he came here that he was going to dump Tammy and he didn't dump Tammy until he was into this project. So Tammy would come in here and sob her heart out and Ben thought I had told Tammy that he was going to dump her even before he got here. That made him incredibly insecure. When I did eventually get to talk to Ben I said, "Ben, d'you think she is going to come in here upset, and on top of her pain I am going to tell her that you were going to dump her anyway?" Then there were other things he told me about his family, and so on. Then he heard something like I was complaining that he only had to fart and it was filmed. And he just got incredibly paranoid, because things like that came from the Corrigans coming to me and saying, "You and Ben are the stars of the show. You've only got to fart and you're filmed. We feel really left out and our contribution is not valued." So I brought it out into the open. But by the time Ben hears about it, I'm not in the picture. I'm not making the same accusation against myself, it's just him. He's a very insecure young man. He just bought into a lot of what he had heard and thought there was a lot more going on than there was. But it's all stupid kids' stuff – so boring. It's not the stuff a forty-three-year-old man wants to be involved in – it's so provincial.'

Dez had an interesting take on all this. 'I'm afraid to say,' he told me, 'the green-eyed monster was alive and well on Taransay. Basically, there was all this stuff in the newspapers saying Ben this and Ben that. To the likes of Ron, who is so egotistical, he wants that to be him. So Ron is there angling at anything to give Ben a fall from grace. Tiny things, it's pathetic.' Dez then gave me the example of Ron's attempting to usurp Ben in the affections of the increasingly popular Pat and Gwyn Murphy. 'On the advance party Gwyn took Ben under her wing like another son. Now I could see Ron edging in, deliberately trying to push Ben out of the frame, because Ben was getting all this praise. Ron worked like mercy on Pat and Gwyn, working with them in the kitchen, being really pally pally and this, that and the other. But early on, at the beginning, Ron was so dismissive of Gwyn. He said, "She's a fake. She doesn't know what she's doing. All this herbal healing bollocks. It's a load of rubbish. She's a complete freak." So when I hear Ron saying that about her in January and then being best buddies in early March, I think, Hang on, something's going on here.'

A Wonderful Reality Check

The mid-March days passed. As the various teams in charge of the animals got used to regular routines, milking morning and evening, collecting and signing in eggs to the kitchen, or rounding up the sheep, work on the infrastructure of the site continued. Mike laboured on the slaughterhouse with Gordon, Pat and Colin. The garden sheds that had originally housed the builders and now contained the chickens were moved. Poor old Ray's remaining unwanted constructions were demolished.

There were some frustrations at the demands placed on individuals by the agreed rules of the community. 'Here's an example of the kind of silliness you have to be able to let go,' wrote Julie Lowe. 'It is not permitted for an ordinary person to collect eggs from the chicken shed. A "chicken person" has to do it otherwise war breaks out. I was nearly hung, drawn and quartered when at around 10.00 one morning I dared commit this particular crime. I'd been up since 6.00 for milking, and got fed up with waiting for a chicken person to get out of bed! The milking crews had offered to let the chickens out and put any eggs in the kitchen as we're up first thing anyway, but there was a sharp intake of breath as this offer was rejected and classed as being "controlling" and alas these poor chickens are often still imprisoned in their sheds nearing lunchtime, and a hungry hardworking person has to find something else to eat!' (The chicken group comprised Ron, Gordon, Peter and Warren.)

Thank God for occasional distractions from the daily round! 'It was a

Monday morning,' Julie Lowe continued. 'This saw me in the MacKay House teaching the little ones in the sitting room as usual. The cry went up "Journalists" and it appeared that there was a whole troupe of them walking across the field towards the steading. "Same old same old" I thought and got the children back to work. Rosemary then came in and said that they weren't journalists but visitors claiming to be related to me! I couldn't believe it. Got the wellies on and went outside only to find my uncle Jonna, cousin Bertie, and a crowd of Bertie's friends from St Andrews!! What a wonderful surprise. Talk about an adrenaline rush! I couldn't keep still, I couldn't talk sense (no change there then!) I didn't know who to hug first, what to ask first, or what to show off first! I took them everywhere – all over the site and would have dragged them all over the island if I'd had the time. I hadn't realised that I was so proud of it – of what we have achieved here and of being a part of it all.

'Six of them had come over to Taransay from Tarbert, in a small open boat, with an outboard, and landed at "Pig" beach. It had taken them two hours and it wasn't warm either. The poor things were absolutely frozen. They'd brought a picnic lunch with them (which earned brownie points among the residents) but luckily there was plenty of hot soup and bread that day – enough to share. It was great. In his typically generous fashion, Jo had come bearing gifts – bottles of wine, whisky and chocolate. He also shared his cigarettes round – there were castaways almost fainting with delight of real fags instead of grotty old roll ups.'

'It was fantastic for Jules,' wrote Mike, 'and most people were really buoyed up by having guests especially as three of them were young women. Trevor went running around like a hormonal madman shouting "Girls, girls!" followed by

"Aftershave! Where can I get some aftershave?" Whilst that was going on Toby was caught looking in a mirror and checking out his hair.'

'I told Jo about the whole dog issue,' Julie concluded, 'about how dogs now always have to be accompanied – we are not permitted to allow them to just run about – and how we have to do regular shovel and bucket "poo patrols". He thought the whole thing ridiculous and had a complete rage on camera about it, which was very funny. "It's a bloody Outer Hebridean Island for God's sake – not Holland bloody Park!" A wonderful reality check. I wasn't sure if I'd been thinking unreasonably and it was very reassuring to know that I hadn't!'

A week after Ray had flown the coop the fortnightly mail and supplies boat arrived. 'I wanted to be there when it was being unloaded,' Mike confessed, 'in case it was carrying the beer I had handed Angus £30 for several weeks ago. We unloaded coal, cement, timber, animal feed, food, straw, hay and most importantly, mail. In a cruel sort of way I find it amusing to watch people, particularly men, who cannot lift a 25kg bag onto their shoulders without help. That is pretty pathetic for a well-fed adult male when there are several here who can lift at least twice that amount and make many trips.'

It was a tiring trudge, thirty yards up from the flat-bottomed boat over the rocks and onto the grassy dune above; then a hundred-yard hike from there across on the flat to the steading. 'As usual,' Mike noted, 'there are those who come down at the beginning and stay until the job is done. There are those who come along for half an hour and then there are those who don't show full stop. It's hard work and you end up all sweaty, covered in hay, straw, cement dust and sand.'

The reward of mail-opening was, by general agreement, kept until the goods-shifting was complete. 'Everybody looks forward to mail day,' Ron told the video diary. 'The big bag arrives and there's this mad rush to see what's for you, and then you sit down and read your letters. The other day, instead of doing that, I sat and watched what happened. You get people laughing, you get people looking pensive and you get some people bursting into tears, because something has been said – well I'll speak for myself, the last mail I had, a friend of mine was incredibly upset by the way the programme chose to show who I was. He actually said that it was as if all the nice things about me had been left at home and the television only showed me as either being funny, camp, or complaining. It upset me because there's nothing I can do while I'm here to help my friend not being angry.'

Ben wasn't the only one to get letters from strangers. Trevor had been written to by a class of psychology students, who said they were looking at leadership, 'and can I give them any information or feedback on what's happening here?' Patrick and Gwyneth had had a letter from a Bristol lady called Maggie, who worked, like Pat, in the Post Office. Julie Lowe had had thirty or forty letters after the scene had been screened in which she'd cried over her smashed crate. 'They asked if there was anything I would like, which they could send for me. I had a lot of those – from teenage girls, some men, a few couples, some families. The best one I got said, *Julie Lowe, Castaway 2000, Somewhere In The Sea.*'

Today Mike was happy. He had sixty letters, a couple of small (unsolicited?) packages and a birthday box from home. 'I collected them all together and went to my room trying to look as inconspicuous as possible.'

The Taransay Five

Along with the supplies and the mail came, as usual, members of the production team, this week not just producer Chris Kelly, but executive producer Jeremy Mills, up from London to answer castaway criticisms about the manner of Ray's departure at the regular Thursday night meeting. 'Ray was on the agenda,' wrote Mike, 'and they explained the reasons for his removal from the island: i) using the satellite phone ii) contacting the *Mirror* and iii) using what Lion considered to be blackmailing techniques. They are also trying to decide what to do about the *Stornoway Gazette* as they printed an article which they had said they would not print.' (This being the celebrated 'exclusive' on Ray's escape, out that very morning.) 'After the meeting I hung around and had a brief chat to both Jeremy and Chris on my own.' Lion had already taken advice on the matter of the *Gazette* from the external lawyers, so at the meeting they discussed what legal action might be appropriate.

Mike wasn't the only one to talk to the two producers that evening. 'Whenever the production team come over here,' says Ben, 'we all want to speak to them, because we all have things we want to talk about. For the first time there is a new face that you can talk to about problems that are going on. It is so incestuous here. Everything that goes on is so focused. The production team are part of the community anyway, they have to be really. They live it through videos and coming out here. So when Jeremy and Chris came out I spoke to them. I had already spoken to Paul about the jealousy thing, and how people had been complaining about me being filmed too much, and being on television too much, so I'd had this idea of trying to step back, because I just wanted it to stop.

'So they arrived, obviously very hurt by what Ray had done. I'd be hurt, if I'd dreamed up this wonderful concept and managed to find all the money for it and then all the people for it and everyone loves it and you feel really passionate about it and then one of the people suddenly goes off and blackmails you and sells the story and then you find out that all the community on the island were worried about was, "How dare you make this statement. It's another untruth from Lion." No one said, "I'm really sorry about what happened."

'So they had various chats with everyone. I told them what had been going on here: milking the cows, the pigs arriving. I told them how I felt another post-Windermere effect, as if it was a "them and us" again, that the project wasn't going forward, there was a negativity remaining; how people had said that they would leave the room if something was filmed. I told them that there had been threats by people saying, "I refuse to let anyone film me because I'm so disgusted by the way Lion have reacted." But that's fact, it's happened, I'm not being a tell-tale tit. It was said in front of every other person in the community. I didn't ever mention specific names, I told them events that had occurred. Even with the whole Ron situation I never specifically ... OK, well, I explained how I saw his involvement with Ray, but I know that Ray had already told Chris that Ron had been an influencing factor.

'So maybe I told the wrong person, but when there's only thirty-six of you here and someone else comes onto the island and it happens to be Chris, who is actually a friend of mine now, I don't see a problem in sitting down and talking to him, in what I considered a relatively confidential conversation. I didn't think it was going to be used as ammunition, for what it was used for. I didn't say anything not every other single person on the island knew.'

'Ben,' says Chris Kelly, 'wasn't the only person who said all this. He was just the most extreme case. He was down and miserable and talking about leaving, which was something he'd never done before.'

'I said to Lion,' Peter was to tell me later, 'that I thought that Ron had been leading Ray astray and that he had manipulated Ray and the whole blackmail thing was fabricated mostly by Ron, rather than Ray. I said this in front of a group of the youngsters, like Trevor and Toby. At that time I felt very much on my own. But they all came up to me and said, "We agree with you one hundred per cent."'

The producers continued their chats with the castaways, both in the steading and in individual pods. 'Chris had conversations,' says Jeremy Mills, 'and I had conversations. We got together about midnight and were really disturbed to find that, from a lot of people, great unhappiness was emerging – terrible, genuine unhappiness about particular people. As well as Ron other issues were coming up about people who weren't felt to be supportive of the project, but who, at the same time were not allowing these negative feelings to be filmed.'

'The anti-Lion feeling and the mistrust and the sabotaging of the filming was stuff we already knew about,' says Chris Kelly. 'Some of it from video diaries, some from watching footage of meetings. I hadn't at that stage isolated the five as much as I knew Ron was a problem. And that some of the families were. I wasn't sure which.'

'So we had various people,' Mills continues, 'and it was a real mixture, saying it's all very disturbing, things have been manipulated, people are saying things to individuals in a way that was not being filmed, but that was making people very unhappy – and Ron came up time and time again. It had got to the stage where some people were not prepared to even talk about the fact that they were being made unhappy on camera. Which is, from our point of view, the worst of all scenarios. Because you had a situation where interesting things were happening, people were trying to use influence, people were being affected by their interaction with other people in the group, but it wasn't being recorded on film. Neither the actual stuff, nor the effects of it. And yet it was creating an atmosphere in which some people were saying they were going to go. And that is just not on. That is not the ethos of the project.

'We heard that there had been a meeting where it had been decided not to film the proceedings. Our reports of it were that it was Warren who was saying they shouldn't film it. He denies that and says it wasn't true, so we will probably never know what really happened. But this decision was to us a key thing that we just couldn't have, their self-censoring, in that way.'

'Warren was accused of turning the camera off at that meeting,' says Julia Corrigan. 'But he wasn't even filming that day. That's how things get muddled up. There's a big Chinese Whispers problem on this island.'

'It was basically the people who had been off the island at the beginning of the year,' says Chris Kelly. 'There was still this resentment towards us. Everything that happened was our fault – it was all part of some calculated scheme. If they were two pounds light on their potatoes or the carrots were a bit manky, it was all because we hate them. And the mistrust these people had towards us and the project was exacerbated by the fact that there was some jealousy after seeing the programmes between Ron and the Corrigans and Ben. Paul had gone down and shot hours of the Corrigans' wedding, which we never used, for example.'

'Chris and I sat up in the steading,' says Jeremy Mills, 'till about two, two thirty in the morning, just talking through what we should do about it. Because clearly it was untenable, it was in danger of wrecking the project. Initially our reaction was we had had enough – of all the rubbish that was going on, and we were going to throw those people off. Full stop. And don't worry about it. But then the following morning we decided that wasn't fair and we would go round and take soundings from other people. So we saw seventy-five per cent of the people and tried to talk to them individually. Because clearly what was happening was people weren't saying things in groups they were prepared to say privately, because of the pressure from the group dynamic.'

'Jeremy and I had agreed the night before,' says Chris Kelly, 'that before we did anything we needed to speak to some of the opinion leaders, those who in our eyes were significant people in the community. Gwyneth was one of those for me. But I hadn't realised until then how supportive she was of Ron. She loved Ron. She said, "He's a pain in the arse, but he's a loveable pain in the arse and we can cope with him." I'd already spoken to him, mid-morning, in the steading. We had a twenty-minute conversation about all these issues: trust and his role in the community. And in outline I explained what I thought needed to happen: that people needed to reassess why they were there, whether they wanted to be there, what they were willing to put into it in order to get more out of it. It might all have seemed a bit abstract to him at that stage. Then I went to see Peter, who said, "Come into the polytunnel." I spoke to Dez briefly on the way.

So Chris Kelly sat for an hour or so with the bearded lecturer in the warmth of the polytunnel and got his overview of the developing dynamics of the community. 'I spoke to him,' says Chris, 'about how this mistrust thing was becoming a problem, which he agreed with. His big thing was that people weren't buying into the project, and if they weren't going to they shouldn't be here. I then said, "What would happen if we were to have a bloodletting of sorts? What would happen if we lost five?" He immediately said, "Which five?" Because he had also identified this coalition of interest which was holding the thing in check. But it was always purely hypothetical.'

Jeremy had meanwhile gone to talk to the doctor. 'Roger is usually the troublemaker,' he says, 'but he hadn't come up in any of the conversations, for being manipulative, because his moans are open. And I really wanted to make an effort to forgive and forget. I made a conscious decision to try and move on from the old antagonistic relationship we'd had. OK, I didn't necessarily agree with him, but I always felt he'd been open and honest in what he'd been trying to do, and I respected that. I wanted to re-establish trust.'

'On the way up to the MacKay House,' says Roger, 'Jeremy started on, "Now Roger, there have been some people who have been really endangering this project by interfering with filming." I said, "If that's an accusation against me, I'm off." And he said, "No, no, not at all, nothing like that, let's put aside our differences." And we sat down here and he basically asked my opinion of whether Colin, Julia, Warren, Monica and Ron – who subsequently became known as the Taransay Five – had been endangering the project. I think Ron was slightly separate in that he's far more threatening, vocally threatening. My opinion was, "Don't risk losing Ron, because he will be far more dangerous to you off the island than on it." Secondly: "How can you level accusations like that against Colin, who is really a great member of this community? He is so valuable to us all." To level that sort of accusation at him, even if it were true, would be desperately counterproductive – but it's untrue as well.

'My other point was that generally when he – Jeremy – or Lion are around, all sorts of feelings are whipped up. We're stirred up into all sorts of things. I explained that anything, therefore, presented to him late at night in pod culture should be taken with a slight pinch of salt. Having got the doctor's angle, Jeremy Mills now joined Chris Kelly in the polytunnel, where the two producers finally confronted the individuals who were to become known as the Taransay Five.

'Bad decision,' says Jeremy Mills, talking over with me later about how this series of meetings got exaggerated into an island myth. 'To do it in there, in the polytunnel, in that way. Crass. Physically, where it was. You are in a situation where everybody can see inside. It was silly. Hindsight's a great thing, isn't it?'

'I originally went to the polytunnel,' says Chris Kelly, 'because Peter said it would be warmer in there. It was a drizzly, coolish day. That was the significance of that, but then it becomes described like some torture chamber. When I'd spoken to Peter, I went and got Warren. I couldn't find Monica, she was teaching. So Warren came in and sat down. I said, "Have you forgiven us yet? Are you over what happened in the New Year?" He was like, "Well, yeah, but no." And we had this very honest conversation about what he should have done and what we should have done. Basically I said to him, "Look, you've got an added interest to be here because you want to do the filming. If you want to be here, stick around. If not, leave." He was like, "No, I'm very happy to stay here." Then we had a similar conversation with Colin and Julia. Bearing in mind, that the one time the community insisted on the cameras being turned off, in a meeting about the Ray press release thing, Julia had been the most vocal supporter of that. We said, "We understand why you wanted to do that, but you simply can't." We said, "Look if you want to be here and whine through the year, then it's going to make life a misery."

'Basically,' says Monica, 'Chris and Jeremy came over here, talked to a few people and picked up the idea that there was something going on in the community. That a group of people, who were described as being more confident than others and possibly a little bit more intimidating, were having a negative influence over the community.'

'In marketing terms,' says Chris Kelly, 'they're opinion leaders, those few. They would express a view in a meeting and are sufficiently mature and strident in their means of expression that they prevent other people from speaking out. That was what was happening. It was basically the people who have their support in a couple. That's the other thing we were learning, the people who can most fully express themselves on this island are the people who are in relationships. If they fall flat on their arse they can go back and have a cuddle.'

'They talked to me about being intimidating,' says Monica. 'Chris said some of the younger members of the community had found me intimidating in meetings, so that they didn't feel they could speak up. He said there were people who still had negative feelings towards Lion and he was implying that I was one of them.'

'He was talking about the saga that occurred in Harris,' adds Warren. 'I turned round and said that was all old hat. I said I wasn't holding any grudges.' The artist felt particularly hard done by over one piece of evidence of his supposed 'negativity' that the two producers presented to him: the scene where he and Colin Corrigan had rebuked Andy the architect about the unfinished schoolhouse (which was screened in Programme Seven). It had been, Warren insists, a meeting arranged by Paul Overton. 'I'd had nothing to do with the schoolhouse previously,' he says. 'I hadn't been one of the people complaining it wasn't ready. Paul asked me to come up and have a word with Andy as to why it wasn't ready. I was happy to give them what they wanted. But once they get that they turn round and tell me I'm negative. That annoyed me.'

'Chris said if there were still negative feelings,' Monica continues, 'it was probably time to think about leaving. I was just laughing, because I can't take Chris that seriously, to be honest. I have quite a matey relationship with him. It's only a TV programme. He also mentioned that I hadn't been doing a video diary. He said he could enforce that on me if he wanted to. I took that point, but that was the only thing I accepted from him.'

'The whole thing was a game of good guy, bad guy,' says Warren. 'Jeremy was the bad guy and Chris was the good guy. Chris was trying to be nice and Jeremy would swoop in with the blows.'

'I'm flattered,' says Mills, when this description of events is put to him. 'Absolutely delighted, I really am. Honesty is difficult. Telling somebody something unpleasant is a difficult thing to do. I was trying to be straight. Trying to address the issues that we felt were important in a way that was truthful.'

'Jeremy started saying,' adds Warren, '"You the families have a lot of power here." I asked him if he wanted me to use that power to benefit him. He said he did. I couldn't believe what he was saying. I was joking. Then they talked to me about the filming. They made some quite insulting allegations about me. One was that I had been deliberately sabotaging the filming and actively preventing people from doing their video diaries. I said I was not even going to ask them where they had got the information, because I knew they wouldn't tell me. I said it was absolutely crazy. If they knew what we had been doing here to try and get things together. What we have been trying to develop in the filming, to get the community to embrace it. They just said that they didn't care.'

'I wanted reassurances from them,' says Jeremy, 'that they were going to be less negative about the process of making the programmes. There was a feeling also that Warren's camera work wasn't very good. That was an irritation. Some of the stuff was unusable – heads chopped off, things like that.'

'They didn't actually highlight what I'd done,' says Warren, 'which they defined as sabotage, but they did highlight what they thought was sabotage to other members of the community. Things like cropping heads out of shots. But everyone has seen the proof, which is contrary to that. I've no idea where this idea comes from. Because it was a film-related incident, I would imagine it could only come from people who I work with in relation to the filming: Tanya and Trevor. I was training Trevor to be my soundman.'

'I never said he sabotaged the film at all,' says Chris. 'This "sabotage" was something that was reported among themselves. "Warren is being accused of sabotaging the filming." It's bits and pieces of conversations. They've nothing better to talk about. What we did say to Warren, to his face, was that some of the stuff he was shooting was unusable for us technically, because of how he was shooting it. Now that's entirely to be expected, because he's not done it before. The only thing he was guilty of was beginner's technical deficiency. I never said that his shots were cropped deliberately. We were constructively critical of him, but only between him and us, not to anybody else. And all in the interest of improving the quality of his filming.'

'Chris said to me,' says Peter, '"do you think Warren is deliberately sabotaging the film?" I didn't have a clue what he was talking about. I said, "I don't think so, no." About half an hour later they accused him of that. He was mortified, shattered.'

'We only found out after they had left,' says Monica, 'that they were actually considering removing us from the island. Peter told us that they'd asked him about it. They had said to him they wanted to remove five people from the island and he asked which five. They told him. He said he could understand Ron being removed, but not the other four. Peter publicly told us everything Jeremy had said, after they had gone.'

Julia and Colin hadn't realised the seriousness of the warning either. 'We thought we'd just been having a conversation,' says Julia. 'Then we suddenly found out that the others had had an extreme bollocking. So I ran after Chris. They were going for the boat to leave. I was absolutely aghast. I said, "Is it true?" They seemed really embarrassed by then, because they had spoken to us and realised that obviously it had all been overblown.'

'In the intervening period,' says Chris Kelly, 'lunch had happened. Colin Cameron had tipped up and addressed the community with Jeremy. At this point I was in the polytunnel with Ron and Patrick, because as soon as I'd had that earlier chat with Gwyneth, she'd run straight to Ron and said, "Ooh, they're not happy with you." Gwyneth dropped me in it with Ron. So Ron said, "Listen, I need to talk to you and I want it to be witnessed." He suggested Patrick, which was a very shrewd and calculated move because Pat was the most respected person on the island at that stage. So I told Ron how I felt he had let us down, and he was manipulative and negative, and erasing the tapes was one of the most serious contraventions. He was saying, "I can't believe you're saying this. I'm full of love. This island is full of love. We could be full of love." All the stuff he'd written me in endless letters before. Then Jeremy and Colin came in at the end of it. By this stage things had got fairly heated between me and Ron. He was shouting at me and accusing me of this, that and the other – portraying him in the programmes as only being the joker, not having any depth.'

'It was basically a witch-hunt,' says Ron. 'Jeremy and Chris came over and I think they had an agenda. I reckon they think that I masterminded Ray's departure. They came in here and went and had their own conversations with various people. They spoke to Toby, Ben, Trevor, Julie Lowe, Peter and others. Some of those people stabbed me in the back and said that they thought that I had incited Ray to do what he did.'

'Yes, we did have an agenda,' admits Jeremy Mills. 'At this point we thought Ron had wiped the tape, which is a serious matter.'

'Chris said to me,' Ron continues, '"Over half the people on this island want you to leave. You are a controlling, negative influence." This was in the steading. Then they accused me of sabotaging filming. They said I intimidated people so much that they were afraid of doing video diaries. They gave no evidence.'

So, as the producers left for the boat back to Harris, Julia Corrigan came running after them. 'The question she asked,' says Jeremy Mills, 'was, "Were you considering it at one point? Throwing me off?" And the answer to that was, "Yes, we were." Because it was the truth. But by the time we talked to them there we had already made our own decisions, that they were not involved in that sort of group.' 'I said to her,' says Chris Kelly, "Julie, you're still here. We had a chat this morning and you're still here. You know we've got concerns. We felt that if people wanted to leave, they should leave. So we're happy that you're staying." She was like, "Oh, all right, OK" and toddled off back.'

'I asked Chris, "Did you mean us as well?"' says Julie. 'Chris said, "Well, yeah." I could see he felt uncomfortable. He put his arm round my shoulder and said, "Oh, I'm sorry." Obviously at that point he'd realised that certain people were being accused of things that might not be true, or that they, Lion, had taken it more seriously than they needed to. Also he wasn't clear enough about the fact that it was all about the turning off of the camera at the Ray meeting. Since then it has become clearer that that's what really upset them. We thought they were talking about everything in general.'

'Then, afterwards,' Julia continues, 'we found out they had actually been going round asking various members of the community how they would feel if they released five people from the island, and we were among the five. We were absolutely shocked, stunned and horrified. A couple of hours later I went storming in and had a go at Ben. It had all bubbled and bubbled. People were saying, "We think it was Ben. He was whinging to Chris." We believed it basically, and went flying in to Ben and had a real go at him.'

'The incident tipped off that night,' says Chris Kelly. 'It's all on film. Peter, in a quiet one-to-one conversation was telling Ron about the chat I'd had with him. Ron told Monica, then it opened up into fifteen or sixteen people listening to Peter presenting his version of what I'd said, correctly by and large, but saying that it wasn't hypothetical, which was the most important thing. By then it had become a statement of intention – that was what was lost in translation. What a lot of them didn't like, I think, was the fact that I chose to have that conversation with Peter. In the same way, when they knew that Ben was one of the people I'd spoken to, it brought out all the jealousy and presented a chance to vent their steam at Ben, which they'd been longing to do. So when it came out that Peter had been viewed as unofficial community head, they all reacted and it became this big thing.'

Ben Fogle had been for a walk up to the hydro with Hugh Piggott, the renewable resources expert, who had accompanied the two producers on this trip over. Afterwards Ben spoke to the video diary: 'Hugh said, "I think big, big things are going to happen today." He'd been spending time with Chris and Jeremy. He said, "They've come here with this blatant agenda that they've got to sort out this trust thing." If we don't have a mutual trust with everyone, their argument went, there's no point in those people that don't trust us being here. It's obvious. If you own a shop would you go and employ people that didn't trust you, and therefore you didn't trust them? No. There'd be no incentive to sell anything. So with this massive £2.4m project, what's the point in Lion having people who don't trust them?

'So I came back from the hydro and saw lots of people miserable. Although I wasn't fully aware of what was going on, I heard snippets that people had been taken into the polytunnel and had various things said to them. And that was it, though I had a strong feeling that people were looking at me all day. Strange reactions. Colin Cameron arrived and left.'

'It was as if civil war had broken out,' wrote Mike, who had spent the day writing in his pod. 'I half expected to see Oliver Cromwell and a load of Roundheads coming up the beach. The afternoon was like a witch-hunt to find out who it was that had spoken to Lion and what it was they had said. The finger was pointed primarily at Ben, Trevor and Toby. Whether it is selfish to say it or not, I am glad that I had absolutely nothing to do with the whole affair. Even so, with friends in both camps the negativity took its toll on me, too, and I am now mentally and physically exhausted.'

'In the evening,' said Ben, 'I came down from my pod. I was going to take Inca to feed her. And Julie Lowe came up and said, "Ben, I think you should know that Julia's in tears and your name's been mentioned and there's lots of people talking about you in quite strong words." So I went down to the steading, thinking, Gosh, I'd better find out exactly what's going on here. I walked into the kitchen, Julia was in tears and everyone was just scowling at me. I said, "Is everything OK?" and Gwyneth just said, "No, Ben, she's not OK. She is *not* OK!" And Patrick pulled me to one side and said, "Ben, I think you should go in the other room so we can sit down and have a serious chat." My heart just sank, because I knew that stuff had gone on that day. So I went into the other room where a conversation was already taking place. Monica and Ron and Rosemary and everyone were all talking. Peter was in there telling his side of the story, what he had said to Lion. As I came in, Monica said, "Ben, we need to know what you said to Chris." So I started telling them, word for word, because it had only been the night before. I told them exactly what had gone on in the conversation. The next thing I knew Colin came running in and screamed at me, "What have you been saying about my wife?" He was drunk. It was St Patrick's Day. It was horrible, really horrible. This was Colin whose wedding I'd been to. Everyone was going, "Colin, Colin, calm down." He was looking really scary. I can't tell you. Eventually he left and I was just shocked. Absolutely shocked. Literally the whole community was in there, sitting down staring at me. I don't think you would be able to see what it felt like – on camera. Having everyone looking at you as if you were the criminal. Then Julia came flying in and just burst into floods of tears, saying, "How could you do this to me? I can't believe you would do this to all of us." Then I just lost it, because it was so unfair. The reason I had spoken to Chris was because I had been having hell from one person for about a month. If I had known that was their plan ... I didn't say it so they could then go straight back to the person and tell them. That is what hurt, because they had insinuated to the families that some of the younger people had said things. They said, apparently, "Some of the young men feel intimidated." Which basically could only be me, Toby or Trevor. It all got too much for me sitting in there, especially when Julia came in. I was so completely gutted. The one thing I had always trusted in my life was that no matter how bad everything was I could always get on with everyone. Suddenly it seemed like that had gone completely, that nobody believed me. I don't know if I burst into tears there, but I certainly did just as I got out of the door. Patrick rushed out after me and Gordon and Cassie were there. I ran up to my pod. It was a really emotional night.'

There was a further twist to the story that Ben only found out later, but which explained why the accusations of treachery had been so firmly focused on him. 'Two people were at the bottom of that,' he told me, in a later interview. 'Ron and Tammy. Tammy was still a bit upset about everything not working out and she had Ron behind her. That day, after Julia Corrigan came back from talking to Jeremy, Tammy was in the room with her and told her that it was me that had said it all, that I'd got Lion to do all this. The reason I know that she did is because she came to apologise about three days afterwards, because she'd been told by a lot of people that she had to. She didn't quite know how to say it, but she said she was very sorry. She admitted that she had maybe wanted to try and hurt me a little bit in that way. Then there was Ron as well. It was brilliant for him, because it was a perfect way of him trying to put me down. Patrick and Gwyneth, who I absolutely adore – who are the wise ones of the group – were convinced through Tammy and Ron that I had done it.'

'The next thing I heard about,' wrote Mike, 'was Ben running out of the steading crying. I was not there but heard about it from Dez and Liz. So later I went to see Ben to check how he was doing. I had no idea that when I entered the room there would also be Pat, Gwyneth, Julia, Tanya, Trevor and Dez. Trevor got verbally violent, not at anyone in the room but at the situation in general. Dez was crying his eyes out and banging his head off the wall.' ('It was the sheer injustice that got me,' says Dez.) 'I felt a bit like a spare part,' continued Mike. 'Pat and Gwyneth had been previously unaware quite what most people thought of Ron up until then. The one thing the rest of us are having trouble with is working out what the problem with the families is. Even the three accused Lion informants have said they have no issue with either of the families. One theory is that they are simply guilty by association. It's all rumour and supposition at the moment. No one here knows the whole story and that is something we must not lose sight of. If we become too inward looking and too self-analytical we could implode. Many things happen here which you simply would not tolerate at home. I guess that is part of the study. At home I would make efforts to remove myself from a situation such as this. Here, though, there is no running away and nowhere to hide. Some may say offence is the best method of defence, so when Lion came after them they went after someone else. Those three in turn have directed it almost all back onto Ron.

'I have made big efforts to be friendly towards Ron but there are still aspects of his character which are repulsive to me. Only last night he was saying how he had written down all conversations with Lion and that he would "have them". He also intends to get his book serialised in the papers and not worry about the contract with Lion. Perhaps most serious of all is the fact that he said he is already planning his revenge. Although he did not say so I suspect he meant against Ben, Toby and Trevor.

'I cannot but think that Ben and Dez will be shown on TV crying their eyes out because it is what the public will want. It will have a Gascoigne effect but it will not be an accurate reflection of what has been going on here. We have a complete lack of trust now amongst many of us and towards Lion, resentment, fear, guilt, tears etc. It's been a bitch of a few days. To quote someone (I think Jules), "It'll stop him prancing around like a happiness fairy." The reference was to Ron.

'This up and down cycle, like the teeth on a saw, is something that I suspect we shall go through many times this year. This one has really shaken us to the core and if it never happens again I shall be grateful. I have never seen so much emotion in one place. How people deal with emotion and stress is also

Paible – Taransay's homestead

TOP Working against the clock in gale force winds in December 1999

MIDDLE Battening down the hatches against the bleak midwinter

BOTTOM The end of the rainbow – The Mackay house and steading in Spring

Day to day life on Taransay:
Padraig doing his washing; 'True
Casterways'; Ben on an early
morning milking shift; Julie
delivers piles of post to the
castaways, from viewers, families
and fans; Philiy feeds the cows;
the boatman, bringing timber
across the straits; Roger, Padraig,
Dez and Tanya on kitchen duty –
rustling up sandwiches for 36.

ABOVE AND LEFT The castaways with
the surprise puppies and the
'stunningly beautiful wilderness'
that has become home

CLOCKWISE FROM OPPOSITE PAGE, TOP The changing faces of Taransay, from Sheila Jowers' notebook: the schoolhouse in moonlight; a view from the pods looking south; sunset from Sheila and Peter's window; Paible - looking across the sea to Harris; looking west from the pods

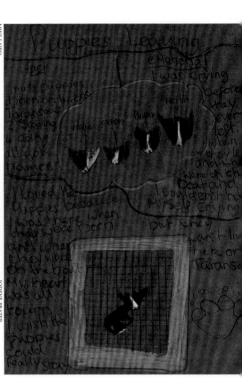

MIKE LAIRD

JODENE PRATER

PADRAIG NALLEN

CLOCKWISE FROM ABOVE Jodene's diary of May Day; the Wicker Man – May Day; Jodene's diary of the day the puppies left; Philiy, as drawn by Padraig; the school house and its teachers and pupils

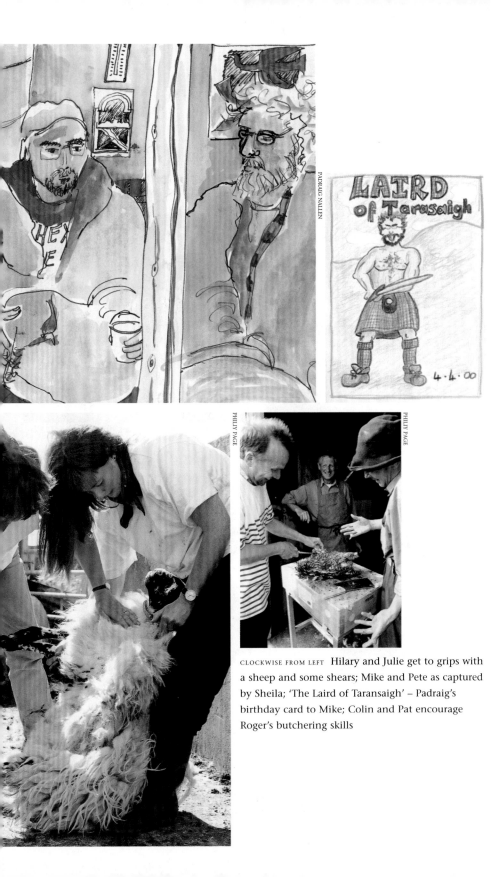

PADRAIG NALLEN

PHILLY PAGE

PHILLY PAGE

CLOCKWISE FROM LEFT Hilary and Julie get to grips with a sheep and some shears; Mike and Pete as captured by Sheila; 'The Laird of Taransaigh' – Padraig's birthday card to Mike; Colin and Pat encourage Roger's butchering skills

Ray Bowyer (58)

Cassie (41), Gordon (51), Yoneh (5) and Aaron (3) Carey

Liz Cathrine (30) and Dez Monks (36)   Tanya Cheadle (26)

Sandra Colbeck (58)   Monica Cooney (38), Warren Latore (31) and Ciara (4)

Ron Copsey (43) and Charlie   Julia (42), Colin (46) and Natasha Corrigan (7)

Benjamin Fogle (27) and Inca   Hilary Freeman (51)

Tammy Huff (27)   Peter (52) and Sheila (51) Jowers

Mike Laird (31)   Trevor Kearon (35)   Julie Lowe (36)

Gwyneth (54) and Patrick (57) Murphy   Padraig Nallen (27)

Philiy Page (25)   Patricia (37), Jodene (11) and Michael Prater (9)

Roger (44), Rosemary (38), Oliver (7) and Felix (5) Stephenson

Toby Waterman (24)

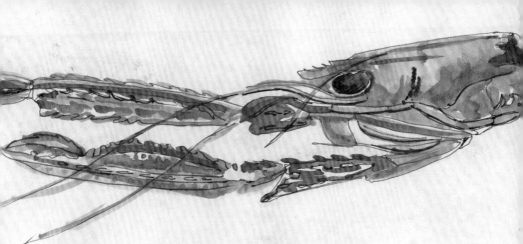

CLOCKWISE FROM TOP LEFT The wildlife of Taransay: seals in the sunshine; shells – each one unique; a lobster; Bol mushrooms; wild flowers; mackerel; diving gannets; mussels

The castaways gather on the
beach to say goodbye to the
Careys (above) and Hilary (right)

Quiet moments, public moments, competitive
Scrabble and a drastic haircut for Colin

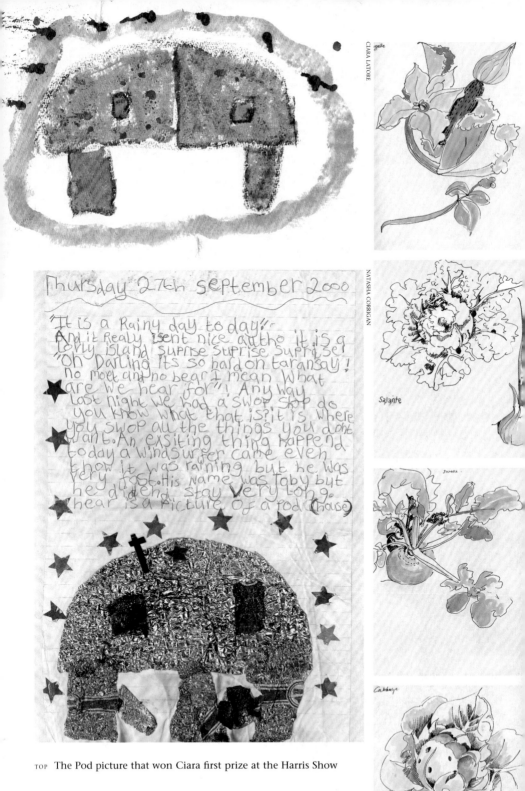

Thursday 27th september 2000

"It is a Rainy day today"
And it Realy isent nice autho it is a
Iorly island suprise suprise suprise!
"Oh Darling Its so hard on taransay!
no moet and no bear I mean What
are we hear for". Any way
last night we had a swop stop do
you know what that is? it is Where
you swop all the things you dont
want. An exsiting thing happend
today a windsurfer came even
thow it was raining but he was
very fost. His name was toby but
he didend stay very long.
hear is a picture of a pod (chase)

Salante

Cabbage

TOP The Pod picture that won Ciara first prize at the Harris Show

ABOVE Natasha's September diary

SIMON ROBERTS

SHEILA JOWERS

PHILLY PAGE

PHILLY PAGE

Peaceful pigs, prolific chickens, a swede surplus and some experimental arable crops: as the year develops the island becomes almost totally self-sufficient and the castaways are able to sell surplus vegetables on the mainland

'There has been a huge amount of fun and camaraderie: the kids' enjoyment of their vast but safe open air playground; the adults growing love for the beautiful island they all now unselfconsciously call "home"; the ready-made social life, from tensely competitive games of Scrabble in the steading to wild parties in the schoolhouse.'

interesting. Couples and families have each other to turn to. Singles do have people to turn to but it is not the same as a loved one or a family member. In that respect, Ron may also have an added difficulty. He often refers to the gay community as a community within a community. They are not here to offer him the support they normally would. Mind you, none of the issues here are or ever have been to do with Ron's sexuality.

'Another interesting point to note,' Mike continued, 'is that all of those that Lion had words with were those who were on Harris for some time. On the other hand Toby, Ben and Trevor were on the Advance Party. Is there an underlying division?

'Toby told me he was glad his inner thoughts were now out in the open. He admitted having said something about Ron but added he had said nothing about the families. Trevor's opinion was pretty much the same. Ben was in such a state that I don't know what he thought. The only good thing is that he has plenty of supporters to give him comfort.

'Later in the evening I went to Colin's to see how he and Julia were. When I went in Warren and Monica were also there. They were all very drunk and very upset. Colin seems to have taken it the hardest. I listened to their side of everything without saying too much and got to bed just before 3 am. I was exhausted.'

'It's amazing,' commented Jeremy Mills some time later, 'how our different reasons for talking to five people about their participation in the project were all lumped together. It wasn't the Taransay Five it was the Taransay One, with four others we had some things to talk about. Was it Ron who came up with the name the Taransay Five?' It was; and the idea of the flag the group were soon flying from their pod.

'The biggest explosion yet,' wrote Julie Lowe a few days later. 'There were furious altercations and accusations and tears and confrontations – it was horrible. It got so bad, one castaway took to her pod and didn't come out for three days. One week on, the situation has calmed down a bit, but there is still an atmosphere of suspicion. Two of the "Taransay Five" have taken heed and are different people – much nicer to have around. One was unjustly accused anyway and luckily is still nice. Two are still carrying on as before and one of these has handed his notice in, not that this means a great deal as it has happened before. We'll see. Are you exhausted just reading about it? Think what it's like to have to live through it, and the endless boring analysis and discussion of it that follows. The sooner my dog grows big enough to go out into the hills, the better. I wish I'd brought a tent!'

Chapter 10

Calm Blue Skies

A tent was the last thing Mike Laird would be taking with him as he headed off into the hinterland of Taransay a few days later. It was the first of his long-planned 'survival exercises'. Although he'd never made it on the Army Officer course, he and a fellow reject had made a habit of spending their holidays going on tough, some might say foolish, adventures: they had walked across the Sinai desert without a guide; hitched along the Syrian border; and found themselves facing the wrong end of a gun barrel while on a jaunt into Cambodia. The lure of *Castaway 2000* for Mike had always been the survival aspect, and the demands of the softer participants for mod cons and what he saw as luxuries had irritated him. Now, at last, he was getting a chance to test himself in the way he'd wanted.

His rucksack was not, he confessed to his diary, as small as he'd hoped, containing as it did, 'rod and fishing tackle, sleeping bag, bivvy bag, tarpaulin, spare thermals and socks, reindeer skin, two books, writing paper and firelighting equipment'. In the pockets of his jacket, furthermore, he had sunglasses, camera, spare film, balaclava and skinning knife, ropes and his 'magic bottle'. This last contained his entire food supply: chilli powder, garlic salt, three sachets of sugar and three Oxo cubes. He had eaten only a bowl of muesli for breakfast. 'The temptation was to eat as much as possible. I refrained as I knew it would make the sensation of hunger greater later in the day.'

With him were good friends but rookie survivalists Trevor and Toby, 'in great spirits'. 'We maintained a very good pace,' Mike reported, 'and got to the furthest part of the island in less than ninety minutes, which certainly amazed me. Trevor and Toby are faster walkers and perhaps slightly fitter than I,' he admitted ruefully, 'so I had to ask them to slow the pace at times.' The trio found a suitable base on the edge of a bleak, pebble-strewn beach, in the ruins of an old 'black house'. A huge section of washed-up pipe nearby, thirty metres long and one wide, provided, Mike reckoned, an emergency bivouac. The Action Man now got going on the first crucial task: lighting a fire, using wool from a handily placed dead sheep. Toby and Trevor meanwhile built a shelter from driftwood and Mike's tarpaulin and then went foraging for food and water, returning with a selection of mussels, limpets and cockles. 'We cooked some of them but not many. I guess the reason was that we were not really hungry enough to find them all that attractive.' Huddled up against the wind and rain in their shelter they read to each other until it was time to sleep. 'We all prayed that the tarpaulin would not rip or blow away.'

The next morning the group leader was up at 8.30. After some false starts, Toby soon had a roaring fire on the go. On went a pot of assorted shellfish, then all three sat on the pipe sharing the contents, crunching their way through the 'small pearls and bits of sand'.

By the following evening, having nearly been washed off the rocks by a wave like a 'mountain of water' but nonetheless having failed to hook a single fish, the trio were starving. They could of course have walked the three miles back to Paible, but that would have spoiled the whole exercise. Instead, Mike asked the others what they thought about catching a sheep for dinner. 'They seemed up for it,' Mike wrote. 'I had a length of rope with me and figured we could catch one with it. We came across three sheep, two ewes and a ram. As we closed in we pushed them down onto a shingle beach. We managed to separate off the ram and closed in further on the ewes. We went for one and I threw the rope. I missed. The only chance now was to tackle it down.' Mike threw himself at the animal and held it down by sitting across its back.

'I had one hand under its chin and my knife ready to cut its throat. I asked the boys to commit, yes or no, and they both said no. I got off the sheep, slapped its back and it got up and walked off. I would have expected it to run but I think it was rather stunned. Toby and Trevor gave a very valid reason for not killing it. They said that we could only justify killing a healthy sheep if we were prepared to eat most of it. As chance would have it, as we approached Black Pipe Beach, we spotted an ailing sheep. You could tell it was ill because it was stumbling around and kept falling over. With thoughts of lamb still fresh in our minds I said to the guys that we could kill two birds with one stone. We could put the poor thing out of its misery and also have a meal.'

The others were now in agreement. The trio gave chase, down onto another beach, where they 'closed in bit by bit'. Then the unpractised slaughterer 'got across its back, got my big knife out and pulled and pulled. I expected some audible click or a gush of blood but nothing happened. I knew I had to act quickly to minimise any distress the animal was in so I put the knife down and decided to break its neck instead. It took all my strength to lift the chin and pull the head all the way over until it was flat on its back. I got Trevor to hold the head still whilst I got the knife and slit the poor beast's throat for good measure. Blood spurted everywhere.

'I was not sure how to feel. I had never killed an animal this size before. It certainly didn't feel good, but on the other hand I was actually quite proud that I had managed to go through with it and not bodge it up. It was a kind of great white hunter thing. I have always wondered if I could do it and now I know that I can.'

Having hacked two legs off for their supper ('I did feel pangs of sadness when I started as I was fairly certain this animal was pregnant'), Mike dragged the remains of the corpse to the water's edge and let the tide carry it away. The trio suspended their prey over the open fire and cut the meat off piece by piece 'like a kebab'. After the meal, they read to each other again till darkness fell. 'A great evening.' Rising early, they returned to Paible by 8.30 a.m., only to discover it was in fact 9.30. The clocks had gone forward and winter was over.

Forget the Buts

As if to indicate the start of spring a period of calm weather marked the last week of March on the island. The rumpus over the events of St Patrick's Day, ten days before, was gradually dying down, though the specially made 'T5' flag was now flying from Pod Two, where the accused gang (plus Sandy) all resided.

Ron was now talking seriously (it seemed) about leaving the project. 'After the T5 thing,' says Chris Kelly, 'there was a series of phone calls from the island between him and me. He kept repeating, "I'm leaving." He was encouraging the community to have a vote as to whether he should stay or not, and being totally miserable when they didn't want to get involved. He was trying to use it as a platform to rally support for him, which had been waning before. That was another negative upshot of T5. It re-empowered Ron, because it gave him something else to be a martyr about.'

Had there been a vote, Pat and Gwyn would have wanted Ron to stay. Previously they'd only seen the side of him that was 'the bit of the clown act'. But, said Gwyn now, 'we've got to know him and he's a very sensitive person and he's got a lovely side to him. He's understanding and he's as straight as a die, he'll tell you black is black and white is white. I hope he stays.' Ron's view of the Murphys was just as warm, if not so undiscriminating. 'Some of the people here,' he told me in a later interview, 'are very simple people. I don't mean that in a demeaning, critical way. It is just fact. People like Gwyn and Pat, for example, whom I am incredibly fond of, are just very simple folk. They have brought up their families, but they are not political. Pat came in here and said, "You think too much." I just said, "I think and you don't think like me, that's the difference."'

Julia Corrigan had, like the three musketeers, also removed herself and her family from camp for a while. 'We spent some time at the bothy,' she told the video diary, 'because we needed to get away and think about ourselves. We wanted to try to calm down, because there was so much talking, talking, talking going on about who could have been the people that had said things about us.' She had remained 'baffled' by the criticisms of her as intimidating. 'I like to think of myself as an approachable person. People say I am fairly assertive and strong-minded, but my own opinion is that all that's balanced by the fact that I'm very warm-hearted – I think. So all this stuff about being intimidating and negative or that I make people feel isolated – I don't think they're talking about me. Everybody I have asked has said, "No, no, you're very friendly, you're our friend."'

Julia accepted that Ron had had a problem in his relationship with Ben, but she hadn't let herself be influenced by that. 'I mean,' she elaborated, 'Ron isn't some kind of Mesmer character, who hypnotises his mates into believing everything he says. In fact, I think I've been able to influence Ron's thinking on occasions, for the better of the community.

'So I feel sad that, because of the fact that I'm friends with Ron, Ben has been feeling unable to come to myself and Colin in friendship and talk to us as he might have done if there had not been a problem between Ben and Ron. I really like Ben. Before all this happened I'd been saying how much I like him. And I love his dog and I think he's really trained her well and I think they're a great couple together. Sorry,' she said, breaking into laughter, 'it makes it sound like Inca's his wife, but they go around the place, Inca on the lead, bouncing around like a puppy and frankly Ben's a bit like a puppy as well. He's eager to please, very friendly and he wants to be liked by everybody. He is generally a well-liked person.

'I had noticed that things weren't right between myself and Ben and I could have done something about that, but I personally was intimidated because Ben's so popular and I'd think, Well, he doesn't want a middle-aged woman banging on his door, saying, "Oh Ben, don't you like me any more." So I didn't do anything about it. I hoped that things would improve.

'And just because somebody like me can be very articulate about something and make a good case for something, that doesn't mean to say I'm full of confidence and that I browbeat everybody else. Actually Ben is a very articulate person, so I don't know where all this stuff about some people can't express themselves comes from. Ben can express himself very well.

'As for Trevor,' she continued, 'there's been a lot of talk that Trevor is the main knife man here, the main person that's stuck it between the shoulder blades of the whole group – the Taransay Five as we're calling ourselves. I don't have any idea whether that's true. I know very little about Trevor. I see him as being a bit of a nervous person. He seems to speak in strange cobbled-together phrases to me. I don't see myself as having much in common with him, but that doesn't mean to say he isn't a nice, good person.

'So I'm just shocked,' she concluded. 'The idea that some people here might not want me to be on the island is just a mystery to me and nobody owns up to saying anything about us. People are willing to own up to saying things about Ron, he seems fair game, and truth to tell there's been a lot of vitriolic stuff spewed about Ron the last few days. But I don't think we try hard enough to understand why people act in particular ways. And I think if people tried harder with Ron they would find out what was going on. It's just a defence mechanism with him I think sometimes.'

Like A Child Again

This first big bust-up had affected the community in radically different ways. While good-hearted Julia took it badly and allowed herself this mighty bout of self-analysis, and Sandy Colbeck, who wasn't even implicated, retired to her pod for three days, 'Knifeman' Trevor gave the impression that he hardly realised he was in the frame. 'Obviously,' he told the minicam, in a joint video diary with Mike, 'I'm not one of those who've been accused, so it's easy for me to say that hopefully we can get over what's happened and go forward.' Indeed, the gregarious driving instructor was one of the few who claimed to have enjoyed the situation. 'When the shit hits the fan, I love it in a way because – this sounds awful – the motivation of everybody drops, so nobody notices when I go missing and start writing me scripts.' But under the jaunty exterior, the misplaced criticism of him from the Taransay Five had clearly reached Trevor and stung. Much later in the year, in July, when the saga was dead and buried, and Ron had gone, Trevor brought it up again. 'I *know* I didn't say anything about the families,' he reiterated in a video diary. 'I was getting on really well with Warren and just starting to get to know Colin. But there was mistrust in the air and nobody really knew why. I feel Ron had a lot to do with it. I think he was whisking it up to suit himself.'

Ben, though he'd accepted his part in the censure of Ron, had been as mystified as the families where the criticism of them had come from. 'Colin's still blatantly really hurt and thinks it was me,' he told the video diary. 'And all I can say is, "Why would I say something bad about Colin?" I went to his wedding, I really like him, I love Tash, Julia's so lovely as well, of course she has her whingeing moments, but why would I say I want them all off the island? I still feel like I'm being used as the scapegoat, I'm still having people blanking me. Which for someone like me that's not so used to it is horrible, horrible, horrible.

'That sounds really childish, but it's really weird, I do feel like a child again, like I'm back at prep school again. "Mum, Mum, he's been mean to me, he's been bullying me" – that's what it feels like. Half of me thinks, I should be able to put up with all of this, I'm twenty-six-years-old, I've worked at Vogue House, I've done things in the Royal Navy, I've been mugged in Latin America, had my ribs broken, held up at gunpoint. I may be young but I've experienced a reasonably large amount of the world.' When he had come on the project, he continued (not specifying whether Vogue House had been a tougher deal than the mugging) he had imagined it was going to be hard physically. He was going to have to stand up to wind and rain and raging seas, lack of food and boredom – the obvious adversities. What he hadn't bargained for was the psychological side. Of course he knew there would be arguments, but he had never imagined himself at the centre of them – 'especially unfairly'.

'Well,' he concluded in freshly gung-ho fashion, 'I've got another nine months and I'm not going to leave for anything. I had a dark day after that whole experience the other evening, but look how beautiful it is again, it feels like spring today, a fresh clean day, flowers are coming up, it's really sunny and not that cold, there's a bit of a breeze, so it's wonderful today.'

Let's Have Some Fun On This Island

The weather was so lovely, Trish had decided to do her video diary outside. Despite the dramas of the previous week she was 'having an absolute ball'. The only conflict she'd ever had was with Peter, 'and now things seem to be getting better between Peter and I, which is great. He actually took me aside yesterday and said, "Look if I get too overpowering or I say something that sounds nasty or comes across wrong, you must tell me." And I went ahead and told him that he did frighten me, because I vowed that when I left this year I'd go home loving myself and being strong, and if anybody said anything that I thought was not right, or unjustified, I would stand up and say so. So simple things that I wouldn't have stood up and said before have started to happen now.'

The only cloud on her current horizon was the community's attitude to animals, including the rule that the pony was not be ridden, even by the children. Right from the start Peter had said to Trish: 'I hope you've not got a saddle on that horse. That horse is here to work.' 'The other morning it was beautiful,' Trish went on, 'and I thought, Stuff it, I'll go over Peter's head this time. So I said to Jodene, "Let's get that pony tacked up and let's lunge her and let's quieten her down – don't leave her sitting in a field doing nothing." Jodene jumped on her back and took her away up the hills. "How is she?" I asked when they returned. "She's great," Jodene replied. So I said, "Right, let's get these kids on this pony, let's have some fun on this island for goodness sake." So we threw the kids on and had the parents on as well and had a wonderful day. Then we saw Peter appear and start to shout down, and it was like, *Oh no, here we go.* But he apologised to me. He said, "I'm sorry, it was great seeing you all riding the pony. If I do that sort of thing again tell me off." And that means more to me than anything, because that's what this experiment's about. People from different walks of life getting used to each other.'

One particular family she had been worried about, she confessed now, was the Carey family. When they had been at Keswick on their selection course, Gordon had brought up the fact that he couldn't work on a Saturday. 'We all thought, Oh for goodness sake, we've got to be working, what d'you mean you can't work on a Saturday? We thought, That man'll never survive. And when they were chosen we couldn't understand why.' But now she was really happy the Careys were part of the project. They were absolutely fantastic, and when she ate with them now she would even join them in saying grace. On their Sabbath, she would cook and give them some of her food and Cassie would return the favour on a Sunday. 'And gosh, it's really worth it, because you get it repaid a hundred times over.'

So who else did she approve of? 'Liz and Dez. They've turned out great. Dez has got a dry sense of humour, but it's funny. Trevor's turned out trumps. Wasn't too sure about Toby but he's turned out to be an absolute stormer. Tanya's a cracker. Philiy's a cracker. Padraig's an absolute cracker. I love everybody really.' After a telling pause she mentioned the trainee psychotherapist. 'Ron is a powerful man,' she mused, 'and I told him to his face that I would be scared to say the wrong thing to him and for him to rear up and point in my face and swear. Wowee! To be here on a cut-off island and for that to happen, you would feel so insecure.' But when she'd said that to Ron, he'd agreed to approach her in a different manner; so she'd taken her hat off to him then.

'It's absolutely gorgeous here,' she concluded. I'm a woman of few words, but the only way I can describe it is this: imagine you're sitting in a traffic jam and you're pulling your hair out, your phone's going, and you've just remembered you've got to pay this bill and oh gosh your money's not in the bank and the car's going to be repossessed. Then, all of a sudden, somebody knocks on the sunroof and you open it and they say, "Right, how would you like to go and live on a Scottish isle for a whole year, do what you like, reflect on your life, write books, build up your confidence, even just get up in the morning and stare around you for a whole year?" You would shoot through the sunroof in a minute. You wouldn't look back, you'd just leave your car there on the M1, wouldn't you?'

Personal Appearance

Tanya Cheadle's hair had followed Liz's in going green, a change she found 'fantastic'. She had had it cut the night before by Gwyneth, who was now established, not just as the community's chief masseur, but also the resident hairdresser. 'Quite interesting,' Tanya observed of her trim, 'because it was right in the middle of the steading, quite a contrast to how it's normally done at home, when I go to a posh London salon and it takes about two hours and costs, with highlights, over a hundred pounds. But I much preferred the night before last – and my hair looks fine.' Tanya had been prompted by this to reflect on her changing attitude to personal appearance. 'When we first came here and were all living in the schoolhouse in the first month, we were grubby and dirty and weren't washing our hair that often and wearing no make-up and no one cared. For the first time in a long time I had a real sense of freedom, from the burden of all that. I found it astounding that people were accepting me without all the paraphernalia that you normally use to boost your confidence – make-up and hair dye and so on. My insecurities told me that when all that was taken away people would find me less attractive and likeable. But that didn't happen – and I made all the solid friendships I have now in that first month. I thought, Fantastic, I don't need all that stuff for people to find me attractive.'

Recently, though, the youngsters had taken a group dip in the sea off the schoolhouse beach, and that had highlighted rather more atavistic attitudes. 'There is also,' Tanya continued, 'a very laddish culture towards the girls, especially amongst the youngsters. You get lots of comments all the time, and I'm not used to that. I'm sure it's to do with limited numbers of females here, so that any young female is pounced on in a way. So what I initially thought of as a sense of freedom from all that sort of getting wolf-whistles walking down the street, has actually become far more pressured than at home. It all culminated for me when everyone went swimming. I decided not to go, and it's easy for me 'cos I can say I have to film it, and I used that to hide behind. But I suddenly felt this huge pressure of, Let's see what Tanya looks like in a swimming costume. And then, at the end of the day, I was standing near a couple of the lads and they were making very lascivious comments about Tammy and Philiy and I thought, That's not what I'm about, I'm not here to be leched at.

'I go out walking in the morning and I get this great sense of release from caring about that side of myself. Then as soon as you come back into the community all eyes are on you. There is absolutely no escape, from anything. So the fact that I didn't go swimming was noted and commented on. There's nowhere to hide.'

More of the Physical Side

Dez and Liz, meanwhile, had been concerned about the continuing prevarications of their one-time friend Ron, who had now formally handed in his notice to Lion. 'He's got eight weeks notice to run,' said Dez, as he sat in his pod with his girlfriend enjoying – on camera – their first glass of home-brewed rice and raisin wine. 'I'm sure we'll be in a situation of: Does Ron go or does Ron stay? Or: Who wants Ron to go and who wants Ron to stay? Very soon a lot of people are just going to say, "If you want to go, Ron, go. If you don't, don't. I'm not bothered one way or the other."'

Dez felt increasingly that the emphasis of the project was becoming more 'on the psychological side of it, and to me I just want to see a lot more of the physical. I don't spend all my life analysing myself and other people and what they say and exactly how that relates to me. I'm very different to Ron. Maybe that's been at the heart of our falling out over the last few months.'

It was a friendship that had been caught on camera in Programme One, with Ron joking suggestively about having to share an eco-cabin with Dez and Liz on the CAT week. It had continued on throughout the summer and autumn, with regular phone calls being exchanged, and the couple going over to Ron's flat for dinner on a number of occasions. He had even invited them to Christmas dinner. 'We're good mates,' Dez had told me in January. Now, though, in the pressure cooker of the island, the relationship was slowly souring. 'I'd rather be *doing* things,' Dez told Liz now, 'than sitting dwelling over who said what, because to me that's very debilitating.'

Dez's solution to the recent upset was clear. He wanted the community to be working harder; so that they stood a fair chance of achieving the self-sufficiency that had been one of the original aims of the project; that had been reiterated in one of the Monday evening ethics meetings they had been having over the past month. An important ally for Dez in all this was Peter (whose room, as it happened, was back to back with theirs in Pod Three). 'I heard yesterday,' Dez continued, 'that people say, "Oh, we hate Peter because Peter tries to get us to work too hard." I'm sure people would say the same about me. But I think a lot of people don't understand how much there really is to do over the next three months. Peter's getting a bit of a raw deal from a number of people for very petty things. They're just not considering the fact that Peter has got a very big picture. He's looking at the whole thing, the whole horticultural agricultural aspect of things. He's trying to give some direction, too.'

Julia Corrigan's diary gave a different view of the same picture. 'Peter gets a lot of bad remarks passed about him from people in the community,' she told the minicam, 'like Tammy, Philiy, Ron, Trish – they all feel that Peter is quite an intimidating character. Somebody has only to be walking across a field and Peter says, "Oh, that makes me so angry, I'm working my guts out here and look, they're doing nothing." Never mind the fact that that person may have just been banging hell out of a fence somewhere – he doesn't know that, he just makes assumptions.' In fact, she went on, there were things being built and jobs being done all over the place. There were cows being milked, pigs being fed, chicken houses being cleaned out. The compost toilets (which she had now taken control of) were being maintained. The steading was being cleaned, the children were being taught, meals cooked twice a day. 'But we don't all work at the same pace, some of us possibly don't do as much manual work as others. For instance, I work a lot in the school, but you're made to feel as if somehow working in the school isn't quite as important as being on a roof, or shovelling shite, or deer fencing. It hurts people – that they feel criticised all the time, and Peter is a main voice in this criticism. But if you get people enthusiastic you get better results than if you kick people's arses all day.'

Jankers

Was it partly because he was aware of this gathering criticism that Peter had decided to slow down a bit now that the weather had improved? 'It's been a week of calm blue skies and spring warmth,' he wrote in a letter to his mother. 'We've had the most fantastic mackerel sunsets over a limpid sea. We can sit on the rocks outside our pod, it's a suntrap on still evenings. During these warm days the arctic terns have arrived, they skim and dart around the rocks with the most beautiful cheeping, trilling calls. So quiet is it here that we can hear any birdsong within a mile.

'I've been taking it a little easy this last week. Perhaps it's just a rhythm, but I felt like a small rest – so I've been enjoying myself immensely, realising a few desires untended for many years. I've been doing a lot of woodwork – pegged joints, complicated mortice and tenons – all out of driftwood. It's really lovely when stools and benches you have made become used as second nature by people who hardly notice them – good job considering how poor some of the initial joints were.

'Sheila is reigning artist here – me, I'm just a crabby old bastard who makes people feel guilty by working – perhaps it is "Jankers" vibes coming through. I often converse with him – esp. when watching the birds. He would have loved that side of things – the rest of the "community" would have driven him to distraction.'

'Jankers' was Peter's father.

Happy and Free

Rosemary and Roger had been having, at last, a busy and encouraging time. The schoolhouse window had finally been fixed and the 'school' was able to move in. 'I feel as though this project has just begun for us,' wrote Roger.

Coincidentally, the weather was now warm enough for an alfresco music lesson. 'Wednesday,' the doctor continued, 'was one of those rare, still, sparkling Taransay days. Stillness here is very powerful, and with sunshine as well there is a glistening sheen over all the lines and curves of the land and sea. After our opening sing-song around the piano – we are learning a variety of songs – we were drawn inevitably outwards. Just beyond the beach is the Ogeis Bhuailte (= Smitten rock, I gather from some potted history of the island; apparently the site of some ghastly massacre in the 1600s). In the centre of this promontory is a small circular depression, the perfect size for eight children and three adults to sit around. Heaven knows what awful atrocity – or perhaps homely pleasure – it represents, but for now it is the ultimate setting for a music lesson. We are surrounded by the vast marine crescent of the sound of Taransay and face the majestic mountains across the water.'

In contrast to this rhapsodical account, Gordon Carey was not so approving of the schooling arrangements for his kids. 'They're only getting two and a half hours a day maximum,' he grumbled in a rare video diary, 'I would like them to spend more time in school so they can learn a lot more. My fear is that they will get to the end of the project and when they go back to the mainland they'll be a year behind. When we were told about this schooling thing, I thought, Well, it's a great opportunity, we'll be having two teachers here and eight children to be taught. I thought they'd be getting a great education, being in a class of three or four as opposed to thirty or forty, but it doesn't seem to be turning out that way.'

Rosemary wasn't talking about this gathering conflict on video diary. But in a later interview with me, she gave her side. 'The Careys came here expecting there to be some ready-made primary school,' she said. 'They wanted their kids looked after all day. They not only do not want to get involved in any way, but also feel resentful because we are not providing more for their kids. They see that as our job, which is extraordinary. What they want is the 9.30 to 3.30 school day. They haven't quite grasped that that is just not what this is all about. We can't possibly provide that. We are not teachers, we're just parents. The school is as experimental as the windpower.'

Peter, frank and to the point as ever, had told his mother what appeared to be the hard-to-talk-about truth of the matter. 'Another issue,' he had written, 'surrounds Gordon and Cassie, the black 7th Day Adventists. They just abandon their children for hours on end – this doesn't really affect us, but the other parents get quite worked up about it. To be fair, Cassie, the mother, is affectionate but in thrall to a very old-fashioned sexual division of labour where she kow-tows to him. He too has nice sides (to men) but is rather arrogant to many of the women.'

Without (as yet) naming names, Monica Cooney had also tried to address this problem on her video diary. 'Another thing that is potentially difficult here is that there are some quite different parenting styles. For those of us that don't believe in smacking our children when they've been naughty, it's quite hard to witness. I had to bite my lip because I felt like jumping up and saying something. For the other children as well who don't get smacked it's quite strange and then they ask questions. Then the children who are smacked ask us why don't we smack our children. But I have stopped trying to be judgmental. We all have our different ways and I'm sure that those people certainly believe that they're doing the right thing. Who am I to say they are not?'

The fortnightly boat on Thursday 30 March brought not just the production crew, Cynthia the psychologist and Carol Knott the archaeologist, but the Head of Education for the Western Isles, accompanied by educational psychologist Ruaridh Martin from Stornoway. 'They came on a sort of inspection visit,' Rosemary reported, 'which was slightly daunting since we have only just moved into our school and I feel we are very much feeling our way.' All went well, however. 'They were really impressed. I could tell they thought it was fantastic.

They said the kids seemed happy and free. What more can you ask? I just felt really proud of what we had created. In fact they were sort of envious, both of them. They said, "We would love to come and spend some time here," and Ian said, "Would you mind if we sent our difficult kids over here for a little bit, it might be good for them" – so that was encouraging.'

That evening Carol gave the castaways an archaeological tour of Paible, pointing out the three churches, the black houses, the mediaeval graveyards and the remains of a Viking house. On the Friday morning there was a further excursion. 'She took us on a walk up to the Dun Loch, which has a little fort in the middle of it,' Rosemary continued. 'I'd not been there before. On the way she talked about various piles of stones that we saw, explaining how these could have been evidence of old settlements. It was fascinating, it just opened up a whole new perspective on the island.' Arriving at the dark waters of the loch, Carol had taken the party out over the narrow causeway of stepping stones that led to the remains of the little fort or 'dun'. 'It's two thousand years old,' Rosemary went on, 'which is amazing, it adds a completely new perspective to the island to think of people living here then and having to protect themselves from invaders. Oliver and Michael were really gripped by it, asking all sorts of questions. I thought, Where else could a seven-year-old have that sort of experience, to be taken by a professional archaeologist all over an island learning about something he hadn't even heard of a few weeks ago?

'Then after lunch he spent the afternoon doing art with Sheila in our new schoolhouse and all the kids were making Mother's Day cards and so he had a completely new experience there. It's what we wanted – for them to be exposed to lots of different things, people and skills in a quite unstructured way. I just thought, Yeah, this is a really good day, this is what we brought our kids here for.'

Chapter 11

Homophobia and Foreign Muck

April arrived on Taransay with a cold snap. 'Taransay has had a rest,' Julia Corrigan reported, 'and now it's lashing us again. I'm absolutely frozen. I can't describe how stunningly disappointing it is to have that respite from the bad weather – with everyone going around thinking, Oh summery weather, spring is here – only to be back to square one today.'

Julie Lowe was making the best of things as always. If the weather wasn't quite what the doctor ordered, it was clearly time to make use of that luxury item that she had so laboriously lugged to Taransay. 'Let me set the scene,' she wrote. 'It's early on Mother's Day morning. I've just about managed to get up the hill with the barrow of pellets to feed the sheep. It's blowing gale force 8 and there's a blizzard that completely cuts off the island. We cannot see the mainland at all.

'I get my sponge bag, thick fluffy towel, and clean undies from the pod. Bent double against the force of the wind, I just about make it down the walkway back to the shelter of the steading. I lock the cubicle door, prop the bath diagonally across the shower tray, fill it, put some lavender oil in, strip off, and prepare to lower myself into the steaming water to enjoy being thawed in warmth.

'The first thing I notice is that I'm sitting on grit and sand. This, although unfortunate, is not terminal. I'm sure all of us have experienced sand in our swimsuits on the beach at some point in our lives. No, what really upsets me are all the coarse, fair hairs floating on the surface of the water. It gets worse. I then remember that the slaughter boys borrowed the bath for some reason that I didn't inquire too much into, but which had something to do with the dastardly deed of dispatch of a pig. Gentle reader, this was not nice.

'It shows what a tough old Taransay bird I'm getting to be, that I didn't instantly jump up screaming, but instead, skimmed off as many of the hairs as I could, added more lavender oil, filled the tub up with a *leetle* more hot water and just shut my eyes! Do you think the old saying "look before you leap" could have been invented just for me? I will be more careful next time – believe me.'

For Monica Cooney life wasn't so carefree. In this weather, everything took longer if you had a child. 'It was a nightmare getting her dressed in the morning, because of all the layers of clothes that you have to put on, the waterproofs and everything. Then getting her washed and getting her to go to the loo, because you have to walk down the path to the toilet block. Then there's breakfast as well, so you have to fight your way into the kitchen. You have to get there before 10.30 because that's the rule we've come to. It might sound quite late, but when your child sleeps for about twelve hours from nine till nine because she's so exhausted, it isn't. I know some of the single people think it's incredibly easy to be up and out and down and have breakfast and be ready for work by ten, but it's not that easy with a kid.'

Seeing her walking up and down the walkways with full potties in all weathers perhaps, she thought, gave the singles a glimpse of what life was like as the parent of a young child. 'Today it was just so bad because the wind was so strong. I was trying to hold this potty walking down the ramp and the wind was blowing it all everywhere. I should have given up and chucked it to the ground, but that wouldn't have been very nice, would it, for everybody?' As for mealtimes, the community setting made everything harder too, because her child had to eat what was offered. 'There's no "I don't like this" or "I don't like that" and you can't just get up and say, "All right I'll go and make you an omelette."'

Rosemary's video-confession that week contained almost identical concerns. 'We've had this cold snap and suddenly the prospect of being here becomes far more challenging again, you're really thrown back on your own resources, you can't use the outdoors. I suppose that's particularly a problem for people with children. You really feel it when the kids can't go outside, the tension and the friction is noticeably different.'

Because everything was so public, she went on, any disagreement or scene was much harder to deal with than it would ever be at home. With other parents observing, you had to manage things in a very public way, to show that you were dealing with the situation. 'I find that difficult,' admitted Rosemary, 'because the way I would deal with it in the privacy of my own home may not be how I would deal with it when I know lots of people are watching me. I feel inhibited and I find that stressful. You're being judged, as we are judging other people, I suppose, in the way they manage their children.'

Without kids of their own, Tanya and Philiy were indeed somewhat critical.

'This pickiness over food is a very modern phenomenon,' said Tanya in a joint video diary with her Pod One chum. 'I'm sorry, but kids a hundred years ago didn't say, "I don't like porridge." You eat it or go hungry.'

'Yeah,' Philiy agreed, 'I remember sitting at the dining room table with these crème caramels, and I just couldn't eat it and I was made to. Everyone else was there and I had to force it down me just to get out of the room. OK, that may sound cruel, but I think with commercialism and consumerism there's too much greed and wastage. I didn't come here for that. I came to realise what's important in life.' She laughed. 'Like polos and whisky.'

Hurting

Padraig was depressed. 'Been pretty much happy non-stop for the last three months and now I'm not, haven't been this low in a long time. I'm not sure how to deal with it. It's like I don't feel like getting out of bed in the morning, but I can't sleep, just keep rolling over and crawling out of me own head and it's not nice in there right now. My best friend used to be a manic depressive and if this is what his life was like all the time then it must have been terrible for him.

'Don't take this out of context,' he told the Lion production team beyond the lens. 'Don't cut and paste it to suit yourselves. I'm real and I'm hurting at the moment. Sometimes I think about my life and wonder what's going to happen, how it's going to work out. I thought coming here might make it a bit clearer, might give me ideas to proceed but at the moment I can't even see my way out of this room. Sitting on a chair looking at an impassive camera, just a cold eye that doesn't look, doesn't blink, just sits there wide open taking not giving. Don't even know why I'm talking to it.

'Trust,' he went on. 'I want to be able to trust people. Even when I know they don't mean to hurt, they still do. They're not bad in their hearts but they can't help themselves. Then it gets very hard to allow yourself to open up again and get close with someone and trust them.' Though he wasn't going to talk about it specifically on camera, Padraig's relationship was in trouble again. On the previous week's visit Cynthia McVey had raised the possibility of doing an interview about their relationship, and once again Philiy didn't want, in Padraig's words, 'to countenance anything like that'. 'She didn't even say "hello",' Philiy complained to me later. 'The first question was, "Would you and Padraig do an interview on camera?" 'I was asked by Lion,' says Cynthia, 'if I could ask them if they were willing to speak about their relationship. Clearly they didn't want to and I could understand why.' 'So a break-up was in the offing,' Padraig told me much later in the year, when he could view the situation with equanimity, 'but it wasn't me who was contemplating breaking up. That wasn't entirely why I was depressed,' he added, 'but it got me down and I started thinking about other things.'

Even as an established relationship experienced a wobble, another growing attraction had become the subject of community rumour. 'Because the community's so tight knit,' said Trevor to Mike in a joint video diary, 'you can't really do anything without everybody else knowing, which in some ways is good. If someone isn't feeling too well then everybody notices straightaway and they're up there to help. But in a negative way if you're just having a quick snog with somebody, then somebody spots it, say Toby for example was out on a snog ...'

Mike was laughing. 'With?'

'I don't know, you could say Tammy, I suppose ...'

'OK, for instance ...'

'Use them as an example,' laughed Trevor, 'then basically everybody knows, including maybe nine million viewers.'

'Just want to say a little thing about Tammy,' Toby told his video diary later. 'I quite worry about Tammy. When she's in a good mood she's great fun to be with, but I think she has worries with her mum so she tends to get upset more than I would. Of course I help there where I can but sometimes there's just nothing you can do, the person has to sort it out for themselves. But yeah, I have to keep an eye on it.' He'd always liked the girl, but this level of concern from the Leeds pensions analyst for the Sandy secretarial assistant was, it has to be noted, relatively recent.

God Love Him

Still undoubtedly single, Mike had allowed himself to be given a severe haircut. Tammy had done most of it, with Toby recording the trim on camera and Trevor pissing himself laughing in the corner of the room. 'It was then off for my first shave of the millennium,' Mike wrote, 'and a nice hot shower. Turning up for dinner was fun and I received some very complimentary remarks, not least from Ron. It felt fantastic.' Indeed, the old antipathy between macho man and gay man seemed to be fading fast. 'He has often joked with me about fancying me,' Mike noted in another diary entry, 'in my kilt or wetsuit. Well, tonight he told me that I was his one chance for sex on the island. He says he is going to get me drunk one night and try his luck. Not knowing quite how to take all this I said that I was flattered and left it at that. I must say that it would have been a lot better for me if such comments had come from one of the girls.'

Tuesday 4 April was the Action Man's birthday. 'Happy Birthday to me,' he wrote in his journal. 'The minute I got into the steading people were wishing me Happy Birthday and the feeling of being special and fussed over lasted all day. Handmade cards and presents came from almost everyone. The creativity was amazing. Painted stones and jars, clay figures, cards made from shells. It was very different from home in so far that people had thought and then sat down and made all these things. Most of the materials came from the island too.

'Weatherwise the day outside was fantastic. The sun was shining and giving off some warmth, the air was still and the sea calm. I floated around on a cloud all day.' After dinner and a bottle of port in his pod with Liz, Dez, Trevor, Wee Mike, Padraig and Tanya, there was a quiz in the steading, hosted by the birthday boy. 'The questions were desperately difficult which led to me getting loads of abuse.' But the evening ended happily with a cake donated by Sandy, 'which was split between 24'. 'I had been invited up to Ron's for a drink,' Mike concluded, 'and so that is where I headed. As I approached I noticed his light was out, so I didn't bother going to investigate.' There was one birthday present the Action Man clearly wasn't ready for.

The dreadful winds and blizzards of the weekend had passed and the spring sun was shining again, even if it remained cool. Mike, Colin, and Gordon worked on the slaughterhouse, putting the inner plywood onto the frame. Trevor laid flagstones near the watertower. Hilary redid the walkway between the polytunnels. Rosemary and Peter dug over the polytunnels, in preparation for the season's planting. From bits of old plywood Dez and Trish made a kids' cart for Aillie the horse to pull, with old, washed-up buoys for wheels. And Ron pulled himself away from his indecision about whether to stay or go and did the first ever drama class for the children. It was a huge success, remembered by them in detail for the rest of the year, especially the bit when they were pretending to be a kitchen team and there was a leak in the roof and he threw the water all over the place – and then! an earthquake! and he was throwing the food everywhere!

Now that the schoolhouse was up and running properly, a series of evening classes had been arranged. Rosemary was teaching French, Ben and Monica were going to teach Spanish, Philiy was leading a creative writing class. A reading group, an art class, and an adult drama class were all planned. 'The really beneficial aspect of this,' wrote an enthusiastic Rosemary, 'will be that we'll start to mix a bit more. It'll break down the groups that have developed, the factions.

And people will start to see each other in a different light, sharing talents and skills. Which again is one of the things I came here for. What I find exciting is that we have to provide our own entertainment, it's really up to us to do it. Either we all just go back to our own little pods and chat with the same people every night and play cards and read a book, or we can actually create something much more exciting. Until recently, I was beginning to get concerned that we were all a bit withdrawn, and there wasn't really the motivation to do anything more. But this week it's beginning to seem more possible. '

Even though she wasn't part of the cow group, Julia Corrigan had been helping Tammy with the small herd. 'I thought it would be an easy task,' she told the video diary, 'we'd just open up the door and the cows would be really pleased to get out of that cooped up place that stank of cow poo. But no, they had other ideas and we had to literally wrestle them out. You have to get your arms round a cow's neck and yank it and pull it and bang its bum and heave it with your shoulders to try and get the damn thing into the field. I was doing all this to Angel and she wasn't having any of it. She just did a sideways step and turned her bum and swiped me with one of her big bony hips, throwing me into a wheelbarrow full of sand.'

Padraig's depression had gone with the wind. He popped his tousled head into the video diary booth in an altogether cheerier mood. 'I don't want people at home to be thinking, Poor Padraig, God love him, has he got nobody to talk to, apart from the whole world. Or that I'm in a blue funk all the time, because I'm not. I was for a little while, and I'm not any more and I anticipate remaining happy for the rest of the year.' In short, he was back on terms with Philiy.

On Wednesday 5 April Molly the sow gave birth to ten little piglets. 'You notice the children are over the moon,' said 'Pigmaster' Pat Murphy. 'I was looking at Yoneh and Aaron. They're from Handsworth in Birmingham and I bet it's not every day they can see a piglet the day it was born.'

No Restraints At All

While others had made regular use of the video diaries to record the details and grumbles of their lives, Cassie Carey had been even more reticent than her husband Gordon. Now, at last, frustration with her island lot had led her to address the minicam. 'At home,' she complained, 'I am accustomed to do what I want when I want to do it. To eat when I want to. Here you are not allowed to, because these so-called bossy people are making rules and telling you what time you have to come down for breakfast and what time you should be there for lunch and supper – and it's really annoying.'

Perhaps she hadn't quite bargained for what community life would be like. But it had been Cassie who had been the Carey who had been keen to come on the project; and when she had first arrived the beautiful island had reminded her of home, of days when she'd gone fishing with her dad and been left to play in rock pools on the beach. Originally from St Vincent in the Caribbean, Cassie had been in the UK for twenty-six years. At one time she had hoped to go to college and study nursing, but her parents had put a stop to that. 'They were afraid that instead of studying I would go just for the boys,' she laughed. Instead she had ended up going to work – in a sewing factory, in a supermarket, silk screen printing. At the age of twenty she'd fallen pregnant by her then fiancé. 'But he was messing with another girl and he says he cannot choose between us because he loves both.' In the end they had split up and, after another unhappy relationship, Cassie had been wary of men for a while. She had met Gordon some years later, in Birmingham, when he had come from the council to fix something in her flat. For a long while she wouldn't even give him her phone number, but in the end he had got to her through her son. 'Every time he saw Jamie in the road, he says to him, "Tell your mom to give me a ring." Two years after she had refused to go out for fish and chips with him, Gordon and she were married; she had become a 7th Day Adventist after that.

'Aaron and Yoneh,' she went on now, 'they keep on asking when are we going home and all I can say is, "Not yet." I am missing all my friends at home. I am missing church especially because we don't go to church on Sabbath. The majority of people here they don't believe in going to church, a lot of them are saying they don't believe in God – and what can you do when people are talking like that?

'As for the hygiene – the kitchen stinks at times. Then some people they just peel the food and they put it in the pot straight away without washing it. The meat as well. To me it is disgusting and it's not nice to be eating and then all of a sudden be crunching on a mouthful of stones. Some people, they are in the kitchen and they are using the same spoon to taste the food as stir the pot and that's disgusting, it's like me going in there and spitting in the food. Yuk. I haven't said anything. As usual I keep my mouth shut.'

Gordon, too, hankered for his life at home. 'I miss so much the friends I have at church and the fellowship we have in each other, and the camaraderie that we have, when we go to church and pull each other's legs. Sabbath is just not the same without going to church, it's just not Sabbath and, oh my goodness, I wish I'd brought a lot of sermons with me. So I could listen to them. Or some music.

'This morning I went over to the schoolroom and Roger was in there and he plays the piano very well and he was saying to me that if I would like him to play any hymns he'd be happy to do so. So I ran back and got my hymn book and he was playing and I was singing and it was wonderful. He was enjoying it too. Even though he's not a Christian he was saying how some of the songs are really beautiful songs. When I get back home by God's grace I'm gonna *live* in the church I think, 'cos the way I feel at the moment, it's as if I'm in a desert without any water.

'There are some wonderful people here, who you would have as close friends, and I thank God for them because they make this experience a lot easier to bear. The Bible says you must live, where possible, in peace with all men. But I'm sorry to say it's not always possible. There are some others who are so negative, trying to cause trouble, to interupt the community, poke their nose into your affairs. My beliefs are totally different to theirs. And they think they can do anything and say anything, go anywhere they like, say whatever they like, no restraints at all.

'If I said to them, "I'm gonna go and drink myself silly with alcohol," they'd think, Yeah, great stuff. But if I say to them, "Well I don't drink alcohol," they think I'm mad. "Why don't you drink alcohol? Why? Why?" To them, I'm an oddity. A lot of them here like to have any excuse for a good booze-up. One of them said to me, he couldn't drink enough alcohol. That's the kind of mentality.'

Just over the water on Harris, where the Wee Frees kept their Sunday Sabbath so religiously that Stornoway airport was closed and no boats were out working, Gordon might well have found some soul mates. But here on the island, where the more contemporary mores of the cross-section of British society held sway, his traditional views and beliefs were indeed those of a freakish minority. And he and his family were missing out on many of the key events that were bonding the rest of the community.

In Hysterics

After the boat came in on Saturday 8 April there was an early celebration of Trevor's birthday. The main man was already pissed before the evening began. Having drunk three-quarters of a bottle of whisky with Tanya, he elected to stay in bed rather than help the others unload the cargo of building materials: wood for the slaughterhouse, and posts for the all-important deer fence, without which the community's serious horticultural efforts couldn't begin. When Mike popped in to see his friend later with some birthday present sweets, 'it took a bit of time to get him up. I fed him some peanuts, bread rolls and water and stayed with him until he looked a bit more human. All he could do was giggle.'

The Action Man then took his mate to Toby's pub-style pod, where the Yorkshireman was discovered drinking with Tammy. 'This was the beginning,' wrote Mike, 'of what would be a fantastic evening. Not long after we got there I convinced Toby to go to the steading and get the command stereo up to the room. As soon as he left I suggested that those remaining all change clothes. Trevor was caught by Tammy staring at her minimalist underwear. What made it really funny was the fact that Trevor had no underwear on at all and had to pull his T-shirt down to protect his modesty. When Toby came back in it took him a minute or two to work out just what was going on. Then we all fell about in hysterics. The funny thing about changing back was that Toby joined in even though he was in his own clothes to begin with.'

Tanya joined them shortly afterwards. Then Philiy appeared, but not to join the party, rather to complain about the noise as she was ill. 'This was followed by Toby making gestures at the door once it was closed behind her,' wrote Mike. 'So often she has a self-diagnosed ailment, sprain or generally wants to moan. Ben, Toby, Trevor and myself all feel sorry for Padraig as she has him running round after her. I fear there will be so much that he misses this year.

'Amazingly, Padraig came in shortly afterwards armed with some homebrew and Guinness for himself and Trevor. I suspect that had it not been Trevor's birthday then he would not have been with us. To avoid upsetting Philiy any further we decided to move room and Tammy's was the chosen venue. Ben found us there and brought in some champagne. I had given a bottle of Jack Daniel's to Toby on the promise of its return to me. That too was produced and drunk. I went to my room to get some cans of beer and some homebrew and we all set about getting more and more drunk.

'Hilary and Tammy carried me to my room to ensure I got to bed. I was told it was quite an effort and I nearly dragged all of us down the steps. The focus was once again kindly taken off me. This time by Toby who went to Dez and Liz's room and did a moonie. After that Toby and Trevor went to Peter and Sheila's and climbed up the stairs to get into bed with them. The rest of the evening I know nothing about. I drifted towards unconsciousness.'

Trevor's birthday had been a key incident for all of them, Tanya reckoned. Everyone else in the community was under the impression that Pod One, 'Serendipody', the infamous party pod, were a tightknit group, but of course they had their own shifting relationships within that, and Tammy and she had never really clicked, perhaps never trusted each other. 'Then Trevor had his birthday and we all got hammered and it was just really relaxed and open and Tammy and I got on really well and we have since then.'

I had, in fact, been present myself when Tammy and Tanya had first set eyes on each other, in November 1999, in the lobby of a central London hotel. Four of the castaways – Ben, Mike, Trevor and Tammy – had been brought together to do interviews with the press and at the same time meet the writer and the filmmaker. Tanya had arrived late and there had been a certain amount of amused speculation as to which of the many women passing through the crowded room might be she. When it finally transpired that it was this neat young blonde with a fetching laugh, the excitement of the men present was tangible. Tammy's feelings were less clear, but I guessed then that she would have been happier with one of the other less obviously attractive possibilities who had circled previously near our corner of the vestibule.

Poor old Philiy hadn't in fact spent the weekend in a hypochondriac sulk; she'd had food poisoning after eating a bit of uncooked cream coconut on the Friday evening. Having thrown up four times in the night, she'd stayed in bed on Saturday and in her pod on Sunday. With time to herself, she had been thinking a lot about her role as a strict vegetarian. 'I've lived with vegetarians and vegans for so long that I've forgotten what it's like to be with so many meat eaters, and I'm actually finding it very hard.' She'd known from the beginning that they would be eating the animals. But when it came to the fact that Taran the calf was going to have to be slaughtered in due course it was hard to accept. She had tried to give the facts dispassionately at last Thursday's meeting and someone had accused her of not behaving like a vegetarian. 'That really hurt me,' she confided, 'because I love that cow. I go out there and he's got these big blue eyes and he looks like Bambi, he's beautiful. He used to suckle my fingers when I was feeding him and he looks up at you with these eyes and you just think, How can people eat you?'

A Pack of Lies

The next week began with a thorough clear up of the site. A press visit was scheduled for Thursday, prior to the first series of four programmes going out at the end of the month. After the Ray furore the *Castaway* story had gone fairly quiet. But when the new programmes went out Lion didn't want a repeat of the January madness, with journalists landing at will. The idea was that by giving the press formal access to the castaways for a day, the guerrilla boat trips would cease. And this time Lion was letting the castaways take charge, deciding amongst themselves who would be showing them round and what they should be saying.

For the first time, the doctor had a nice word to say about the production company and the BBC. 'They organised it reasonably,' he said. 'They actually asked us which of us wanted to speak to the Press, and it worked out fairly well, because only about 12 or 13 people were willing to do it, and that's all they wanted, and that was wonderful. And that,' he added pointedly, 'came, I'm sure out of our little rebuke consequent on the Ray press release.' 'I would certainly like to be involved,' wrote Mike, 'as I find it quite exciting.'

On the Monday morning of the clear-up, the Action Man was up at 7 a.m. and spent the morning with Toby and Ben, removing a fallen fence, ditched iron doors, concrete posts, pallets and large pieces of timber. 'Most people,' he noted, 'were doing something of worth.' Peter and Sheila had put the finishing touches to their self-shutting flotsam-and-jetsam gate, which now closed off the area round steading and polytunnels from the rough grass up to the pods. Tammy had decorated the inside of the shower block with colourful paintings. Irises had even been planted. However Mike noticed a predictable absentee: 'It came as little surprise to see Ron emerge from his room slightly before 11 a.m. All that he did as a contribution was the windows of his pod room and then he disappeared inside. He has decided that until he has had an answer from Jeremy he will not do anything towards the community.'

The trainee psychotherapist was still after an apology for the accusations about tampering with film made by the executive producer during that dread morning in the polytunnel over three weeks before. 'I found out later in the day,' Mike continued, 'that he tried phoning Jeremy but only got through to his secretary. He had abided by our house rule of getting three others to agree to the phone call being made, but in my opinion he fell short on the fact that his whims and whinges do not constitute an emergency. What is the difference here, in some ways, to Ray having used the phone. Not an emergency, therefore also gross misconduct?'

Even as Ron tried to get through, a call came the other way, but not for him, rather his rival in the TV celebrity stakes. 'Lion did actually give me a call about the Press Day,' said Ben, 'and basically said that all the papers that had been invited had mentioned my name and wanted specifically to talk to me. But it was suggested by Lion – or I was probably told rather than it being suggested – that they didn't want me talking to them. They didn't want articles dominated by me, because of the whole jealousy thing that had been erupting here over the first few programmes. So they asked whether I would mind stepping back. I said,

"Yes, that's fine." I was disappointed, because I thought it would be fun to speak to a journalist at least once in my life, because I'd never done it before.'

'We suggested,' says Jeremy Mills, 'that maybe Ben shouldn't be in it, because he had already expressed his own fears about being too exposed, that maybe for his sake, and the group's sake, this would be a chance for him to take a back seat.' 'I thought,' says Chris Kelly, 'that all these journalists would go up there and just want to speak to Ben. Was Ben Getting Any? would be the whole mission of the press thing. He understood that.'

The build-up to the Thursday conference continued. 'Shall we feed them gruel,' asked Julie Lowe, 'or put something slap-up on?' The decision was made to give them just the normal food the castaways were going to have anyway. 'By Thursday,' calculated Julie, 'it'll be two weeks since our last delivery and we'll be down to potatoes and parsnips again, I reckon, so it'll be potato and parsnip soup.'

Gordon had already made his mind up about the visiting hack pack. 'We are expecting some reporters across,' he told the video diary, 'which I'm not looking forward to because they are people who see one thing and report something completely different, they never seem to be able to tell the truth. You know, why spoil a good story with the truth? So it's a pack of lies and that really annoys me.'

'I'm a bit apprehensive,' reported Rosemary to the video diary, 'because I think it's inevitably going to stir things up. I feel that any sort of intrusion from the outside world is going to have some sort of impact. So I hope people can remain fairly philosophical and not worry too much about what's written and just keep their heads focused on what's going on here.'

But as it happened, the disruption of the community's peace was to come not from without, but within. Things had been going so well, Julie Lowe reported. Yoneh had turned five and been introduced to the delights of musical bumps at her first ever birthday party. Floozy was beginning to use her sandbox. Ben's puppy, Inca, had made great friends with Taran the calf and they were making the community laugh with their racing up and down the field and tugs-of-war together. Dez had got the community motivated to put in the deer fence posts round the area that was to become the crop field by setting the task up as a competition between teams (Mike's managed 56 posts in four hours). The weather was beginning to improve and the chickens had started laying more eggs. 'And then,' Julie's letter went on, 'our gentle domestic harmony was shattered by Cassie, Mrs Seventh Day Adventist, having a major scrap with Castagay, Ron.'

Padraig had actually been in the kitchen when the incident kicked off. 'Normally we've pretty relaxed banter going on with our kitchen team – Ron, Cassie, myself and Ben – and it's good fun and we make cracks and innuendo, whatever, and it always works and you're always laughing – but this time something happened. Roger had come in and made a slightly off-colour joke at Ron's expense, went over to apologise, hugged him and in the process Ron patted his bum. So then Cassie says, "Ron, that's disgusting, you shouldn't pat another man's bottom." Cassie's someone who's got a sense of humour, as is Gordon, they can laugh at a lot of things, themselves as well, but she really exploded about Ron patting Roger on the bum. She started going on about it not being natural and being wrong, immoral, against God, against Nature etc. Ron said, "I don't fucking care," and then she took the use of the F word as a personal affront and got even more irate and finally stormed off out of the kitchen. I think the last words she said as she slammed the door were, "It says so in the Bible." And I was quite shocked really because they've known Ron was gay since they got here, and it may not be to their liking, but he wasn't coming on to him, it was just a friendly pat on the bum.'

Julie's Lowe's letter took the same line: 'Ron had given Doc a friendly hug and tweaked his bottom. This is not unusual behaviour here between friends and I don't think anybody thought twice about it. But Cassie then threw a major homophobic wobbly and called him disgusting and unnatural etc etc. Now, as you may have gathered, Ron and I are not what you could call friends. Even so, I still don't think he should have been subjected to this kind of discrimination. Ron can no more not be gay than I can not have size seven feet. How sad for someone from one persecuted minority group to so actively persecute and discriminate against another.'

'I think there has been trouble brewing between Cassie and Ron for awhile and this small straw set it off,' she continued. 'It would be highly unlikely that a 7DA family, let alone a black 7DA family would get through a year without clashing with someone, and a flamboyant, gay man who demands attention and is noisy, frequently outrageous and provocative is a prime candidate.'

'Obviously Cassie and Gordon, being fundamentalist Christians, don't approve of homosexuality,' said Padraig, 'and I being an atheist don't approve of fundamentalist Christianity, but I'm not going to try and convince fundamentalists that their beliefs are to my eyes incorrect. So I don't see the point in trying to persuade Ron, who's gay, to change his entire being because it doesn't fit in with what was written down by a widely disparate group of people many hundreds of years ago.'

'We'd had a row earlier in the day,' Cassie told the video diary, 'but we'd ended up being friends again and everything was going on fine until Roger Stephenson came in there. Then "this person" was hugging him up and kissing him up and actually having a good feel at his bottom. To him it was one big joke, but to me it was very offensive. So I had a go at him and told him it was disgusting, filthy, it's a disgrace that that kind of thing should be going on round here. Even though I know what he is, it should never be done in the kitchen. Then he started swearing at me. If he'd said, "OK, Cass, I'm sorry, I shouldn't have done that," maybe I wouldn't have carried on shouting at him – but I did. I told him a few home truths and he didn't like it. Now he is not talking to me and I am not talking to him.'

After Cassie had left the kitchen, Padraig, Ben and Ron had continued with the preparation of the meal. When it came to serving up time at six o'clock, Gordon had given Ron 'a stare-out', Padraig reported. 'Ron just stared back. I suppose it would have been within his rights to throw a bit of a wobbly but he didn't. He restrained himself admirably, I thought.'

'Well, Cassie has opened up a can of worms,' wrote Mike. 'Ron and several others, myself included, have noticed various things about Cassie and her family but kept quiet in case accusations of racism were levelled against us. The children are badly behaved and this is probably down to the lack of attention given to them. As a family they eat much more of certain foodstuffs like eggs and sugar than anyone here. It is not uncommon to see Cassie cook eight eggs for their breakfast, which is totally unacceptable to the rest of us.'

Things were warming up nicely for the arrival of the press the next day – Thursday 13 April. But as it turned out the weather was too poor for the assembled journalists to make the crossing. On the mainland, the production team and BBC press officers rescheduled the Sundays and dailies to come together the next day. 'At the hotel,' wrote the Sunday Herald's wry Hebridean correspondent, Torcuil Crichton, 'we have exhausted all topics of conversation with resident psychologist, Cynthia McVey. It is a very good service for a hotel to provide a psychologist to comfort the guests marooned inside by the weather, but I am feeling guilty for all the other people on the island who have to sort out their own problems over the dark winter without this kind of support. In the bar, one jealous islander was telling me he is fed up of his television licence subsidising the lifestyle of media types and their unsustainable projects when his crofting grants are being cut every year and the price of lamb is falling and the BSE scare is finishing off the beef market.

' "Wake up and smell the black pudding," I was telling him. "Agriculture is the past, think of the tourists and other television companies that will want to come and see our unique way of life long after crofting is gone, and all thanks to the Castaways."' On the island, meanwhile, Rosemary Stephenson had more serious concerns. 'The boat should have come today,' she told the video diary, 'but there's a gale blowing and it's freezing cold and we haven't got enough food. It's the first time this has happened and there are real worries, from the parents particularly. I've been concerned for the past week about our diet, because we're getting very few fresh vegetables; there's been no fruit for ten days. We've had no cheese, no meat for a while, no butter. Basically, we've been living on bread and potatoes and lentils, onions and celery, and I have, for the first time this week become quite concerned, not about myself, but about whether the kids are getting a decent diet. So we had a crisis meeting yesterday with Sheila and Sandy, who are in charge of ordering the food, and several parents, just to try and work out how we're going to manage the food in the future. Now it seems like when the food arrives, either there isn't enough, or it's not being managed properly, or there's a problem with ordering, because we're asking for things that just aren't arriving. We're having to go through Lion in Glasgow, but we need a direct link to our suppliers, because trying to order things through an intermediary is a very inefficient way of doing it. It's all been heightened by the fact that the boat that should have been coming today hasn't arrived and the forecast says it's not going to come tomorrow.'

With thirty journalists champing at the mobile at the Harris Hotel, however, Lion had hired a helicopter, and the following day the media pack arrived, plus producers Chris Kelly and Jeremy Mills and attendant production team. 'We have separated ourselves into two groups,' Julie Lowe's circular letter continued, 'one to talk to the Sunday papers and one to the dailies. We talk for around an hour, giving them wonderful stories of our "community togetherness" with a common goal of self sufficiency. Conflict? Well, teething problems, but all over now! Sex and scandal? What us, surely not. We then give them the guided tour, which focuses strongly on the ecology of the settlement, and of course, the puppies!'

'They did two absolutely brilliant press conferences,' Jeremy Mills told me. 'Funny, witty, talking about the things we hadn't heard before – about them reflecting on life, on their jobs, their friends, what it was like to be there. We just listened. We said nothing. We didn't tell them what to say.' Mills didn't, he added, at that point even know about the Ron/Cassie fight. 'It was their choice not to talk about it,' he stressed.

Not all the castaways had volunteered to be interviewed. 'I didn't really want to have much to do with them,' reported Monica. 'But it was weird when they were wandering around. Because there were loads of them, really staring at you. I felt like an animal in the zoo.'

'The Press Day,' said Ron in a later interview, 'was just a fiasco. Because people were made to lie. Jeremy was there at the press conference and questions were asked and everything was fudged. It was like Little Fucking House on the Prairie. I was told not to talk. They said, "Ron, can we talk to you?" And I said, "No darling, I'm gagged. I've been a naughty boy, my bum's been spanked. Ben can't talk to you because he's been a very, very good boy."'

'Ron was in the middle of saying, "I'm off. I'm leaving. I've had enough",' says Jeremy Mills. 'It wouldn't have been the right thing for him to be talking to them. Knowing what a manipulative person he is, we didn't want him at the press conference.'

As for the now-famous heart-throb: 'I was just wandering around,' said Ben. 'I suppose in hindsight I should have completely gone away, gone to the bothy or something, but I find it really exciting when suddenly twenty-five journalists descend here. So I sat outside and I heard Toby and Trevor and Padraig all together laughing and all the journalists in hysterics and I did feel really left out.'

'One of the BBC Press people came to me,' says Chris Kelly, 'saying, "Listen, if we don't give them Ben, the story is going to be 'BBC gag Ben'." And Ben was doing his Ben bit in the background. Mooning around, looking like something out of a sailing catalogue, looking a bit left out of it with Inca. So we said, "Fine, give them five minutes with Ben." They got five minutes with Ben and then all the press cuttings are all Ben. I felt sorry, because the press conference that Trevor and Toby did was really funny. People were popping questions and every answer was a wisecrack. "Why do you think Ben gets more fan mail?" "Because they can spell Ben." Things like that.'

The press conference wasn't the producers' only headache that day. Ron was still on the warpath about the Taransay Five allegations. 'There was a lull,' Mike wrote, 'whilst Jeremy was dragged off to Ron's pod. Cynthia was having her ear bent this way and that.'

'Jeremy came to my room,' Ron told me later, 'and I challenged him on the accusations and he apologised and said that they had realised very quickly that they hadn't been fair. I pointed out to him that this was the last in a whole line of incidences where they had treated me like that. When he apologised, I said I wanted him to do it in front of the community and that's when he snapped. He said, "Well, I've done it now." I said, "Well you made the accusations publicly, so you'd better make the apology publicly." He said, "I might forget something. We've talked about so much today." I just looked at him and said, "I'll prompt you."' This was not quite the way Mills had seen the encounter. 'I never apologised to him for what we said,' he told me later, 'But I did apologise for the way in which it had been said – in haste, moments before we left the island.' 'In the meeting that followed,' Ron continued, 'he did try and squirm and backtrack and get out of it and look as if he was being the tough executive producer. I just looked at him and said, "That's not what you said in my room, Jeremy. Now say what you said, otherwise this is not going to work." And there he was squirming like a little slug. Some of the younger ones said afterwards, "I don't know how you did that." I said, "Well, I'm not afraid of him. You are and I'm not. He has no control over me and I'm not in awe of him because of his position."'

A rather different perspective on this scene was given by Julie Lowe. 'The moment the Press are off the island,' she wrote, 'we have a huge meeting with Jeremy, head honcho of Lion TV, at which Ron demands an apology from him *re* the Taransay Five stuff last month, where he was accused of being intimidating and manipulating the Ray debacle and being a negative influence on the community. Ron wants a retraction of Jeremy's statement that half of the community would prefer him off the island. He says that he wants a public apology as he was accused in public. As I recall, he was taken aside into the polytunnel quietly, and if he'd said nothing, no one would ever have known, but there you go! Jeremy, brilliant master spin doctor/manipulator that he is himself, manages to appease Ron and yet make it perfectly clear to all of us that he still believes that Ron is guilty as charged.'

Having dealt with the provocative psychotherapist, Mills then reiterated what he'd said in a letter that he had sent to the castaways a few days before: that the three firm rules they had all agreed to at Windermere – no parcels, visitors, or personal radios – should be stuck to. He didn't particularly mind, he added, small transgressions; the major crime was not to film them. 'I think the phrase I used,' he says, 'was "minor naughty things". I had in mind, I think I even said, "A bar of chocolate that arrives in a letter." The only point of doing all this,' he adds, with mild exasperation, 'is to try and make the whole experiment work. There's no point in doing it if all they're doing is living a nice life on an island for a year. A lot of them feel that as well.'

That afternoon, finally, the weather had improved enough for the boat to land. As well as the castaways' fortnightly food supply, there was a load of animal pellets, hay, straw and more posts for the deer fence. There were three mail bags, of which half one bag went to a delighted Mike. Trevor got a birthday box with six bottles of Scotch. The vegetable selection was disappointing. 'Only one bag of carrots,' wrote Peter, 'and one tray of broccoli arrived – for 35 people for 2 weeks. Some Lion cock-up.'

Becci White, who as Production Coordinator was responsible for food deliveries to the island, gave me her angle on what was going wrong. 'Initially,' she said, 'the food ordering was all over the shop because they weren't consistent in their orders. I would get a phone call here, a list here and a scribbled note here, no matter how much I said, "It can't work like that, it's not reliable."' Combined with problems with the suppliers, whose deliveries often differed from the orders, it was a difficult situation.

It was a tension that was soon to blow up into one of the most symbolic events of the castaway year. In the meantime, however, food delivery issues took second place to the major drama of the Ron/Cassie bust-up, which had still not been resolved. 'He's been making sly remarks within earshot,' Cassie told the video diary the next day. 'But I can hear what he's saying, things about me, and it's very, very annoying. If he's got something to say to me he should come and say it to my face. I'm trying hard not to get upset – but how long I can keep it up for I really, truly don't know. The children, they're very fond of him and I haven't stopped them from talking to him, but he's been doing annoying things. Today is Sabbath and he was singing an MC Hammer rap song and telling my children to sing it and they were singing it. I shouted at them not to, because it's the Sabbath. He didn't say anything to me and then about ten minutes after, my daughter came in and says that he was outside talking about me and saying these things, so I told her to tell him that if he's got something to tell me come up and tell me to my face.'

Community opinion was much divided over the rights and wrongs of this thorniest of issues. Julia Corrigan – perhaps surprisingly considering her friendship with Ron – spoke on video diary of her sympathy for Cassie. 'It seems to me that this came out because it's all been building up for a while. Cassie told me that when she's in the kitchen with Ron, even though Ron knows, or should know, that it's difficult for her dealing with his gayness, he still flaunts it openly. On top of that he constantly talks about sexual subjects, in a way that she finds offensive. And asks her sexual questions. I know this is true because Ron's told me that he's asked her about oral sex, whether she gives it etc etc. Cassie laughed it off, but underneath I think she found it deeply offensive. On top of that he has criticised her cooking. He said, "Oh we don't like all that foreign muck you serve up." Then he tried some of her sweet potato pudding and spat it into the bin and said, "This isn't fit for human consumption." I know he did all this because he told me, he seemed to think it was a bit of a joke, but Cassie found it deeply offensive. Her most important job as part of her family unit is her cooking. So this is attacking something very fundamental about Cassie.

'I think it's very important that Cassie understands she shouldn't have said those things, but I think it's equally important that Ron understands that his behaviour is upsetting for Cassie because she doesn't have the kind of worldly experience that many of us have. Is it fair to condemn people for not being as worldly, broadminded or as able to speak about sexual matters as other people? I know if my mother was in the kitchen and a heterosexual couple started feeling each other up, she would say, "D'you mind, that's disgusting in the kitchen." So what would you say, she was anti-heterosexual? I don't think so.

'We can't condone this anti-gay stuff, but if we're going to get anything back from this at all and rescue the situation before we lose the Carey family altogether, then we need to compromise.'

On the evening of that same day, Saturday 15 April, a group of the castaways decided that a delegation should be sent to talk to Cassie and Gordon. Padraig told the video diary that it would be about 'their treatment of Ron on Wednesday and subsequently, and about their obvious difficulty about fitting in here. The main point being the display of prejudice they've both made, because it would be equivalent to somebody calling them a nigger, which would be utterly unacceptable.' Patrick Murphy was going to go and sound out the ground with Gordon first, and then Padraig and Sandy were going to follow as ambassadors. 'I like Gordon and Cassie a lot,' the Irishman continued, 'but I don't like what they've done, and I don't think it's tolerable and they need to know that. That's why I'm there on the delegation, because I'm a friend of theirs and hopefully somebody they can trust. I'm quite nervous,' the diplomatic Irishman admitted, 'very nervous in fact, I don't want to have to do this, but it needs to be done. I don't think that prejudice should be permitted in this place.'

Tanya had arrived at a similar view. 'We're trying, perhaps, to set up some sort of model community for the first year of the twenty-first century, the new millennium, and British society has reached a point where we say we don't accept homophobia, we don't accept racism, we don't accept sexism. So I think it's vital that we make a statement that we will not tolerate prejudice of any kind.'

Finally, the community was doing as Jeremy Mills had hoped, way back at the conception of the programme: it was wrestling with the big issues of contemporary life. But had the volunteers realised how painful a process this would be? Catching up on his voluminous correspondence in his pod, Mike Laird overheard Padraig and Sandy calling in to see Liz next door. 'They were asking whether she was prepared to be part of a group to go and see the Careys in an attempt to find a solution to the recent upsets. She said that she did not have the mental energy and I can hardly blame her.'

'Everyone is emotionally exhausted,' wrote Julie Lowe. 'The truth, no matter what we say to the Press, is that here the conflict never stops. It's just one confrontation after another. I understand there's a four-step concept of creating a community, labelled as follows:

Forming
Storming
Norming
Performing

We're still definitely in stage 2. Roll on stages 3 and 4! Do you think we'll last that long?'

The Bothy

Chapter 12

Escape From Escapism

Padraig's delegation had agreed to call on the Careys at two o'clock on Sunday afternoon. But the plan was unfortunately foiled by Gordon, who, having been sounded out as agreed by Patrick Murphy, had gone off fishing with Colin.

In a long video diary recorded on the Saturday evening, Gordon had expressed his feelings. 'For the first time since I've been here, I'm really seriously considering leaving,' he began. 'I just don't like some of the issues that are happening here, some of the people I'm finding it nigh on impossible to get along with. There are too many nasty things going on and we seem to be singled out for a lot of the negative and horrible stuff.

'There's one man who this week has been particularly nasty,' he continued, as ever naming no names. 'And I've decided from this week onwards I will have nothing further to do with him. I don't like the way he spoke to my wife and called her a female dog. With the F word as well – I'm not standing for that. If I continue to associate with him and he's talking to my wife like that I can see us getting into a fight. And I'm not here for that. I didn't come up here all the way from Birmingham to fight anyone. But it could very easily happen. So I just don't feel I could remain here the rest of the months.'

On top of all that, Gordon had discovered in the Friday mail that his bank card had been stolen. 'Somebody has been using it to run up debts.' He now owed the bank £1800 and despite the fact the police fraud people were looking into it, it was 'very very worrying', as his mortgage was now also three months behind. Then he had received a clipping from his local paper, the Birmingham *Sunday Mercury*, reporting that his family were having difficulty with people on the island because of their religious beliefs. 'That they are up in arms against us because of what we believe and because we won't work on Saturday and this sort of stuff. I don't know where they got this story from because I have never told anyone this is true.' The article had further alleged that the family had demanded to be taken off the island just after the New Year, which was 'a total and utter lie'.

'I cannot tell the last time I've been so unhappy as I am right now. It's hard, it's hard, it's hard. I sometimes wonder if it's because we are black people why this is happening, but I don't want to get on to thinking it's a racist thing, because it's too easy to say that. Many people in the past, as soon as something is wrong they said, "Well, it's because I'm black," but I'm very reluctant to say that. But it makes you wonder if that really could be the reason. I don't know, I just don't know.'

Even as her husband tried to forget his woes and catch his first fish, Cassie had moved on to Round Two in the Homophobia Stakes. 'It really kicked off in the steading this afternoon,' Mike wrote that evening of Sunday 16 April. 'Cassie offered Ron outside for a fight. It is hard to know exactly what went on but the current rumours are that the gay comments made by Cassie the other day have been countered by Ron making racist comments to Cassie. I cannot actually believe this for two reasons. Firstly Ron comes from a community that are themselves often subject to prejudices, and second the fact that Ron is too intelligent to become involved at that level. He knows that if he made racist comments he would be off the island in a flash.'

'Ron supposedly disparaged the food Cassie was cooking,' wrote Julie Lowe, in another version of the story, and Cassie (all of 4' 11") declared that she wasn't afraid of Ron and if he would come outside she'd show him what for, which I understand to mean that she was going to resort to fisticuffs!'

With Gordon off fishing with her husband, the ever-concerned Julia Corrigan had called on Cassie earlier in the day. 'I said to her,' she reported, 'that she had no right to say Ron's being gay is disgusting. It shouldn't be seen as some kind of choice. He is gay – that's it. And although this may be her private opinion, to actually publicly declare it is a very, very unfortunate thing to do.' Julia had hoped that progress had been made. 'I thought that she was thinking that yes, she would need to talk to Ron in a group, and try and sort out the whole thing, but then on Sunday there was a big blow-up – it's unclear as to why it started. They were just both ready to go – powder kegs waiting to explode. I did say before that they should meet in the middle, now in the light of things she's said since Sunday, I really can't support Cassie now. I also can't condone her threats of violence against him. She said she was going to pick up something and do him an injury, if he carried on like that again, and that if they have another argument then Gordon would step in and flatten him. So I think she's dug herself a very, very big hole and she's in it now up to her neck.'

Cassie was now, Julia added on the Tuesday, refusing to work with Ron in the kitchen and telling her children that they shouldn't speak to him. The school had broken up for the Easter holidays and on the Monday Cassie had kept Yoneh and Aaron in their pod all day. But Ron was now getting more involved with the school. So what was going to happen? Was Cassie going to take her kids out of school on days when Ron was there – because he was gay? It was, after all, she who had made the comments. 'It's beyond my understanding,' Julie concluded. 'There's nothing in my life that I can draw on that has a parallel with this. And I'm afraid that if we don't sort this out at the meeting on Thursday, there will be an almighty explosion.'

Meanwhile, on the mainland, the results of Friday's press visit had been published. Despite Lion's attempts to keep Ben Fogle in the background, the tabloids weren't going to let their gorgeous creation get away. 'His efforts to avoid the media were rather half-hearted,' reported the *Observer*, 'he perched himself in the middle of the community and played forlornly with his black labrador Inca. Alone, but for all the world to see.' The photo coverage was almost entirely of the blond heart-throb, and most of the headlines focused firmly on his (and, as a sideline, the other castaways') celibate state. NO SEX PLEASE WE'RE CASTAWAYS, was the *Sun's* effort. CASTAWAY FROM LOVE managed the *Mirror*. In their allotted five minutes, the press had done well with quotes from their hero. 'It's very strange,' Ben had told the *Sun*, 'in a way I'm gutted because I spent my last year hoping to find a nice woman without much success. It's only now I'm isolated on this island that I'm told everyone fancies me and I can't do anything about it.' He added: 'It's the same reaction for any suggestions about me getting together with Tammy. We just laugh it off and she's too busy milking cows anyway.'

Hmm. The conference that had seemed such a success to both Lion and the castaways had in fact produced a rather bland collection of articles. None of the hacks had rumbled Philiy and Padraig, nor Ben and Tammy's bust-up, nor the island rumours about Tammy and Toby. Instead they had been forced to dwell on such topics as ghosts, puppies, weird mail, creepy visitors, and the slaughter of '15-stone porker' Heathcliffe. 'We haven't seen people leaping into bed with one another because it would be a nightmare,' Philiy had told the *Observer*, managing a level of spin to put the Lion gang to shame. 'You are not going to risk getting into something that could just fall apart. We have to live with one another.' 'The closest anyone has come to scandal,' reported *The Times*, 'was Sheila Jowers, who recalled walking into the pod of Trevor Kearon when he was naked. "I don't know who got the bigger shock," she said.

'No one really believes any of this, of course,' wrote the *Independent*'s reporter, 'and yesterday as the self-selected volunteers chatted to the media, it was clear that there were tensions simmering. While Trevor Kearon, the chirpy scouser from central casting, joked about what a great time he and the others were having, Gordon Carey – the Seventh Day Adventist who disapproves of drinking alcohol – sat looking on, his face sullen and heavy. At another table, Ron Copsey, the trainee psychotherapist from Twickenham, West London, looked equally forlorn. "I've been told by Lion that I'm not to speak to the Press," he explained.'

The Stornoway Jaunt

Even as the Ron/Cassie dispute began to die down, another island saga was hotting up. The concern of the parents and others about the lack of a balanced diet and the most recent incorrect delivery of food had decided two of the castaways to take matters into their own hands. The unlikely partners in crime were Dr Roger Stephenson and Sandy Colbeck, the granny of the island.

'Sandy and I,' Roger wrote when it was all over, 'have just had a wonderful little adventure. A succession of events and coincidences produced the motivation for our escape, and however deeply it divided the community, for us, and I suspect for the television programme, it was a total success. And I still don't know,' he crowed, not unlike a schoolboy who had got one over the headmaster, 'whether Lion know about it.

'Jeremy Mills visited us recently and said, with a twinkle in his eye, he would like us to do "naughty things" as long as we filmed them,' the doctor continued. 'We could then keep the tapes until the end of the project, he said. That set us all thinking, but I never imagined it would produce something like our expedition so soon.

'A few days ago we received notification that the deficit in our most recent food delivery would not be made up until our next supply run, despite being dangerously low on particular vital food supplies. Now this was not just a temporary problem. Time after time supplies have failed to match our orders, particularly in the area of fruit and veg.'

'Next, a meeting to discuss both the failure of our horse and plough and the serious food situation gave Dez and Sandy a mandate to phone Lion urgently and get a food and tractor/rotavator delivery as soon as possible. They succeeded with the latter, but failed with the former.

'So with a succession of Lion/BBC failures it was time to act. Then a series of coincidences made a surgical strike on a Stornoway supermarket possible. Firstly, friends of ours rolled up on Ruari's boat, the Leverburgh guy who spent time building on Taransay – yet again chickens coming home to roost! It was Richard and Sarah, our neighbours in Devon, who had arranged a few hours on the island. Secondly, the crucial phone call, with the news of the food failure, happened two hours prior to our friends' departure from the island. Thirdly, Ruari had to go to Stornoway the following day to swap a friend's car for his own, newly MOTed. Fourthly, Ruari owned a bunkhouse in Leverburgh where we could keep our heads down overnight.

'Sandy, in charge of the stores, and I decided to act to correct the deficit. We loaded a light overnight bag, collected £442 (including a cheque for £170 from Ron) purely for "contraband" and set off to the bothy with cheque book and credit card, ostensibly to say goodbye to Richard and Sarah. Ruari's boat was moored there and the cash was supposed to be given to him for contraband. Clearly we would need a Lion camera for such an operation and we had to persuade someone to let us film it ourselves. There was no time to consult the community properly, and therefore the fewer people who knew the better at this stage.

'It was a glorious day and we had a real sense of escapist adventure as we sped off from beneath the bothy. Of course it could be seen mechanistically as a forty-minute boat ride and a drive to a supermarket, but in the context it was so much more. The oldest person on the island, who fears water, speeding off for a day trip to a supermarket from an island where she was supposed to be incarcerated for a year. The Harris coastline was stunning, with gannets diving over us and seals popping intrigued noses in our direction.'

After forty-five minutes the group arrived in the little port of Leverburgh. After a quick trip to a shop, during which the mutinous pair kept their heads well down, they headed for Ruari's bunkhouse, where they spent a discreet evening with Roger's friends and a touring American cyclist who was kept in the dark about the daredevil island-break. 'It was good to taste so many strange phenomena,' Roger wrote, 'a bath, pasta, cheese, wine, warmth, washing machine, and to cap the list a phone call and an e-mail to friends. I slept terribly. I was very proud of my role in this. It was great for Sandy, and for me, for the television, and I thought, entirely within the spirit of the project. Escape from escapism. More and more the producers have been saying the filming is the most vital part of the project – the television project. That fits with failed food deliveries and we were putting two fingers up to the failures, while paradoxically creating a lovely little storyline.

'At breakfast over the *cafetière* coffee there was exciting talk of cars, MOTs, supermarkets. It was the first time in my life I had been excited by a supermarket. It was transformed from rushed drudgery to a glistening, forbidden treasure trove, full of unimaginable riches.'

On arrival in Stornoway, the escapees ran a couple of errands before hitting their Aladdin's Cave, taking their camera with them. Even if they hadn't been recognised from the television, their supermarket sweep was hardly an inconspicuous outing. 'We tried to persuade the manager to put everything on Lion's bill without success; so wound up paying with our own money, £214. As we left Sandy spotted a garden centre where she added a bag of compost (to placate Peter) and her own addition a garden statue of – a Lion!'

Meanwhile boatman Ruari had switched cars. 'In fact,' wrote Roger, 'for mundane MOT reasons, but it gave the escapade a James Bond touch. A pint of Guinness and a prawn sandwich later, and we were returning to Leverburgh with a car complaining of the weight round every corner and over every bump.

'The pace of our adventure was maintained, after a quick nap on the journey, by Richard and Sarah helping with the transfer from car to boat in freshening weather. We had reached a crucial point. Could we get back tonight and avoid the sort of Press horde that Ray Bowyer had been subjected to? As loading and weather anxiety progressed Ruari delivered the *coup de grace*. He pointed to some large crates on the quay labelled "Stolt". "If you go up there you could get some salmon," he said. A trawler was offloading loads of enormous fish. I was passed around four different people before finding someone – Roddy, I think – willing to phone the boss to ask if I could buy some. A few minutes later and Roddy opened a Stolt box and delivered five huge salmon without the merest suggestion of me having to pay. He wouldn't even take a tenner for a few drinks.

'Just before departure there were a couple of clues to slight anxiety in the boatmen, Ruari and Donald. First they drove off for a final weather forecast and also they took the boat for a little run to test the handling. They were anxious (in their cool way) about the weight in worsening weather. It was wet on the way back, and how happy Sandy was is difficult to judge. I just remember her shielding herself from the oceans of spray with a hood down to her mouth and a survival suit up to her eyes. There was nothing of her to be seen until we reached the relative calm of the only west-facing little bay on Taransay within reasonable distance of home. Here we offloaded our cabbages and contraband and stored it behind a rocky outcrop, covered in a tarpaulin.

'By sheer coincidence, Colin and Patrick were walking past, towards the bothy, hoping to get tobacco off Angus MacKay's shepherd (lambing was imminent). You can therefore guess whether food or drink went home first. The rest remained, covered, till the following day.

'I was thrilled to arrive home, not only because everyone had given us up for the night, but also because Sandy and I had made a great little contribution to the television project and the community. I was therefore surprised, the next morning, to discover unwillingness to join the party to collect the remaining goods. But it was a wonderful scene, when I had got ten of us together; trudging off with empty backpacks to a grey windswept rocky outcrop to find the appropriately grey tarpaulin undisturbed. What did we find? Booze, tobacco, jewellery? Ancient artefacts? No – cabbages, broccoli and oranges and – a model Lion! It was the perfect finish to a wonderful expedition!'

Not all the castaways shared Roger's upbeat view, however. 'When we arrived at the steading,' Mike had written the night before, 'it was obvious there were serious undertones. Roger, who had friends visiting, had gone across with Sandy to get some provisions. He is currently obsessed that his children are about to suffer malnutrition due to a temporary shortfall in green leafy vegetables. As the boat was around he took the opportunity. I don't blame him and in view of what I may be involved in later in the year I am certainly not going to make any adverse comments about it. Some people laughed, some don't care and some are livid. Dez falls into the latter category and this surprised me as he, too, is involved in plans for the same thing as me later this year.' Mike and Dez had been secretly planning to build a raft, with the idea of surprising Liz with a visit to a pub on Harris for her birthday. 'But it transpired,' Mike continued, 'that leaving the island was not what annoyed him. Rather it was the fact that Roger had directly contravened something that was agreed upon in yesterday's emergency food meeting.'

'I think reactions to their action are going to be crucial to me,' a 'lonely' Rosemary had reported that same evening. 'So far I've had a reasonably positive response from people. There's been a mixture of amazement – "My god! They've dared to do that!" – some wholehearted support – "Good on them!" – and admiration. I've not had any direct hostility but I know it's also there. But I feel really, really proud of Roger that he's stood up for what he believes. And I hope most of the community will understand that, although I'm sure some of them won't. It will be a real test of our position in the community and how people see us. It'll also be, for me, quite a test of whether I really want to be part of this community.'

The Blonde Waiting to Get Out

If the trip had been 'escape from escapism' for Roger Stephenson, it had surely been an adventure within an adventure for Sandy Colbeck. She had been one of the keenest to get on the *Castaway* project, having been dreaming about such an enterprise since she was seven. At that impressionable age she had met an emigrant aunt called Jess, who had returned to the cold shores of Blighty just after the war for a one and only visit from her new home Down Under. 'I can remember we had this big party, as a way of welcoming her here,' Sandy recalls, 'and I was just knocked out by this lady. They had originally gone in a boat that took them three months to get to Australia. It was an Immigration Scheme, so if you didn't like it when you got there – tough, you couldn't come back. And that to me was so exciting. My dad said, "She's almost a pioneer." I didn't know what a pioneer was and he said, "Well, the pioneers go to these new places when the explorers have been, and found them." I just said to myself, One day I'm going to do something like her.'

But it had taken her fifty-one years to realise her ambition. She had led a life she describes as 'very conventional', married to a naval instructor near Gosport, who was, she says, 'almost Victorian in his views, he had very fixed ideas on men and women's places – and I wanted partnership.' Then, when they had finally parted in Sandy's thirties, she had stayed in the Portsmouth area, getting a job in a pharmaceuticals company while she finished the rearing of her two children. 'Although I used to think about Aunt Jess and what she'd done, it was always going to be something for the future.'

Her sense of adventure nagged her, though. 'I remember, one year, there was this massive music festival on the Isle of Wight, I could almost have swum across there if I'd wanted to, and I thought, Gor, I wish I could be there.' But even when her children left home in her forties she didn't do anything about her fantasy, returning instead to college on day release and getting an HMC in microbiology. When she was made redundant she took time out and did a City and Guilds course in fashion design, but she still hadn't been any further north than York. Only when she returned to a 'mind-numbingly boring' job as a lab technician did she start to look around. Then she saw the *Castaway* ad. 'And I thought, This is the adventure I've been looking for for fifty years.'

But her early time on the project had proved hard. First she'd been so ill she'd had to join the offshore contingent in the Harris Hotel. Then, once on the island, 'all I can remember about February and March was bad weather. Which affected me quite badly, because it was very grey, there were very strong winds – it was awful, and I couldn't really rise above it. I just kept thinking about what the locals said, which was, "If you can get through February and March, you'll make it through the rest of the year." So I just gritted my teeth and dug my heels in and thought, "It's got to get better" and it did.' One day Sandy got sick of her own depression. 'I started thinking, "God, this is awful. You shouldn't feel like this here. This is what you want to do. This is where you want to be." I looked at myself in the mirror one morning and I thought, My God, everything looks grey, including you. Your hair looks grey, your face looks grey, the sky outside is grey – I'm going to do something about this. I know what I'm going to do, I'm going to lighten my life.' So, with a bit of advice from Trish, Sandy went blonde. 'It's been the turning point for me,' she said. 'I can't believe what a difference it has made. Each time I look in the mirror my face looks smaller and my chin doesn't look so big. It changes my appearance so much, everybody says the same thing. I think this blonde has always been here dying to get out.'

Equal Opportunities

Meanwhile, in the runaway pair's absence, the Ron/Cassie fight had reached its climax at the regular Thursday afternoon community meeting. 'No one wanted to go,' said Monica, 'people just can't face heavy situations. No one wanted to have any involvement with racism, which is what it was all about. So me and Julia had to go round encouraging people to come. Gordon and Cassie weren't even going to come. But we went to them and said, "It's really important. You can't just bury your head in the sand. You're living on this island. Ron's living on this island. We've got to sort it out." '

'It was up to us to hear and resolve,' wrote Mike. 'Mmm, what fun. Gordon just kept on saying that all he wanted to do was leave the island. He says it is not a place for him and his family and that they have never fitted in since they arrived. He says that they feel like outsiders.

'Discussions ensued about the fact that they have been invited to various things like quiz nights. The night for this was even changed so that it did not conflict with their Sabbath but they still did not attend. There are many issues relating to their religion, the fact that Ron is gay, that there is alcohol drunk here and that there has been some soft drug taking.

'An equal opportunities declaration had been drawn up by Monica and Julia and was read out at the meeting. We have all been asked to agree it and sign it so that any future incidents can be dealt with in a prescribed manner. I have no great problem signing it (anything for an easy life) but some people did.'

For Liz, it was 'a brilliant meeting. People really opened up. I think Gordon has felt totally outside the community, for whatever reason, and he's obviously been building things up in his mind, because he hasn't been talking about them and he's felt less and less part of anything. Yesterday was a breakthrough because he finally admitted it.'

'The tension was absolutely palpable,' reported Padraig, 'a lot of people, I suppose, were afraid to speak because sometimes saying something can be more damaging than helpful. But there was even a round of applause when both parties gave a little ground each.'

'The outcome of the evening,' wrote Mike, 'after two and a half hours and a lot of tears all round, was that Ron has been asked to modify his behaviour in front of Cassie and she was asked to apologise for her comments, although I cannot actually recall her doing so. Ron stayed until the end of the meeting and then got up and stormed out. He felt that they had turned the meeting around so that they were seen to be the victims rather than him. He also felt betrayed that he had not had more attention. To me it was about fairness rather than attention but I don't think that is the way that Ron's mind works. He could burn a lot of bridges.

'Gordon has now left the group looking after the chickens, because Ron is in it and Cassie has made it plain that she will not be in the same cooking team as Ron. They have also said that if Ron is teaching drama they do not want their children to be there. It also appears that they have told Yoneh to have nothing to do with Ron, which is very sad for her as she is only five and does not really understand what is going on. In any event Ron disappeared to his room and did not answer the door when someone went up with his dinner.'

'He just got up and walked out,' said Gwyn. 'He looked quite upset and he did look across to me and I think he felt there was more support going to Gordon and Cassie. But I felt that knowing Ron as I hope I do, and his intellect especially, eventually he would see that that was the only way that meeting could have ended. Gordon and Cassie needed that little bit more support than Ron.'

'How could it be resolvable?' Ron asked me later. 'They have views about the very core of my being. In some ways I'm ashamed of myself that I did all the running to make the compromise, and I was the victim, although I hate using that word. I have resentment towards them because they used the race card. Cassie did. She justified her comments by saying I made racist comments, which wasn't true.'

'Nobody bothers Ron until lunchtime the following day,' wrote Julie Lowe, 'when it turns out that either he is very quiet in his pod or he's disappeared off somewhere, presumably to the bothy. The problem with that, is that Angus is over there. He's had a Portaloo and Portakabin delivered by helicopter as he's going to be there for the next few weeks. This is the start of the lambing season and he's got a hundred to do. Ron has an un-sheep-trained old London collie dog that is a certainly not to be trusted around pregnant ewes. Oh dear.'

The Consulting Thing

Meanwhile the Doctor and the Blonde had discovered that their merry trip to the mainland had not (in the final analysis) gone down well with a good number of the castaways. 'This trip caused a great furore on the part of some of the younger ones and myself,' wrote Peter. 'How castaway are we? So we refused to eat any of the frozen rubbish or stale veg they returned with.' 'Why I feel so angry about what Roger and Sandy did,' Tanya told Philiy, in a joint video diary, 'was that I was really looking forward to the point where we were pushed into using our creativity.' 'Exactly,' Philiy agreed. 'There's nettles growing out there. Pretty soon they're going to grow big enough that you can take the young shoots and we can have nettle soup, which is full of iron. I'm sure there's fungi, which will be coming on in the autumn.' 'There's wild carrots around,' agreed Tanya. 'I've seen wild onions as well,' said Philiy. 'I mean *hello*.'

'I was annoyed,' said Ben, in a joint video diary with Toby, 'because everyone was always saying we should make this what we want it to be for ourselves. That was taken away from us by two ambassadors going over and shopping.'

'Yeah,' Toby agreed.

'But when you stand back from it,' Ben added, 'it does seem like a pretty trivial thing.'

'It does, yeah.'

'But for us here, who don't have anything else to talk about, it's pretty big, it's the equivalent of a ... Middle East crisis,' finished Toby.

Mike Laird had been 'arsing around' doing formation barrow pushing with Trevor and Toby when Roger appeared at the gate by the steading. 'He asked all three of us whether we would come up to the bothy to collect all the food and booze that he had brought back. We all flatly refused, which really pissed him off. I wanted nothing to do with it as I was not sure how he had paid for it etc. For all we know Lion could kick Sandy and Roger off for gross misconduct although this is rather unlikely.'

Julie Lowe was, perhaps surprisingly, among the critics. 'Of course they had been recognised,' she wrote. 'All the Press articles are out after our "self-sufficiency seminars". We don't know if the people that recognised them informed the Press, but I can just see the tabloid headlines – "CASTAWAY CO-OP COUP". How stupid do we all look now? We were furious with them. What's the point of even trying to attempt a measure of self-sufficiency let alone advertise this as our *raison d'être* if at the first sign of difficulty we run off to the supermarket? What is the point of all of our efforts to run things as a community if people can just take it into their heads to do something big like this off their own bats without consulting first? I hate having to do the consulting thing – truly, loathe and detest it – but I go along with it because for this year, I'm living in a small society that can only operate if we do it this way.'

Inevitably a meeting was called, though not all attended. Mike and Trevor took the afternoon off. 'No one noticed that we were not working anyway,' wrote Mike, 'as they were all busy in yet another meeting to discuss the rights and wrongs of the trip across to Harris. Even though I was not there I could see the debris falling out of the door in tears. Liz was really upset because Roger had laughed at her. I was outside when she came running out and I gave her a hug until she calmed down. It's very hard to explain how people react to situations here. Liz is a management consultant back home and yet here she seems vulnerable and quite fragile.'

'There were all kinds of fireworks at the meeting,' wrote Julie. 'Roger was totally unrepentant – wouldn't accept the possibility at all that he had over-reacted and didn't give a stuff about the community. Said he'd do the same thing again without consultation and if the community would not accept him and his right to do it – yes, you've guessed it – he'd leave! How many does that mean we've lost this week?! I like Rog in many ways, but sometimes I just want to smack him! How Rosemary stays so sane and lovely, I do not know.'

'Then it was time to face the flak,' wrote Roger. 'Loads of pompous stuff about ruining the integrity of the project and failing to consult the community. I tried hard to explain that of course we didn't consult the community – we would have lost the opportunity if we had. I had expected a little opposition, but I was dumbfounded that half the group could not see the simple humour and escapism in the oldest member of our community braving such an expedition. Sanctimonious, grey, humourless claptrap poured forth from half the group that met to discuss it. And it was split mainly down the lines of those who had young children here and those who didn't.'

'So Roger and Sandy went shopping in Stornoway,' Toby reported, 'without a care of leaks to the Press or going against a community decision. If I was at a meeting and something was decided, however much it annoyed me, if it was a decision made by the majority I'd stick by it. But they went against that and removed some of my castawayness. Now they've brought back lots of lovely food, salmon and veg and this is a problem for me. I could be childish and say, Oh I don't want to eat that or I could be a hypocrite and eat it. I'd rather be childish than a hypocrite, but it's a no-win situation for me. But it's fine, we addressed it quickly in the open, I said what I felt to them and Sandy was fine. We had a good chat and just said, No hard feelings. But Roger was a bit different, he was a lot more stubborn in admitting that he might have upset some people. He's not thinking communally, he's thinking for himself and his family. I can appreciate that his kids must come first. But I just wish he'd talked about it beforehand. Anyway, I shan't be eating the food.'

'He did what Cynthia accused me of doing in the first programmes,' said Dez. 'Going against the community and going off and doing his own thing.'

'So I lived for a week,' wrote Peter, 'on fruit, muesli, bread, pork, lamb, spinach, radish, dried apricots, dates and loads of milk – seems a pretty healthy diet. What is dispiriting is how, after months of lovely bread of the highest quality, they bring back steam baked supermarket hot dog rolls and half those here are excited!! I despair at this type of thing.'

Wind-up merchant Pat was not taking the boycott too seriously. 'We were in the kitchen yesterday,' he confided to the video diary, 'and we cooked the bacon and Peter's wife Sheila came in, asked what we were cooking. We said some quiches with bacon and tuna and she says, "Oh, that's very nice, the bacon isn't what came back from the mainland is it?" I said, "No, no." So Peter queued up with the rest of them and ate it and Toby ate it, so they've all eaten it.' 'I happen to know now,' Sandy reported a fortnight later, 'that both the individuals who took that stance both ate and drank contraband food, which is even sweeter, shall we say?'

When Jeremy Mills had conceived his TV *Lord of the Flies*, could he have anticipated what was going to emerge: instead of a group of children behaving increasingly like adults, a group of adults behaving increasingly like children.

'I heard gossip that a handful of dissenters had "come round",' wrote Roger, 'and I gained reassurance from Rosemary, Sandy, Colin, Julia, Warren, Monica, Gordon, Cassie. But the truth is that Sandy came out of it all rather better than I did. And that's as it should be – it was her expedition, her story. Ultimately, I would not have gone if she hadn't.'

'It was my idea,' admitted the Blonde With Attitude. 'We got to the stage where we had virtually nothing. We hadn't had poultry for nearly a month. We'd got down to just potatoes and the last few onions.' Flour was low; there was no fruit; no salad; no fresh tomatoes; almost no pasta; one sack of rice. 'We have got children here who are growing. We can't afford to do this. The point was made when we came back that there was no consultation. I will accept that. But the chronology of the incident meant that it was impossible. The last information I had by phone was Wednesday morning, and I was told categorically that there would be no boat with food for at least a week. I thought,

"Well, I don't care. From this point on I feel a degree of responsibility for this."'

'Roger got into a whole lot of shit,' commented Ron, 'because he didn't ask the community if he could go. I say "bollocks" to that. It was fantastic for Roger and Sandy. People like Dez and Peter and Toby and Sheila, who have a very concrete and fixed idea of what this project means to them, have to comprehend and understand that that is their definition and it might not be ours. They say it's against the ethos of the project to leave the island. But my belief is that there are as many definitions of the ethos of the project as there are people on the island.

'They came back with some great food that we're really grateful for and haven't had for a long time. A decent piece of strong cheddar. A piece of turkey. Some nice broccoli. It was great and I really admire them. If I hadn't been in the middle of my own controversy I would have gone with them.'

But for the time being this was not an opinion that was being heard, because Ron was indeed away in the bothy, thinking things over. 'Everyone agreed he was best left to his own devices,' wrote Mike.

The others, too, were worn out by the rows. 'Maybe I was naïve,' said Tanya, in her joint diary with Philiy, 'but I never envisioned this level of stress. You know, normally I'm quite mellow. But this is making me slightly hysterical.'

'You go from laughing to crying to chocolate,' agreed the vegetarian.

'You have to turn it to humour, don't you?'

'It's the only way you can survive. I mean like what blew up this afternoon about food. I went to clean the toilets, I've never been so happy cleaning a toilet in all my life. I was singing while cleaning the toilet because I knew what was just literally a metre behind another wall was more stress, more hell, more shouts, more of the same crap and yet I was happier with my loo brush.'

LUSTAWAYS!

One thing Roger and Sandy had failed to notice on their trip to the mainland was an article in Monday's *Daily Mail*. Ray Bowyer had finally sold his story: CONFESSIONS OF A CASTAWAY. *Drink, sexual tensions and petty rivalries – the truth about the BBC's castaway island by the man who fled in disgust.* Criticising the project as 'a shambles from day one' Ray claimed that Lion had 'purposely picked characters who were bound to clash and create friction in order to make good television. I think they forgot that we were human beings.' Other revelations: 'Token gay Ray [sic] Copsey allegedly has a "soft spot" for Taransay's acknowledged heart-throb, Ben Fogle'; 'University lecturer Peter Jowers longs to be "king of the clan"'; 'if any of us complained about the food the production company just sent over another crate of alcohol'; and last but not least, 'romance has blossomed between Irishman Padraig Nallen and 24-year-old student Philly [sic] Page, the dreadlocked vegetarian trapeze artist'. 'I caught them in bed together,' the ex-builder elaborated, 'wrapped in each other's arms, at 3 pm. They are made for each other.'

It was the Easter weekend. Tanya decided to relax. 'On Thursday night,' she reported, 'at the meeting between Ron and Cassie, I had a bit of a funny turn, nearly dropping the camera, so I thought it was time for me to take a couple of days off. So Saturday was my best day here. I've got this little hollow in the rocks, just up around the corner, where you can sit and watch the sunset, so from about four o'clock onwards I just watched the otters play down on the rocks below and read about half a book and did a lot of writing and watched the mountains and the islands and the sunset and paddled in the pools and it was like being seven again. Then on Sunday I went on a big exploration of the island, 'cos I haven't really seen much of it. So I trekked off all round the western section, out past the isthmus and beyond. It's fantastic here, because you can go for a walk and not see anyone. Normally if you go rambling in the countryside you're constantly bumping into people. That's absolutely magical, to feel that sense of freedom that you're the only one for miles around.'

'With Ron at the bothy,' wrote Jules, 'and Roger a.k.a. Mr Negativity – "I can't wait for this year to be over so that I can go home" – keeping a low profile, the sun came out and we had a brilliant time. Me more than most.' Ruari the boatman had brought her a pair of unexpected visitors, who had been staying at a holiday cottage on the neighbouring isle of Scalpay. With them came the ex-stockbroker's first ever shipment of contraband, which she dipped into rather too freely that Saturday afternoon during a barbecue the castaways had decided to have on the beach. 'I don't know what's happened to my alcohol tolerance level,' she wrote, 'but I got pickled very, very quickly. Fortunately I'm a happy, affectionate drunk, and next day when I surfaced around two o'clock, people just looked at me and laughed.'

'Jules got horrendously pissed at the barbecue,' wrote Mike. 'She couldn't sit up straight, was laughing hysterically, snogged Toby and even had a cigarette. The seals were close in to see what was going on, the waters were fantastically clear and turquoise and all the children were enjoying themselves. A great time was had by all.'

As well as Ruari, there was a boatload of Harris builders who also, surprise, surprise, had brought some booze. 'So a few people got a little bit tiddly on that,' reported Ben. 'They stayed till five or six, begging me every other minute, "Ben, get your shirt off, we can make loads of money." ' The heart throb had cooked up a plan with pranksters Pat and Col. As they got in their boat to go, Ben would strip, but the two men would jump in front of him and obscure the view. But Ben had underestimated Pat, who 'did a double trick and jumped away'. Not content with that, the wind-up merchant had a much better hoax up his sleeve. Having headed off in Ruari's boat with Roger, his family and assorted rucksacks to pick up the final bits of food from the Stornoway trip, Pat had returned alone, on foot. 'Something very strange has happened,' he told Ben. 'Roger just turned to me and said, "Patrick would you mind getting out of the boat please?"'

'So, of course,' said Ben, 'I put two and two together and made twenty and shouted, "They've gone! Oh my God, they've just left – what are we going to do?" So I was running around, picked up a camera, started filming everyone, asking them what they thought, and of course it was one of Patrick's pranks. Which I still fall for, hook, line and sinker every time.'

On Easter Sunday the children had an Easter egg hunt and spent the rest of the day, wrote Mike, 'gorging themselves on chocolate and squabbling'. Ben, off for an early Sunday walk with Inca, ran into Ron, returning from the bothy. 'I just didn't know what to say. We managed to talk for about half an hour without mentioning anyone's name in the community, without talking about *Castaway 2000*, we literally did some small talk, about mink, birds, dogs, what he'd eaten, the weather. I got the impression that he didn't want to talk about anything that had gone on. So he walked back here and he closed himself off. He blanked lots of people. A lot of people were a bit hurt, because of the effort they'd put in to try and resolve the Cassie and Ron situation. And his response to that was, "You obviously aren't on my side."'

Julia Corrigan served him lunch that day. 'I wasn't properly on conversational terms with him,' she reported. 'It was "Hello" and "Do you want some more salmon?" or "D'you want roast potatoes?" but there was an atmosphere between us and after that session I suddenly developed a horrible feeling of nausea and tiredness. Utter exhaustion just washed over me. On the second day of feeling ill like that, in the afternoon Ron and I had a chat and I was able to tell him how I felt about the various things that had happened and how he'd gone off without speaking to us and how we'd been so upset about the whole thing. Miraculously I recovered by the evening and was as right as rain.'

'He had the attitude,' said Liz, ' "It's me that's hurt. I'm the victim here." He wanted sides, and you can't do that.'

'I think Roger is the only person he's speaking to,' Toby reported. 'He didn't tell anyone when he got back and I think he's having a very hard time. But when Ron first came to this island, he was in my room, he just sat there and said, "Toby, there are some people on this island that I will be friends with and some I won't be all year. Now I like to see our friendship as a little present I can unwrap later in the year." Which basically means "I don't want to be your friend," which was fine by me, but he must be miserable now because he's alienated himself from everyone. And you know, when you've said something like that to me, Ron, I'm not going to try and help you out, mate.'

Meanwhile, the first of the new batch of programmes had gone out nationwide, taking the story from Millennium Eve up to Ray's departure at the end of March. *The People*, picking up on Ray's revelation about Padraig and Philiy in the *Mail*, had a celebratory central page spread. LUSTAWAYS! read the headline. *First romance for TV Castaways as veggie former trapeze artist Philiy romps in bed with meat-munching Padraig who hasn't had a girl in years.* 'She fell under Padraig's spell as he sang her Irish folk songs and played her haunting tunes on his penny whistle,' wrote the inventive hacks, who had managed to bulk out their story by tracking down a former college pal in Dublin, mum Maura, former flatmates of Philiy in Manchester and the spokeswoman for the trapeze school she had attended in Rochdale, as well as some usefully anonymous Tarbert locals who had noticed the pair looking 'comfortable together'. The *News of the World* had a similar piece of rubbish.

To coincide with the latest batch of programmes, the BBC had launched an official *Castaway* website. On its first two days, Easter Sunday and Monday, it was to receive 2 million hits. 46,000 e-mails followed.

Chapter 13

The Big Picture

'At this moment,' said Toby to Ben on Easter Tuesday evening, 'we're sat here while all across Britain *Castaway 2000* is being screened.' 'Which is really, really, really strange,' said Ben. ''Cos it's like our parents and families and friends are all finding out a version of what's gone on here.' 'And they'll have our letters,' said Toby, 'and they'll be reading those beforehand and matching it up to what happens ...' 'And in my case,' laughed Ben, 'suddenly realising what did happen ...'

'Although we don't know what's in the programmes,' said Rosemary Stephenson, in a joint diary with Ron later that week, 'we know they're going out and there's a sort of feeling that everybody is being exposed to the nation and you've no idea what they're seeing – or thinking about you.' She and Roger had talked to the coastguards that morning on the satellite phone. 'We said, "Did you see the programmes?" And he said, "Yes." We said, "What did you think?" There was a pause and he said, "Interesting" and you're left thinking, My God, what do they think of us?' There had as yet been no feedback through letters or press cuttings. But a remark made by Terry Wogan on his morning show had been heard on the communal radio in the kitchen. 'It was something,' said Ron, 'about "that narky doctor" and "Who'd want to be his patient?" If Roger's patients know him just a little bit they're going to think that's so funny because I think people would be lucky to have Roger as their doctor.'

A New Beginning

After the dramas of the previous fortnight the controversial gay castaway was feeling altogether better about things. Indeed, that very morning he'd had something of an epiphany. 'I'd just finished working with the chickens and cleaning them out and feeding them and watering them and I was walking across the steading field and I saw one of the sheep. Well, I thought she was in distress or she was ill, 'cos a lot of the sheep here have fluke or some other dreadful disease and anytime you go walking over the island you see sheep on their knees they're so weak. The next time you see them they're dead and their eyes have been pecked out by the birds and their guts have been ripped out by the mink. Anyway, it wasn't a sheep dying, it was just about to give birth. I suppose to farmers and people who see it all the time it's just another everyday occurrence at this time of year. But to see this beautiful animal pop out and the mother's instant and natural and organic love and attention, and within minutes of being born to see the little thing struggling to its feet and wobbling around like Bambi, was just so moving. I know it may sound really pathetic, but for me that was more symbolic of a new beginning and a new start than New Year's Eve. I just love that little lamb, because its birth gave me a sense of why perhaps I'm here.'

Ron wasn't the only castaway male to be affected by the new births. 'The lambing has just started,' reported slaughterman Colin Corrigan, 'and it's really weird because I'm the man who goes round killing the animals for people to eat. And if there's a problem with one of the animals, people come to me and I either put them out of their misery or give them advice about what I think is wrong. But tonight I was having my dinner in the steading when Gordon came up to me and said one of the ewes was ready to give birth and had been struggling away for three hours. In the back of my head I remembered that in one of the books I'd read it said you should leave them for an hour and then try and give them a hand. So I left my dinner and went up to the MacKay House and looked at this ewe that was trying to give birth. There was a little nose peeping out and I put my hand in and pulled the lamb out and it just lay there on the floor. I thought it was dead. Then I gave it a real good slap and breathed down its mouth and gave it another slap and pulled away some mucus from its mouth and it got up and had a waggle. It was really great to actually give a bit of life on the island rather than take it away. Found it quite emotional. I think there's a few people here who may look on me as being good old Col, who can shoot anything, can't feel anything, and I tend to put up a bit of a barrier about that. I don't know what to say – I'm beginning to question lots of different values.'

'Suddenly,' said Julia, 'we've got a great change in Colin, who's questioning everything about being the butcher on the island. He's intending to make a collar for the lamb he delivered so he doesn't accidentally pick it out and kill it by mistake. But I don't think that'll happen because it's so tame already, it follows Philiy and Padraig around constantly wagging its tail.'

'His mum's not very well,' Philiy reported of her new charge, 'and we're trying to get some milk out of her to feed him but he's having cow's milk at the moment. The kids have named him Scraggy and I've been bottle feeding him. He's just had his second dinner. He's been wandering around following me everywhere, so I guess I'm his new mum, which means I have to get up every two hours and feed him. I think he's all right, but I wonder if he might have a bit of brain damage and not be as quick as the other sheep.'

'This is a new beginning,' Ron reiterated to Rosemary in their joint video diary. 'That little lamb might survive or it might die and my presence on the island might survive or it might die. You know, I've put my crate together and threatened to leave a few times because I've never quite known what I'm doing here.' But despite his new-found enthusiasm for the project, even Ron's closest supporters were now getting fed up with the psychotherapist's endless changes of heart. Apart from everything else, reported Julia Corrigan, it was affecting her daughter Natasha. 'Children do pick up on the anxieties that are floating about. The other day she came into the pod and said, "Why's that crate up outside the pod?" And Ron had actually been nailing it together ready to pack it. I couldn't lie to her, I had to tell her. She's already been overhearing people saying that Ron was going or not going – and she adores Ron. She's been very emotional for two days now.'

Having returned from the bothy and re-established relations with his core circle of friends, Ron had recovered his equanimity enough to write a letter to the Careys about the events of the previous week.

Dear Gordon and Cassie,

I've been thinking about our recent events and I still feed sad and unresolved about them. Mostly I feel that as the two minority groups on the island we have not been particularly understanding, tolerant or kind to each other over the past few weeks. I worry what message this will send out to people watching the programme. We have been partly chosen for this project to represent our minority groups in Britain and perhaps we have a bigger responsibility whether we envisaged this or not. I am frustrated that we do not talk at all and I feel this creates a bad atmosphere and situation for the people who like us both. If we really care about these people then surely it is another good reason to move towards a more positive result to our problems. After a difficult start to this project we managed to overcome our differences and have a friendly association. This gives me confidence that we can do it again if we can put our pride and anger aside and think of the big picture. I guess that any new relationship between us will be different from before and perhaps this is wise. I gather that, like me, you are still considering your position on the island, so perhaps we could talk soon in the hope that we can show that we are bigger than this unfortunate problem. Please let me know if you and Cassie are willing to meet with me in the hope we can salvage something that is a bit more human than we have now.

Yours sincerely, Ron

This had been delivered to the Careys' pod, all of twenty yards away across the rough green grass of the upper settlement. 'Gordon has shown me the letter that Ron has given him,' wrote Mike, 'and I actually think it was rather nice. Strange after all the recent goings on but nice nevertheless. Basically what it said was, "We had a friendship, so let's try and have one again." Ron left it open for Gordon and Cassie to go and speak to him.'

'Gordon came up to me rather aggressively,' Ron explained, 'and said, "I got your letter. I'll find some time to talk to you about it." It was just how he said it – not, "Hello, Ron, thank you for your letter." I nearly said, "If this is the attitude, Gordon, just let's forget it."'

Troubled Eyes

This last was not to the video diary, but to me, as I sat at the psychotherapist's feet in the pod that he characterised, when asked for a description, as 'Small. Claustrophobic. Dingy.' Despite that, it was, with its pink, purple and blue walls and peach ceiling, considerably more colourful than most of the other homelets I'd visited, as I trooped round with my tape-recorder listening to the twenty-eight adult angles on the developing story.

I had arrived on the morning of Thursday 27 April, delayed by a day because of bad weather. Twice on the Wednesday assistant producer Paul Overton and I had driven hopefully down to the little car park in the dunes at Horgabost, only to find Angus MacKay, the tall and taciturn owner of the island, looking out dourly across the turbulent water of the narrow Taransay Strait. No, he told us, with a convincing shake of the head, it wasn't feasible tonight. I for one was not going to try to change his mind, especially when there was a pint of Velvet and a pepper steak back in the warmth of the Harris Hotel. Over supper Paul and I laughed about Harris now having mobile phone coverage: in January the journalists had been fighting to use the one public phone in the lobby of the hotel; now virtually every school kid in Tarbert seemed to be carrying a colourful pay-as-you-go. Afterwards we sat in the TV lounge and watched the seventh programme go out. It was one that Paul had filmed parts of, but had had no hand in editing. A father with two turning-teenage children sat with us. 'Is that all they ever do? Whinge?' he said after watching the bit where Warren and Colin berate Andy McAvoy about the unfinished schoolhouse, a scene that Paul had organised. A little later he got to his feet. 'It's a bit dull, isn't it?' he said as he left his children quietly glued. I'd raised my eyebrows in what I hoped was a sympathetic grimace at Paul. Then he showed me the clipping from the *People* that he was going to have to give Padraig and Philiy the next day. LUSTAWAYS!

The pair were barely aware that Lion knew about their liaison, let alone that they were a centre spread in the tabloids.

In the morning things hadn't looked much better for Angus and the fortnightly supply boat. Our visit was saved by the *Daily Mail*, who had hired a larger inflatable from Tarbert to transport their award-winning animal photographer out to the island for the day to take snaps of the five Taransay puppies who were being given away to lucky *Mail* readers. 'This project gets more surreal by the moment,' Paul said, announcing this news with a grin. Down by the quay an enormous boatman in a wetsuit tied us into our lifejackets and explained that if by any chance we fell in we were to sit tight, 'an' I'll come and get ye'. As we bounced over the alarmingly large rollers at speed, I became the award-winning photographer's new best friend, so keen was I to avoid the thought of what might happen if the tiny craft suddenly flipped over into the icy drink.

Then suddenly you're there again, wading the last few feet through the waves, looking up from the beach to the dunes. A little silhouetted figure way up on the grass sees us and waves. It's Trish. And with her Tanya, who is visibly chubbier and less-kempt, no longer the well-groomed and petite city creature I remember from my last visit, in January, when the whole place was still a mad building site. They both seem slightly stunned and distant, like residents of a mental home, with slightly haunted eyes.

We embrace. I kiss Trish, surprised that she's a real person, not just a face from the screen. To her, of course, I'm a virtual stranger. To me – well, I know more about her private feelings than many of her fellow islanders. Paul and I head up along the fence to the MacKay House to dump our bags. It's such a contrast to my last visit. Then it was the main centre of the island, with Trish cooking away non-stop for the streams of 'pod men', the front room piled up with boots and sleeping bags and mattresses. Now it seems empty and cold. Pushing open the old front room door I find Ron and Rosemary doing a joint video diary. 'We're just saying wonderful things about each other,' says Ron. He grabs me and pulls me, just as I am, with thermal rain hat on, in front of the camera. If I'm going to be seen on screen this is *not* how I want to be pictured. But Ron's got hold of me, is immediately quizzing me about the programmes, what's in them. 'They're good, they're good,' I mumble feebly, aware that Lion will view this footage, looking over at Rosemary, thinking of the portrayal of the Stephensons. 'Am I going to be unhappy again?' asks Ron, and suddenly I'm trying to think why he should have been unhappy last time. Wasn't he portrayed as quite a fun figure?

Down in the steading I find Gwyneth. She, too, has – it seems to me – the same troubled eyes. They've had a hard time over the last two weeks, she says, with the row between Ron and Cassie, 'the worst yet'. I've heard nothing of this, of course. Transcripts of the relevant video diaries won't arrive in London for weeks. I'm stuck in a different time, with lots of leading questions about Ray's departure and the Taransay Five. But things have moved on, of course. They're real people.

I start talking to each individually for up to an hour, in pods that vary from Dez and Liz's, filled almost entirely by the double bed, to Trevor's, which has no decoration at all, is just a bare space to write scripts in. Tanya takes me out to a favourite sheltered spot on the rocks, looking southwest towards Uist. Among other things, I ask her about Valentines. Did she get any unexpected ones? 'How did you know about that?' she asks. Well, Mike's diary is very frank, I say. We laugh.

The *Mail* photographer has long gone. Trish has told him that the puppies are known as the Taransay Five! And when Molly, Merlin, Bruiser, Duke and Ryan appear in the *Mirror* two days after the *Mail*'s CASTAWAY CAST-OFFS, it's under the banner SAVE THE TARANSAY FIVE.

On Friday afternoon the sea has calmed enough for the supply boat to come in. 'Come on Mark, lend a hand,' shouts Pat Murphy, as I stand recording the scene. So I put my camera and notebook down on the rocks and lug bags of animal feed, sacks of mail, and box after box of cauliflowers (do they really need all these cauliflowers?) up the long steep slope from the boat. At last I understand, viscerally, the anger about work. Ron, for example, is nowhere to be seen, while this exhausting unloading process is going on. When I eventually excuse myself from the group effort and head up to the pods, ostensibly to get on with an interview, I find him emerging from his pod, yawning. 'Oh, is the boat here?' he says vaguely. Suddenly I feel like Dez.

Paul leaves on the boat and I stay a second night. I manage to talk to all except Toby, who is in the steading by the time I get to him, grinningly pissed. 'You can interview me now,' he groans, barely able to articulate his words. With the supply boat has come the 'personal allowance' booze, and it's been a long evening. Trevor is on the floor beside him. I've never seen the Scouser silent before. He smiles quietly to himself, way beyond his usual patter of one liners. I wake very early in Ray's old pod with a whisky hangover, creeping out to pee in the dawn, hoping that none of the castaways is yet up to see. I'm praying that by not trekking down to the smelly compost toilets, I'm not about to fall foul of some terrible castaway rule and be reduced to tears at a meeting. As I cross the field to the MacKay House to get my washbag the sheep gather round me, bleating eerily, 'Mark, Mark, Mark, Mark.' Will this be what it's like when I'm turned on by the castaways after some perceived failure of trust further down the line? The chorus of disapproval, the once-welcome author chased to the beach.

When finally I leave on an early boat, it's a blessed relief to be rippling out over the (now) millpond of the Taransay Strait and back to reality, even though it's so breathtakingly gorgeous up here that at any other time you'd want to stay.

Islanders Now

Also on the Friday supply boat, of course, had come the mail, bringing with it not just LUSTAWAYS! but other clippings from the press conference a fortnight before. 'Bit embarrassed really,' Ben told the video diary, 'there were lots of rather big pictures of me. I wasn't supposed to talk to all the journalists, but I did because I was told to by the BBC girls. But I still find it extraordinary – humungoidal pictures of me. But what can I do about it? Nothing.'

Except perhaps stay away from the cameras in the first place. Ben was surprised, he continued, that Ray had sold his story. 'Because in the last post I got a letter from him saying "I promised you I wouldn't". Just before he left I sat with him early one morning outside the schoolhouse, it had snowed all around, and he said, "I'm not going to speak to any of them. I hate the Press. I promise you Ben, I will not jeopardise you or the project or anyone here – I just want to leave." I trusted him. I'm probably slightly too trustworthy a person.' Not, the heart-throb went on, that Ray had revealed any secrets except Philiy and Padraig. 'Which wasn't such a big secret because I didn't understand why it had to be a secret anyway.' Or been desperately rude about anyone. 'I was really flattered he said I was the best of the bunch.' But money talks, I suppose, for a lot of people. Although, Ben went on, he couldn't believe he'd got that much for it. 'It was Page 30 or something. Which makes it even more of a shame really.'

Dez, meanwhile, was particularly taken with one of the selection of e-mails that Paul had brought with him. *One of the most fascinating things* (it read) *that I have seen on all of the programmes so far is the way that people seem to hold onto the ultimate threat, when things go wrong, of leaving the island. Ron has threatened this several times, in fact left at the selection stage, then came back. The Doctor and his family are constantly on the verge of leaving. Ray has gone. Is threatening to leave the community the equivalent of suicide? i.e. those who express such a threat imagine the effect that leaving (dying) would have on the others, i.e. they imagine how the 'others will feel sorry when I've gone' or is it more a way of trying to manipulate people by getting them to feel sorry for you in the here and now, and alter their behaviour to suit yourself. It seems something like that. An adult version of 'I'm not playing any more, but you can try and persuade me' left over from the school playground. How do Castaways feel about this? I believe that when people are really feeling part of a community or committed to it and when they feel safe and accepted for who they are, threats to leave will stop happening. It seems to me that those who express that are expressing something on behalf of the whole group, i.e. that at some deep level the community doesn't yet feel a very safe place and that it is necessary to have the option to leave held in reserve. How can you create some more safety for people? Do you have any regular meetings where people can say how they are feeling? Or do you just wait for these feelings to emerge when they are not containable any more? Finally, why is it that it is the men who are the ones who threaten to leave, rather than the women? Would the women miss the men if they left? Far less aggro I suspect.*

'Very apt actually,' Dez said. 'That is the one that caught my eye.'

Mike Laird had received far fewer letters than he'd expected. 'Everyone came to the conclusion,' he wrote, 'that Angus has probably not been to the Post Office for a while due to the lambing season.' Nonetheless, he had thirty-five replies to write. On the Saturday afternoon he headed over to the computer on the

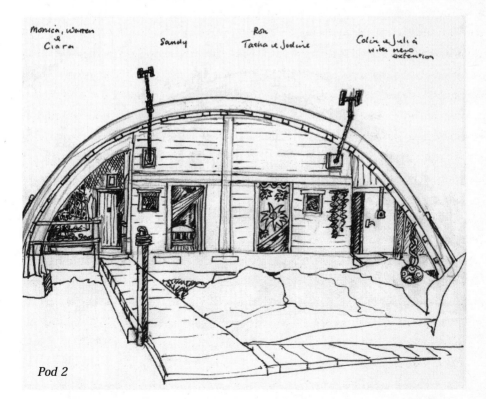

Pod 2

schoolhouse and got stuck in. 'An hour or so later,' he continued, 'I was casually staring out of the window and noticed that there was a small boat about to land. The five guys in it made their way up to the schoolhouse and came in. The first chap through the door put out his hand and said, "Hi Mike". That felt really weird to me but I guess we have lost our anonymity. He did add that he had served me a few pints in Tarbert. I was introduced to his four friends and they all asked if they were welcome here. I said of course, as long as they respected the private areas. They then said they had a load of booze in their boat and that if I helped them carry it in we could all go and have a drink in the steading. There was tons of the stuff.

'Once it was unloaded the pilot went back to Horgabost to get a few more people. They were all playing with their mobiles, which are a brand new distraction for the folk up here. Pat went to get anyone from Pods Three and Four while I went to Pods One and Two. Soon enough there was a large gathering in the steading. They had said they were only going to be here for an hour, but stayed about four and were absolutely cabbaged by the time they left. So were all of us. One thing that they did say was that they intended to bring more people next time and a band. I guess we had better get used to this as it will happen all summer. They had spoken to us all as if they knew us well which was rather weird.'

Padraig knew one of the visitors, Angus McLeod, who ran McLeod's motel in Tarbert. He was the landlord who had hosted the karaoke night at the end of December, and subsequently protected Warren and Monica against prying journalists back in January. 'He's a sound man,' Padraig reported.

Ben had been for a massive walk with Tanya. 'Came back at five, gasping for a cup of tea, walked into the steading, all these strange faces and suddenly I was confronted with this magazine with me on the cover. For surreal days that has to be one of the biggest. Here's us just cracking on with our lives on the island, and then suddenly you're given this magazine with a big picture of me on the cover, saying, EXCLUSIVE – POSH BEN TELLS ALL. Then one of them came up to me,' Ben continued, 'and said, "Gosh, Ben, you're so shy, I thought you were going to be far more extrovert and talkative and everything." I didn't even think I was being shy. Hope I'm not. Well, shy is OK isn't it? But what really brought goosebumps on was when I was saying to them, "D'you still feel that we're all just strangers up here for just the year to get our fifteen minutes of fame and then go off and that's it?" Because there was a time when the locals all thought, Ugh, these Southern softies, coming up here thinking they can make this programme about how harsh it is to live on these islands when we've been doing it for years.

There was a lot of resentment. But now they actually said, "No, no, we genuinely feel like you are islanders now. You are part of the whole big community up here." And I just thought, Oh my gosh, I'm so flattered. I love blending in.

'It was lovely,' Ben concluded, 'to see new faces, but I couldn't help but think this could start the ball rolling as far as people coming over and visiting us now.' As for his picture on the cover of *HEAT*: 'I barely slept last night, just thinking, Oh my gosh, what is going on? There is obviously this big thing tumbling out there. It's snowballing.'

'A rollicking good time was had by all,' said Julia Corrigan. 'Lots of singing, lots of laughter, lots of us asking what the programmes were like, what do people think of us over there and how did we come across? Lots of people did get very drunk. I was leaping around like a wild woman and people were falling all over the place. Pat apparently had to be helped back to his pod because he couldn't walk. And we let down our defences. We were very trusting. They were a nice bunch of people and we trusted them completely, but now we are beginning to wonder at the wisdom of this, because any of them could go and sell their story to the newspapers.'

In his cups, Mike had been speaking to his one-time love object. 'I do remember having a relatively serious conversation with Tanya about the fact that I sent her a Valentine's card but that we don't speak much any more. I wouldn't say we don't speak, just that I tread lightly so as not to offend. The card was obviously not well received and the last thing that poor Tanya needs is to feel uncomfortable with me around. She has made it plain, though, that that is not the case and she wants to put matters to rights. I cannot remember how the conversation started but do think that it had a bit to do with Mark having been across recently.'

Ninety-six Lettuces

As it turned out, my instincts about the number of cauliflowers were right. 'We asked for four cucumbers,' reported chief housekeeper Sandy, 'and we got four boxes of twelve; we asked for six lettuces, we got a hundred.' 'We now have a food surplus,' reported Rosemary, 'which is very ironic since this time last week we were facing a food shortage. We've got 96 lettuces, masses and masses of cauliflowers – I've never seen so many cauliflowers. There's absolutely no way we'll be able to eat them all before they go off. We're not sure what's gone wrong. Again, it seems to be something happening on the mainland – I really don't think it's a problem of our own making. Sandy's been very efficient with her ordering, so somewhere there are crossed wires. One's instinct is to send it all back – is that the best thing to do? Or is it perhaps better to feed it to the pigs here? The most worrying thing is that we're paying for it and it's coming out of our ever-dwindling budget. It makes rather a mockery of trying to manage our finances.'

While the women worried about trivial things like food deliveries, the men had a more urgent preoccupation. Monday was May Day, and they were determined to celebrate the start of summer in style.

Wicker Man Ray

'We allowed ourselves a holiday on 1 May,' wrote Julie Lowe, 'and treated ourselves to a day of festivity. Sandy, Hilary, Sheila and Gwyneth got together and made the girls beautiful May Day dresses out of scrim (white plasterboard fabric). As well as a posh frock, every May Queen needs a crown and suddenly there they were, fashioned of straw and festooned with ribbons and shells. Think Christmas-wreaths-on-doors-type circlets and you'll be very close. If you saw them in Harvey Nicks they'd come with a very hefty price tag! Sheila is hugely talented and wonderfully generous with her gift. Our home would be very dull without her.'

The day, Julie elaborated, had dawned bright and clear. After the surprising heat of Saturday and Sunday, the castaways felt lucky to get a third consecutive day of good weather. 'The sun sparkled on the water, the wind dropped and Roger faced the sea and played his heart out. Careful there Rog, anyone would think to look at you that you're actually beginning to enjoy yourself!' 'People were in shorts and shades,' wrote Mike, 'and others were dressed up (well, as dressed up as we ever get!). All the girls put frocks on and I decided it was time to don my kilt and polished boots. The atmosphere amongst people was so good today.

'Trev and I headed down to the schoolhouse to see the children singing. The piano had been taken outside and it was all going swingingly. Just as the children had finished a dog fight began. As I have done before I bounced in without being concerned by their ferocity. No one else really seems to fancy it. Strange that! This time, though, I paid the price as Clare accidentally bit my hand. One of her canine teeth sank right into my palm whilst several others dragged across the back of it. I am very glad it happened quickly as it bloody well hurt. I hung around for a minute whilst people asked me if I was all right. Funny how people do that when they can plainly see that you are not. I know they were only showing concern but the only person whose advice I wanted was Roger's and he didn't initially notice.'

'The day continued with dancing round the Maypole,' wrote Julie. 'The men were definitely the best – well, the funniest anyway. This was followed by a kind of "primary school sports day" up on the field behind the MacKay House. We had potato and spoon races, wheelbarrow races, sack races and tossing the wellie competitions where all the men tried to show off. Good old fashioned fun. I do realise that one could get very sniffy about it, going "Oh my God I'd rather die" or "Darling, too tediously provincial for words" but if you throw yourself into it wholeheartedly, it's actually great fun. Trish and her team were on kitchen duty that day and provided pretty well non-stop sustenance (pizza) which was fantastic. Our motherless lamb, Scraggy, provided us with more entertainment – his vertical take off when pursued by Floozie is a thing of wonder to behold.'

'The rest of the afternoon was great,' wrote Mike. 'I was slightly miffed that I could not take part in the races because I am trying to rest my ankle and also because of my hand. I spent a fair bit of time with Ron as he was not too bothered in taking part. I did go back for the pig races in the afternoon. Poor old Toby had spent ages setting up a wee race track for them to run round and doing a board displaying their names (Spam, Javelin, Molly's Pride, Carnivores Delight etc) and the odds on each one. Sadly, though, there was no way the little piglets were ever going to do it. They kept on jumping over the perimeter fence or going the wrong way round the course.

'The last event I can recall was dancing round the Maypole. All the children did it in their outfits, which looked really sweet. Then it was the chaps' turn and I think it's fair to say we all felt suitably daft as we pranced around and horsed the whole thing up, but it was a great giggle. Then the girls did a bit and showed us up good and proper. They made it look as though they almost knew what they were doing.'

'It was the sort of May Day I remember as a very young child,' said Tanya, 'when we used to live on a green and the whole village would get together. I think it's what people miss in our individualistic society. It's the idyll that people imagine when they talk about community living, when they get nostalgic for the way we used to live. My feeling was: is one day worth four months of bickering and squabbling and arguments? The answer's no, but things are looking up. Maybe today is the first proper day of the project.'

The evening ended in spectacular, if controversial, fashion (this was Taransay, after all). 'Inspired by the cult film *The Wicker Man*, Warren, Padraig and Colin had built a fifteen foot fertility idol out of straw, facing the mainland. It had started off being Ray,' wrote Julie Lowe, 'complete with beard and pot belly, but was transformed into a pregnant woman when it was pointed out that Ray may be upset if he saw an effigy of himself being burned on telly. We had a visitor that day, a Dr Aitken, whose retirement mission is to visit every inhabited Scottish island, who said that the locals were wondering what on earth we were up to, as from over there our figure looked like a crucifix. This was worrying. The last thing we wanted to do was offend the locals by appearing to burn a cross à la Ku Klux Klan.'

'The only sore point is the wicker man,' Philiy told the video diary. 'Which is a shame. Some are upset by it, think it's a pagan, whatever. To me it's just a big scarecrow and we're going to burn it. Yes, to begin with we were going to burn Ray, but we don't want to do that any more. Ray shouldn't have gone to the papers, but he doesn't deserve to be burnt.'

'We built it,' Colin Corrigan told me later, 'and some people wouldn't come to it, because they didn't know whether it was the right thing to do. Ben walked up and said, "Is it OK to be seen near here? Is it dodgy?" He was being serious. I said, "Ben, make your own mind up. Either look at it and say what a brilliant thing it is or don't bother coming."'

Julie Lowe was not among the doubters. 'As night fell,' her enthusiastic description continued, 'the eerie sound of a heart beat echoed across the water. It's the first time Warren had played his drum and possibly the first time anything like it had been heard on Taransay. As a small robed procession approached the headland, a torch was lit and ceremoniously applied to a long straight pathway, which led to a wide circle surrounding the figure. Unbeknownst to me, this had been impregnated with something flammable, paraffin perhaps. The flame raced along this pathway and around the ring, igniting at its completion a firework, which exploded into the heart of the straw figure, setting it alight. Hugely dramatic. Definitely Pagan. Primeval and slightly menacing. That visual impact of the burning effigy, the smell of the gunpowder, the powerful, vibrating beat of the drum assaulting the night sky, all made an unforgettable start to May 2000.'

But even with the Ray element removed, the ritual did not go down well with all. 'I went to have a look at it,' reported Gwyneth the next day, 'and I really didn't take any offence to it, it was a wicker man and they enjoyed building it. But when it came to the evening part Warren was banging his drum and Padraig was playing his flute and Peter was there with his mad monk cape on, and his guitar, and it really seemed to get to me that it was, as much as they'd dressed it down, a pagan ritual. I was only there a minute; they hadn't even lit it when I sensed what it was all about. So I came away very quickly. I got quite upset, actually, at the thought of it being a pagan ritual. That goes against everything I believe in. I just went back to the pod and Patrick came with me and we talked about how I felt. I got the impression that maybe there was a few more people there that felt quite uneasy about it. This morning my first sight was looking across and because it had been burnt it left the structure underneath which was the emblem of a cross. So I just wanted it taken down.'

When Pat had reassured her that the structure was to be dismantled after lunch, Gwyneth had gone off for a walk with Inca, up into the now-green interior of Taransay, to think about why she had been affected so deeply. She spoke to the video diary later: 'There's Gordon and Cassie here,' she told the video diary later, 'who have a deep religious belief and, apart from their Sabbath, they don't impose it on anybody. Myself and Patrick, we're both Catholic, and we have our own quiet belief in what we think is right and wrong and we wouldn't impose that on anybody, either. We do it quietly in our own way. I go off to a little place each day and say a little prayer. I usually talk to Our Lady. I say a few Hail Marys. Most of the time it's for us all here and our loved ones at home.

'Then on my walk I started to think about what May Day meant to me, and I related back to when I was a little girl, and it was all to do with the crowning of Our Lady in church. When I got back they'd taken the structure down, so I went and said a few Hail Marys and sang a little song we used to sing at the crowning.

Oh Mary we crown thee with blossoms today
Queen of the angels and queen of the May

'Apparently Gwyn didn't agree with it,' said Julia Corrigan, 'and had turned up with a candle and said she thought it was dreadful because it was pagan – this was some kind of affront to her Christian beliefs. I have to say I disagree with that completely. It was just a bit of fun. We didn't have incantations, it wasn't witchcraft, we didn't slaughter animals and offer up burnt offerings, we didn't do anything dodgy. Monica is absolutely right to call it performance art – it was a fantastic display. Gwyneth didn't show her face all of the next day and some people like Padraig and Philiy were quite upset because they said she was very offish with them. It caused an uneasy feeling and a feeling of defiance in the people who had enjoyed the display. We hadn't intended it to be taken in any serious way – it was just meant to be a really uplifting experience. I'm sorry that she was offended, but I can't square it with her dancing round the Maypole somehow.'

'The "pagan symbol",' Colin Corrigan told me later, 'was just a circle with a line and three other lines underneath it.' He chuckled. 'It's the common sign for electricity. They thought it was something pagan to be really scared about, but every one of our pods has probably got four or five of these behind the plugs – that's what's so funny.'

The Growing Season

The fine weather brought new problems for the fridgeless castaways. 'Milk's going off,' reported Ben, 'vegetables are going off quicker. Flies and insects are starting, so midges arrive soon.' 'Now it's back to reality,' Rosemary reported on 2 May, 'and actually there are a few clouds on the horizon because we're now facing, for the first time, a power problem. Our hydro seems to have stopped working, we haven't got enough water to run it and the wind power has stopped as well. Over the weekend there were times when we had no power at all.'

It was a 'power crisis', she went on, and a few priorities were going to have to be thought about. It was only the start of May and water levels were already worryingly low. 'I'm not sure that many people have realised what that means in terms of the growing side of things. We've got to get planting, we're incredibly late on that, and if we don't have enough water to nourish our plants it's going to be critical. And any hope of becoming self-sufficient seems pretty remote.'

The Horticultural Group, when it had first met in mid-February, had comprised Peter, Sheila, Rosemary, Liz, Dez, Hilary, Gwyneth, Philiy and Padraig. Padraig and Philiy's interest, Liz told me, had waned fairly early, and Gwyneth's attendance had been sporadic because she found Peter hard to deal with. Together the group had decided what seed to buy, what area to fence and what to plough. But it was the Gloucestershire lecturer, with years of experience of growing his own vegetables at his communal house in Gloucestershire, who was the Great White Chief of the operation. Now, with the growing season upon them, his input was crucial, as spuds were 'hectically' dug in and seeds planted. For management consultant Liz it was all exciting and new. 'Today's been busy sowing carrots,' she told the video diary midweek, 'working as a group in the field. In fact there were only six of us, but working in a team makes it a really pleasurable activity. We've been turning the earth; the soil is really light and in a stony environment it's wonderful to work with such friable loose soil.'

It was hardly a surprise that Ron was nowhere near the action. 'Today's been potato planting day,' he reported. 'Thank God I've managed to get out of that because I was in the kitchen, but I'll have to do it tomorrow. I can't think of anything more boring than planting potatoes. I'd rather go to Sainsbury's and pick up a bag. I just don't see the point of putting potatoes that are this big into the ground to get potatoes that are this big. I really don't buy into the self-sufficiency angle of the project.'

It was hard to know what angle the psychotherapist did buy into, unless it was the perfecting the art of introspection angle. By the weekend, his and similar attitudes had driven Peter to despair. 'My first real depression,' Peter wrote in a letter to his mother, 'amazingly for me to have none so far. It was about "lost illusions". I always feel that "if only ...", together we could move mountains but then people have different work interests, no capacity for sustained concentration and are generally bone idle, careless and self-centred. Then I find myself sounding censorious to myself, then I think that perhaps I'm just an old puritanical chip off Jankers' block – but I get tired of being "long stop", of having to "pick up", check, think ahead, take responsibility. Hope this doesn't sound arrogant – but even though we were told this was going to be physically demanding, very few are interested in that side (wimps). Anyway, that's the area of depression and the pressure to get crops in etc.'

It wasn't just Ron not taking a full part in the planting. Mike's bitten hand ruled him out of such hard work, he reckoned. In any case, 'there was no way that I was going to go out and do potatoes with Hitler working there. He is forever coming over to people and telling them how he would do it. Well, bugger him, I've had enough. I refuse to work with him, as do many other people. Even Pat and Gwyneth who are so kind, good-natured and forgiving will not work with him. If it weren't for the cameras and publicity I would have told him to fuck off ages ago.'

Memory Days

Despite individual quibbles, in general the community seemed to have followed the weather and settled into a period of relative calm. Trish had started a daily walking regime. 'It's been a week now, since I've been positive about myself and my confidence,' she told her video diary, 'and I've been walking down to the Spit and up the hill, which is quite a climb.' She'd been doing this twice a day: the first day had been easy; the second, not bad; on the third, she'd really, really had to push herself; and then on the fourth she'd suddenly noticed the difference. 'I was actually kind of running up. It was like that scene out of *Rocky*, when he's going up the stairs – well that was me over the lazybeds.'

The biggest issue at the regular Thursday meeting on 4 May was whether Ron, like Julie, should be allowed to reverse an earlier community decision and keep a puppy. 'The total was fifteen in favour (myself included),' reported Mike, 'four against (Roger, Rosemary, Sandy and A.N. Other) and six abstentions including Jules, which is odd in view of the fact that we had to vote for her to keep her puppy. In fact, no, it's not odd as she and Ron don't get on too well at the moment.' Her vote certainly hadn't improved their relationship. 'She knows what it's like to want to keep that puppy,' complained Ron, 'but she abstained from the vote. I think that's pretty selfish.' Trevor couldn't see why the issue had been debated at all; the vote had already been taken. 'The community has to work as a whole,' he said, 'not as a person. Once a decision has been made we should stick to it.'

The meeting had been interrupted, Mike reported, by several phone calls from Lion. The newspapers had got hold of the story of Roger's supermarket sweep and Jeremy was 'not amused'. 'For me,' wrote Roger, 'the most enjoyable aspect of the Stornoway jaunt (apart from actually eating the food) was that we kept it quiet from the Lion top brass for so long. At last Jeremy Mills expressed and felt a little of the anger that he had been provoking in me at times over the last few months. Three weeks after the event he phoned me, incensed more, I suspect, by the fact that he hadn't known than by the event itself. He slammed down the phone on me saying, "I'm thinking about what action we are going to take." I understand that he and Colin Cameron wanted me – and therefore, I assume, Rosemary, Oliver, Felix and Sandy – off the project.'

Friday 5 May brought yet more visitors: two archaeologists, plus Mike from the Uist 2000 Project and James, a ranger from the Scottish Countryside Association. 'Every "burrocrat" (Burroughs) around finds an excuse to inspect us,' wrote Peter. 'We disarm them with cups of tea, witty and intelligent conversation, at the same time we learn more about this area and islands – Sheila is often our "ambassador" on these occasions.'

After lunch, James the ranger had given the castaways a talk on Taransay and its surrounding islands, speaking on everything from the size of the Hebridean Bumble Bee to his memories of the days when you would walk to a neighbour's house carrying a lump of burning peat as a torch. When you arrived, you added it to the fire, and when you left, you took another peat with you. Those were the times, he added, when a fisherman would expect to find three or four lobsters in one creel. Now, due to overfishing, you could lift eight creels before finding a lobster.

'Such a wonderful man,' enthused Philiy. 'He looked at Scraggy and thought he was wonderful and wanted to take him home. He gave me a lambing diary and a bit of information – more than I've got from Angus or anyone else. We've got no books, I didn't know what we should be doing. I've never looked after sheep in all my life. I just feel like we're in the dark half the time and I don't want to be doing something wrong that is going to hurt those animals.'

The boat had also brought a caschrom, or foot-plough, that Peter had ordered. Roger had been experimenting with the bent-handled spade-type device on a lazy bed he planned to cultivate, 'when James appeared to point out that I was in fact digging up a peat bog! I had stumbled ignorantly on next winter's fuel supply!'

On the Thursday Toby and Trevor had taken off up the island on a camping expedition. 'If I'm honest,' wrote Mike, 'I am saddened by the fact that they didn't even ask me. They are entitled to whatever time they want without me, but I just found it odd.' By Friday evening the Action Man had realised that another camping party had headed off without inviting him along – Liz, Dez, Trish, Tammy, Jodene and Wee Mike. He was reduced on Friday night to having a drink with Hilary, Sheila and – good God – Peter. 'I do find it odd that I'm invited there,' he observed, 'because I spend so much time disagreeing with Peter. I have my suspicions that he actually rather relishes it and likes the banter. Tonight he commented on my good relationships with people here, which was flattering. As he is blessed with a fair bit of the grey matter (and I am not talking about his beard) he tends to scare people off as they feel they cannot take him on mentally. Ben was there, too, and the evening was spent once again discussing all that has been going on recently: the fact that we have sold our souls and there is nothing we can do about what they do with the footage; the fact that Trev is upset about the trailer showing him swearing his head off; Ben's disapproval of the T5 flag; and the fact that the arrival of Lion and Cynthia has been cleverly planned for Thursday, as that is when the first post-programme mail arrives.'

By the following evening, Saturday 6 May, poor Mike had been abandoned. 'It was dinner time when I left the school house and being the weekend everyone had eaten in groups. No dinner was kept for me and no one offered. The four remaining youngsters who were left here (Ben, Tanya, Philiy and Padraig) had dinner together on their balcony. It didn't make me feel too special. So much for community spirit.' He was saved from total solitude only by Hilary, who came round to his pod with a present, the first of a series of shelves she was making. 'She also brought a can of Guinness for each of us so we sat and chatted till bedtime.'

'Me, Ben, Tanya and Padraig had a dinner party on the porch,' Philiy reported the next day. 'It was so lovely and we had music and me and Tanya cooked and we had miso soup and then deep fried tofu on lettuce leaf tops, followed by a Christmas pudding that I'd saved since Christmas and some coffee that I'd brought with me that we ground up. We sat there with the sheep running around under the table and Ben telling wonderful stories about his travels and we were looking out across at the sea and Ben said, "This is what I thought it would be like." Those are memory days, times that you will always remember. There's some really special people here.'

So why hadn't they asked Mike to join them? OK, so he wasn't exactly one of the happening Pod One 'youngsters' – but was there another reason?

Oh the Guilt!

The start of the next week brought a huge surprise, and an explanation – of one mystery at least. Aillie, the horse that had been so useless at ploughing, suddenly gave birth. 'We were sent,' wrote Julie Lowe, 'what we thought was a strong working horse. Sadly, she has not been a great success due to being too small and not nearly strong enough to plough or carry great loads. We have tried really hard to work with her – I mean, really, really hard – never having the slightest inkling that she was pregnant. Oh the guilt! At the crack of dawn one morning there was a banging on Trish's door (next to mine), which was the early milking crew coming to inform her that Aillie had just produced! The foal is beautiful and both mother and son are in excellent health. Perhaps we should call it Leo!' (Julie, at least, had been keeping in touch with events in the outside world). 'No, the children want to be the ones to name him, but have decided amongst themselves, that to do this they "need a meeting to discuss the relevant issues"! Oh dear, what are we inflicting on these kids?'

'It was so unexpected and beautiful – rather like this whole enterprise, which seems to lurch from one ridiculous event to another,' wrote Peter. 'That poor horse,' said Philiy. 'I felt awful because she's been trying to steal the cows' food and I've been pushing her away and calling her greedy and we put her on a diet because we thought she was so fat.'

Padraig was indignant. 'We've got a foal out there,' he told the video diary, 'from a mother who's been pregnant for eleven months, which I believe is the gestation period of a horse. Which means she was more than halfway gone by the time she got here. There was no way we could ever do any proper work with a pregnant horse. It's not fair on us. We've received the horse in good faith. And we've done our best with her. And she's been no good at all. Now it becomes clear why. So we've basically been supporting the horse from February till now to no avail.'

Another, more private, mystery was solved that evening. 'Whilst at Toby's for a chat with him, Ben and Tammy,' Mike wrote, 'the subject of my diary came up. It ended with me saying "I can write what I want" and Tammy saying something snappy and slightly rude and storming out. Tuesday lunchtime Tammy came up to me to explain herself from the night before. The long and the short would seem to be that Mark (the book's author) asked them (the youngsters) all some leading questions in his interviews and they have concluded that the info leak came from me because I keep such a detailed diary. They have not yet considered what others have said to him, written to him, put in their diaries or said on video diary, which he also gets to see. The crunch point, apart from concluding that I have conveyed all this info, is that they now feel they cannot talk openly in front of me. What this effectively means is that they no longer trust me, which pisses me right off.

'I thought that the censoring side of things would have been done in more depth (see Cynthia) and I would also have hoped that Mark would have used a lot more tact (kick his arse). I do not need all the shit and might just as well write "I got up, had lunch and went to bed." There are many others that write nothing and I'll bet they get their royalties.'

'Everyone started getting agitated and fidgety,' Tammy was to tell me later. 'Saying: "What's he writing?" So as a friend I took Mike to one side and said, "Mike, I have to tell you this, but a lot of us are thinking, What can we tell you? If you tell us something really deeply personal that's got nothing to do with the project, are you writing it down, is Mark seeing it, is it going to go in the book?" I hugged him at the end and repeated that I'd told him this as a friend, but he didn't speak to me for days.'

As it happened, in this instance, poor Mike had been victimised unfairly. Though I perhaps shouldn't have discussed his Valentine's card with Tanya, the 'leading questions' that I had asked Ben and Tammy about their relationship at CAT and afterwards (which is what Tammy was concerned about) had hardly been prompted just by Mike's diary. Though not spoken about to the participants, the affair was known about, not just by myself and Cynthia, but at all levels of Lion. Even acquaintances and strangers I had met and discussed the programmes with in London had asked what had happened to 'that pair' who seemed to be getting on so well at the end of the first programme. Tammy's body language had unfortunately given away her secret, long before Mike or anyone else confirmed it.

In any case, as ever on Taransay, things were already moving on: 'Tammy's a great girl,' reported Toby in a video diary, 'and I've been spending time with her. Go on, speculate on that! Everyone here bloody well is!'

Named and Shamed

The grumblers didn't have to wait long before they would be able to address their off-screen masters face to face, both about the pregnant horse and the erratic food ordering. On Wednesday, 'a glorious morning', Chris Kelly appeared with project psychologist Cynthia McVey. 'Whenever they arrive,' complained Peter in a letter, 'all hell seems to break loose as Roger and Ron get their paranoias fed.' This time it was the Stornoway jaunt that was rumoured to be on the agenda. 'Lion are livid!!! Apparently the "Beeb" even more so,' wrote Peter. 'It looks very much as though Chris will be giving us a talk following Roger and Sandy's trip,' wrote Mike. 'There are also rumours that they are likely to stop contraband. This will be a big blow to many.'

This time the rumours turned out to be true. A Stornoway local had shopped Sandy and Roger to the press and a story had duly appeared in the Scottish *Sunday Post*. It was only a single column under the small headline, SHOPPING TRIP FOR CASTAWAY DOC. But the leaving of the island by the ever-difficult doctor had seriously got Lion's goat. 'We had a very heavy session in the MacKay House kitchen,' wrote Rosemary. 'Chris accused us of wanting to live in suburbia, of not being cut out for this, of deliberately trying to undermine the project. We explained the real reasons for the trip: the repeated failure of Lion to sort out food supplies and our genuine concern that our kids would not be guaranteed a decent diet. I am quite sure now there was no deliberate manipulation of food supplies. Of course, Chris knew nothing of all this and did take it all on board and toned down his criticism. He was genuinely apologetic for his heavy-handedness. I had got very upset and left the room in tears. I'm so fed up with being accused/portrayed as somehow inadequate simply because we have the guts to speak out and take action to make things happen.'

Another story had also reached the papers. The visit of the group from the MacLeod motel in Tarbert had been reported in lurid terms in the previous weekend's Scottish *Sunday Mail*. Under the headline ISLAND INVADERS, readers of the rag had been told of a 'mob of drunken revellers' who 'stripped naked and hurled abuse at TV's Castaway's stars in an early morning raid on the docu-soap island'. As Padraig was to point out, the report was 'ridiculous, absolute lies, bullshit'. There had been no abuse and no stripping, unless you counted one of the gang removing his jeans to wade into the sea to bring his boat in. 'They were very welcome, very nice people and we really enjoyed their company.' It was to lead to much anger on Harris, and a letter to the *Stornoway Gazette* from the MacLeods, putting their side and saying they wouldn't visit the island again because they didn't want to be subjected to this sort of gutter press treatment.

On Thursday 11 May the mail and supply boat followed, bringing with it Callum, an officer from the Scottish Society for Protection of Cruelty to Animals (SSPCA) to remove the puppies. 'The SSPCA man,' wrote Julie Lowe, 'was the best possible person for the job. Their departure was a huge wrench for Jodene, she was terribly upset, although aware that it had to happen and that it was the best thing for them.' Ron took time off his kitchen duties to bid the little darlings farewell and, Mike reported, 'there was a good deal of sadness and tears'. Though not, of course, from Roger.

That evening (even as the famous pups flew, courtesy of British Airways, first class into a media frenzy in Glasgow, where over two thousand people had offered them new homes) Chris addressed the gathered community. 'He made a big thing of the parcels that keep coming,' wrote Julie. 'It's always something – they can never leave well alone! The parcels were piled stage centre and the names and addressees were called out. Needless to say, my name came up a couple of times. After we'd been "named and shamed" and roundly chastised, waggy finger and all, he tried to discourage us from taking possession of our gifts. The implication was that we were greedy and avaricious and a wounding disappointment to him.'

'They handed out the parcels,' wrote Mike in his diary, 'whilst the camera was rolling. Lion want us to go back to basics and what they think the project is all about. Chris did say something along the lines of the fact that they have not used certain footage that they could have. This to me was both him giving us a chance and also putting the frighteners on. If we don't play ball then we will be hung out to dry on TV as a 'can't do without'. I have no intention of that happening to me and shall write to all my friends and family asking that they stop sending chocolate and booze. I think that it will split the community to a degree.'

This was not of course quite how the producer saw his appeal. 'We had got to the stage,' he told me later, 'where we couldn't tell them – nor should we be telling them – how to live. We would always insist on the rules being observed – even though they were clearly transgressing them – and ultimately whatever happened we would put in the programmes. If they wanted to be seen throwing away this opportunity, then we would show that, but not gladly, sadly. We tried to appeal to their better nature, which of course went in and out of the ears of some of them.'

'I do find it bizarre,' Julie protested in her letter, 'that he can select a bunch of adventurous, independent mavericks and yet not understand that he can't wind us up and expect us to go like obedient little robots in exactly the direction he points us. It seems that he has very clear pre-conceived ideas of how he wanted the year to go, and is unhappy that it isn't working out according to his plan. He tried to manipulate me by working on my fear of looking ridiculous. He said that people would say about me, that you can take the girl out of the home counties, but you can't take the home counties out of the girl. People would think less of me because I'm not entering into the proper "Castaway experience", because I don't want to forbid people to send me little jiffy bag luxuries, such as chocolate bars, conditioner sachets, Earl Grey teabags and little packets of dog chews for Floozie. Chris's strategy didn't work in this instance because: I don't think being a home counties girl is so very terrible; I think that whatever castaway experience I am having is going to be unique to me and therefore not to be compared to anyone else's; and given that we're all hand-picked stereotypes, purpose built to appeal to different categories of viewer, I don't think behaving true to type is necessarily a problem.'

When Chris had finished, psychologist Cynthia got to her feet. 'I asked,' she wrote in her notes later, 'how many reckoned they had more parcels than they thought they would have when they arrived and many put their hands up. I also mentioned the idea behind the project that all would be equal and that this was evidently not the case as some could afford to buy litres of gin and so forth and others did not have that kind of money at their disposal to spend on contraband.' The 'What is a castaway?' issue was discussed at length. 'It seemed a pity to act like schoolmasters in laying down rules for children and it was interesting to see how they dealt with the situation,' wrote Cynthia. 'Some of the behaviour has been childlike in the not speaking (not playing) type of thing that seems to have gone on. All this was supposed to be part of the experiment – to see how they sort these things out. Therefore, Chris left it to them to decide what to do about parcels etc. and handed the remaining parcels out. Ron received a very large box from Fortnum and Masons and gleefully carried it away.'

Ron refused to return his gift. 'He said he was going to keep it,' wrote Mike, 'and he didn't care how they portrayed him on TV. Chris said he had more front than Brighton.' Unbeknownst to the producers and castaways the champagne was from a national newspaper editor, an old friend from Ron's journalist days.

It was a shrewd investment, because when Ron did eventually leave and tell his story, it was to the *Mail on Sunday* that he sold it. 'Ron and his cronies proceeded,' Peter wrote, 'to quaff the champagne in full view of the cameras and Lion people. It was like a red rag to a bull.'

Ignorant, Arrogant and Reprehensible

As well as the parcels and newspaper articles, the mail had inevitably brought reaction to the second batch of programmes. Mike was very flattered to receive letters from women he had never met and even the offer of women's underwear. 'It's quite interesting,' Ron told the video diary, 'what friends have to say about various people in the programme. This is what my friend Caroline had to say: *The Stephensons are a pain in the arse, I really don't know why they are there and they don't seem interested in surviving or living as part of the community.* That's not true. The Stephensons are very interested in being here and – especially in the education of the children – they play a vital part. It's a shame that Rosemary and Roger are only being seen as whingeing. *Peter should not be allowed in the kitchen without a hair net or a beard net.* Agreed. *Liz is very impressive and seems hard working and a real member of the community.* Hmm. *Ben and Julie Lowe are so irritatingly cheerful and optimistic and jolly hockey sticks that I want to slap them both in the gob. I really liked Ben in the beginning but his cutesy little boy chats to the camera are wearing very thin, Ben shut up.* We don't ever see these cosy little chats to the camera so all I can say is that sometimes I also want to tell Ben to shut up.'

The castaways' friends were not the only ones to have intense and critical feelings about these people they had never met. In their mailbag Roger and Rosemary had received an upsetting letter, addressed to 'Stephenson and Wife'. *Your behaviour*, it read, *up till this evening's programme has been most reprehensible, incompetent, lazy, arrogant and a complete antithesis of what is the expected behaviour of an English trained doctor. Your performance during the meningitis scare highlights the peril the rest of the community are in if you are both allowed to stay on the island. You're just an ordinary woman and your treatment of the possessions of Mr Laird shows the same traits as your partner. Get out, both of you. Taransay needs and deserves better.*

The cold turkey of the TV high that Roger had talked about all those months before was now truly kicking in. 'I suppose it's the power of television,' he mused, sanguine as ever, it seemed, about his public image, 'but a few little tiny snippets of our existence here are blown up into such an almighty sense of disgust, really. I worked out the amount of time that the most avid *Castaway* watcher would have seen of our joint lives here – it is about one four-hundred-and-fiftieth. In fact, we sleep, eat, communicate, talk, laugh, cry, run around, play, teach, learn – all that as well as deal with meningitis scares in arrogant, incompetent, lazy, reprehensible ways.'

Rosemary was more visibly upset by this harsh criticism. 'I've been thinking about what it feels like to have adverse publicity,' she told her video diary. 'Since the programmes have gone out we've received lots of press cuttings and I've had lots of letters from friends, I think really quite upset about the way that Roger and I have been portrayed. They feel quite angry about it. It's very frustrating, because I can't pick up the phone and say to people, "Well actually, this is the full picture."

'At the same time, I do recognise,' she went on, in a fashion more understanding and reasonable than perhaps could have been dreamed of by the writer of the hate mail, 'that in a TV programme it's very hard to show a complete person, and really show the complete picture of any situation. It's better to be more entertaining, to pick up on the more dramatic moments.'

Rosemary wasn't the last to realise that the castaway experience was turning out to be more about surviving contemporary media fame than anything mere Nature could hurl at them.

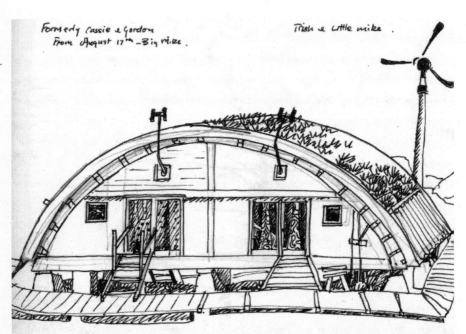

Pod 4

Chapter 14

Death of a Castaway

Even as the mutinous trainee psychotherapist mocked the producer's initiative by guzzling the Fortnum's bubbly, others among the community were reacting to Chris Kelly's message in a rather more proactive fashion. On the Friday evening after his departure, the 'youngsters' from Pod One found themselves sitting around in the steading talking about the aims they'd had when they'd first come on the project. 'We'd lost pretty much all of the principles we thought this project would be founded on community-wise,' said Padraig. 'We thought we'd have to rely on our own inner strength, resourcefulness and tolerance to get by.' The tolerance, he reckoned, was still there, but the way people had been getting anything they wanted sent to them, or delivered by local fishermen, had removed all the resourcefulness and self-sacrifice the project had initially entailed.

After a long discussion, the Pod One group – Tammy, Toby, Tanya, Ben, Padraig and Philiy – decided to make a pact. They would stop receiving parcels, even the compromise jiffy bags; and they would try to encourage the rest of the community to do the same. Padraig was going to write to his sister and tell her to spread the word at home. 'From now on,' he asserted confidently, 'the only alcohol I'll be drinking is home brew and what I get in my birthday parcel. The only fags I'll be smoking are the ones I've already got and when they run out,' – was his will already faltering? – 'well, if anybody wants to give me a fag now and again, maybe I'll smoke it, maybe I won't. But I won't,' he continued decisively, 'accept gifts from people or get parcels. I won't leave the island for any reason. I'm also not going to get any contraband any more. I think it's a pity,' he concluded, 'that we've had to do this in the way we have, but it's the only way to maintain some dignity, because otherwise there's no real point in being here.' Acting on his words, he was going to return the bottle of champagne that Ron had given him the night before.

'Last night was a real watershed,' said Tanya. 'Tammy's saying that today feels like the first day of the project. I can understand where she's coming from.

It's been like a holiday camp here. Everything's been far too easy. Thank goodness there are still seven, eight months left and that we've realised in time. It's going to be a real struggle because idealism doesn't go down well here.'

On the Saturday morning, once Pod One's pact became Taransay news, others in the community declared their support for the idea. 'It seems that we weren't the only people thinking that way,' said Padraig. 'Dez and Liz, Peter and Sheila, Gwyn and Pat – various other people have been thinking along the same lines.'

'This episode,' wrote Peter, in a letter to his mother, 'has led to a real division in the camp between those wishing to stick to the core ethos of this experiment and those who do not seem to give a monkey's. So, Sheila and I have decided – no more parcels please!' The university lecturer's involvement and support was not welcomed by all, however. 'The whole thing went wrong,' Gwyneth told me, 'because Peter came into it, and in my view he used those youngsters. He took over. And then some of them started getting upset about things he was saying and it just went totally wrong.'

'This morning,' reported Tanya on the Saturday, 'once it had become generally known what we'd decided, there was a backlash. It snowballed, everyone talking and discussing and being very forthright.' The camerawoman was immediately worried about her role. 'I should have anticipated it,' she berated herself. 'Suddenly for me the alarm bells started to ring, because I'm a filmmaker here and I'm not supposed to get involved in controversial issues.'

A good half of the castaways were not, Rosemary wrote to me, joining in this 'back to basics' campaign. 'It has come mainly from Pod One and seems to encompass most of Pod Three (Dez and Liz, Peter and Sheila, Hilary, Trevor – not sure where Mike stands). As you can imagine Pod Two, most of Pod Four and us lot across the field are not sharing in this mass repentance from the true Castaway path.'

Ron, meanwhile, had been none too happy about his boomeranging bottles of champagne. When Padraig and Philiy had given back their bottle, Philiy reported, he'd taken it as an insult. 'People have been handing their champagne back to Ron,' wrote Mike. 'I can see why they have done it – to avoid being implicated in its consumption. What they have not reckoned on is the fact that to give back a gift for whatever reason is very hurtful. Personally I would have kept it until the project was over.'

Though they didn't, for obvious post-Supermarket Sweep and pact reasons, take the raft Dez had been secretly building across the strait to the pub in Harris, Liz's birthday party that Saturday night of 13 May was, Mike reported, the best the community had had since the New Year. There were fairy lights, Warren's strobe bicycle light and two CD players. Warren was the DJ. Was this a final fling with their existing contraband before the pact took hold? Dez and Liz 'brought loads to drink as did almost everyone else. Alcohol,' Mike continued, 'is a very important factor here.' 'They made it a disco night,' says Paul Overton, who had stayed on over the weekend. 'They got dressed up in all these clothes, which God knows why they thought they would need in the Outer Hebrides. There was some note about the figures who were missing. Ron again. Roger and Rosemary weren't there. Colin and Julia turned up for a short while.' Peter and Sheila were present, though, and Sheila loved both the dancing, which she'd been missing since she'd been on the island, and the dressing up. 'There's a great need to have some sort of transformation of yourself on these special occasions,' she said, 'and I was thinking next time it would be nice to have a masked party, just so that we could have that feeling of meeting new people.'

Old and New Friends

Sheila wasn't the only one who could have done with some new faces. Not only did Ron's bubbly continue to bounce back from self-depriving pact signatories, his well-established friendship with Roger seemed to have come to an end. This had nothing to do with the champagne, rather because of the meeting on 4 May, where the community had voted in favour of allowing Ron to reverse an earlier community decision and keep puppy Boo Boo. 'The repercussions of keeping that dog,' Ron explained, 'have been that Roger has ignored me for a week and a half. I've said to him, "Can we talk about it?" He said "Yes" but he had conditions. I can't believe that somebody of Roger's intelligence is so overreacting about me keeping a puppy. I know he feels very strongly about dogs and dog mess, but I'm just a bit tired of so much debate and bad feeling about a puppy.'

This withdrawal of friendship had caused Ron to consider who his real supporters on the project were. Julia and Colin Corrigan, in the next-door pod with daughter Natasha, were two of his best chums. 'You probably don't see much of Colin,' he told the viewers. 'He's the butcher and he keeps a fairly low profile really, he's one of the most popular men on the island. He's great friends with Patrick and Gordon and me and Warren, and I don't think you could get men more different than that. We all think a great deal of Colin – he's got a great sense of humour. On top of that he's a great dad and he makes sure he gets valuable time with Natasha,' Ron continued. 'He makes up songs with her and paints with her and tries to create some magic on top of the magic that she's already getting living here on Taransay.

'As a team Colin and Julia are great. Julia, I suppose, is Mother Earth of the island, she's known as Old Mother Corrigan and she's genuinely warm-hearted and she's a great mum and she's real. She can also drink as good as any bloke that I've ever seen. She's very funny when she's had a drink and she's very funny when she's not had a drink. She's also very good with the kids as part of the teaching team.'

Those Ron loved, he loved a lot; they came in for his wholehearted approval and his kindest nicknames. He and Colin had now come up with handles for just about everybody in the community (as the butcher was to explain to me later). Colin himself was Skinner 'for obvious reasons'. Julia, as well as being Old Mother Corrigan, was Bucket-and-Chuck-it, because she was head of the Poo Committee. Sandy was Smash-and-Grab or The Catalogue Queen, because of the endless demands for tupperware and gadgets she put in with the regular food orders. Warren was Bunny, because of his name; Monica, Hipster, because of the trousers she wore. Rosemary was Field Too Far, because of the position of the MacKay House, way out across the community's big central field. 'She's always up at the house,' Colin elaborated, 'and it's hard to get her across. Roger and her do miss out on a lot of things that happen in pods, like instant parties. It would be nothing for me to walk over and see Murphy and take him a drink, but to walk over to the house, there seems to be this barrier.'

Moving onto the less affectionate monikers:, Roger was Pooper Scooper, 'because he's obsessed with dogs' poo', Tanya was Evil Camera Woman, Ben was Golden Rivet, and Toby was Pig Boy. Padraig was Tin Whistle and Philiy Her Indoors. Because laughed Colin, 'Padrig can never actually do anything without checking with her that it's OK.' Peter was Fat Boy Grim; his wife Arty Farty. Hilary was the Work Bench. Dez and Liz were the Care Bears, 'because they care so much for the community'. Mike was Rambo, Trevor was the Bat, 'because you never see him by day'. In Pod Four, Gordon and Cassie were the Scary Careys, 'because everybody's afraid of them'; Gwyneth was Miss Tea Tree; Pat Murphy Pig Master; Trish Miss Teetotal, 'because she likes a drink'; and Julie Lowe, most endearingly, was Von Trapp on Speed.

The only one Colin didn't mention as having a designation was Ron himself. 'A masterpiece of manoeuvring,' observed Chris Kelly, 'that he, individually, has become responsible for the nicknames for the whole community. Normally nicknames would evolve, you would get your name from the people you were with, but he had sat down and come up with a list, which just encapsulates Ron for me. And of course a lot of them have stuck and a lot are very funny.'

As some of Ron's earlier pals grew fed up with him, he was quick to warm to others he had once not so obviously been bothered about. Rambo Mike was blatantly one such. Another was Miss Teetotal Trish, with whom, at Windermere, he had barely exchanged a word. Looking out of his pod window, he told his video diary, he could see her now, returning from a long walk with her dogs. 'I love Trish,' he said. 'She came here wanting to make the most of it and discover things about herself and to move forward and I suspect to heal some pain. And she's great. I haven't had a cross word with Trish. I've had a few heart-to-hearts with Trish, you always know where you are with her.'

Continuing his friend-inventory (not mentioning Roger and Rosemary for the time being) there was of course Pat and Gwyn of whom the psychotherapist was increasingly fond. 'They're really special people,' said Ron. 'Being around Pat has taught me to hush up and maybe look at something and think, Is it worth it? Is it worth saying anything? Is it worth getting upset about? Pat lives very simply and that really works for him. I look at Pat and I see a man who is happy and content and has a great friend in his wife Gwyn.

'If there was a poll taken then Pat would probably be one of the most popular people on the island. I think that's because he leaves people alone. He realised that he's not perfect and therefore doesn't really expect you to be perfect. That's a great quality. She's a great support to him. She told me the other day they went off to the bothy and they were strolling along on the beach and she was in front of him and she looked around and he had taken all his clothes off and was just running naked through the surf. She said she just stood there giggling. He knows how to enjoy himself, whether it's with a drink or without a drink, ten o'clock in the morning or ten o'clock at night. And sometimes I think he's a bit of a father figure to some of the men on the island, even though he might not be old enough to be their dads.'

As for himself, nearly half a year of community living had convinced him he needed a bigger community. 'There's not enough space. There are times when I'm in the steading or the kitchen when I wish my arms could just extend and push people away. Seeing and hearing the same thirty-odd faces and voices, day in and day out, is a huge lesson in tolerance. I want to be a kinder person. That doesn't mean to say I'm not kind and tolerant, but it's about degrees.'

So he was staying, he'd decided; staying and becoming a more tolerant person.

'Something good has happened for Ron today,' reported Mike on Monday 15 May. 'He has agreed with Cassie to take Aaron for two half-days each week. She has also retracted the racist allegations and said that when she was upset she just said anything that came into her head. I am so glad they are on better terms with each other.'

'As time passed we began to talk,' Nothing had ever come of Ron's reconciliating letter. But he told the video diary. 'Not as we were before and not overly friendly, but with some degree of humanity. I think that's the best we're going to get to.'

Happy Days at Last

With most of the big infrastructure projects now completed, the May days passed contentedly for the castaways. The rolls of wire for the deer fence had been delivered on the Friday boat, and were carried over the weekend to strategic points along the boundary of the large crop field ready to be attached to the already dug-in posts. 'When that's up,' said Sheila, 'it will prevent the deer and sheep from raiding the produce. The deer are already sniffing around, but are sent off by the children (as it is described in stories of life in traditional black houses).'

The field had now been completely rotavated and Peter, Sheila, Hilary, and the rest of the Horticulture Group had been supervising the transplanting of vegetables – tomatoes, cucumbers, aubergines and more – from polytunnel to field. Nineteen rows of new potatoes had been planted, together with peas, beans, carrots, beetroot, parsnip and onions. 'I knew absolutely nothing previously about vegetables,' reported Trish, 'so that's been interesting, learning about that. Been shovelling loads of manure and pig shit as well. Ha! What an exciting task!' In the yard at the back of the steading, Colin, Pat and Gordon had got the last part of the slaughterhouse frame erected and concreted in.

'The weather has been gorgeous,' wrote Julie Lowe, 'warm, sunny, hardly windy at all, and people have all of a sudden started being more laid back, far less sensitive and chippy and are being nicer to each other. What a relief. At last.' 'Taransay life has moved outdoors,' wrote an ecstatic-sounding Roger. 'Early May has glistened and sparkled and warmed our hearts and souls. We did some fantastic hikes and the island seemed to enlarge each time we ventured out. It doesn't look like much on the map, but the terrain makes you work for your joy. Just as Ben Raa has false peaks, teasing you to the top, the island has false headlands, which trick you ever further round its coast.' 'God, I wish I had a girlfriend here,' wrote Mike. 'Not just for the sex, but for all sorts of reasons. To walk with, to share things with, to sit and watch the sun go down, to hold my hand and be warm next to me.'

Even the fortnightly meeting on Thursday 18 May went smoothly. The key issue, about whether organic or cheaper non-organic vegetables should be bought for the community, was eventually settled. 'The outcome,' wrote Mike, 'was that we shall move to seasonal vegetables, buy organic where possible, source them all in the UK and be budget conscious.' Mike's suggestion that fishing be considered 'as a job for the community' was accepted and, much to his delight, he was appointed to lead this new group. 'I have been in and out of the water every two days for the last month and am now quite possessive of the lobster pots,' he wrote. 'I would like the recognition for any success.' Toby even proposed that suntan lotion be paid for out of the capital budget, which was also cheerfully agreed.

There remained only the problem of a potential water shortage. The little loch on the hill behind the MacKay House, which measured twenty of Roger's paces by ten, was running seriously low. If it didn't rain for a week, Liz suggested, the community would have seven to ten days' supply left. There was a long discussion of the extent to which 'grey water' from showers and kitchen could be used to water the polytunnels, before Liz, practical as ever, proposed three options. 1) ignore it; 2) install a pump to get water from the well; 3) get water from an alternative loch. Option 3) was most highly favoured, with the suggestion that the community get on and order the necessary piping and pump – at the cost of £1000 – to enable them to take water from the big loch on the way to the bothy, soon to be nicknamed Loch 'na Budget.

Controlling Influences

The champagne might have come boomeranging back, but for the irreverent psychotherapist that only meant more for him and his best mates to drink. Fuelled up with bubbly, weren't he and Julia Corrigan having a great bitch!

'Tell me,' asked Ron, 'who you think are the most controlling influences in the community? Because some people have said we are. But I don't think we are. I think there's a more subtle enemy within.'

'I think,' said Julia, 'there are people who are attempting to wrest control – essentially there are three people. One of them is Peter. Another is Dez – and Liz. But I think a lot of their ideas have the backing of a number of people here. I'm not sure if that's because people are ... '

'Gullible?' prompted Ron.

'I wasn't going to say that, I don't disagree with a lot of what Peter says, I just don't agree with his way of getting results out of people, which is to kick people's arses and moan at them all the time that they don't work hard enough.'

'Mmm,' Ron agreed.

'And Dez's idea is to run around like a wind-up clockwork toy with his mainspring on serious wrench and expect everyone else to do the same. And Liz is in there controlling in a different way. She's very much this dreadfully level-headed voice of wisdom ...'

'She reminds me of one of those plants ...'

'The Triffid?'

'No, Venus Flytrap,' said Ron. 'What gets me about her is that when the cameras are there she's very sort of together and Miss Middlestream, Miss Middle-of-the-Road, Miss Well-This-Is-The-Scenario. It's all very, what's the word I'm looking for?'

'Reasonable?'

'Reasonable. Amenable. But they don't ever see her flying into the kitchen calling people See You Next Tuesday's. She's flown off the handle at me, at many people, screaming and shouting ...'

'Who else besides you?'

'Jules. Quite a few people. Dez.'

'Dez doesn't count, though. They're living together.'

'No, Dez probably needs more of it.'

'Yeah, he probably deserves it.'

'I tell you what,' opined the psychotherapist, 'I think he is the oppressed one in that relationship. She definitely wears the trousers and she gets him to do her dirty work.'

'Well, I think she is a controller,' agreed Julia. 'She's certainly very good at summing things up and then saying things like, "Well, shall we move that argument on to the ethics committee?" Then everyone's sitting there, desperate to have a vote about the dogs or whatever and she sidelines it into another meeting.'

'Unless it's a decision they want,' said Ron. 'Then they push it through. Did I ever tell you they manipulated and controlled the allocation of the rooms in the pods?'

Now Colin joined the pair, the trio had another glass of the *Mail on Sunday*'s magnificent Moët, and the talk got even looser. 'The only plus point,' said Col, 'about Dez trying to take over the island and run it, is that if he's thinking long term he's going to be dead by the time he's forty. Of a heart attack, probably.'

Another glass of the much-rejected case went down. 'The funny thing tonight,' laughed Ron, 'was Liz saying there were three options about the loch drying up. One: we ignore it. Is that an option? I thought, you silly cow ...'

Julia laughed. 'I think it'd be great if you were at the meeting and you said, "Is that an option, shut the fuck up you silly cow!"'

'I want to.'

'That would be so cool.'

When that laughter had died down, the agenda moved on to another Taransay Five figure of contempt. 'You're turning into Trevor, you are,' said Julia.

'Do I look like the barnacle stuck to the bottom of a boat?' laughed Ron.

Oh, how relaxed they had all become with the Mini-DV cameras that Lion TV – at Tanya's suggestion – had now provided so many of, so that anyone could have one just lying usefully around their pod, ready to pick up and film with whenever, even as they got drunker and less and less discreet, forgetting in their Hebridean isolation that they were in fact performing in front of eight million plus people.

'I think some bonky bonky has been going on recently,' confided Ron. 'Because there's something between …'

'Who?'

'I was sworn to secrecy on this, but I don't care. Toby, Padraig, Philiy …'

'Don't tell the story on camera,' said Julia suddenly.

'Well, all I will say is that there is a secret we have regarding Toby, Padraig, Tammy and Philiy.'

No, it wasn't an orgiastic foursome, just the rumour that Toby and Tammy had now – very discreetly – moved on from snogging and got it together properly. If they had, they certainly didn't want to end up on the centre pages of the *News of the World*. Indeed, their secret remained safe from the wider world until the day before the next series of programmes was screened, Monday 11 September, when the gossip-hounds of the *Daily Mail* finally busted them – under the headline HUG THAT SHOWS ISLAND CASTAWAY HAS DESERTED HER OLD FLAME.

Desperate for Attention

'I'm definitely off the idea of ever having children,' wrote Julie Lowe in her monthly circular to friends at home. 'Oh, I like them well enough in small doses, but to live with full time? No thanks. It's quite a shock for all of us single people to suddenly live with eight kids and it has brought my previously fuzzy attitude towards children into very sharp focus. I see how the different families work, and what leaps out is how much time and attention and unselfish love and care and commitment the children need if they are to be happy, secure and fulfilled. Some of them don't always get it, and it matters. I think I'm too selfish and that I'd resent the constant requirement of emotional output. The children come up to me all the time here and want me to do things with them and while sometimes I'm happy to, other times I really can't be bothered and just want them to leave me alone! Not exactly good parent material.

'Predictably, we've got extremely different styles of parenting here,' she went on, addressing an issue that had also been looming ever larger in the minds of the Taransay parents. 'Some of the children have so much freedom that they are sometimes a bit lost. They don't appear to have much in the way of boundaries – are not sat with at mealtimes or put to bed at night. They are grubby and unkempt, tired and underachieving at school. Others are at least washed and fed but are continually told to go away and to shut up. They're desperate for attention and try and get it from whoever is around. And they can be incredibly loud. Very sad.

'I see and disapprove of various things, but who am I to make a value judgement? I would like to say to certain parents, "For heaven's sake, can't you see your children are confused, sad and exhausted. Listen to them, talk to them, play with them, read to them, value them and for God's sake tuck them into bed before they get so tired they fall over. But I have learnt not to intervene. If there's one thing I'll come away from Taransay knowing, it's that interfering in other people's affairs, no matter how well meaning your intention, causes resentment and nine times out of ten doesn't change anything anyway.'

Mike Laird had been one of those who'd taken on the one-to-one teaching in the school, in his case with Trish's Wee Mike (who seemed to look up to him as some sort of role model). On a practical level he was experiencing the problems Julie and the more productive parents had been worrying about. 'He had not done any of his homework,' he wrote on Monday 15 May, 'was half-asleep and did not concentrate. I put the pressure on with more homework and the threat that if he does not do it then I shall resign the post.' He had spoken to Trish about it, but, 'it is a difficult subject to tackle with any parent because it could be seen as a reflection on her. But I fear that he is too much for Trish to handle and misses the stability that a father would bring.'

But it wasn't Mike who was going to fit into paternal shoes. If anyone, it was his old mucker Trev, who, the community had been noticing, had been spending more and more time in Trish's pod. When I'd visited in April she'd laughed about their close friendship, pointing out the sleeping platform Trev had built for her, the fireplace he was going to brick in for her. 'I came in one day,' she laughed, and all his CDs were in here. I think he thought he was moving in. I said, "On yer bike, Trev."'

Since she'd appeared on TV and in the papers in January, Trish's 'lying, immature, ducker and diver' of a husband in the Isle of Man had been 'desperate' for her, so much so that he'd put his name to an article headlined CAST OFF – BBC WRECKED MY MARRIAGE TO CASTAWAY ISLAND TRICIA. Then he'd been writing her eight-page letters. 'The man is on his knees,' she'd told me in April. 'He just keeps saying, "Please come back, the place is falling apart without you."' But she wasn't interested. She had written back telling him to sign the divorce papers.

On Saturday 20th May, exactly a week after the famous pact, the self-denying Castaways were doubly tempted. First, the Pulteney whiskey company dropped off a case of single malt on Pig Beach. Padraig managed to resist the temptation, and not be too too upset when Ron decided it would be hypocritical of him, after receiving his champagne, not to accept the obvious PR plug. Liz was furious. 'It makes a laughing stock of us here,' she reported.

Then a Coastguard helicopter appeared, and offered the castaways free rides over the island. While Pact member Ben resisted, Tanya gave in. It was 'an absolutely fantastic experience', but it left her feeling dreadfully guilty. 'I'm glad there aren't many mirrors here,' she reported, 'because I'm not sure I could look myself in the eye.'

That night it was Warren's birthday. There was a fire round the back of Pod Two, and while music blared, whiskey was drunk by non-pact members. 'Those who were not invited,' wrote Mike, 'got very annoyed by it all.'

The Castaway Philosophy

Ron and Col were still enjoying their case of champagne – on camera – and had developed their earlier inebriated video diary sequences into a sort of Derek and Clive act, in which they pretended to be two world-weary socialites enjoying a glass of bubbly après-ski. 'I left Colin out on the slopes again,' sighed Ron. 'Nothing you can do about it, either you have it or you don't, it's one of those things, the old skiing. Little drop of Moët, darling?'

'Little bit on the warm side, darling.'

'Well, we are castaways, darling.'

As some tried to restrain themselves and others mocked, hypocrisy was increasingly a charge being bandied around the community. But whatever herbal pleasures he indulged in the privacy of his pod, Peter, like everybody else, had developed his own ethos and was sticking to it. 'I make a distinction,' he told Ben on another joint video diary, 'between stuff that is solicited and commercial – and gifts. I don't mind somebody like the man from Edinburgh University or the fireman or James or Lion coming and bringing something. I think it's pleasant actually and a form of social exchange. It's a very generous-spirited thing and in that case I'm happy to receive it and share it among friends. And the ideological thought-police can fuck off.'

'This place is all about survival of the head,' wrote Mike. 'It is a "head fuck". There is just so much going on and it gets churned over and over and over. Blame is thrown and guilt is felt. I can think of no one here who is one hundred per cent clean of presents, smuggling, contraband, etc. Some people try hard to seem righteous, but they are all tainted in one way or another.'

Swill Tins

Meanwhile, the serious question of the water supply hadn't gone away. 'Can you believe,' wrote Julie Lowe, 'that here on Taransay, which must be one of the coldest, windiest, wettest places in the UK, we have a water shortage? May has been sunny, warm and dry and not only has our brook dried up (causing problems for our free ranging livestock) but the loch supplying all of the settlement's water has shrunk to a mere puddle. The Poo Committee has removed the swill tins from the loos, the twin tub has been Sellotaped shut and we've been warned not to shower more than once a week and advised to do it with a friend where possible! We are desperately trying to cut back on our domestic usage in order to be able to water the crops we have worked so hard to plant. If we can't water them, all our rotavating, deer fencing and hard graft will have been for nothing and we can write off our attempt at self-sufficiency.'

The solution decided upon was to run a new pipe from the huge top loch down to the settlement. But previously a helicopter had dropped sections of pipe into place for them; this time it was going to be a big job.

Ben, who under Warren's expert supervision had taken charge of water, walked up with Trish to 'the puddle' to check out the current supply. 'I'd say we probably still have a week left,' said Trish. But trying to get people to modify their use of water proved difficult. 'Some people take note and others just carry on using it willy-nilly,' said Trish. 'I think the only way those people will find out what it means to have no water is when there *is* no water.'

A Fleece-Lined Coffin

Thursday 25 May brought the fortnightly boat, the mail, and the Lion gang. Chris Kelly was unwell, so there was no official development in the parcels clampdown. When the production team left the following day they took Ron with them. Not that he had changed his mind again and was finally leaving; his elderly dog Charlie had not been right for some time and he was worried. A report came by phone later that the dog might even have a tumour. Becci's weekend and planned house-move was cancelled and Assistant Producer Paul Overton took an overnight ferry to Tarbert.

On the Monday morning the news came through to the island that Charlie had inoperable cancer and was to be put down. Colin and Pat got to work immediately on a coffin for the beloved animal. As for the rest of the community: 'We all concentrated,' wrote Mike, 'on how to cope with Ron.'

At two the school was closed for the day and everyone headed for the beach. 'Why?' asked Peter of Hilary and Sheila, as they analysed in a joint video diary the 'right over-the-top' sequence that followed. The trio were on kitchen duty that day, so didn't directly participate. 'Why d'you think there was so much waiting, what were the motives behind the waiting?'

'Just to be there when he arrives,' said Hilary.

'Is this out of sympathy with Ron or a desire to be on camera or something?'

'It could be a mixture of the two,' said Sheila.

Around five, the boat finally arrived. Peter and his supporting ladies had looked out of the kitchen window and seen people coming up from the beach. 'Ron and Becci,' said Hilary, 'and it was like—'

'A funeral march,' said Sheila.

'With Ron,' Hilary continued, 'bringing Charlie up in the box, with Paul and the camera team following ...'

'I just thought,' said Sheila, 'This is right over-the-top.'

'It was very significant,' Rosemary told me later, 'that Ron brought Charlie back to bury her here, because we'd all assumed he'd just go straight home – would just snap. But he came back saying, "This is my home." That's what's so extraordinary. "You are my friends. I want to bury her here." People were amazed. But at the time, because of the tragedy of the event, people rose to the occasion.'

So the dead dog was carried off the boat by Ron in the vet's cardboard box. Followed by Becci, Paul and a reverent procession of castaways, he then proceeded up through the settlement to his pod. A grave was dug a hundred yards west of the pods just above the stone- and seaweed-strewn beach, while Charlie was laid on a fleece in the coffin that Pat and Colin had made. 'Charlie' read the box on the outside.

'We all stood looking on solemnly while the box was lowered,' wrote Julie Lowe. 'He'd brought a wreath of white flowers, which he put on top of the grave after the turf had been replaced. To my mind it was all rather elaborate and over the top, but it made Ron feel better and isn't that what funerals are for? Poor beggar. I found myself putting my antipathy towards him into the "on-hold box" and was just sorry for him.'

'I did not go to the funeral,' Mike wrote. 'It was relayed to me that Ron said, "All Princess Diana got was a little island in a lake. Charlie has got Taransay."'

After a short and emotional speech that had both castaways and Becci from the production team in tears, the first sod was thrown on the coffin. 'The best fucking friend I ever had,' cried out a distraught Ron.

'Were there a lot of people weeping?' Peter asked Hilary on their video diary.

'Yes, I think that happens. It rubs off and people feel as though they have to be displaying sorrow, like they did with Lady Di.'

In best Taransay style, a party followed. Mike stayed for hours and was 'absolutely ruined' by the time he went to bed. Padraig, despite the pact of a fortnight before, took a drink of whisky. 'There was a bonfire and people were sitting around toasting Charlie's life. I had some of what Ron was offering, even though it was contraband. I decided it wasn't an occasion to be a stickler for principle.'

The only trees on the whole island, growing out of rocky cliff, looking through the spit.

looking up at tree

Chapter 15

Dodgy

A few days later Peter wrote to his mother: 'Last week endless boats began turning up at the bothy. This is the season to be in the Western Isles, dwarling! It seems that Taransay has been added to part of the route of touring vessels – they come from another island, Berneray, to the south of us and go off to St Kilda's, which is sixty miles out, a World Wilderness Centre and host to huge numbers of nesting seabirds. So gwarking at gannets has been entwined with gwarking at *C2000* geeks.

'Ben was out walking the other day, way into the interior of the island, when someone with binoculars came charging out of the hills crying, "There's one! There's one!" And then asked for his autograph – he politely declined. On Tuesday I was out in the field and was just turning to come into lunch when at a far fence I see someone waving and beckoning to me – so I go over and this young man (a bit spotty) says, "We've been touring around and thought it would be a nice gesture if me and my father give you a bottle of whisky." Unthinkingly, I accepted it. I then asked where he was from – Surrey – what did he do – he worked for his father's company – what did they do – oh PR! I should have given the bottle back, but didn't smell a rat.'

Somewhat guiltily, the university lecturer carried the pact-breaking donation up to his pod ...

Two days after Charlie had been laid to rest, on the last day of May, it was Ron's birthday. There was a small gathering of his chums in his pod and the psychotherapist made a speech. 'He said he wanted this to be a new start for him and us and with Lion,' wrote Mike. 'He told how kindly Lion had treated him on Harris. He said, too, that he realised just how special some people here were for having helped him through the toughest day of his life. He was given all sorts of home-made presents and these were scattered around the room but mainly on his desk, which is now a sort of shrine to Charlie. He told me he was going to light all his candles for thirteen nights, one for each year of her life. I had given him thirteen josticks to add to his pyro-tribute.'

Colin had made Ron a wooden boomerang with MOET written on each side, to remind him of his returning champagne; Warren, a birdcage from wire and bone; Tammy, a framed picture of Charlie. Rosemary had gone one better, putting a photograph of Ron and Charlie in a handmade frame covered in seashells. Trish brought him a dish full of winkles she'd caught that morning; Hilary, Philiy, Pat and Gwyneth had all crafted something individual; little Natasha had stuck shells on a stone; Wee Mike had carved a bird Ron described as 'a dove of peace' and Wee Mike as 'a seagull or something'; and the other kids had done birthday cards. Ron may have lost a beloved dog, but he had regained his popularity. Soon there was not enough space in his pod and the party moved to the steading. There was a table laid with nuts, crisps, sausages and cakes, plus an assortment of contraband booze.

'How many of the people,' wrote Mike, 'who attended still had their principles intact at the end of the evening? Few, I suspect.' Padraig certainly hadn't, having taken yet another illegal drink, whisky this time. 'I told myself I wouldn't be doing it again,' he confided to the video diary. Ben, however, had stayed pure. 'I said no to absolutely everything,' he told the minicam. 'I was the only person in the room who did. I sat drinking a cup of tea.'

Ben was being particularly careful about charges of hypocrisy, having been the subject of them over the previous weekend, after Inca had come back limping and collarless from a ramble round the Taransay hinterland. Soon her damaged foot had swollen so much she couldn't walk and Ben had decided that Inca's wound, which could have poisoned her whole system and killed her, constituted an 'animal emergency' and merited finding the requisite four people to give him permission to use the satellite phone. But he couldn't get through to either vet or production team. At this point James the ranger, who had stayed over to spend Saturday on the island, offered the use of his mobile. Poor Ben had agonised over breaking his pact, but Inca's welfare had won out. When Roger had been told about this by the ranger he had accused Ben of hypocrisy. 'He categorised it,' said an upset Ben, 'in the same boat as him going to the mainland, because, he said, he utilised the resources that were available.'

It was in such a climate, where astonishingly petty accusations were being traded around the community, that the celebrated contemporary rock band Dodgy decided to land and treat the castaways to a free concert on the beach.

Why are you living in this way?

'We were just beginning our fortnightly meeting on 1 June,' wrote Julie Lowe, 'when the shout went up, "There's a band turned up on the beach wanting to know if we'd like a few tunes to relieve the boredom." Don't you just know that this is going to cause trouble?'

The castaways abandoned their deliberations and hurried to Pig Beach where they found the band, a manager, and several hangers-on. Ben, amongst others, smelt a rat. 'Perhaps I'm more cynical about these things,' he told the video diary with well-chosen words, 'but I think there's something slightly dodgy about a big band just turning up out of the blue to play you some songs – that's not a natural thing to do. So I couldn't help but see this as another PR exercise.'

While Dodgy waited on the beach in the rainy cold, the castaways reconvened. 'It was decided to leave them on the beach,' wrote Mike, 'while we all went indoors and made a decision. It all seemed rather rude to me. Who the hell do we think we are to go and debate something like this? But that is the way the majority round here seem to work. Yes, I know it's bloody PR, but why don't some people here pull their heads out of their arses and see the sun sometimes.'

'I'm Chairman of the meeting,' wrote Peter. Having brought along his free whiskey planning on a *mea culpa* he now found his intended confession completely upstaged. 'We rush a discussion. It's quite clear that this is a PR stunt! So the "hardliners", as our group know ourselves, vote to have absolutely no dealings with them. 10 are in favour, 8 vote to let them play – madness – 5 abstain, others aren't there – our lot are disgusted. The most vociferous in their favour are, of course, Ron and Trish.'

'I couldn't care less whether the band played or not,' said Trish. 'All I knew was some of the lads were frozen and it had been a really cold day and they were tired and cold and the fact that I offered them tea was questioned. But that's just my motherly instinct.'

'Trish has a lot of care and love inside her for her fellow man,' said her platonic intimate Trevor. 'If more people in the community had that, it'd be a better place to be in.'

'I found the whole situation really difficult and upsetting,' agreed Ron. 'Two of the band members were absolutely gobsmacked by the degree of paranoia on the island. One of them cried. He said, "Why are you here? Why are you living in this way?" And it made me ask myself, Do I want to end up as paranoid as some of the people here?'

'About an hour later,' wrote Peter, 'they announce the band will play at 6.45. More disgust. Then the phone goes. Chris Kelly on the other end. Ben answers and discovers that band have phoned Radio 1 and want to transmit live!' 'Chris was FURIOUS,' wrote Julie Lowe. 'He had just been told that Radio 1 had announced it on air, that they were on a live link up from the *Castaway* Island of Taransay. What the hell did we think we were playing at? Of course this put a different complexion on the matter. What I had thought was a few local lads, turned out to be an invasion force of around fifteen blokes, including sound engineers with big boxes of electronic kit.'

'It's then,' Peter's letter to his mother continued, 'that our lot flip and decide it is time to kick them off – politely. So we zip over to the schoolhouse. I go in and say – sorry – time to go – out – now – and they begin to leave. Thinking there were about three of them, I'm amazed to find there are about twelve people. Some very nice, but the actual band, absolute louts. They had been drinking, had a crate full of beer and whisky. All this in the schoolhouse with Trish fawning all over them – ugh – I know this all sounds judgmental, but the schoolhouse is a very "innocent" space – it felt as if it had been violated. Anyway they eventually left, just as the evening sun began to appear. The whole episode seemed to have crystallised something – it was as if some sort of boil had been lanced. A distinct sense of shame, or contrition, seemed to have appeared. Some form of resolution of the, by now, deep and simmering differences seemed to be hovering into view. A subsequent telephone call from Chris Kelly that evening showed how utterly p.....-off Lion are. He and the mega big cheese Jeremy will turn up on Thursday to read the riot act.'

Most Blatant Acceptance of Gifts

No, it never rained but it poured on the beautiful island of Taransay. The very next evening, Friday 2 June, Tammy, Philiy and Padraig were walking on the beach, when yet another boat appeared. This time it contained familiar faces, the ISLAND INVADERS from MacLeod's Motel in Tarbert. Despite their letter to the *Stornoway Gazette*, they had decided to give their mates on the island a second visit.

The castaways went over and tried to explain. 'Look, you've come at a really bad time,' said Philiy. 'Also we can't accept anything off you.'

Padraig said he'd have one drink in friendship with them and that they were welcome to sit on the beach. Philiy then went up to her pod and got a bottle of her own homebrew, thereby sticking to pact principles. 'I didn't have a drink with them. I sat and drank that and they played guitar and sang and it was really nice. Then it got very cold so we moved into the schoolhouse.'

'Sheila now returns to the pod,' wrote Peter, 'to announce that Toby, Philiy, Padraig and Trevor are on their way down to meet them! Shock, horror – hardliners – our people – socialising with visitors. Only twenty-four hours after the Dodgy episode!'

Once in the schoolhouse, Philiy and Padraig 'were offered and accepted sweets', said a disappointed Sheila. 'This is something we've just talked about, not receiving gifts, and it's the most blatant acceptance of gifts. I thought they were hardliners.'

The pact members had known at the time, Padraig told the video diary later, what a delicate moral situation it was for them. Nonetheless, they had invited the MacLeod gang ashore, and told others in the community that they were there. When the Harris men had landed their booze and after Padraig had had his can of friendship, he'd had another, then another. But it wasn't, he stressed, as if they were encouraging the visitors to make a habit of turning up: 'Basically we conveyed to them the difficulties we're in, as a community, regarding this question of visitors,' Padraig said. 'They said they wouldn't come again and that they'd spread the word in Harris. I just wanted to be able to tell them face to face, because they're sound guys, they're local, and they're not here to abuse us. Unfortunately the drink was almost unavoidable but they know not to come again now.'

Ben, on the other hand, managed to remain true to the agreement. 'They were stepping very lightly when they first came,' he told the video diary, 'so it was never going to be a big issue to say, "Thank you so much for last time, really nice of you to turn up, feel free to visit as much of the island as possible, it's yours really, rather than ours, but we can't have a big party with you."' That, Ben argued gently, would have been the line even before the youngsters' pact; which had been a serious and sober agreement, and one of its *specifics* had been that if MacLeod's people came back the youngsters would, as a group, go to the beach, explain the changed situation, thank them for writing their letter to the *Stornoway Gazette*, and ask them to leave. 'Instead of which,' continued a baffled Ben, 'everyone was running around going, "Gosh, what do we do?"'

So he himself had gone down there, thanked them for everything and then left. 'I was there for about fifteen minutes, then I went up to my pod – it was about ten o'clock. What happened after that is not for me to criticise, but it did go against the agreement, and I know you could argue I went against the beard-growing agreement, but I felt this went slightly deeper, it was more significant, because it's about why we're here.'

'I'm not being holier-than-thou,' said Dez. 'But what I find difficult is that some people, who two weeks ago were openly saying that they wouldn't take things from visitors and have cigarettes or drinks, are now being quite blatantly hypocritical. So you think, Maybe they've got less integrity than Ron, who has said all along, "I will do what I want."' 'A sniff of booze and a bit of company and they gave in,' agreed Peter.

The community was now rife with special pleading and condemnation. 'Some of the people that had partied with the MacLeod boys appeared tired, hung over and aggressively, self-justifyingly, guilty,' wrote Julie Lowe of the next morning. 'Some of the others that hadn't, are angry, deprived and self-righteous.' 'Now there's huge debates,' reported Philiy, 'because we let them into the schoolhouse. There's a lot of self-righteous people muttering that, "I've not ever accepted da da da," when they've accepted bottles of whisky off other visitors before.'

Even as Philiy moved the argument away from facing up to the breaking of the pact, Padraig had found another source to blame for his recidivism: the television overlords who had created the situation where the poor castaways were swamped with all these visitors and so much temptation. 'Now we're surrounded on all sides with people just throwing stuff at us,' he complained. 'It's not easy. It's not what this project's supposed to be about, because there were not meant to be any shows going out *this year*,' he stressed. 'We were meant to be here in isolation and nobody was meant to know about it. But instead the entire world knows about it now and they *want to come*. So what are we *meant to do*? We weren't anticipating having to put up signs round the perimeter fences saying PLEASE RESPECT OUR PRIVACY AND DON'T COME ANY CLOSER. It's thrown a real spanner in the works: by observing us, you destroy us.'

He was entirely right, of course; but it still didn't absolve him. The BBC's decision to show more programmes during the year may have had an affect on the nature of the challenges entirely; but they were still challenges. In this instance, challenges that most of the youngsters had failed. 'Tammy I know is absolutely guilt-ridden,' Ben reported.

'Then,' Ben continued, 'as if nothing else could happen, Hilary came back having found a dying sheep on the beach. This happens all the time, but this one had been attacked. I rushed down to have a look at it and – oh, it was just so sad. It had obviously been brutally attacked by an animal and was still alive and had clearly been suffering for hours. So we got Colin up and he came and put it down. Then there was this whole debate about what could have done this, because the night before Trish had been in the schoolhouse with the MacLeods' people and her dogs were running around outside and this sheep was found outside the schoolhouse. Colin and Warren had seen her dogs in a frenzy and I'll admit it did look like a dog attack.'

Oh dear, oh dear, oh dear – would there ever be peace on Taransay?

What is a Castaway?

Mike Laird had missed all the fun. At Ron's suggestion, he had gone off on the Friday evening to spend a night with the psychotherapist at the bothy. This was an entirely platonic friends outing. While Ron lay in the sun, Mike had tried in vain to catch a fish. Then they walked together to the Natural Arch, 'which Ron loved', then chatted over a meal round the fire. 'It was good to be away from the madness of Loonyville,' Mike reported. 'The place is just so intense and in your face all the time.' The night before, after the Dodgy fiasco, he had seriously contemplated leaving. 'I could not sleep,' he wrote, 'as there was a war going on in my head. I was thinking that I could just as easily leave and save myself all this shit. What would the papers and the BBC PR machine do to me? Would I be another sacrificial lamb like Ray? My guess is I would.'

Certainly the press hadn't lost interest in the island story. The next morning the Scottish and national tabloids were full of the Dodgy incident. TOO DODGY FOR US SAY TV CASTAWAYS was the *Sun* headline; while the next day's Scottish *Sunday Mail* congratulated the castaways on their decision. 'They displayed impeccable taste by throwing this bunch of losers back into the sea.' Other recent pieces had been written about the bothy, which the MacKays had decommissioned for the year for repairs (FURY AS TV CASTAWAYS TAKE OVER BOTHY); the unburied sheep carcasses found littering the island by Stornoway-based photographer Derick Mackenzie (TAPEWORM SCARE IS LATEST THREAT FOR BBC CASTAWAYS); low-flying RAF pilots buzzing the settlement (CASTAWAY ISLE HIT BY A TORNADO); the water shortage (CASTAWAY DROUGHT); and the news that day trips were now being offered to Taransay by Stornoway yachtsman Donald Wilkie (CAST OFF FOR THE ISLAND).

After his night away Mike returned to find the schoolhouse 'trashed' and 'people milling around in moods ranging from grey to black. Few smiles and little talk.' He learnt that Dez and Liz had threatened to leave, 'Because the project was such a farce'. The Careys, Ron and Trish had all told Mike they were thinking of going. 'I have caught wind of the fact Tammy and Peter and Sheila have said the same, but not directly to me,' Mike reported.

Julie was also thinking of home. 'I was upset,' she wrote, 'because it was 3 June, my grandmother's eighty-ninth birthday and I felt I was stuck in this ridiculous TV La La Land, imprisoned in a virtual Alcatraz, with a load of moody, touchy, alcohol-dependent manic depressives, while real life was happening hundreds of miles away. I am missing hugely being able to pick up a phone whenever I want, and being in proper touch. Letters and photographs are good, tapes are even better, but neither are enough. It's that lack of instant, two-way communication and feedback that I find most difficult.' Desperate for some contact, she managed to get the requisite four castaways to agree to her using the 'emergency' phone. 'I think they were quite shocked to see me in such an unusually upset state, because nobody turned me down and I rang home.' But there wasn't anybody in, which was 'gut-wrenchingly disappointing'. 'I had a really lousy day. I seemed to bump into all the other people who were wanting to go home too and we empathised with each other about how awful life was, and queried whether we actually wanted to spend another six months in this madhouse.'

Was this to be the community's nadir? The pervasive unhappiness that had been caused by the recriminations over the Pulteney's Whisky, Dodgy and MacLeods episodes had thrown many into acute bouts of self-analysis. Those who weren't planning to leave were wondering exactly what they were doing there.

Peter was questioning the very concept of *Castaway*. The normal sense of the word, he noted, was to be 'castaway' from society, whereas this project seemed to be standing that idea on its head. 'It seems to be us trying to cast off or castaway the frivolities and trappings of society and that society tenaciously attempting to hold on to us and not let us be fully castaways. So the challenge is increasingly becoming: how much can we forgo and how can we actually arrive at a position where we are castaway? Of course the role of the media and our contradictory position is bizarre. Anybody could say, "What a foolish idea to try and get away and at the same time expose yourself to television."'

'Yesterday,' Ben reported, 'was the first time people realised just how sad I am that this project isn't what I applied for. It's like applying for a job and suddenly finding out that it's a completely and utterly different thing.' Part of the problem lay, he felt, in the community's lack of discipline and structure. None of the rules laid down at the outset had ever been adhered to. There were too many strong characters, who would automatically rebel against any form of discipline. 'When we first got here the mere mention of constitutional rules got the reaction: "Well, no, I don't want to live in a society like that." The way we've evolved is we're now divided into the half that want to stick to rules and the other half that don't. So because we have no rules, we have no one to enforce any rules. We are such a completely democratic community that everyone has to have their liberty and we can't accept that anyone can possibly be wrong.'

Dez was thinking along similar lines. He had made a promise to Jeremy and Chris to stay on the island for the whole year, he told the minicam, and he didn't want to let them down. But, he went on, 'I'm wrestling and Liz has wrestled with her conscience over the last couple of days about our promise to you. We're not going to give up, we are going to stick to it, but it really is quite frustrating. Bearing in mind that you cannot impose rules on a group of people in this environment I honestly think it's time that certain things were done and certain things were said.'

TV Fodder

As they thought further about this strange little society they found themselves living in – democratic, certainly, but equally, anarchic and impotent – many of the castaways began to question precisely what they had let themselves in for. There was nothing, many of them said in their video diaries, uniting them except the fact that they were in a TV programme. And what kind of TV programme was it? 'We don't have anything really pulling us together,' said Julie Lowe, 'other than the one fact that we all applied for this advert. We do not have work ethics in common, we do not have standards of hygiene or cleanliness in common, we do not find the same things funny. And if the TV company is going to come and give us a right old rollicking, it will shake things up, but I don't know what direction it will shake them, it might just trigger a whole load of people saying, "Well, that is really it. I really have nothing to stay for now, so I'm going to go." There are a few of us thinking that perhaps our lives could be better employed than providing television fodder at the cost of being away and so out of contact with our friends and family and the real world.'

'We know this is a TV programme,' said Peter, 'but is it a TV programme with any integrity or is it a TV programme just to see what events and what drama you can get?' Monica had actually written me a short piece on the subject, entitled *The 'reality' of being in a docusoap.* 'It is very difficult to explain,' it read, 'what it really feels like being involved in a TV project of this nature, but as the year hurtles along, careering from one bizarre event to another, and we become increasingly embroiled in a media frenzy, one becomes more and more cynical about the whole damn thing.' Having described the Dodgy and MacLeod mob episodes, she mentioned the latest rumour, 'that the *Sun* newspaper is planning to drop some Page Three girls on the beach to chase Ben – our supposed heart-throb. Not your everyday run-of-the-mill occurrences, are they? One begins to get the feeling that we are just pawns in a game – a media game that we are not familiar with and have no control over. We have entrusted a year of our lives into the hands of a media mogul. Can they be trusted? I sometimes wonder if we've sold our souls to the devil!'

Lion's representative on earth, however, was thoroughly delighted with the way things were going. 'I think the filming's going better and better,' Tanya told the video diary. 'People here are now very open to the cameras and there's an awful lot of filming within the community, i.e. not by me, which is brilliant and exactly what I wanted, people recording each other's experiences as well as me recording them.'

We've Really Got There

Part of the group depression which now seemed to have settled on the castaways had to do, surely, with the fact that the community's infrastructure was now virtually complete. The deer fence was finished and the large field within rotavated and planted with carrots, swedes, turnips, peas, French and dwarf beans, onions, Red Baron and Rjinsburger cabbages, beetroot, parsnips, sprouts, calabrese, celery and cauliflower. In the two main polytunnels were aubergines, tomatoes, cucumbers, lettuces, leeks, runner beans and sweetcorn; the third contained a nascent herb garden: with parsley, coriander, dill, fennel, origano, basil and marjoram. Colin's slaughterhouse was finished; the hen houses were full; the routines for looking after the animals long-established. 'We've worked really hard,' said Dez, 'and we've really got there. The whole thing is pretty much done now. We've just got to wait and hope that things we've put in the ground grow.' He was going to need, he recognised, a new challenge. 'I don't feel there is going to be anything on the island for the rest of the year to really get into, unless it is, I don't know, making wooden fish or whales for the kids.' 'The work's run out,' concluded Trev. 'There's no big jobs to go out, even Dez says it.'

Roger, however, was quietly conceiving a major future project. 'I instigated the first round-Taransay walk last week,' he wrote to me. 'The whole coast in nine hours. I invited Hilary and Dez to come in on it too. A fantastic day – and it has sown a little seed in my mind ...'

Shove it, Peter

Despite (or perhaps because of) the fact that Ron wasn't present, the ethics meeting on the Monday night after the MacLeods debacle – 5 June – was, Ben told his video diary, 'brilliant'. 'We had this big meeting that everybody had been waiting for for ages, when we were going to decide how we would cope with PR stunts, visitors, friends and family visiting, everything really. This came on the back of people like myself admitting how disappointed with the project I am. It was good and I really felt we made some progress, although there were certain people that weren't at the meeting, like Ron, and unfortunately on this island the Ron factor is huge. Every decision we make has to take him into account. We came up with these guidelines, which is more than we've done for the last five months, but we haven't got anything to sanction them because no one wants to kick anyone off the island.'

It was Julia Corrigan who introduced a more incendiary subject. 'I was trying to say, Look, we need a project that can pull us all together, such as May Day, and can we please stop carping on about who does what, because it's affecting the whole atmosphere.' She was talking principally about Peter, whose open criticisms of how little work the other castaways did had been annoying many of them for a long time. 'I know Philiy and Tammy and Toby and most of the younger people feel very upset at the level of criticism they get from him,' Julia went on, 'and it's not just them. He's always asking, "Why is the slaughterhouse taking so long to build?" – well, what's it got to do with him? Colin's been having a fine time building it with other people in bits and pieces, he doesn't kick people's arses, he just has a laugh and gets on with the job.' 'Peter seemed to burn a lot of bridges at this meeting,' wrote Mike. 'He was making various accusations including the fact that the youngsters don't do enough work. The truth of the matter is that they all refuse to work with him because he is such a pain in the ass. Everyone says that if he left the project, the productivity of so many would rise with their morale.'

Warren Latore, sitting to one side of the steading after the main meeting was over, found himself being dragged into the continuing discussion. 'Basically Peter was losing the argument,' he told me. 'And he just turned round and went, "As we're on the subject, you Warren, you didn't clear up that grey pipe next to polytunnel three?" And I just went, "Hold on! No way! I'm just sitting here minding my own business, Peter. And you just turn round and start attacking me." I just went, "Look, Peter, you're an arsehole. I don't care what you say, I'm never going to do what you want. You're not going to be the leader here. If I want to leave anything outside I will."'

The video diaries of the next few days echoed with anti-Peter complaints. 'When I got to the steading,' Mike wrote of the next morning, 'everyone was discussing Pete and the fact that they are disgusted by his continual attacks on people. Ben put up a sign this morning which said, "Ben is working" just to get Pete off his back. Once again Pete was up at 10.20 and once again seven out of the eight youngsters were up before him and working. Wake up and smell the coffee, mate.'

'We were talking yesterday in the meeting that none of us have got a common goal to hold us together,' joked Trevor, 'but I think Peter gives us a common goal: to say, "Shove it, Peter, we're not interested in your attitude."'

The person who had most difficulty with the censorious university lecturer was Lancashire dinner lady Gwyneth Murphy. 'He has Gwyn in tears so often,' Julia reported. 'She can't even finish a sentence and he's jumping down her throat. He's admitted to me it's because she tries to be too nice to everyone and that's not a natural thing to Peter. It irritates the hell out of him and the body language when she speaks up at a meeting – he starts turning his head away, rolling his eyes up to the ceiling, he's so irritated he starts wagging his foot – it's just so obvious. Of course Gwyn picks up on that because she's a very sensitive and lovely woman. She would never do anything to hurt anybody, but he makes her feel worthless.'

'He speaks so badly towards Gwyneth,' agreed Tammy, 'he uses fancy words that he knows she doesn't know. I've had one person do that to me before – not here – and it's horrible. You feel this big when people use their book knowledge to put you down.'

As for Gwyn herself, she still couldn't bring herself to name her tormentor on camera. 'For the first time in all the months I've been here,' she reported, 'somebody actually got to me yesterday to the point where I walked away from it, not because that was the most sensible thing to do, but because if I'd stayed I might have done something I'd have regretted. There's an arrogant, self-opinionated pompousness around here sprinkled with a bit of self-righteousness that is really getting up my nose.'

It was interesting that the island had turned Peter into this hated figure of authority, for back home in the Forest of Dean he had always been very much on the left of things, against traditional right-wing structures of British authority, in a 'very creative community of people who mostly headed for the hills at the end of the sixties and seventies'. At the time Cruise missiles had arrived in this country, he had started the local branch of CND. In the eighties he'd been heavily involved with the world music group WOMAD.

How are the funky fallen! As with Ray before him, the ruthless scrutiny of Taransay was stripping away the layers of myth and self-myth, revealing the fiftysomething intellectual to others and himself in the most unforgiving light. Would Jankers's son survive?

Ants Becoming Butterflies

As Peter's star sank, Ron's rose. Even though he had openly flouted the visitors policy by meeting a gay friend, Paul, at the bothy and then letting him stay over the weekend in his pod room, there was little expressed disapproval. 'I couldn't really care,' wrote Mike. Nor was Ron a slouch in joining the anti-lecturer dynamic. 'I'm increasingly disillusioned with him,' he told Trish in a joint video diary. 'I find him self-righteous, supercilious, pious, condescending, chauvinistic, bigoted, I don't like the man really if I'm honest.' And when was the psychotherapist not honest?

One evening Ron had returned from a walk. 'I went into the steading,' he told the video diary, 'and it was like The Twilight Zone, there was this really awful atmosphere. I sat down and had my dinner, listening to Peter ranting and he said something to Gwen and she ended up in tears again. I just lost it. I stood up and told him what I thought. He gave me some backchat and I said if there weren't women and children in the room, I'd wop my plate in his face full of mashed potato.'

Things were now much better for Ron again. 'It's a really beautiful sunny day,' he told a video diary on 8 June. 'I sat here in my room last night feeling very comfortable and peaceful and happy to be here. Not everybody is feeling that way at the moment. There is a shift happening, a division in the community, between the people that I call the ants who just run from A to B to C to D, busy, busy, busy, doing, doing, doing, and the butterflies who I feel are the more flexible and creative people here. And I think more ants are becoming butterflies and they want this to be more than a work experience, a YTS. I think people like Peter, Dez, Liz, Hilary and Sheila are now in a minority, and they're finding that quite hard. Relinquishing the hold that they've had on the community is proving very difficult for them. People are putting their foot down and, realising that the project is nearly half-way through, they have decided that they must get something of what they came for. I think that's a really positive thing.'

'The only problem,' said eleven-year-old Jodene Prater on 11 June, 'is all this argument about Peter. I'm sorry to say this Peter, but Gwyn and Pat are the bestest people here, they're like a nana and grandad to me – and I love them. And I didn't like the way he made Gwyn cry like that.'

Julia Corrigan was keeping it all in perspective, though. 'It will all come out in the proverbial wash,' she wrote to her friend Sarah in Cheltenham. 'Despite this seeming disharmony there are times when it feels fantastic to be here – in fact, I've never felt any other way. The beauty, the peace, the loneliness! Leaving this place is going to be the hardest thing I ever do.'

Chapter 16

The Rules

The carefully chosen cross-section of society were now almost half-way through their year on the island. Their crops were flourishing, their animals producing, their infrastructure all but complete, and despite individual squabbles and their private complaints to letters and video diaries, they were, by and large, gelling and getting on. Yet still they hadn't worked out an effective form of government that they were all agreed on. Many were starting to question whether they were a genuine community at all, or just unwitting mugs in a preposterous media game. In Glasgow and London, meanwhile, the producers were worried about their creation. Right from the start it had proved to have a horribly unpredictable life of its own. Wild weather had made a difficult project even harder, creating an unwanted late start that had led to a level of press interest in a single programme unprecedented in the history of television. A decision to capitalise on that interest by showing rolling programmes throughout the year had been taken against the wishes and instincts of the programme's producer. That in turn had led to still more interest and a series of stunts that had spawned yet more press. Was the monster running out of control? Both castaways on the island and production team off could hardly be blamed for thinking, *Whatever next?*

On Thursday 8 June the supplies boat was over once again, bringing producer Chris Kelly and hydro-electric expert Hugh Piggott into a community wondering what the official line was going to be on their latest misdemeanours. 'I think they will be swinging a large hammer,' predicted Trevor.

The meeting that evening went pretty much as the Scouser had anticipated. First, the castaways were told about the latest schedule of programmes: three more in September, plus the possibility of live broadcasts on Christmas Day and New Year's Eve. Then there was some discussion of the upcoming Visitors' Week, which was the plan to gather all the visits of castaway families and friends into a single, separate, manageable, indeed filmable, occasion. 'Then we entered the real meat of the evening,' Mike noted afterwards. 'Chris read a final draft of a letter telling us that unless we signed it we would have to leave the project. It went on about the ethos of the project, i.e. that we were to do without the trappings of twenty-first-century life, friends and amenities. The project was to assess what value these had in our lives etc.'

'There was the predictable dissenter,' wrote Julie Lowe, 'noisily digging his heels in and talking lawyers, original contracts, changing of goalposts and the usual persecution mania and no, I'm NOT talking about Roger, who, once you get to know him, is lovely.'

'Ron said that this was in fact an addendum to our contract,' Mike continued, 'and that he would be speaking to his lawyers. Then Roger objected: because it was a draft, not signed and not on headed paper. He rambled on about all sorts of other things. Peter, on the other hand, did what is so typical of him on camera, saying that it was exactly what he thought the project was about and that he would sign it. I shall sign, even though it is not my recollection of what happened at Windermere. I just want a stress-free existence. Not long after this Ron stood up, made a comment to Peter about drug taking and stormed out. This place is one huge fucking teacup and there are plenty of storms in it.' 'Ron came up,' Peter explained to me later, 'and said, "You violate the biggest rule of them all. You smoke drugs!" Fucking hypocrite!'

Ron's leaving was not the end of the stormy meeting. Gordon then protested, Mike reported, that the project had been hijacked, and it was the hardliners who had driven the BBC to it. Gwyneth agreed. 'Whether they have or not,' Mike continued, 'this is something we have to deal with as they are our masters. Like it or lump it. As Chris said they have paid in excess of £380,000 to set this up and given us about £75,000 to spend so they can do pretty well what they want. They protected the image of the programme during the last four episodes but could have been a lot more hardline and really stuck the knife into some people but chose not to. The pressure is now on to claw back some integrity with the advent of more *Big Brother* and *Shipwrecked* programmes.'

'It got to the stage,' Chris Kelly explained to me, as we sat discussing the situation in a Glasgow pizza restaurant a couple of weeks later, 'where the BBC was starting to get some comparative press with *Big Brother* and *Survivor!* – all these other reality genre programmes, and a couple of those newspaper reports were hinting at the fact that maybe they didn't have it as tough as they should on the island, which led to this whole reiteration of the rules. The rules were always no visitors, no parcels and no electronic goods, which have been the main areas of contention between us and them. The BBC said, "Look, these need to be enforced, and we know they're not." So we went in with a document and it was, initially, "Sign this or leave". Of course that was Ron's dream scenario, because he won't do anything under duress or under deadline. That was his big thing. Ninety-nine per cent of the rest of them were all very supportive of it. Even Roger felt the rules were fair and reasonable. Ron went off into this big legal thing about – if the rules were so important why hadn't they been written into our contract? – a typically long and tawdry Castaway incident, but the upshot of it was that Ron was isolated to a degree over this issue of signing the document.'

'The BBC,' wrote Peter to his mother, 'are quite clearly pissed off with all the antics and breaking of the rules – so Chris appears with a letter asking people to sign an agreement. I say outright that I'm prepared to sign! All holy hell breaks loose. Ron is literally inches from my face screaming at me and Gwyneth (Postman Pat's missus, I call her "lavender drawers") starts ranting at me about wanting to kick Ron off and charges out of the meeting!'

'Gwyneth came to me after this meeting on the verge of tears,' says Chris. 'She tells me that she has no problems signing this piece of paper except that she wants to leave the island! I think, Gosh, where did that come from? "Let's take five minutes," I said to her. So she and I went for a walk. We were joined by Pat. Then she basically explained that she thought this initiative of reimposing the rules was only going to create conflict and that she wasn't going to be able to deal with the amount of issues that was going to raise. It was about Peter basically. So we had a summit in the MacKay House: Pat, Gwyn, Roger and Rosemary talking about Peter. They said, "We think Peter's argumentative, patronising, we don't like working with him." In very strong terms Roger made it clear that Peter has made life a misery for him and a lot of other people in the way he speaks down to them and judges them. Pat had by now decided that if his wife left because of another individual it would be very difficult for him to continue living with that individual in the community, so he was feeling that maybe he should leave, too. I said, "Surely you need to speak to Peter about this, first and foremost?" So Rosemary and Pat went over to see him.'

When the meeting had ended, Peter and Sheila had retired to their pod, to chat with alternative energy expert Hugh Piggott, 'a lovely, lovely man'. Happily gandering away about Piggott's recent trip to Peru, windpower and other mellow matters, the trio had been disturbed an hour later by a knock at the door. 'In comes Rosemary and Pat,' Peter's letter continued. 'Could they have a word? Yes. I'm then told that Gwyneth is leaving – because of me. She is obsessed by the way I supposedly speak to her. I interrupt her, talk down to her etc etc. I'm accused of being calm in meetings, of being able to speak, of using long words, of being loquacious, I suppose. I cite in my defence those here who I get on well with. Anyway Ron, ever acute and deviously manipulative, has spent hours cloistered away with Gwyneth prior to all this. So the story, much more protracted than I can indicate here, leads to a very head-on polarisation – but as I say to Rosemary, it's like a wave crashing against 3 billion-year-old gneiss – I'm not too upset – just very cold – I'm not called Petrus for nothing.

'Two days later, after much hot air about lawyers, the letter being a draft, not on headed notepaper, blah, blah, everyone bar Ron is willing to sign it. Chris Kelly departs, due to return the following Thursday. Gwyneth looked like "death warmed up" – she hasn't looked me in the eye since.'

'Peter offered to speak with Gwyneth the next day,' Liz told me, 'but Gwyneth just snubbed him and said she didn't want to talk to him. For three weeks she didn't utter a word to him and he tried to be very friendly and polite with her. She just blanked him.'

For a moment it even looked as if Gwyneth might be leaving right there and then on the Friday boat with the Lion team. Mike was in the kitchen the following morning when Sheila came in and burst into tears, saying that this was the first time she had felt emotional here. 'She said it was effectively blackmail when someone said they were going to leave because of another person,' Mike wrote.

But when the boat arrived just after lunch, carrying fourteen rolls of water pipe for the planned connection to Loch 'na Budget, Gwyn had decided to stay.

Reactions

Despite all this drama, Liz was relieved that things had finally been made clear. Since the very beginning, she told the video diary, certain castaways had gone around saying this or that was never in the rules. And because the BBC and Lion had kept out of it, had even watched while people broke what she had always understood were the rules and not done anything about it, she and the others who cared about the integrity of the project weren't able to act. 'So I'm really relieved,' she said, 'that we've finally got this message from the BBC saying, "Yes, this is what you agreed to." Because I'll tell you I was beginning to think I was going potty.'

Rosemary, like the rest of the families, was less impressed. 'Now we've got the BBC laying down the law,' she told the video diary, 'and I can't see why they're doing it. I'm not convinced this will give them what they want. It's creating a feeling of suspicion in the community.' She felt, she said, like she'd never felt before in her entire life: that she was going to have to be careful what she said. She didn't want to be responsible for someone being victimised and chucked off for the transgression of some rather artificial rule.

In any case, she felt strongly that the whole 'visitors issue' had effectively been sorted out before Chris Kelly's draconian statement. The castaways had come up with guidelines at their ethics meeting the previous Monday and they were ready to tackle the situation. Indeed, on the very morning that the Lion boat had come over, those guidelines had been put into practice when a couple of journalists turned up from the *Daily Mail*, bringing a hamper from Harrods. 'I think a few weeks ago somebody would have rushed out and taken the hamper and the consequences would have been more adverse headlines,' Rosemary continued. 'But we dealt with it really well. Two people went out, talked to them, told them to go away, and within ten minutes the whole issue was sorted. We dealt with it satisfactorily, we were putting our own guidelines into practice.'

For her husband Roger, the crucial issue was not so much the rules themselves, which were 'fair and reasonable', but the fact that under the new arrangement, breaking any one of them would be deemed 'gross misconduct' and therefore a dismissable offence. 'I am not sure of the legality of this,' he said. Sandy Colbeck agreed with him. She particularly disapproved of the 'one strike and you're out' provision. 'None of us liked that,' she told me later. 'And I wasn't prepared to let them trample all over us. Having read the first draft of the letter that came to us, there were a lot of loopholes there. I was convinced there was room for negotiation, so I spent about three days putting something together, then asked people if they would read it. There was a great deal of despondency. To my surprise, the majority didn't think there was any point.'

Ever-influential Julia Corrigan and Monica Cooney, however, were in general agreement with Sandy's stance. 'We went around,' Julia told me, 'saying to people, "We don't think it would be good if Lion controlled this. We think it would be better to set up our own judicial system, however stupid it sounds." First of all people didn't want to talk about it.' But the two women had worked out how to operate in a democracy. 'Monica and I,' Julia confided to me later, 'have got quite good at moving behind the scenes. We've realised that if you go to a meeting and say, "I propose this" there is a big debate and you don't win. Or you only win sometimes. So what we do now is we move around a lot within the community and try and canvass opinion.'

Murphy's Law

The new pipe was just in time, because that very afternoon the water stopped flowing in the system and the castaways were thrown back onto the big green reserve tank just above the steading. Liz and Warren then disconnected the supply from the small loch to stop people taking showers and make them realise the seriousness of the situation. This being Taransay, however, the Island of Absurdity, even as these dramatic measures were taken, the already windy and wet weather turned worse. By the Saturday there was a force eight gale and it was pouring. 'It feels like January,' reported Rosemary. 'I've just spent nearly two hours emptying water baths, filling wheelie bins and buckets and troughs and barrels and anything we can lay our hands on with water because despite the fact that it's been raining a lot in the last few weeks, we have a water crisis, and in order to water the polytunnels we have to gather rainwater. So we're in the absurd situation where we can't have a shower or wash our clothes and yet there's water everywhere.'

'Murphy's Law,' observed Ben wryly. 'If we hadn't bought the piping, we wouldn't have had any rain and we'd be without water. But because we bought the piping, we've had lots and lots of rain.'

'Rain drove us all indoors,' wrote Julia Corrigan to her friend Sarah, 'and the children, bored, dragged each other up and down the steading in cardboard boxes, which makes an infernal racket. You could see some of the adults wincing at the repetitive noise of cardboard on gritty floor and the children's screams of laughter, which seem to get shriller as the day labours on. The rain hammers on the roof of the steading like steel pellets. Outside, a few sheep wander around in the blast looking for shelter. One of them is a thin, scraggy-looking thing in what looks like a ragged fur stole. Actually, it's the remains of its fleece; the rest has moulted away for some mysterious reason. I feel sorry for that poor sheep. It must be freezing.'

Stormy Skies

By Monday 12 June it was an official force eight gale. 'Somebody asked where the sun had gone,' joked Trevor. 'I said that Lion had pinched it. We'll have another meeting about that later tonight.' He was right. Another Ethics session had been convened that evening, this time to try – finally – to develop and implement some sanctions for breaking the newly re-established rules.

'Powerful driving rain and stormy skies,' reported Sheila, 'pretty well reflecting the feeling here in the community. We were re-read the rules for the project, rules which I certainly thought should have been in place all along. Not everybody has accepted the wording but now they've been re-established there is some sense of agreement over them. How they will be implemented is another matter; how we can actually say that certain people should be off the island is very problematic.'

As it turned out, the discipline suggestion put forward (by Julia Corrigan) was one that had originally been mooted way back in January, after Ray's Burns Night extravaganza. The 'three strikes and you're out' proposal was a clear improvement on instant dismissal. Moreover, the idea of policing themselves was more appealing to the castaways than being told what to do by the BBC. It now only remained to work out penalties for misconduct. Monica suggested 'peak-knocking' (spreading the peak of the pyramid of excrement in the compost toilets, a necessary castaway duty, currently the weekly cleaner's responsibility), which reduced Roger, then the meeting, to laughter at the 'Pythonesque' nature of the proposed punishment. Ben pointed out that in the real world the ultimate sanction was prison. Roger brought up his experience on Pitcairn, where the prison he said was 'rusted up', yet they somehow managed to be self-governing. Ron suggested voting one person off per month and the meeting ended inconclusively, with the familiar suggestion of pod meets and a reconvening later.

That night was the worse summer wind the Hebrides had seen in years. The pods 'rolled and rattled', Julie Lowe was unable to sleep, the castaways' cows didn't return to fold, and the newly planted crops were seriously damaged. 'It's absolutely devastating,' reported Rosemary on Tuesday morning, 'everything has been destroyed. I'm sure some of the plants will recover, but it looks like a few have been completely killed. I worked really hard putting out a whole load of tomato plants about a week ago; all now look completely dead. Then a whole row of sweet peas that we planted from seed – we'd planned this amazing avenue of sweet scented flowers – the whole lot have gone. You begin to realise,' she went on, 'why many of the Hebrideans didn't bother; they just grew potatoes, cabbages and crops that could survive such conditions.'

When the cows still hadn't returned in the morning Colin and Pat headed off to fetch the lost beasts and bring them back for milking. Lady was particularly full, Sheila reported, 'busting an udder even'. As for herself, milking over, she was off to prepare some fleeces for dyeing. 'A time has come when, especially after the last few days and the different disagreements we've been through, I feel less motivated to do jobs I would normally consider doing.' She was going to make some cochineal dye and then collect other local materials, like nettles and lichen, for other colours.

Others were also quietly opting out. Rather than sit in the steading listening to 'further debates on BBC issues' Mike had escaped to the schoolhouse to catch up with his diary. But returning from a post-prandial game of cards with Toby, Trev and Tammy ('I kicked her ass') he saw that Ron's light was still on and popped in. The reluctant castaway wasn't doing too well, Mike reported, and saying that he now just wanted to go home. 'He was just like a wee laddie missing his mum. He said he had cried wolf several times before but this time he meant it. It is to do with the BBC letter. He will not sign it and he will not go peacefully. He wants to be forcibly removed from the island for all the coverage that he hopes it will bring. He intends to go to the papers and talk about the injustices of people television and how the participants are exploited.'

Four-part Harmony

By Wednesday 14 June the storm had blown itself out. The sun shone again and an eager gang of castaways came out to lay the newly arrived waterpipe – Mike, Roger, Sheila, Ben, Dez, Liz, Tammy and Jules. They carried the pipe across streams, bogs, fences and walls to reach the natural granite dam that enclosed the hundred-yard-long stretch of water now nicknamed Loch 'na Budget. 'Whenever one of the girls met an obstacle,' Mike wrote, 'they would let go of the pipe increasing the load on the person in front. The guys didn't do this, though, and remained attached to the pipe for the duration. There was very little filming done,' he added, 'and that which there was focused on Ben again.'

'In the afternoon,' he continued, 'we went back to do the last two sections. They were the easiest as they had to be carried the least distance and it was flat ground. As ever, once it became known that the cameras would be around, more people wanted to help. I do think that's unfair to Roger, as he put in so much effort in the morning and the filming doesn't represent that.'

Despite his continuing pernickety attitude to Lion and all its works, Roger's popularity was on the up and up in the community. Wednesday had now become a regular 'choir night' in the schoolhouse, an event increasingly well attended. 'Roger really is in his element,' reported Julie Lowe, 'absolutely loves it and radiates enthusiasm, energy, and positivity. It's infectious and we all come away on a high, which is wonderful. Word that it's fun is getting out and the choir seems to grow by another member every week. We've got a dozen now and who knows how many we'll end up with. It starts off in the schoolhouse at 7.30 and officially finishes at 9.00 except that it hasn't yet! We then leave the schoolhouse and come down to the steading, make tea and then keep going around the fire. I love it. If only we could enjoy working in big groups with each other in the same way that we enjoy singing together perhaps we could make a community.'

'I think it's really taking off,' Roger wrote to me. 'I start each session with a "barn-stormer" that everyone can sing in unison. Then rounds – the easiest way to start singing in harmony without quite realising it. Finally we attempt "Silent Night" in four-part harmony. It's incredibly impressive how people who don't read music can learn to sing in harmony by rote. My aim is to have fun; though above and beyond that to reach for our souls – to make us laugh and cry; to tingle our spines; to stir us up, and to calm us down. Ultimately I dream of a carol concert with some "a capella" four-part singing, and on the stroke of midnight on 31 December, as we prepare to leave our Scottish home, I want to see tears in castaways' eyes as we all sing "Should auld acquaintance be forgot" in four-part harmony.'

What a contrast that would be with the doctor's previous New Year's Eve!

Trish's regular daily walks had been paying off. 'The difference is just absolutely fantastic,' she told the video diary. 'I've actually looked in the mirror today and for the first time in about four years I said, "Hey, Trish, you're looking good!" I feel just fantastic and everybody's noticed the difference. I don't want to bore people with my weight problem but for me it's a big, big thing. Next year I'm going to look back on these video diaries to prove to myself that I can stick at it.'

What else could be making her so happy? None of the castaways thought that she was actually 'in a relationship' with Trevor, even if her kids now called Trevor 'dad' (a titbit Ron was to tell me with some glee). But they were very good friends. 'I suppose the rumours will start,' Trev told the video diary, 'even if they haven't started already. We enjoy each other's company. From the first time we met at Keswick we clicked straightaway.' The pair made up a happy foursome with Toby and Tammy, something Tammy was enthusiastic to discuss on my next visit. 'I've got a small circle of friends,' she told me, 'that I'm fantastically happy with. I can say anything to them, have a moan or a waffle on about nothing and they don't judge me. We have a laugh. If anything happens we can turn it around and giggle about it and that is one of the best things – you've got two girls that can talk about girl things, and two boys that can talk about boy things. Being single, if something happens here you come back and you're in a pod on your own – now all of a sudden there's four of us and you can discuss it.'

'Our social groups,' said Trevor to Trish in a joint video diary, 'are built up of people that either want to get something against Lion; or against somebody else; or that want to work; or just to have a laugh.' This happy foursome was in the last category. The previous Saturday the group friendship had been cemented with a candlelit dinner party where the lads had courted the girls in an almost Edwardian manner. 'We've tried and tried and tried and tried and tried and tried and tried,' Toby jokingly complained to the minicam in a joint video diary with Trevor, 'to get these ladies to love us and have a romance with us. Nothing's worked so far, so we're doing a candlelit meal for four. It's our last hope. We've got lots and lots of red wine, which we're going to try and force these girls to drink – and hopefully we'll get somewhere.'

Despite the wine, and the home-made pizza, and flowers with condoms in their petals delivered by Philiy, and a couch brought up from the steading for the ladies to recline on post-prandially, the gents did (by all public accounts) once again retire to their own beds that evening. 'Did we pull?' asked Trish of Tammy the next day. 'I think we could have,' she replied. 'They tried hard enough, didn't they?' 'Oh, did they try!' said Tammy. 'It was hilarious. So much so that my cheek muscles here started to cramp up with all the laughter we had.' 'But it was just so nice,' she elaborated a little later, 'knowing you're having this tender loving evening with two guys that you really know and feel safe with and you don't have to have your barriers up and think, Oh, what are they after?'

'Well, I don't know about that,' laughed Trish, 'because I went for a walk today and came back and Trev was in my bed.'

As for the lads: 'I did feel a bit cheap afterwards,' Toby told Trevor.

'Used?' Trev asked.

'Yeah. I mean, I like both of the girls, they're really good friends, but they cooked us a meal and wined us and dined us and plied us with booze but we're just not like that.'

Kangaroo Court

Over the other side of the little compound, in Pod Four, Gwyneth, meanwhile, remained seriously unhappy. At the regular meeting on Thursday 15 June she again told the community she was intending to leave the project. 'For people to have got to her that much and for her not to feel supported by the rest of us,' said Julia Corrigan, 'it's a real failure on the part of the community. She's such a nice person and I'm going to miss her a lot.'

The meeting had been enlivened when two-thirds of those present suddenly burst into song, a bit of high spirits that had been planned on choir night and put down on the agenda between *3. Budget Update* and *5. Compost Toilets* as *4. Light relief.* Ron was unamused. 'He stormed out, saying it was inappropriate, childish,' said Ben. 'But it was for fun. It was just a joke.' The psychotherapist's reaction was 'absolutely barmy', Ben added. His idea of a joke was miming sex in front of some devout 7th Day Adventists. Ben was fed up with it, and him. 'I've done my best to be pleasant, but when you're blanked and ignored ...' He threw up his hands at the minicam with exhaustion. Now it had even got to the point where Ron was refusing to work with him in the kitchen, because he was labouring under a delusion that Ben had written to the BBC demanding the reinstitution of the rules. 'Incredible!' he concluded. But whereas in March it had got to him, now he didn't seem to care. 'If he wants to blag me, he can blag me. Obviously it bothers me a bit, it's not particularly pleasant – but then neither's Ron.' (That terrible thing had happened that Gwyneth had told me, back in January, she hoped would never come to pass: Ben had lost his innocence.)

After discussing *Personal Allowance* and *Fuel* and *Water* and *Horticulture* and *Health and Safety* amongst other matters, the castaways returned at the end of the meeting to the vexed question of their judicial system, under the heading *BBC Letter and Filming.* The BBC proposal to use film as evidence would totally compromise her and cameraman Warren's position, said a vexed Tanya. It was unanimously agreed that film be removed from the sanctions procedure. The castaways would rely on witnesses of misdemeanours, but obviously, argued Sandy, not just on the strength of an accusation by a single person. 'The claim,' read the minutes' account of her contribution, 'must be substantiated in some way or other as in a County Court.'

'So what d'you think about this kangaroo court thing,' said Ron to Tammy on video diary a little later, 'that if you don't do what the die-hards say you have to go to court?' 'That wasn't the outcome of the meeting,' Tammy corrected him. But the term 'kangaroo court' stuck.

Get the Bailiffs In

Friday 16 June brought the long-suffering producer to the island for the second week running. 'I stayed out of the way,' wrote Mike, 'as I knew Chris would be getting a hard time from the likes of Ron. It didn't take long to confirm my suspicions. Half an hour later Ron was shouting his head off at Chris by the tool room. Chris was in for a very stressful day today and I feel sorry for him sometimes.' After lunch Kelly discussed The Rules with the gathered castaways again. 'Roger and Ron made dicks out of themselves as always,' wrote Mike, 'and tried to pick arguments that a seven-year-old could have defended. They just drag everything out and waste so much of everybody's time. It really pisses me off.'

'I was going to walk out,' Ben told the video diary. 'It's the nearest I've been to it. I just can't understand the problem of those people who, six months into this, are making a big hoo-ha about signing something that is basically the spirit of this project anyway. The idea of coming here was to see how we interact with each other, how we reflect on family and friends that we *didn't* have coming and visiting us all the time. So part of me wants to say, gosh, if they really can't live without them, perhaps they shouldn't be here.'

Ron had told Chris Kelly that if he wanted him off the island, it would be 'kicking and screaming. "I will not sign your piece of paper. You'll have to get the bailiffs in."' The producer, meanwhile, had flown back to Glasgow with a copy of Sandy's self-governing document in his pocket.

Half-time

Saturday 17 June saw celebrations of Toby's birthday at the schoolhouse. Padraig had written him a song, which he sang to the tune of *The Limerick Rake*.

The Taransay Rake

I am a young fella that's easy and bold
I hope to get laid before I get old
But here in the wind and the rain and the cold
I've been doing my lovin' right-handed.
There's girls that'll have me, they've written me so
But they're all girls who've seen me on this TV show
What I want's a young lassie who'll never say no
When I try to get into her pod room

The three following stanzas developed the theme. And much did everyone laugh at Toby's predicament that night. But all too soon romantic situations were to be cruelly reversed.

Sunday was another wet and miserable day. Peter and Sheila remained pod-bound till half seven in the evening, when they decided they really had to get out. They walked together towards the Spit at Roa, 'seeing it in totally different weather, through mist and rain and clouds hovering over the surface of the sea,'

Sheila rhapsodised to the video diary. 'It had an amazing beauty of its own and there were dark, dark clouds hanging over the mountains on the north side of Taransay. The sea was so calm it looked like oil had been spilt across the surface. It was like moiré silk. On the cliff face before you get to the spit we saw the rooks that had nested on the rocky ledges – and they were going crazy, announcing their presence with raucous calls. You can actually see the territories of the different birds. And as we walked out along the spit the whole surface was shimmering with sand eels, they looked like sardines flickering. There were seagulls and terns that had been fishing, and as you saw these sand eels you realised that that's what they were after. They were having a feast.' But for Sheila the enjoyment was tinged with sadness. 'It made me feel,' she went on, 'how much I'll miss this island when the year's over. We've only six months to go now. It makes you appreciate even more what's here because soon this will be in the past and these will just be memories. So I want to savour each moment.'

As the Summer Solstice approached, many of the others had been having similar 'half-time' thoughts. 'We're half way through,' Julie Lowe told the video diary, 'And boy oh boy what a learning experience the first twenty-six weeks have been. What I've learnt is that the way to keep going in this community is to keep your head down, keep out of things as much as possible and just try and maintain an equilibrium that's all your own. Otherwise your life is up and down like a rollercoaster and you spend your time being upset. But I've spent too long being concerned with things that in the real world you wouldn't give a moment's thought to.'

'I was just thinking,' Ben told the video diary, 'how strange it'll be to leave here and suddenly hear all those noises again. And the fumes. The air's so completely and utterly fresh here. For six months I've been away from urban life and rural life as well. I haven't bought anything for six months now, haven't used money, and that's a weird concept. For the last few weeks I've been thinking, Could I genuinely settle down somewhere like this? Live here? I think I'd be very lonely, just me and my dog. But my idea of a fairy-tale life would be to go back to London, work, earn lots of money, meet a beautiful, beautiful girl and – this is another thing I've been thinking: do I want lots of children? Having lived with eight for the last six months I've reduced the number I want. Think I'll stick with three. More could drive you absolutely bonkers. So, anyway, meet beautiful woman, really lovely, wonderful girl, get married, have some children, then move somewhere like this.'

'It's the half-way mark,' reported Philiy. 'And people have been reflecting on that and we seem to be talking about going home a lot more, what people are going to do when they go home. But to me, we've got six months to go, and that's a long time. I'm not thinking about the end just yet.'

Monday 19 June brought summer weather again. Sheila and Peter were back out in the field – today accompanied by Ben – planting cabbages and cauliflowers and broccoli. At four, when they'd finished, they went for a swim. With a wetsuit against the cold of the beautiful turquoise sea, Sheila felt she could have been in the Caribbean.

Trev, Toby, Trish and Dez were in the kitchen. Hilary and Julia were teaching. Colin and Pat killed another pig. Mike sat in the schoolhouse working on the budget, prior to yet another meeting that evening. He was taking over from Toby and taking stock of where they were, which seemed, he told Trevor, to be basically about eight grand over. 'Which takes us, basically,' said the ever-cheery Scouser, 'to the first week of November when we'll run out of money. Some people aren't bothered and some are. I am concerned and I'm going to start

The slaughter house

saving up some of my Personal Allowance so when the money does run out I can get some rice, say, or pasta.'

The seed planted in Roger's mind during his round-Taransay walk was growing. 'My other project?' he wrote to me on 20 June. 'Fuel self-sufficiency. It has become very obvious that we could easily be self-sufficient in fuel. There is masses of peat and driftwood, but because of our predecessors, it is, of course, distant from our dwelling. So today I called a meeting to discuss our approach to peat cutting, which is the first, most urgent job and already a little late. In a few days' time a small party are going on a survey to prospect for the most appropriate source – probably along the north coast. Once our peats are cut and drying, we can then concentrate on driftwood.'

In the schoolhouse Mike and Trev had set up a mock court. 'With dolls as the jury,' wrote Mike, 'me as the Judge and Trev as Clerk of the Court. We tried Ben for trying to be too much of a castaway, Gwyn for overuse of Tea Tree, Roger and Rosemary for damage limitation, Padraig for possession and concealment of a girlfriend, and Sandy for the purchasing of excessive tupperware.' Why damage limitation? I asked him later. Because ever since they realised how bad their initial TV image was, he said, Roger and Rosemary had been setting up scenes for camera where they would be seen in a good light.

Meanwhile, Philiy was worried about Angel and her calf Taran. They had been separated for nearly a week and Angel had been crying every night. 'She's been pacing the fence till one o'clock in the morning,' the sensitive vegetarian reported, 'and she's cried so much she's lost her moo, she can't even moo any more, she sort of goes *ooogh*. That's the only sound you hear and it's heartbreaking. She's barged through gates and trashed the garden trying to find him. And when I finally got him he came running round the fence through the gate, nearly squashing the sheep in the process, and ran straight to her, onto her teats, and she was licking his back while he was getting some milk. It was quite emotional, really. I felt close to tears. It's quite an eye-opener and it does make me think why I have my attitudes to meat-eating.'

Hopefully, she said, the blue-eyed calf was leaving the island on Friday. 'We're going to let Angel see him onto the boat so she knows he's gone. In my self-sufficiency book it says that after five days she'll forget. Or rather after five days she just accepts that he's gone and stops crying. But it's sad. People get a pint of milk delivered on their doorstep and they pour it on their cereal and they don't really think. They don't realise that a calf's had to be taken away, and the mother will cry for a week for her child.'

Rather more robust about animal matters Trish had proposed in a meeting that another animal be sent back to the mainland: Aillie the horse. She wasn't working and was still getting fed twice a day, using valuable resources.

Padraig had been hoping that Summer Solstice on Wednesday 21 June would be a celebration equivalent to, or at least in the same spirit as, May Day. The plan was to work as normal till lunch, play rounders if the weather was nice, maybe do a bit of welly throwing, followed by a performance by the singing class, a barbecue, then up to the top of the mountain to watch the sun go down, before returning to Paible for another bonfire spectacular. He, Warren and Colin had laid out a circle of stones in the exact positions of Stonehenge (Becci had downloaded the details from the internet for them). Then they had made a huge central dolmen out of corrugated iron, with the word LIFE cut into the lintel stone and a sun and crescent moon on the uprights.

But though in no way a flop, the event didn't match the carefree communal harmony of that earlier day. 'It had a milder vibe to it,' Padraig told me. The weather was 'crap', Mike reported, until the evening. Toby had been distracted by the arrival of some visitors from home, who stayed for three hours of the afternoon. The children didn't want to sing. 'Rather than push them,' said Julie Lowe, 'I said, "No, we won't do it."' And not everyone turned up to or bought into the entertainment laid on. 'All a bit weird as far as I'm concerned,' commented Mike, on the procession of kids with Chinese lanterns that circled the mock Stonehenge. 'I just hope that the pagan side of it will not have offended any of the Harris folk across the water.'

He stood by with a fire extinguisher as the sculpture – full of wood, straw, pig fat and diesel – was set alight, and LIFE, sun and moon lit up brilliantly, while flames raced down grooves cut in the grass to link up with fireworks at each end. 'Soon the whole structure was ablaze. The fireworks went well and everyone was very happy.'

Rules and Reality

The next day, Thursday 22 June, brought the boat, and for the third week running, the harassed producer, still trying to sort out some workable arrangement about The Rules. With him was Graham the slaughtering inspector. Another pig was to be 'dropped' so that Colin could get his full certificate. The test was successful and Colin, Graham, Mike, Gordon and Ron, who had been assisting on pulley, retired to the shed to drink a can of ice-cold beer in a box with ice packs. 'What a welcome treat that was,' wrote Mike.

The evening saw the culminating meeting of the tortuous governmental saga. 'The long and the short of it,' Mike continued, 'is that we be allowed to police ourselves for a month before the BBC do anything about it. Strictly speaking, that would mean that Toby would have to suffer a punishment for having had visitors yesterday.' A one-page document entitled *BBC Response To Castaway Letter* was the answer Sandy had been hoping for. 'I just prayed all that week,' she told me, 'that somebody would be gracious enough to read what I'd written, instead of just chucking it away. I'm pleased to say they'd looked at it – even passed it to the BBC lawyers – I bet they had a laugh when they read it.' The BBC's response concluded:

To summarise -

A reported transgression will be heard by a panel of 5; good people and true. The defendant may request replacing up to 2 panel members if he/she believes that any member of the panel may not be impartial.

At least 2 independent witnesses are required to substantiate a claim. Hard evidence is not required.

The accused has a right to a defence.

Based on the evidence submitted, the panel of 5 will reach a decision.

If the complaint is proven, a suitable penalty will be implemented.

The next day Sandy had a long chat with Chris Kelly, ironed out a few things here and there, and made some adaptations. She was now happy to type up a final proposal and stick it on the board for community approval.

But even as the castaways finally settled on a theoretical way of policing themselves, practical problems just refused to go away. The following morning saw a 'massive barney' in the kitchen between Liz and – you guessed it – the restless Ron. 'Once again,' wrote Mike, 'poor old Lizzie was reduced to tears. God alone knows what this one was all about. Wee Mike did tell me yesterday that Ron is on a mission to make life difficult for Dez, Liz and Pete. Will things here never be harmonious?'

Ron had been goaded to anger by a sarcastic remark Dez had made at the previous night's meeting. The psychotherapist had been saying he didn't want anyone other than him to open his parcels; there might be something private or embarrassing inside. 'And Peter gallantly said,' Dez was to explain (when I visited a fortnight later to witness the dramatic climax of the Ron soap opera), '"Well, I think it would be a good idea maybe if we could perhaps get someone that the community trusts, is independent and objective, to be there present when people open their parcels." Now bearing in mind all the flak Peter's been getting, I then made a comment, "Well, Peter, why don't *you*, as a trusted member of the community, be there when Ron opens his prezzies." Everyone in the room gasped. It was as much an insult to Peter as to Ron. But it was a complete joke of course. But obviously Ron felt I was being very cheap and nasty about something he feels strongly about.' After the meeting was over, a furious Ron had grabbed the Tanya and headed for Dez and Liz's pod. 'They're sat on the bed,' Ron told the video diary, 'having a little cosy sort of glass of wine, all very friendly, invited me in, had no idea why I was there, then I said I'd come to speak to Dez and Tanya was with me to film it, and Dez basically told me to get out.' The friendship was well and truly over.

'Next morning, I go into the steading,' Ron continues. 'Liz says, "Can I talk to you?" I said, "Yes, I'm going to get a cup of tea first." Before I'd even finished making my tea she was in the kitchen screaming and shouting in my face. I try to point out to her that sarcasm is not considered humour, it's rude and bad manners. Then I told her that the issue I had was not with her, it was with Dez, and what's a man doing sending in his woman to do his dirty work ...'

Oh dear, oh dear. Would the fury never let up? Goaded beyond endurance, Dez had decided, he told me, that he just couldn't be bothered with Ron any longer. 'I won't go and sit in his room and have a discussion about it,' he said, 'because I'm just not interested any more.'

'Which is the worst insult for Ron,' chipped in Liz, 'because he needs attention. So he was running around saying, "I'm going to hit Dez." I let it wash over me most of the time, because he's such an attention seeker, but I just thought "You're not getting away with that." ' If the community's demon had finally threatened actual physical violence, he was, as far as Liz was concerned 'off the island'.

Chapter 17

Get Him Off the Island!

For Rosemary's birthday on Saturday 24 June there was a wonderful party at the MacKay House. 'It seemed like we had all gone out for the night,' wrote Mike, 'because of the change of venue.' Fresh from his success with *The Taransay Rake*, Padraig amused the company with another song he'd adapted from the Irish. Entitled *Rosemary's Song*, it was sung to the tune of *Seven Drunken Nights*.

> *When first I came to Taransay, under great protest*
> *I looked into the schoolhouse and it was a feckin' mess.*
> *So I called up Chris and I said to him*
> *Would you kindly tell to me,*
> *Where is the feckin' schoolhouse roof*
> *Yiz bastards promised me?*
> *Ah, you're spoilt, you're spoilt, you stroppy ould bint*
> *And still you cannot see*
> *That's a lovely open-plan that Bobby built for thee*
> *Well, it's many the years I've travelled*
> *A thousand miles or more*
> *But on a feckin' schoolhouse, I'd expect at least a door*

The following two stanzas, dealing with the leaking schoolhouse window and the unhygienic compost toilets, with their continuing chorus of 'you're spoilt, you're spoilt, you stroppy ould bint', had the gathered castaways, wrung through the emotional mangle as they had been, in tears of laughter.

Padraig was putting a brave face on things, and who knows what private sorrows he endured later in the tiny dark little pod he'd only moved into finally a fortnight before? The night previous Philiy had ended their relationship. It wasn't going to be easy for either of them, interlinked and adjacent as they were in such a tiny community.

'It's been quite a difficult morning,' the beautiful vegetarian told the video diary on the following Monday. 'My kitchen group is me, Tanya, Rosemary and Padraig. Normally if you split up with somebody you would go away, even if it's just for a week, but here even if I go for a walk I can bump into him. Last night I went and sat in front of the schoolhouse and Padraig appeared. So I feel very sad and a lack of space and privacy. Obviously I've had to go round and quietly tell everyone so that nobody makes comments.'

Philiy had spent the weekend cleaning and rearranging her room and giving her ex his belongings back. 'It sounds quite heartless,' she confided, 'but I just wanted him out of my room. I didn't want there to be any part of him there. That was my space and I had to make it mine again.' Why had she done it? They had split briefly on Valentine's Day, then there had been those three days at the start of April where a break-up had been discussed, yet on both occasions they had worked through it. But now it had just got to the point, she told the video diary, where she couldn't have a relationship any more. 'I came here not wanting one. I wanted to be single. And normally if you started a relationship, it wouldn't be so full-on. You'd date each other, and phone each other up and see if you wanted to go out, but you'd have days when you didn't see each other. But here you're with each other all the time and it fries my head. Our friends are the same people, because there's limited people here, so everything we do is the same.'

There was also the fact that she couldn't deal with the publicity. It had been Tanya's suggestion that an interview about the relationship would inevitably be asked for that had caused the first split; and Cynthia's sounding-out of the same possibility the second. Then, when Philiy had seen the articles in the *News of the World* and the Irish tabloids it had been her 'worst nightmare'. 'It really shook me,' she said. 'They phoned Padraig's mother in Ireland and we were on the front page of the *Star* over there alongside Posh and David Beckham, which was bizarre.' Paul Overton had told her that the newspapers had been phoning once a week to the Lion offices to ask about her and Padraig. 'That was really the nail in the coffin for me – I don't want that. You know, fine if they write about me, just me, but I don't want to be just a relationship that has happened here. It was becoming Padraig-and-Philiy, you know, one word.'

This was the first time that either of them had discussed such personal matters in public (however private the video diary seemed). Padraig had always been wary of talking about his private life, insisting, for example, that he would only let me read his letters home if I didn't mention references to Philiy. Even now he didn't unburden on the minicam. But at the end of September he was candid with me: 'I wasn't actually as broken up as I expected to be,' he said. 'Or would have been if it had been earlier. We'd been straining for a while, because of external pressures mainly.'

'So I feel very sad,' Philiy concluded, 'and quite lonely at the moment and I suppose the only way I can describe it is that it almost feels like there's been a death. It's all very sombre and no one really wants to talk about it. I wonder if we had met outside of here how different would it be. I don't think he would have spoken to somebody like me, really. We come from two very different worlds and it was a difference in the end that I couldn't deal with. I thought I could carry on but there was something missing for me. I don't want to say it was because of the animals, because it's more than that, but I was finding that difficult. I am not used to going out with meat-eaters. Or if I do, they become vegetarian or eat meat when I'm not around.'

Voila!

For the rest of the community, though, the sun was shining, and there were new and exciting projects to be getting on with. First, the connection of the new waterpipe to Loch 'na Budget. This was something that Ben, under Warren's expert tutelage, was nominally in charge of; but he was keen, he told the video diary, to give other people a chance to use their imagination, enthusiasm and, 'erm, ideas'. Which was lucky, because when it came to the crunch and the water had somehow to be got from loch to pipe, it was Mike Laird who came up with the solution that worked. Ben's initial scheme had been to make 'a massive funnel', close off one end of the pipe, and pour water into it until it was full. 'Slightly laborious, but I thought that would be a reasonably good idea.' Then Mike came up with a plan to submerge the first hundred metres of pipe under the loch's surface. 'I have to admit I was slightly dubious,' Ben confesses, 'but we popped it all in the water and Roger, Mike and I all went up to the loch's edge and got in. Admittedly I was about to put a wetsuit on because I suspected a loch in the Outer Hebrides might be slightly chilly. But then Roger just sort of jumped in in his pants. I couldn't let Roger upstage me so I had to do the same, without the wetsuit. It was freezing at first.'

'In true Ben style,' wrote Mike, 'he decided that he would not wear a wetsuit as Roger had already got in without one on. All for the camera. I kept mine on and we were all in there for about twenty minutes. I was cold enough and they were shivering and their teeth were chattering. My idea worked and the pipe was filled with water. One end was taken out of the loch and once lower than the loch started to flow. It was a great moment.

'The camera as ever followed Ben. He was the only one individually interviewed, he was focused upon in the loch etc. That really fucks me off. It is not "The Ben Show" and I am not here to be a cameo bit actor. That was my idea and he was happy to take the credit for it. Not much I can do about it, though.'

'So we ran along with the hose and dropped it on the ground and water started coming through,' said a jovial Ben. 'And it was just so exciting that we'd done all that, you know, completely the castaway way, without any pumps or using any electronic things. The water started flowing, so we connected it up to the valve, and then fitted it all together and *voila!* – we've got water from the loch.'

Ponsequences

That same sunny Monday another key project was inaugurated: Dez's raft. Mike was once again at the centre of the action. 'Tammy was in the water with me,' wrote Mike, 'and we were like a pair of engines. Liz, Dez and Toby were on top of the raft using spades for oars. Soon enough we were underway. Dez asked for a name for the raft and the first thing I could come up with was the *Starfish Enterprise*. That is now its name.

'For as long as possible we were attached to shore by a long line which Pat held for us. Soon, though, we had to be released so that we could go further out to sea to clear a headland. The water was so shallow in places that I was scraping over the rocks. Then suddenly it would be six or seven metres deep. There were plenty of fish and I always called out to those on the raft when I saw them. It went very well.'

The next day Ben joined them as they laid out a guiding line and anchor system. 'I have to say,' the now-bronzed Ben reported, 'that the raft is the most incredibly brilliantest most humungoidly fantastic incredible thing that's happened here for ages.' They had made a massive weight, he went on, out of a fish box filled with cement and steel, which they had attached to the bottom of the raft at low tide. It was so heavy it took five of them to carry it, but it had been so exciting when the tide rose, lifting the weight inexorably with it. Tammy, Toby and Mike, all wearing flippers, had provided power in the water, while Dez and Ben had again paddled from the top of the raft with spades. A nylon line had been tied to some rocks on the beach. Five hundred feet out into the sea they fed the other end through this huge pink buoy they had found in Buoy Land and tied it to the weight under the raft, which they then cut loose 'It was so exciting seeing it going *phwwwweer* shooting down. And then the buoy was there, floating on the water and it won't go anywhere because it's so weighted down. So then we were able to heave ourselves along holding on to this line.'

Raft secured, Mike had gone off for a shower, having agreed with Dez that they would attach the first fishing net at 5 pm. When Dez didn't turn up Mike headed down to the beach. 'And there he was with Ben and Gordon paddling out. I was not amused. After dinner I had words with him and told him exactly what I thought about it all. It's all to do with fair portrayal. The fishing project is my baby, just as the water project is Ben's.' Only that morning the Action Man had expressed his frustration on this subject of fair filming to Ben and Warren. 'I have not been happy with the way that a lot of the filming still seems to focus on certain individuals. I just feel that people should be filmed equally if they are involved in a project.'

His argument with Dez had left Mike 'nearly in tears as I am feeling very fraught about so much at the moment'. For several weeks now he had planned to get away from the community on his own and do 'the proper survival bit'. Initially the plan had been to swim to a tiny neighbouring island, Soay Mor, but the mile-and-a-half-long sea journey had been ruled out by Lion on safety grounds. Instead, he had announced to the community that he was off to the far end of the island, that same Black Pipe beach where he, Toby and Trevor had first camped out back in the wind and cold of March.

The Cup of Coffee Incident

That afternoon was the regular Thursday meeting, when, amongst other agenda items, Sandy's 'kangaroo court' proposals were to be finally accepted or not. As the castaways assembled at the snug end of the steading, Ben was working in the kitchen. He was suddenly joined by Gwyneth. 'She came rushing in, tears flooding, and saying, "That's it, I can't cope any more. I'm sorry Ben, I hate him, I hate him. I never even want to see him again."'

The object of her disaffection was of course the bearded lecturer – Fat Boy Grim as Ron had nicknamed him. 'He looked directly at Gwyneth,' says Colin, 'for what felt like three minutes, she says. She then left the table, came over and sat next to me and said, "If he does that again I'll go across and slap his face." ' 'His looks are so horrible,' Gwyneth told me later, 'they actually go right through me. So I just walked out and went for a walk.

'I came back,' she continued, 'just at the point – my own stupid fault, I was still incensed – when Patrick was asking him why he'd done that. And I went straight up to him and he did it again. And Sheila. The pair of them were at me and they wouldn't allow me to say what I think and feel. I called him one hell of a bastard, and I really meant it. And he went on and on, until eventually, out of pure frustration and just to shut the man up, I picked up my coffee and threw it. Then I walked out.'

'The biggest event of the last two weeks,' wrote Peter to his mother, 'was having coffee thrown in my face by Gwyneth (lavender drawers) after the last meeting. She is always tilting at everything I say in meetings – she is inarticulate, hates debate, which she sees as conflict, and as the saying goes round here has been thoroughly "copseyed" (Ron Copsey). He has her in thrall, so any discussion of rules on my part is interpreted as an attack on Ron. She was apparently infuriated by a remark I'd made three weeks previously about people trying 'emotional intimidation'. This time I was looking at her quite deliberately to make the point that I'd stand by my principles rather than be blackmailed by her desire for mushy togetherness. She then charges up saying "What did you mean by that remark?" and threw her cup of coffee in my face, called me a bastard and then stormed out. Next thing I hear she's leaving the island again, isn't leaving etc. I must say I was remarkably calm throughout the whole episode, didn't raise my voice, acted dignified etc. So she is left looking utterly "barking" – which is now the general consensus. At least the goody-two-shoes healing bullshit no longer washes. Actually it has all acted as if it "lanced" a boil – she, as they say, "lost it big time" and has major egg on her face. Of course, interacting in a small physical space with someone you do not speak to lends a certain "frisson" to life here – it will pass – but it doesn't make me (and Sheila) feel all too social.'

'I am hopeless at putting a point across,' says Gwyneth. 'I can't do it. I have it all up here. I can use all the terminology in the world, but it never comes out right. It just doesn't come out. And he knows I'm like that, and he knows how to work it with me.'

Hoist By Her Own Petard

The very day after the community had delighted Sandy by accepting her 'kangaroo court' proposals, who should turn up, unannounced on the island, but her long-lost brother from California. She hadn't seen Hector for seven and a half years. 'All I knew,' Sandy told me, 'was that he was going to be in the UK about now. I'd said, "Don't bother to come, because with these new rules and regulations in place it's not worth it." But he turned up anyway. I was completely knocked sideways. But would you send your brother away if you hadn't seen him for seven and a half years?'

And what did Hector think of this wild new life adopted by his normally conventional older sister? In our first interview, back in January in the Harris

Hotel, Sandy had waxed lyrical as she had contrasted the sixties-style freedoms that her musician younger brother had enjoyed, while she had been trapped in her fifties-style marriage in Gosport. 'They bought vans, they did everything,' she told me. 'You imagine what a real free spirit of the sixties has tried, my brother has done it.' Was she jealous of him, I asked. 'No,' she replied, after a moment's thought, 'I wouldn't call it jealousy, because for me jealousy is tinged with hate, and I love my brother to bits.'

So Sandy let Hector stay, along with his American wife and another cousin and her husband, for a full three hours. 'Then of course the question was, "What do we do now?" I said to the others, "I don't care what you *think* you should do, but I know what you *should* do. We have to have a hearing." People didn't want anything to do with that. But I said, "Well, you've got to. We've got to show that if somebody breaks the rules we are going to use this sanctions procedure." I spent the next two or three days, cajoling people. "Come on," I said, "somebody's got to get this moving." '

The Castaways' Castaway

Down at Black Pipe Beach, Mike was well away from all the legal precedent-setting. He had arrived mid-morning on Thursday 29 June, accompanied by his two 'sherpas', Trish and Trev. Having deposited his stuff near the famous black pipe, the platonic couple headed for home. 'I watched them walk slowly up the hill and over the ridge,' the abandoned Action Man wrote, 'until they could be seen no more. I was all on my own and it's a weird feeling but I'm very happy.'

Having sorted out his bedding and tarpaulin for the night, strung across the beams of the black house as far away from the 'evil-smelling' dead sheep as he could get, Mike cooked himself a quick meal of noodles and then set about finding a suitable site. For at last he was doing that thing that he'd fantasised about from when he'd first heard of the Castaway project: building his own house.

He found himself a nice, flat, stone-free and well-drained area. 'I then went along the beach and carefully chose five pieces of wood,' he wrote in his diary. 'Four were to be the legs and the fifth was the crossbar. I had not chosen wisely. Some of the logs were too heavy to tie securely and fell down. One of them gave me a fair thump on its way but could have been a lot worse. I chose two more pieces and soon it was up. I was chuffed.'

Having watched a 'truly magnificent' sunset and listened to a bit of music on his illegal Walkman he crashed out. By the next evening his little house – complete with pod-style turf roof and raised bed – was ready to move into. The white cross on blue of the Scottish flag was flying from its roof. But in the morning there were urgent modifications to be made. 'The most important of which was to alter the position of my bed as a lot of soil had fallen on my head and got into my sleeping bag during the night.'

No sooner had he finished that task than the castaways' castaway received his first visitors, Roger and Rosemary, with sons Oliver and Felix and little raven-haired Tash, who brought a bag containing four bread rolls. While Roger headed off up the low adjacent headland with a spade to check out peat sources, Mike caught up on the latest gossip with Rosemary. 'Which was interesting to hear whilst being here, but totally supports my reasons for wanting to get out of Paible.'

That evening Mike dined alone on cockles by the shore. He woke to a gloriously hot and sunny morning and, dressed only in boxer shorts, set about making a circle of stones for his fire, erecting a drying line, and making a sun-dial. Liz came to visit him, bearing pasta, cheese and carrots; then Hilary with water, fruit and bread. When they had gone, he decided it was time to build himself a proper toilet, complete with a driftwood back screen so that he wouldn't be caught mid-crap by casual visitors. He need hardly have bothered, as he didn't get another visitor for four days. It was Trish, with dogs. 'The only news she had for me was that Gwyneth was now staying and Ron's an arse.'

The following morning, now splendid in kilt, vest and bare feet, Mike was joined by a peat-cutting party. Roger had found the fuel source he wanted up on the headland and brought back a group of castaways to get to work cutting it – Padraig, Ben, Roger, Gordon and Toby. At lunchtime they repaired to Mike's dwelling for a sandwich lunch, before digging on till 4 pm when they'd all had enough. 'It's dirty, hard work on the back and the sun was hot,' Mike reported.

By the following morning, breakfasting late on a stock cube, pasta and bread, Mike was really missing certain things in Paible, 'let alone the real world'. After his regular hour-long round trip for water, he spent the afternoon building a sun out of buoys on the slopes of the glen he now called Sleepy Valley. As he worked, his head was filled with thoughts of draught beer and cigarettes. 'I can't think of the last time in my adult life,' he wrote, 'that I didn't touch alcohol for five days.'

Judgement Day

Meanwhile, back at the ranch, the kangaroo court had been convened to try its inventor. The judges were five castaways drawn out of a hat at random: Monica, Tammy, Padraig, Tanya and Philiy. Ron was having no part of it. 'There's something really unsavoury about it,' he told the video diary. 'If the BBC and Lion want to impose the rules then let them have the guts to do it themselves. They will not use me in that way. I will not pass judgement on the people I live with here. I find it all a bit pathetic really, I'm not going to obey stupid rules imposed on me to make good television or create an image of this project that Lion wants to portray. The people drawn out of the hat were all the kids from Pod One. Now most of those don't know their arse from their elbow and there's Sandy, who's the oldest member of the community, having to sit and be judged by a load of kids. I think it's absolutely despicable. She didn't invite her guest to the island. She told them they shouldn't be here and then took them to the bothy where she waved them off.'

In his rant, Ron had forgotten that it was Sandy who had been so adamant to be tried. And as it turned out, the youthful justices were lenient with their elderly charge. 'The six of us sat down,' Sandy told me two days later, 'and worked out something that would be useful to everybody, which wasn't too taxing for me. We thought of things like cleaning windows. But some of these windows are a bit difficult to get to and that would have meant using a ladder. Padraig very gallantly said, "I don't think that's a good idea. Not for Sandy."' In the end they came up with a more appropriate idea: that everyone in the community could bring the microbiologist two garments each for repair.

Taransay Sickness

Two days later the Lion boat was in again, bringing with it this time Paul Overton, myself and Louise Halestrop, the Compost Toilet expert from CAT. Chris Kelly was following on after a meeting in Stornoway with a tourism official who had been appointed specifically to capitalise on the interest in the Outer Hebrides generated by *Castaway 2000*. So much for those 'irate locals' of January! As we landed in the sunshine on Pig Beach, we wondered quite what reception we were going to find.

Ron was, to use his phrase, in my face as soon as I sat down for lunch in the steading, sounding off with his attacks on Lion, his fellow castaways and so on. 'Keep it for the tape recorder,' I told him as he frothed on, and around him his associates Monica, Julia and Warren rolled their eyes and laughed wearily.

We sat in his little pod in the same positions as we'd sat two months before, and to me, the outsider, it seemed as if nothing had changed. Ron looked worn out, his blue-grey eyes blank as he gazed out down the walkway to the steading, the Taransay Strait and the mountains of Harris beyond. His fury with Lion was now centred around the fact that there were now three more programmes going out in September, which was not what he'd signed up for. The project had become, he said, a 'trashy voyeuristic soap opera'. Friends of his had sent him audio tapes of the first four programmes and he wasn't impressed. 'It's about discord, it's about bitching, it's about human beings at their worst.' Of the material he'd actually seen, he was equally scathing. There was nothing shown from the CAT week about the alternative technology, he complained. 'It's all people-based. There's nothing about the positive aspects. Now suddenly they come in and institute these rules. They want to make it like *Big Brother*.' Around the time of the Taransay Five, he reminded me, he had given in his notice. It had never been withdrawn. 'So I can leave at any time,' he said. 'I won't even tell Lion. I'll just go. I'll be here one day and gone the next.'

As I went round the other pods that afternoon and evening doing interviews, it was clear that everyone, even his one-time friends and supporters, were heartily sick of Ron. 'He's not the man I knew when I started this project,' said Philiy. 'He needs to go home.' 'As for our little stirrer with the wooden spoon,' said Tammy, 'I think if he pissed off the island it'd be a better place.' Others, like Dez, talked of how they just blanked him now. 'The more you want him off the island,' he told me, 'the more he'll want to stay.' Toby and Trevor just 'keep out of it'. 'He's imploding nicely,' joked Trevor, 'self-destruction is the finest quality you can see in somebody.' 'Why don't you just vote him off the island?' I asked Julie Lowe as we sat drinking wine-box Cabernet Sauvignon under the driftwood mirror in her neat little pod. She explained how, as she saw it, Ron was forever upsetting the equanimity of the community. 'A little poke here, a little word there, a little stir there. A flagrant disregard for anything that other people hold right and fair.' Even as we left the subject and moved on to discuss her ambition to write a Mills and Boon under the name Tara Cast, there was a knock on the glass of the door and a breathless Sheila appeared. Ron had just gone crazy in the steading, she told us. Paul Overton had presented him with the vet's bill for Charlie's last hours and the psychotherapist had lost it, screaming loudly in Paul's face for several minutes, then hurling a chair the length of the steading, 'narrowly missing Aaron'. He'd then stormed out and run amok in the washroom with the mangle.

TV audiences were to see the discussion that later developed in the steading, in which Julie talked of her fears. 'This is no way to have to live. He intimidates the hell out of me,' she concludes as she breaks down in tears. 'I'm scared of that man.' With the cameras off, the idea of actually removing Ron from the island was then mooted by Julie.

I had meanwhile moved on to Liz and Dez, hearing their complaints about the psychotherapist. He had the nickname Thunder Clouds, said Dez, because whenever he was in the village there was just this big depression over it. He incited hatred, said Liz. 'You'll go into a room and there'll be Gwyneth, and Ron'll be bitching about Peter. To me this thing about Gwyneth leaving is that a true friend would have encouraged her to stay and work through her problems with Peter, rather than just saying, "Yes, that horrible mean man. Get him off the island." '

Eventually Liz led out a loud groan. 'I'm just bored to tears talking about this Ron thing,' she cried. It was, it seemed to me, a heartfelt summary of the community's feeling and I felt strongly that something practical had to be done. Of course I was only there to observe, but I mean, honestly …

The next day, Friday, Paul and Louise returned to Harris on the mailboat and I was left alone with the castaways to complete my interviews. I came out of the Corrigans' pod mid-afternoon to see Ron still mooning next door, gazing mournfully out of his window at the sea. He was *seriously* thinking of going, he told me. All he needed to do was make a phone call to Ruari and he'd be off. No bother. 'Well, you could always come with me tomorrow,' I said. 'There's a boat coming over at twelve.' I explained that I was staying on in the Harris Hotel for a few days. We could have a nice slap-up dinner, I suggested. Or I'd put him in a taxi to the airport if he wanted. For the first time since I'd arrived his eyes brightened and showed a little of the old Ron spark.

A little later Rosemary called on him. 'Having heard about the incident where he threw the chair,' she was to tell me in August, 'I thought I'd go and talk to him, because obviously something had cracked. Chucking a chair didn't seem in character to me. I talked to him, and he was very tearful, I think he was a bit drunk already. He was saying Lion were so insensitive, bringing over this vet's bill for Charlie. I see his point, but in the real world you would just get sent a bill. Anyway, he'd opened this envelope and it had brought back all the Charlie dying thing for him. I think he was at the end of his tether in lots of ways, still very grief stricken by Charlie's death. He said, "I gave them so much when Charlie died. They filmed every detail of it and now they're just using me." Then he said, "This is the biggest mistake I've ever made coming here." So I just said, "Well, why don't you go? Go tomorrow." Ron was miserable. "Look, is it worth it?" I asked him. "What are you staying for? What are you trying to prove?" He was saying, "Rosemary, you're the one person … you're so wise." He was pretty pissed at the time. I think he needed pushing, because there was still something holding him. It's just a feeling that you've failed. Eventually he said,

"I think you're right. Shall I? Yeah, OK." Then he started pulling all the photographs off his wall.'

As I emerged from my next interview, I heard the news buzzing around the excited community. Ron was leaving, he really was. He had started giving away his possessions, just as Ray had done before him. While I was talking to Trish, Wee Mike ran in clutching a heavy, secateur-type tool that Ron had given him. Trish was impressed. 'You're joking,' she said. 'Gosh, they're about £60.'

'It was £120,' Wee Mike corrected her.

'Is he drunk?' 'No, he's leaving.'

God, I thought, unaware of the chat Ron had had with Rosemary, what have I done? Had it been my turn to stick my finger in the Petri dish?

As I went down for six o'clock supper, Colin Corrigan approached me. Julia was organising a farewell party for Ron in the schoolhouse. 'Keep it to yourself,' he said.

There was a small post-prandial diversion as Roger was bitten in the arse by one of Trish's dogs and went into an irreversible black mood, hands out on the kitchen table in the MacKay House, muttering about having the animal taken off the island and put down. Half an hour before he'd been genially suggesting I share a glass of contraband whisky with him; now there was not even a glimmer of humour. Rosemary made a raised-eyebrows face and we left him to it, glowering over his diary.

Ron had not yet arrived in the schoolhouse. A small band of friends and supporters were there: Julia and Colin Corrigan, obviously, with beautiful little Tash, seriously upset about her favourite adult's departure; Pat and Gwyn; Philiy; Padraig; Warren and Monica; Trish; Tanya. There were a couple of bottles of the foul, chemical-tasting home-brewed wine, which gives you a hangover before you're even tipsy. Thankfully Louise from CAT had managed to leave some brandy, ostentatiously taking back the bottles she'd brought as gifts, unbeknownst (the castaways crowed) to the Lion police, filled with tea.

We stood and chatted and laughed and then champagne was served, the last bottle of the *Mail on Sunday* editor's gift. A toast was proposed and Ron made a speech, but was by now barely coherent. He had been drinking, someone told me, since the Personal Allowance stuff had arrived on the boat at lunchtime. 'Look at you,' he muttered, tears glazing his eyes, as he looked round. 'Look at you-ou-ou all ...' He collapsed into sobs and Philiy and Tanya ran to comfort him.

Padraig was so drunk he could barely stand. Yet he somehow managed to sing the two songs he'd written about the castaways from memory: *The Taransay*

Rake and *Rosemary's Song*.

> *When first I came to Taransay with both my kids in tow*
> *We moved into the farmhouse, there was nowhere else to go.*
> *So I called up Chris and I said to him*
> *Would you kindly tell to me*
> *Where is the double glazing*
> *That yiz bastards promised me?*
> *Ah, you're spoilt, you're spoilt you stroppy ould bint*
> *And still you cannot see*
> *That's a lovely mansion that ould Angus left for thee.*
> *Well, it's many the year I've travelled*
> *A thousand miles or more*
> *But a mansion soaked in builder's piss I never saw before ...*

Rosemary laughed gamely and Ron sobbed. Pat and Gwyn were dreadfully sorry to see him leave, they told me, and I thought about how Ron had called them 'simple people' and wondered how I was going to deal with that one, since I liked and had respect for the Lancashire pair, and didn't want them to think they'd been, in Peter's phrase, 'Copsied'.

When Ron had gone Julia and I steered Padraig down to the steading kitchen for a midnight snack. 'I won't believe he's leaving till I see him on the boat,' he told me. 'He's said he would so many times.' Up in Pod One Toby's pub was still rocking, but I headed off across the torchlit tussocks of the 'field too far' to my bed in the MacKay House. Julia meanwhile guided Padraig past Toby's and into his own pod, where he promptly lit a load of candles. Was he still lovesick for that beautiful, rangy, gentle, sensitive, talented, animal-lover Philiy?

In the steading kitchen the next morning Pat was making bread rolls and Liz and Julia were frying bacon. They really thought Ron was going this time. Gordon didn't. He'd work out a way to change his mind again, he said with a short laugh, as he strode brusquely through.

The boat arrived at ten to twelve over a flat calm sea. I trudged down to Pig Beach with my cases, the troop of castaways ahead and behind me, all of them on tenterhooks to see if Ron really *was* going to depart. Trish and Jodene were leading Aillie the horse and Arnie the foal, for whom the boat had been originally ordered. Ron was already there, centrally on the beach in the light drizzle. Beside him was Tanya, filming everything assiduously.

Now Ron had got on the boat and was refusing to get off. Angus MacKay seemed uncertain what to do, shaking his head and scratching his windswept blond hair. Eventually he decided to phone Chris Kelly on his mobile. Down the line from Glasgow, the overstressed producer was clearly unhappy. So was the psychotherapist. 'Will you please tell Angus to take me home,' he cried to the general gathering around him on the flat-bottomed landing craft. 'It's a very difficult situation, Chris,' protested the boatman, 'and I'm not going to manhandle him.' Behind the camera on the ramp up from the beach, I watched as the phone was passed from Angus to Julia Corrigan. 'Chris,' she pleaded, 'you've got to let him go, you've got to.'

'He's saying I can't go, he's saying I can't go,' Ron told the castaways on boat and beach, every last one of whom didn't want him to get off the boat, stay, become a martyr, maybe change his mind *again*. Meanwhile the tide was turning and Angus was fretting. From the beach, Trish was shouting about the horse. It needed to go now. Come *on*. Negotiations were still continuing with a clearly desperate Chris. With a clanging clatter of hooves on the metal ramp of the old landing craft, Aillie and Arnie were hauled up onto the boat. 'I refused to get on the boat,' wrote Jodene, in her precociously atmospheric description of 'Aillie's Point Of View', 'and they pulled at the rope. Somebody got behind and tried to push me, but my hooves dug into the sand. They kept trying and every moment that passed got me nearer to the boat. At last they pushed and pulled me until I was actually up on the platform and walking onto the boat. Arnie followed straight away. The humans cheered. It reminded me of how they had cheered when I first arrived and that made me sad.' Now Tanya had put down the camera and had the phone. I dodged past her and the snorting, stamping horses, crouched up out of shot by the cabin. 'Take notes,' Roger shouted over at me bossily, and for a flash of Programme 11 you can glimpse me, out of focus with my shorthand pad, as Jodene strokes the horse and weeps in the foreground. 'Aillie, Arnie and Ron are going,' she sobs, 'and they're the few people who I love.' 'See ya, skinhead,' says Ron, as he pats Wee Mike on the head. The horses continue to champ and clatter.

Tanya has passed the phone to me. 'You've got to let him go,' I explain to Chris. 'They're all gagging to see the back of him, but none of them can be seen to want him to go.' My pleading is irrelevant. The horses are on by now and Angus has started the engine. At the other end of the line Chris has bowed to the inevitable. 'Throw the bastard off the boat into the Taransay sound, would you?' he jokes, as I switch off the phone.

The ramp is drawn up and the boat finally heads away as the castaways stand in a long group, solemnly waving. Monica, I notice, hands on little Ciara's shoulders, is smiling broadly.

Ron leans tragically against the blue rails of the old landing craft, his brow crumpled with emotion, his mouth a flat line as he bites his lower lip to hold back the tears. 'See you, Mr Prater!' he shouts. 'I'll have tea when I get to the hotel, Mr Prater!' He stays at the beach end of the boat, magnificently alone, except of course for the horses, one of which is now crapping furiously. I realise Ron has his puppy Boo with him. 'I thought you were going to leave him behind,' I say. 'Last minute decision,' replies Ron.

The castaways in their colourful waterproofs dwindle on the beach. Ron keeps waving, turning with a tragic self-absorbed look to me at the other end of the boat, before turning back and waving some more. Angus's young lad and an older teenager with glasses, holding the horses, shrug and smile tightly at each other.

After fifteen minutes or so we arrive at Horgabost beach. The lads unload the horse and foal. Then I jump off, then Ron. He smiles a nervous smile as he looks round at the empty mainland. He's already slipping back a little into camp mode. 'I'm going to shop till I drop!' he tells the startled boys.

Up by the empty roadside we wait for Mr Cameron's taxi to take us up to the Harris Hotel. 'You're taking this very calmly,' Ron tells me. 'Well,' I reply with a shrug, 'it's your decision.' He nods thoughtfully. 'Am I going to regret this?' he asks a little later.

In the taxi he's ranting about how terrible the island was. Liz had said to him, when he first arrived, and they were still friends, 'Beautiful island, shame about the people.' She was right, though now he's realised that she, and in particular Dez, was one of those people. God there were individuals on that island he wouldn't share a doner kebab with, let alone an island. He's not sure what he's going to do. One moment he's going straight to friends in Glasgow, the next he's going to hole up with me in the Harris. He's not going to the papers. He's just going to slip away, go back home, maybe go to friends in Queensland.

Eventually he decides to stay at the hotel. 'I need to be quiet,' he says. 'I'll just put it all on Lion,' he adds. Boo is nervous. 'She's not seen cars before,' he points out.

Back at the Harris Hotel, the grey-haired, moustachioed, deputy manager is on duty at reception. His eyes widen visibly as he sees Ron. In the little bar, Ron is suddenly thrilled to be back in civilisation. He orders a pint of Velvet and a pepper steak with glee. He's making plans for London now. He's going to go to the Harrods food hall and just *savour* and *salivate* and just, uum, darling, love it. He's going to come out with so many bags and hail two taxis home. He's going to dress up and go to the opera and give his ears a feast. He's not going to give Lion an interview until they pay him *pro rata* of his end of project fee.

He's not even sure if he wants to give me an interview. 'I might be shooting myself in the foot,' he says. But why, Ron, if you're not going to the papers? 'Well, I don't know that I'm not …' It all depends on how Lion treats him. He wants to keep his options open. Whatever else happens, he assures me, he's not going to write a book. Really, I say? 'No, Mark,' he smiles his sweetest smile, 'not in competition with yours. Maybe in three years time.' We shake hands on this.

I buy him a second pint, then a third. We retire to the TV room for an interview, during which we consume a fourth. Once I've got him on the sofa with the mike clipped to his tracksuit top he's fine. 'How much d'you think I could get for my story?' he asks me.

Relaxed and off the island he is no longer the blank-eyed, simmering pod-occupant, but funny and endearing once again. He wasn't going to slag his fellow castaways off, he told me, because he knew enough about human nature and people to know there were reasons for everything. Stepping back from it now, he could find forgiveness in his heart. Even for Trevor and Toby, who had kidded me they were involved with Trish and Tammy. 'Taransay sickness, darling. Pretending something is happening when it's not. There is no single person on that island at the moment getting their end away.'

His beef was with Lion, he repeated, and once again told me about unfair contracts, tabloid TV and all. 'It is a cess pit,' he elaborated. 'It is incestuous. I think it's destructive.' It was a soap opera, a circus with neon lights and balloons on sale and candyfloss. Being there felt mucky, unclean, dishonest, like he'd been raped. He was glad to be leaving it all behind. 'Friends of mine have written to me,' he said, 'fellow actors that I once worked with. They said, "After this you'll be so famous you can do what you like." I wrote back and I said, "It was a dalliance with my ego and it was a fantasy."' The truth was, he wanted to go back to college and finish his degree and become a therapist.

So he *had* done it, I said, to be on TV? No. 'I saw an advert that said, "Have you ever thought about living on an island for a year?" I have very strong spiritual beliefs and it has crossed my mind in the past that I could end up in a monastery. I suppose my beliefs are closer to Buddhism than anything, and this is something I am going to look into. I haven't given that side of me a life. I went out of curiosity and of course they told me what I wanted to hear, just as they told Rambo it was going to be a survivalist thing …'

At 5.30, worn out, I retire to my room for a bath and a nap. I wake blearily at 7.30. Must get up, I've arranged to have dinner with Ron. But when I drag myself downstairs I discover that the psychotherapist, having paid a visit to the public bar over the road, has crashed out. Meanwhile the newspapers have started to phone. There's a local journalist in the bar, says Sarah the manageress, but it's only a young Tarbert lad who joined the *Stornoway Gazette* a few months ago. 'It's amazing how it gets out,' she says cheerfully. She's denying that he's staying here, of course. 'But if he wanted to keep it quiet he shouldn't have gone to the public bar …'

I have a quiet dinner then sit in the darkened sun lounge with a malt. A group of five holidaymakers come in and sit just round the corner. Their conversation soon turns to *Castaway 2000*.

'It was filmed through there …'

'I saw those bits …'

'The doctor—'

'He was a *misery*, I said all along he was a misery …'

'You don't rate their chances …'

'They're not castaways at all. It's all a stitch-up. It's all a complete fix.'

In the morning, Ron's down before me. I go up to his room. 'Who is it?' he yells through the door. When I tell him he opens up. There've already been journalists phoning him, he says. He's not talking to any of them.

I leave him to it and go painting for the day. In the evening we meet for dinner. Ron has had bad news about his flat. His flatmate (to whom he's been paying rent to hold his room) has sublet it. The landlord's throwing him out and he leaves today. Where's he going to go? He wants his own things around him and he doesn't want to be camping on people's floor. Meanwhile, he's had several more calls from newspapers. There's a fellow from the *Stornoway Gazette* through in the bar, not the young guy, but the older, serious reporter, Iain Somebody-or-Other, who's covered all the *Castaway* stories so far. There being no flights or ferries into Stornoway or Tarbert on a Sunday, this guy has got instructions from nationals to negotiate with him. Ron seems quietly delighted. He's smiling as he comes back from talking to him. 'I've just said I'm not talking to anybody at the moment. I wonder how much he's authorised to pay,' Ron speculates. His eyes dart mischievously. 'Shall I go and ask him?'

He's got the *Castaway* videos from Sarah, but can't work the video. There's a girl in the TV room watching the Wimbledon final but Ron barely seems to notice. 'I can't get it to work,' he grumbles, kneeling on the floor fiddling with the buttons.

We stay up late, drinking and talking. Ron seems to be returning to his old self. The depressed self-obsessive has been replaced by the camp anecdotal charmer. 'I wonder how much Rod *would* pay ...' he speculates of his old acquaintance the editor of the *Mail on Sunday*.

In the morning he's down before me again. 'Oh,' he cries, 'you've just missed a scene.' A table of eight, over the far side of the breakfast room, had been discussing *Castaway 2000*, talking about Roger the doctor, saying what a pain in the arse he was, and Rosemary, too. 'So I got up and went over and said, "Excuse me, you may not recognise me but I'm one of the castaways and I've just left the island and I'd rather you didn't talk about my friends like that while I'm eating my breakfast."'

I laugh. 'How did they take it?'

They saw the point, he says, nodding over at the now cowed group.

When I return from the Post Office an hour later Ron is sitting on the floor of the TV lounge watching the *Castaway* video. He's going to sell his story to the highest bidder, he tells me, and put the money down on a flat.

Eider duck

Chapter 18

A Post-Ron Society

In his self-built house on Black Pipe Beach, meanwhile, Mike Laird was totally unaware of all this drama. On Saturday night he had dined alone on spaghetti and a stock cube. He had been hoping that Trevor would join him, as agreed, bringing booze. But there was no sign of the Scouser, so the Action Man consoled himself by opening a tin of pears. 'I have to say they were magnificent,' he wrote.

Besides copious scribblings in his diary, he had written a short poem. It was entitled *I Love You*.

> *Yesterday we'd not seen each other*
> *Today you're my best friend*
> *To meet you was such little bother*
> *On each other we now depend*

Clues as to the love-object's identity emerged in the second stanza:

> *I sleep between your shapely limbs,*
> *So coloured by the sun*
> *And though you answer none of my whims*
> *You are my number one*

By stanza six, after teasing praise of 'scent as fresh as morning dew', 'hidden curves' and 'short green hair', all was clear:

> *Sometimes you bring moisture to my cheek*
> *But you don't bring kisses too*
> *Oh bloody hell you've started to leak*
> *But my turf-covered hut, I love you!*

The weather worsened. The turfs on Mike's roof having shrunk in the dry weather, the rain swept in, soaking him in his sleeping bag. 'I sometimes wonder why I put myself through things like this,' he mused. 'The truth is I must enjoy it. I went to sleep to the sound of plip, plip, plip on my Goretex jacket.' By Sunday afternoon it was lashing down and the wind was fierce. Outside the sea was dark grey and waves pounded the rocks. 'I could swear that it was growling at me.' He had hoped to stay out alone for three weeks, and so far had accomplished only twelve days; but already he was fantasising about going home: warmth, clean clothes, a shave, a shower, company, a decent meal and a beer. At 9.30 that evening, just as he'd given up all hope of seeing Trevor, who should turn up but Trish, bringing his mail, some chicken and rice from the Careys, and two bits of news: Ron's departure, and, more important for Mike, the forecast of an imminent force eight gale. Some of the community, she said, were worried about him.

Not sure what kind of wind his beloved dwelling could withstand, Mike packed all his gear, then lay for four hours on his plank bed listening to the gathering storm. It was pitch black and raining hard and the Action Man wasn't sleeping. Finally, at 2.15 am, he decided to leg it. Wearing six layers of clothing he stumbled and staggered up the hill with rucksack and three bags. 'The combination of almost no light and rain all over my glasses made it a real effort to see. When I reached the first ridge I was nearly blown off my feet. I actually thought for a while that I might not actually make it with all that gear. I'd have to ditch the bags and come back for them when the storm was gone ...'

The journey, normally 59 minutes, took Mike three and a half hours. He arrived back at quarter to six, to find Sandy in the steading in her nightie having her breakfast, swearing away about someone nicking fruit from the recent delivery. Mike was straight back into the Paible maelstrom, but he didn't care. The hot sweet coffee had never tasted so good. And as the day went on he was greeted with hugs and kisses and he felt 'really special, really loved and it was just so nice'.

Sombreness and Relief

The community were still in a state of half-disbelief that Ron had finally, actually departed. It was no surprise that Julie Lowe happily admitted to being 'extremely relieved. There was an increasing pattern of loss of control going from verbal assault to threats of violence to actual violence ...'

On the day he'd decided to go, she had, in fact, moved to have his Thursday night derangement brought up as a community issue. Ron had got wind of this and screamed at Julie on one of the walkways. Nonetheless, before he'd left, she'd gone down to the kitchen to say goodbye and wish him well. 'Well, good luck, Ron, I hope all goes well for you,' she'd offered.

'I said everything I want to say to you the other day,' he retorted. 'I don't want to talk to you any more.'

'I felt fine,' she told me later. 'I thought, OK, let's leave it there, it's not worth a scene.'

So she hadn't been on the beach. And now, blissfully, he was gone and she could theorise in tranquillity about why he was as he was. 'He's very stentorian about standing up for what he sees to be his rights, regardless of whether they infringe on anybody else's. It's almost as though it's a kind of game where you say black and he says white, you say yes and he says no, just for the hell of it. Perhaps as a gay man he's had his rights infringed upon many occasions, which is why he's so intense about them and so adamant that nobody will actually make him do anything he doesn't want to do.'

The island's other Julie – Julia Corrigan – had a rather different perspective. 'It's very sad about Ron going, but he had to go,' she told the video diary. 'I was just becoming too emotionally hyped around him, because in this strange environment where we all see each other all the time, I was practically living with him. Colin, Ron, myself and Natasha were like one family. I don't know him outside of this project, but I feel fairly certain that he's not normally as on edge and confrontational about things, so clearly it was making him deeply unhappy being here. Basically, I felt as if I was watching somebody slowly unravel in front of my eyes. The various layers of his personality were separating out, so you'd see angry Ron, bitter Ron, funny Ron, happy Ron, depressed Ron instead of it all being a blend. The layers were coming away. That's what this place can do to you, because for some weird reason everything here is bigger than life ...'

'I remember thinking,' wrote Peter to his mother, describing the scene on the beach, 'at last, he's "dead" now, in the Greek sense of exile as death. Because of Lion's stipulation now, leaving the island means the end. So by being on that boat really meant that some end to the nightmare was in sight. Another emotion was not so pleasant. At one moment I saw Roger giving Ron a lengthy hug. I also knew that a month or so earlier Roger had said to Chris Kelly 'get rid of Ron'. It all felt Iago-like. The public schoolboy's capacity for duplicity and hypocrisy never ceases to amaze me. Perhaps I should learn – I get repeated hints about it – a superficial politeness masking vicious competition.

'There is little else to say *re* Ron specifically,' Peter continued. 'In both his and Ray's case something akin to breakdown is figured as a rapid speeding up of emotional states, as they begin to oscillate wildly, to become ever more irrational. Another description which fits, I came across by Sir Philip Sydney, writing of a treacherous son – he has "much poisoning hypocrisy, desperate fraud, smooth malice, hidden ambition and smiling envy as in any living person would be harboured". Seems to sum it up rather nicely.'

Everyone had their angle, but no one disputed that it was time for Ron to go. Most succinct, as always, was Trev: 'I didn't really know him enough to call him a wanker, but from what I've seen of him that was my perception of him.'

The sudden absence of the community's Lord of Misrule created new dynamics. Colin, having wandered around, Julia noted, like a bit of a lost sheep for a while, began hanging out more with Gordon and Patrick. 'We've been calling them Foggy, Compo and Clegg,' Julia said. 'It's very comical, they go off to Buoy Land and hunt around among the debris and try and find things and have little adventures. They're like three old men with nothing better to do. I can see them from the distance, walking around with their hands in their pockets and then all of a sudden they'll stop and pick something up and gather round and discuss what they've just found.'

'The day he left,' reported Tammy, 'there was a mixed element of sombreness and relief. His presence is missed, but there's relief and lightness and people now feel they can speak out. Somehow I think things will now fly unhindered and freer and higher.'

'Since his departure,' wrote Peter, 'the atmosphere has been very subdued. To show too much joy would only inflame the situation further – this is because there are clear "parties" here. Colin (our butcher) lived next door to Ron – he seemed to become his "thing". Because I repeatedly stood up to Ron, in meeting after meeting, and argued for the ethos of this project, those who were in his camp seem to direct their venom and hostility at me. This stems largely from Gwyneth of the coffee fame and Colin, who having lost his frame of reference at the moment – Ron was a much smarter goader of Lion – is bereft, emotionally at sea. The last couple of days it has got so bad that when I enter a room, Colin leaves, along with his side-kick Warren.

'There is a lot of emotional debris flying about so my strategy (actually instinct) is to keep a very low profile. We work hard, we eat fast and then go and lie in the honeyed fields. In the evenings we read.'

Unforeseen Expenses

Though for a while it might have seemed to some that the much-criticised psychotherapist was the author of all their troubles, it wasn't long before new problems sprouted. This time they could in no way be blamed on him.

As Mike had discovered, Sandy Colbeck had now abandoned her duties as the castaways' housekeeper. 'I resign,' she told the video diary, 'from food estimation, purchasing etc, and the voluntary responsibility of generally trying to manage the household element of life here. The last straw was the smallest of incidents, in itself almost a laughable one. I didn't have the foresight to put some fresh fruit into a safe place yesterday, hence when I came into the steading this morning the box had been opened and some of the contents had gone. I'm not interested in the cry of "It's only a few grapes". If you're not prepared to abide by a simple principle that *you* instigated I'm not prepared to do the job any longer.

'This incident,' she went on, 'demonstrates a core of selfishness I find difficult to deal with. In spite of being here for some six months, some people have still not grasped the concept of a little selflessness being a central tenet to a reasonably successful society, not just here but anywhere.'

While the community digested this news, there was a potentially more serious issue over the budget. The castaways were finally coming to terms with just how much they'd spent in their first six months and how little they had left for their second. 'We started off with I think it was £70,000 for the whole year,' Ben reported, 'and it's now the end of July and we have £14,000 left. So we've spent £56,000, which is embarrassing. Well, there you go. I'm not a money person, my exam results will vouch for that as I got a nice big N for Nearly in my A-level economics! So I stayed well clear of any budgets and figures and numbers here and left that to the accountant people.'

These 'accountant people' were Toby and, more recently, Mike. Toby had, by his own admission, just concentrated on entering figures into his spreadsheet, not actually ever advising the community to restrain itself. But recent events had concentrated the community's minds. With Ron going, his allocated £30 a week would now be deducted from the remaining total.

Padraig, in particular, was incensed. 'We're running out of money very fast,' he told the video diary, 'and a lot of it's due to unforeseen expenses, things being sprung on us.'

Trevor had a more reasoned view of the issue. 'It's all about hidden costs,' he summarised. 'Have Lion put a lot of hidden costs onto us? I personally feel not. It might be that one or two things people didn't expect in the budget are here. But in January I was saying about the dogs, do the vet bills come out of the budget? It was never chased, because everybody was too busy arguing. That's all we did, from February, March, April, May; I'd say we argued for three months.'

Meanwhile, schemes to reduce one area of community expense were progressing nicely. Roger's fuel self-sufficiency project was, after his recent visit to Mike on Black Pipe Beach, up and running. Friday 14 July saw the first of a series of peat-cutting parties heading over to 'Sleepy Valley'. It was the good doctor himself, accompanied by Toby, Padraig and the Action Man. At lunchtime the group had taken a long and relaxed break and sat on a rock looking out to sea. 'Half a dozen grey seals popped their heads up and watched us watching them. You could hear the silence,' Mike wrote. 'Roger wondered how long ago it must have been since someone else had sat on that rock and eaten their lunch. Maybe 500 years, who knows?'

Who would have guessed, from his fulminations against the doctor at the end of January, that this friendship between Mike and Roger would have developed so strongly? The next day, Saturday, the Action Man lent a hand taking stuff up to the Dun Loch for a raft that Roger wanted to build for Oliver. 'Everybody carried something,' he wrote. 'It was a really hard slog to get it all up there, but worth it. We then all sat down for lunch. They had a load of smoked salmon that they had got on their personal allowance. What a treat! I really do like Roger and Rose a lot. Roger then asked for some help with the raft so I pretty well built the whole thing. It floats. Yippee!'

The mellow mood continued that evening, with a party that Ben had organised in the schoolhouse. 'A great time!' wrote Mike. 'None of the young children, just Mike and Jodene. The music was blaring. We drank, we danced, laughed and dressed up in some of the stuff from the box. I put on a dress and a blonde wig and swanned around like a right queen. It's cringeworthy to know that this is all on film and could be shown. It went on until 2 am and it came out officially that Toby and Tammy are together.'

At the end of the evening, Toby had asked his girlfriend outside for a kiss. 'Oh, just give me a kiss in here,' she told him. 'I've had enough of trying to keep things quiet.' She kissed him then and there, in full view of the others on the dance floor. With Ron going, she told me later, it was easier. 'Because he would comment on everything.' He'd remarked that Toby was just a rebound after Ben. 'And it's not,' Tammy assured me, with the lovelight in her eyes, 'it's the furthest thing possible from that. Where I am now is the best place to be.'

Custody of the Sheep

'It's sweet,' observed Tammy's long-ago admirer Ben. 'I'm really glad they're together. I think they're quite a well-suited couple and I have a suspicion that it'll get stronger and stronger. A few people have asked if I'm jealous, but I'm not, I'm happy for them. So anyway,' he went on briskly, 'Padraig and Philiy have stopped seeing each other at the same time as Tammy and Toby have started. I think they're having quite a difficult time, but they did have this very intense relationship for about six months. A relationship here is rather different to a relationship on the mainland, because normally it takes quite a while from when you first start seeing someone to when you live with them, and of course here, you're living with them straightaway. And the hardest part of that is that when you finish, you're still living with them. So they're feeling strange about it, which is a shame, because it affects all of us, we feel uneasy when they're both around.'

Trev was more flippant. 'Don't know who's going to get custody of the sheep,' he quipped. 'I think Padraig's going to be seeing the sheep mainly at weekends and the CSA are now after him for more of his personal allowance.' But Trevor continued more seriously: 'Padraig's come back in leaps and bounds. He's absolutely spot on again. I remember when we went to Keswick he was brilliant, a diamond, and then when he got with Philiy he was basically following her around quite comfortably. Which a lot of people do in a lot of cases. He lost himself within her. His personality and his outlook and everything. Whereas now it's like a having a new castaway. It's very strange having a couple who have split. Philiy's walking around, she doesn't look as if she's got a lot to do, but Padraig's back on form and hopefully we'll see a lot more of him.'

The weather continued 'gorgeous'. The next day Trevor, Toby, Tammy and Trish headed off on a round-island walk. 'Absolutely fantastic,' the Scouser reported. 'Glorious day, sunburnt, red raw, dead sore. The views, the chat, the laugh, the crack of it all, couldn't think of a better place to be.'

The days passed pleasantly and quietly in what Julia Corrigan described as 'a post-Ron society'. 'Colin really misses him,' she elaborated. 'Night times we're at a loose end, there's nothing really to do, so we just have more sex.' Monday was Dez's birthday and a game of Who Wants To Be A Taransay Millionaire? was organised in the steading. Padraig won and his million, reported Mike, proved to be homebrew, wine, sweets and tobacco. In the middle of the night the Action Man got up to go for a pee off his balcony and met Trish coming out of Trev's room. 'Hmmm,' he wrote.

Tuesday 18 July saw a little drama when Inca still hadn't come home at 11.30 pm. A search party of Mike, Ben, Padraig, Toby and Tanya was sent off and the dog was eventually discovered in the bothy, where she had been taken in by some visitors. It was 2 am by now, and as Ben shared an early morning cup of tea with the strangers he heard an unwelcome tale. They had seen Fran, Trish's dog who had recently bitten Roger, chasing sheep. 'I mean,' said Ben, 'actually on the back of these sheep ripping at their fur.' It was something that Trish had always denied her dogs did, right from the very first argument with Peter that I had witnessed on 17 January.

Peter wasn't around to hear his criticisms of Trish's dogs vindicated, six months after the event. He and Sheila had gone camping, just to be out of the 'hothouse' that Paible still was for him. For three nights they slept against the ruins of an old black house by a gurgling stream, cooking with sticks in an old catering can of beans on a peat and driftwood fire. 'Quite why I find myself the target of such hostility is something I have had to meditate on long and hard,' Peter wrote to his mother. 'I do wish I had a male friend of my age to discuss these matters with. I suspect it's because I'm not ready to compromise with what I regard as bullshit.'

Sheila, meanwhile, threw herself into observing Nature with her ever-imaginative eye. Wandering over the rocks below their encampment she had looked down into rock pools and seen stones that looked like islands. Each was surrounded by the most vivid lime green tidemark, 'a perfect even margin like a fringe of silk'. She was reminded of the work of the sculptor Christo, who had once wrapped real islands in pink silk. Then there were black rocks with bright orange intrusions and quartz lines running across them, which made her think of paintings by Klein and Jackson Pollock. It had given her lots of ideas for sculptures and paintings she wanted to do once the main community work was over.

Philiy had also gone camping – on her own. 'I just don't want to see him,' she told the video diary. 'We're trying to be friends but we haven't had that important space you need when you've split up with someone.'

Instead she perched above a cliff overlooking the Atlantic Ocean and knitted a scarf and wrote letters and watched the amazing sunsets and thought about her good friends in San Francisco, way across the sea in front of her. 'I just let my mind wander and it was a really nice sort of daydream, thinking about memories and my friends.'

She returned to find herself in the middle of a follow-up drama involving Fran, who had been seen by 'literally everyone', Ben reported, chasing the sheep. 'Trish couldn't deny that one,' he continued, 'because she was there, she saw it. So she disciplined her dog. Now there's different forms of discipline, it's the same with children, everyone has their own technique, and if, say, I catch Inca chasing sheep, which rarely happens, but it's been known, I will tell her to sit down and then I give her a little slap on the nose. But Trish's discipline was – cruel is the only way of saying it.'

'I was walking past,' said Philiy, 'as Trish came in and she grabbed the dogs and picked them up by their neck on the collar and then went round the back of the stables. As I walked up to the pods I could hear her screaming at Fran and I kept walking and part of me thought, Turn round, because if that was your dog you wouldn't want it to be happening to it. Trish isn't a bad woman, she's lovely. But you can't do that to an animal.'

Peter and Sheila returned from their break on the Friday evening, 'much rested, refreshed, happy, fit and well' to hear, first, the shocking Fran-Trish story – and second that Ron had gone against his solemn guarantee of a fortnight before – 'his last words were promises not to say anything!' – and sold his story to the *Daily Mail*. Peter found himself revealed to the nation as Fat Boy Grim. 'He wants to be in control,' revealed the dependable psychotherapist, 'As you see on TV, he's loud, sexist, bossy, intimidating and manipulative. He shouts people down and tries to bully them into what he thinks is right. At first I argued with him, then just ignored him. He had disgusting habits, like soaking his feet in the bowl in which we kneaded the bread.'

Other of Ron's enemies came in for similar treatment. Toby was Pig Boy, 'and not just because he looked after the pigs – he was hardly somebody you'd take to the Savoy. He wore open sandals and would walk through the pig muck, then into the kitchen.' Julie Lowe was Von Trapp On Speed, 'because you'd mention something in passing and she'd turn it into the line from a song and belt it out at full throttle. There was no love lost from the minute we met. I discovered she'd stabbed me in the back many times, claiming I was a troublemaker and before I left I told her what a bitch I thought she was.'

Nice. Roger, Rosemary, Colin, Julia, Padraig, Philiy, Pat, Gwyneth and the Latore family were spared the psychotherapist's scorn. But he was well away now and Peter, for one, wasn't even bothered to read it. 'I'm a fat bastard or something,' he wrote. '*Que sera sera*!' 'Honestly,' Julie Lowe assured her friends, 'it doesn't bother me. He's left the island and now I can get on with enjoying what's left of the year.'

On Saturday 22 July she took to the hills with Floozie. 'Swam in the loch, picnicked, read my book and then played on the raft with Roger, Rosemary and kids. Wonderful!'

Ben, meanwhile, had spent the whole weekend on the big raft off the beach.

'Liz and Dez and I put some roll mats down and just lay and read and had such a lovely time. Then Padraig and Tanya came out and we bought some home-made beer and just chattered for hours and hours and it was so bleep-bleep wonderful.' Ron had described him in the *Mail* as 'a bit vacuous', but, 'so what? I don't care. I don't even know what it means anyway. He said I couldn't peel a carrot. I can now!'

Prizes All Round

On the Sunday the idyll was added to by the amusing spectacle of two microlites buzzing over the strait. One landed on the spit, was unable to take off again and had to be rescued by the coastguard. It was two chaps with more money than sense, Mike wrote, who had come all the way from Edinburgh at an altitude of 7000 feet.

Meanwhile Dez and Liz had returned from a night at the bothy to find Sandy had picked the prize cucumber they had been growing for the forthcoming South Harris Agricultural Show, to which the castaways were submitting entries. 'About fifteen people,' Julia reported, 'said, "Sandy's picked your cucumber. What are you going to do about it?" But they just fell about laughing. They couldn't believe we were all so concerned about it.' How things had changed!

There were quite a few other entries for the show. Colin Corrigan had put in a picture of the Natural Arch and, reported wife Julia, 'a particularly strange sculpture, a whale bone suspended from a piece of fishing twine and surrounded by barbed wire tipped in blood-like red paint'. He'd called it 'Safety Of A Species'. 'It's supposed to be a statement about saving the whale, so it's a bit of an animal rights thing,' Julia explained, 'which is interesting, coming from Colin. I don't know if the South Harris Show is quite ready for this, but we'll see,' she laughed.

Sandy had made a patchwork cushion cover. Hilary entered some jigsaw puzzles. Dez had put in a backgammon board, inlaid with different types of wood he had found; Ciara a picture of her pod; Pat some bread rolls. If Lion gave them final permission they were going to be taken over by Tanya and Rosemary, acting as camera and sound.

Tanya was nervous about leaving the island. 'I haven't packed for a trip for seven months,' she told the video diary. 'And I suddenly started getting really nervous about what I actually need in the real world. Thank God I did my washing yesterday because we've got a level of grubbiness here which is perfectly acceptable. The thought of all those people and cars and noise and hotels and attention is a bit nerve-wracking, but very exciting at the same time.'

It was only tiny Leverburgh they were going to, and they were back that same night. 'It was a very local, quite low-key event,' the camerawoman reported. 'It was good fun, not too weird. Nice meeting and chatting to local people and we were very much welcomed and I think it helped build a few bridges. It made us feel like part of a wider community here on Harris. But to be honest, it was far more exciting coming back here. It was really lovely being in the steading and everyone got just so excited about the prizes they'd won. It makes you realise how much now we are isolated and how things like village fetes and prizes for your breadrolls become huge news for a community like ours. The information that got the biggest roar was that Rosemary and I had eaten an ice-cream, which is something no one has done in the seven months that they've been here. So everyone was extremely jealous. But it felt like coming home, it really did, like coming home to my family.'

And hadn't they done well! First prizes had gone to Ciara Latore for her picture of a pod and to Pat for his white bread rolls. Second prize rosettes went to Sandy for her patchwork cushion, Yoneh for a shell bracelet, Mike for a shell-framed mirror and Liz and Monica for some carrots. Cassie came third in her class with a loaf. Best of all Colin Corrigan's strange sculpture also scooped a first prize. 'We are all so chuffed,' wrote Mike.

Getting Excited Now

The castaways were now just a few days away from an event that they had been speculating about with much excitement for some time – Visitors' Week. 'I'm getting excited now,' said Philiy on the Wednesday. 'I'm really proud of what we've done here and I really want to show people at home, so that when you go back you can talk about it and people understand. At the same time it's going to be chaos, lots of people, lots of hard work.'

Trevor had decided not to have any visitors. 'In fact,' he told the diary, 'I haven't even told me parents that there is a Visitors' Week. I just can't be arsed. There's thirty-four of us, we're going to have over a hundred people, it's a big enough island, but it ain't that big.

'There'll be like a truce when the families arrive,' Trevor continued. 'But behind the scenes everybody'll be backbiting, unloading. I think a lot of people are going to unload on the families, tell them what's been happening, all the problems in the way they've seen them, all their viewpoints. And when they go everybody's going to feel a lot fresher. It's going to be like a big confessional box. Loads of fresh women, should be a good laugh, a good chat up. Tobe and I might go on a bit of a mission to see what we can pull. Padraig's already said we need to have a sister talk before everybody turns up because basically he's got a really good-looking sister and he doesn't want me to be diving in. But I'm going to do me best. I'm going to have a good laugh and not upset anyone.'

'It may turn out to be a real bore,' said Oliver (aged 7).

Having waited 'for weeks' for Angus MacKay to come and show them how to shear their flock, the sheep group had decided to take matters into their own hands. 'I decided today, Let's sort them out, let's cut them,' reported Ben, 'because yesterday and the day before have been boiling here and the poor sheep were sitting there in the biggest, fluffiest coats you've ever seen, just absolutely panting. So – coats off!' He had worked out a system where they could get all the animals into one of the little pens round the back of the steading. Padraig and Philiy had chased them in there first thing on the Monday and then they weeded out all the lambs and the ones that had already been shaved by Angus. 'Then we all held the sheep and basically started using these shearing things to cut them – quite difficult I hasten to add.'

Mike Laird was on hand to help. 'None of us really had any idea what we were doing but we gave it a go anyway. We had traditional scissor-type shears and set to. We got the first one on its back and Philiy started off. Ben held the head and I held the back legs as it was kicking away. It was nowhere near as easy as it looks in the films. The sheep was so stressed that it was grinding its teeth and shitting all over the place. It took almost an hour and even then it didn't look that great. It was like a really bad haircut.'

Taking so long with the rusty shears, the group switched to a big pair of scissors that Ben had seen in the schoolhouse. This was much better. At least they met in the middle. Between the three of them (Mike had now wandered off to write) they managed five further sheep, including the anti-scab injection the vet had shown them how to administer, although Ben managed to inject himself by mistake. 'I'm a little bit worried,' he grimaced at the video diary, 'as it says DO NOT INJECT YOURSELF WITH THIS on the bottle. And also we'd used the needles quite a few times on the sheep, so it did have sheep's blood on it and stuff. So I'm a bit worried I might turn into a sheep now. That will be my come-uppance from the sheep for everything I've done to them over this year. I've been to see Roger and he gave the vet an emergency call and he's going to get back to us. So I hope I don't wake up in the morning with woolly legs and horns.'

But no – in the morning, the heart-throb was still thoroughly human. Day Two saw a much-more-like-it thirteen sheep sheared. Tammy had returned from her camping trip with Toby and shown them all what to do. 'It turns out,' said a bemused Ben, 'that she's actually done a course or she's been a sheep shearer before – all a big mystery if you ask me.' In fact, unbeknownst to quite a few of the others, the Bedfordshire beauty had been taking secret lessons from Angus MacKay and his men up at their shearing site on the other end of the island. It was something, she had confessed to a video diary in early June, she had always quietly dreamed of doing.

Other preparations for the invasion went ahead apace. Padraig had painted the ceiling of his pod. 'That's about the extent of the renovation I'm going to do in my humble abode,' he said. Mike had washed his sleeping bag for his mother. 'I doubt the smell of six months of sweaty socks and camp fires would be appealing to her.' Jules had 'a good old clear out' of her lovely home and repainted the scratched and bitten areas ('that dog again!'). And on the Friday the castaways had a huge site clear-up. Mike finished painting the sign he had been working on for the slaughterhouse. Julia and Monica sorted out the schoolhouse, 'which looked as if someone had thrown a hand grenade in there and left it', while Sandy, Gwyneth and Tammy did a phenomenal job on the steading, reported Julie Lowe. 'It looked superb by the time they had finished. Gwyneth's garden looks wonderful and the sweet peas have suddenly burst into flower. The weather has been gorgeous. Let's hope,' she concluded nervously, 'we haven't used up our "quota".'

Chapter 19

Our Own Family

'In the morning it was just so exciting,' Ben reported, 'we all had our binoculars out and were looking over to Horgabost beach on the other side and you could make out lots of little figures, but not who they were. Then you could see them all being herded towards the landing craft. I was so completely nervous, I don't know why, about seeing my family. I had butterflies and had to go to wee lots of times; it was like before you have an exam. I know other people felt like this as well. So we were all waiting outside the schoolhouse for the boat to arrive and as it got nearer we all rushed down.'

'The anticipation's been incredible this morning,' reported Roger. 'Everyone was hanging around, anxious, excited, lots of hysterical giggling. And when the first boat arrived, it was incredibly exciting – just to see people being reunited was amazing – very emotional.'

The first boat included Padraig's sister Maureen, Mike's twin sister Ashley and her daughter Ilona, and Trish's oldest daughter Joanna, who had been offered the chance of being a castaway, but decided to stay back on the Isle of Man with her grandparents for the year. 'She hasn't changed at all,' reported Trish. 'She's just the same. I'll find out later if she's been drinking or smoking or anything.'

On the second boat came Ben's parents and Mike's closest friend Steve, whom the Action Man had first met when they'd failed the Officer Selection course together. Now a policeman in Weymouth, Steve had been Mike's companion on those daring adventures to Cambodia and Jordan. 'I had already heard that he'd slept out last night,' wrote Mike, 'rather than staying in the hotel. He had also considered swimming all the way over to see me but thankfully in the end only had a short swim. At least the dear chap didn't let me down. He came off the boat in his wet suit with bare feet. Some people here think I'm a bit bonkers at times and maybe now will see why. I think Steve and I get on so well because we both think the same way and like flaunting with danger. It gives us a buzz. '

The visitors were taken up to the pods and shown round the site. They were 'very taken with the beautiful vegetables growing so well both out in the fields and in the polytunnels,' reported Julie Lowe. 'The animals, too, came in for much admiration, the cows in particular proving a great draw, with many spectators enjoying evening milking – some even having a go at hand milking and quickly appreciating the value we put on the milking machine! Fresh milk, fresh eggs and fresh vegetables, together with home killed pork and lamb meant that our visitors feasted royally. It was a huge challenge doing food for seventy people per day – we couldn't have done it without our friends and families mucking in to help – poor Mum stood peeling carrots for three whole hours without complaint (thanks Mum!)'

'My father was just absolutely breathtaken,' Ben told the video diary. 'He couldn't believe how beautiful it could be here. My mother couldn't get over the sea, how clear and blue it was.' While the Fogle parents headed back to their hotel on Harris, Ben's sisters and friends decided to stay over. 'Suddenly my pod had four of us sleeping in it and Inca, which was odd after the number of lonely, well, solitary evenings I've had in there.'

That first Saturday evening there was an impromptu party round a bonfire at the back of Pod Two. 'Lion must have realised that there was an unusually large amount of alcohol and a great number of drunken people kicking around,' wrote Mike. 'Fortified by homebrew of varying strengths and descriptions,' wrote Julie Lowe, 'we talked and sang and were joyous and thankful, long into the night.'

An Extra Visitor

On the Monday I arrived at the Harris Hotel. It was all going well, Chris Kelly told me, in a snatched moment away from his mobile. We drove down in convoy to Horgabost beach, where we were mobbed by a gang of pre-pubescent campers who wanted Ben's autograph. Then it was over the calm strait on Angus's old landing craft.

It was bizarre being just one of many outsiders. The steading was packed with strange faces, and the usual rush of the stranded islanders to tell you the latest news and gossip didn't happen. Only Trevor, who had no visitors, seemed to be actively interested in gabbing into my tape recorder this time.

So after supper I joined a youthful gang (plus Padraig's parents) who were living it up on sickly-sweet 'bilberry wine' on the wooden steps outside Tammy's room in Pod One. There were plenty of pretty young women for Trev to get stuck into, if he so desired, and his platonic chum Trish would let him, including Padraig's sister Maureen, and Peter's two daughters, who gave an altogether more attractive context to the vilified lecturer.

The visitors had quickly got sucked into castaway ways. Whenever Gwyneth went past, the gang on the pod steps shout-screamed 'Silent Night' – some new island joke to do with Roger's singing group that I had yet to catch up on. In return Pat dropped his trousers and waved his skinny naked backside around. 'Did you see that!' cried Philiy as the others laughed.

Tammy, Toby, Trev and Ben, they told me, had been comparing notes on the interviews I'd done with them three weeks before. 'What did he ask you about?' 'Relationships?' 'So we know what you're up to,' teased Tammy. She had no visitors either, as her mother had had a relapse and had to go into hospital.

It was good, Toby told me, to see people's visitors, because it made you see people in the round – Peter and his daughters, for instance. It was a point to be made later in several castaway video diaries. 'So incredible to see everyone's families and friends,' said Ben, 'because it added a whole completely new dimension to them.'

In the morning I walked across the island with Mike and Steve the policeman to see Black Pipe Beach. The relationship of these two gung-ho adventurers was as well developed as an old married couple. Mike spouted confidently as Steve stayed silent, pacing purposefully along a little ahead in his cutaway black T-shirt and dark glasses. Beyond the bothy isthmus we paused for a Mars Bar and a gulp of water from the shallow loch that Mike had used for his drinking supply when he'd been camping out. As we strode on, he pointed out the corrugated lazybeds that swept down to his home in Sleepy Valley.

Black Pipe Beach turned out to be one of the most exposed bits of the far section of the island, an unprepossessing swathe of stones by a bleak shore. Mike's hut was an eccentric mini-pod, cobbled together from driftwood, its turf roof now broken into comic dry oblongs. The Scottish flag flapped in the breeze. 'You're like the Queen,' remarked Steve dryly. 'You fly the flag whenever you're in residence.'

The famous Black Pipe was smaller than I'd imagined, only about two and a half feet in diameter. Mike reckoned it had come off an oil or gas installation. It ran at right angles to the broken-down black house he, Trev and Toby had first slept out in. The dead sheep was still there, as it had been since March. 'It stinks a bit,' Mike observed, 'but it's actually quite handy for taking a bit of stinky wool off and starting a fire.' We walked the fifty yards or so up to the top of the little peninsula to look at Roger's peat-gathering operation. The black cubes had been dug out deep and the top turf replaced. Driftwood had been spread around nearby to act as a drying rack.

As we stood there Angus's rib arrived, bringing Roger, Chris and the crew to film the peat-gathering operation. I headed back over the lazybeds with Charles Guard, a visitor of Roger's, with Steve the policeman pacing silently ahead.

Guard had known the now-notorious doctor since his professional pianist days, fifteen years before. He had been reporting on a competition in the Isle of Man for a local radio station and had been impressed by Roger's piano playing. 'So we had a drink and chatted and found we had things in common, and we've known each other ever since.'

The portrayal of his old friend as an irksome cuss had surprised him. But, he said, 'I can see how it came about. Roger's a bit of a stickler for detail.' As a documentary maker himself, Guard's professional-eye view of the project was intriguing.

What had happened, it seemed to him, was the film company had become like the headmaster in a school. Simultaneously they were trying to film people talking about them, and trying to outwit them by bringing in contraband, and it meant that it was difficult to do a properly detached job.

'It's very odd,' he went on, 'to see adults arguing amongst themselves about how they've outwitted Jeremy or Chris and stolen something in, like naughty schoolboys. And these tiny things become major issues in their lives, because they've lost the swim of taking the kids to school and dealing with life in its wider sense. It's absolutely bizarre. I can't get over some of the conversations I've heard.'

After another gourmet lunch (the castaways were doing their visitors proud, with home-baked pizzas and an impressive range of Taransay-grown salads) I decided to behave like a visitor myself and see the settlement as it now was, with outsiders' eyes.

Dez offered to show me round. So much had changed, even from my last trip up; from my first visit the place was unrecognisable. Here at the back of the steading, which had once been a sea of mud, was 'the fank', where last week the sheep had been sheared; the Portakabin full of 'big foods' – flour, beans, seeds etc; Colin's completed slaughterhouse and adjacent layerage, above which Mike had painted his sign saying *LAST CHANCE SALOON. Prop: Big Mike. Rooms By the Hour.* Round the corner, beyond the store for animal feed, were four stables, which the cows would use when the weather worsened. Hanging against the back wall of the steading were sheep's fleeces, being cured to make coats and rugs. A rusted old filing cabinet had been converted by Colin into a smoker, for pork and, one day, if they ever caught any, fish.

On to the polytunnels, which were as hot and humid as the tropics in the rainy season. Once bleakly flapping polythene arches, they were now cornucopias of fruition. Rosemary, Liz and himself were the mainstays here, Dez told me. He preferred working inside than out in the fields with Peter, who could be a bit demanding. I nodded sagely at this novel piece of information. Polytunnel Three was the dedicated herb tent, with parsley, coriander, dill, fennel, oregano, basil and marjoram laid out in neat rows – and in the damp air, a mixed scent to revive the most world-weary cynic. Outside, in more neat rows, Dez had planted shallots; while Rosemary the Broccoli Queen managed not just that vegetable but rocket, beetroot, outdoor tomatoes, parsley and cabbage.

Round the front of the steading, things were much the same as they'd been for months: the big muddy pig enclosure to the left; the chicken huts central; the little garden to the right. Since Ron's departure three weeks before, the chickens – 39 pullets and 2 cockerels – had been handled by Dez, Rosemary, Sandy and Jules. The adjacent chicken-rearing shed (another Dez project) contained four broody hens and one overworked cock. The cockerel shed beyond, he said, with just the flicker of a raised eyebrow, was Gordon and Cassie's domain. Beyond Gwyn's pretty little garden was the cold store, a turfed arch sunk three feet into the ground – 'Tammy's area,' Dez told me.

Still a couple of months behind with the video diary transcripts, much of this was new to me. Even Philiy's pet lamb Scraggy, with his turquoise scarf tied around his neck, hanging out with the pullets in the main chicken shed, was a *Castaway* character I hadn't fully got my head around just yet. As I left Dez and wandered around jotting down details of notices, cooking rotas, and so on, I wondered how much other stuff I'd missed, would inevitably miss. Perhaps the only way to document the castaways' existence would have been to live with them, to have had my own little castaway writer's pod. But then, of course, I would have become one of them, taken sides, got angry, lovelorn, depressed, or worse. And how would I have coped if I'd been isolated as the *bête noir*, as Peter now was? Badly, was the honest answer. Like Tanya Cheadle, I needed to be liked; I wouldn't have even begun to manage the lecturer's gneiss-like imperturbability. You had to hand it to Lion, whatever mistakes they'd made on the hoof, they'd done a good job in the selection process. The castaways were all, in their different ways, remarkable people. Which, I suppose, begged the question: was this really a cross-section of society?

I was saved from over-introspection by Julie Lowe, inviting me to her pod for a pre-prandial glass of Cabernet Sauvignon with her mother Joy. Mum wasn't staying on the island like the other families, preferring a twice-daily boat trip and the comfort of the Harris Hotel. But she was enjoying her days. 'I know there have been problems, but there appeared to be no conflict.' Having seen the TV programmes she hadn't expected it to be quite so free of conflict.

The conflict went on in the background, I explained, under the calm exterior. On my several visits I'd never once seen anyone actually shout in anger at someone else. The bitching had gone on, privately, in pods, in quiet corners of steading and schoolhouse, out in the field. In any case, we agreed, everyone was putting their best foot forward. 'I just hope this will continue next week,' Joy continued. 'I would like to think it will. I have a *feeling* it will – now certain things have happened.' We didn't mention what those certain things might be.

For Joy, though, the biggest surprises had been what the project had revealed about her daughter. Julie's wonderful descriptive letters had been a huge surprise. 'I didn't think the first one was yours,' she told her daughter now. 'Isn't that awful? I thought you had lifted certain things from a guidebook or something. When you were describing the island it was so well put together, I thought, "This isn't Julie." I had no idea how articulate you were.'

Oh, the confidence of parents!

On the Wednesday morning I continued my visitor's tour, with a look at Peter's famous field. We walked up together along the deer fence and the bearded lecturer was, as he'd always been with me, charming and soft-spoken as he guided me expertly along the cultivated rows. Here was the second sowing of carrots, the second sowing of swedes, the beetroot which did so well in this sandy soil, Dez's withered sweetcorn, which Peter had always known wouldn't do any good in this climate. It was an impressive display, and Peter was clearly in charge, though, with me, modestly not admitting as much. 'I did have the most knowledge,' he told me, 'so I felt that's what I was expected to do. And to bring it off is a nice feeling. Trying to grow in an extreme climate. Of course if you had a second year it would be easier, you'd have learned a lot, you'd refine it.'

In the spreading meadow beyond, the deer fence had allowed a veritable carpet of wild flowers to spring up. Dandelions, hairbell, ladies' bedstraw, creeping vetch, pink clover (which was beautifully scented after rain), yarrow. The flowers changed every two weeks or so, he added.

Down to the left were a row of cultivated lazybeds. They were Roger's, Peter observed, without going into the doctor's motivation for this freelance growing of spuds and oats. Up in the top left corner of the meadow, Dez and Liz also had an experimental patch – oats and barley in this case.

Back in Peter's pod, I found his two daughters: art-student Jessie, 22, and international relations student Henrietta, 20. They were very glad they had made the journey, they told me, when we were left alone. 'Totally reassured,' said Jessie. It had been strange having Peter and Sheila away on an island, in the dark about what was really going on. 'Because they're your parents, you're not sure that what they say in their letters is what's really going on. So to come here and dispel any wild imaginings ...'

'Such as?'

'That people don't like them and they're not getting on with anybody. That was one of the fears. Seeing the programmes and knowing our own parents and how Peter can sometimes come across to people.' She was specifically talking about the arguments with Tanya over the washing up and Trish over her dogs in the first programmes (the others hadn't yet been shown). But her fears had been allayed. People here did realise what he was like.

Henrietta could actually understand Tanya's reaction. 'I've reacted like that sometimes.' Peter had very set ways, Jessie chipped in, and strong ideas on how things should be done, and in the family they always argued a lot, although in a very constructive way; they were more like loud discussions. The thing with Peter, added Henrietta, was if something was going on, he wouldn't want to hush it up.

Over and above these insights into the Jowers' home life, it was interesting to me how much more wised-up to the business of television the daughters were than their parents. Despite what critics in the newspapers and on radio had said, they told me, about how anybody doing the project must have been doing it to be on television, Peter and Sheila really *hadn't* done the project for the TV side. It was Jessie who had suggested that Sheila watch *Paddington Green* before they signed up. 'The thing is they never really watched a lot of television, and for them to come into a docu-drama, which is basically what they did, they needed to see how vulnerable people are. It's a totally constructed thing. We wanted them to see how strong the element that television plays would be.'

They were a protective pair, these daughters, and they cast 'Fat Boy Grim' and 'Arty Farty' in an entirely new light for me. 'It's only because I know that Peter, deep down, is so lovely,' said Henrietta, 'and I think people misunderstand him sometimes.'

Chickens

The sun was still shining from a cloud-fluffed blue sky, picking out the fat white T of the schoolhouse roof against the shimmering blue of the strait beyond. Up in the lush, flower-thick long grass of the meadow Liz was lying with Dez's best friend Debbie watching Dez play football with a bunch of assorted visitor lads. 'That's why Dez likes children,' said Debbie, 'because there's always someone to boss around.'

After lunch I sat with Rosemary outside the steading, at the table made from an old cable drum, with the ex-maypole, still with fluttering coloured ribbons, at its centre. Behind us the Home Education guinea-pigs screamed with excitement as they played with a huge black buoy, 12ft long and 3ft high, which they rolled back and forth, and tried to climb up on. Was I intending to write about the kids? she asked.

Watching them play, I was indeed getting a handle on the kids at last. Chubby little Michael, with his sheepish hang-dog expression, a Just William-like character forever in search of a prank or scheme, was the oldest of the boy gang and a sometime playmate of cheeky Oliver, the nearest lad to him in age; though when Angus MacKay's boy came over from the mainland, Rosemary told me, Wee Mike would drop Oliver like a stone. Beautiful dark-haired Natasha Corrigan was Oliver's special friend (ten years on, those huge hazel eyes of hers would have made him her slave). Moving down, there were the three five-year-olds, Roger and Rosemary's cherub-featured blond Felix, Warren and Monica's skinny blonde Ciara, and the Careys' rumbustious Yoneh. Toddling little Aaron Carey (2) was in a group of his own.

For the adults, the biggest problem came with the three five-year-olds. This was a subject that Rosemary had strong off-the-record views on, but that Monica Latore had been actively eager to discuss with me on this visit. She knew, she said, that Ciara and Felix were a pair together and that Yoneh had slightly become the odd one out, but this had nothing, absolutely nothing to do with colour. 'In any case me and Warren couldn't really be accused of being racist.' The problem was simple: Ciara and Felix were at the same stage at school, a bit ahead of Yoneh, who needed a lot more one-to-one support. All of them had picked up on this, and often asked why they weren't working on the same things. 'Then outside of school,' a concerned Monica had continued, 'there are so many things that Yoneh and Aaron aren't allowed to do that the other kids do, like play on the beach, take their shoes and socks off, go in the sea.' Often they were kept in their pod. So again Yoneh was set apart. Kids being kids, and Ciara and Felix being so close, they could be mean to Yoneh sometimes. Yoneh then felt left out and in order to assert herself and get involved she tended to throw her weight around – she was quite a big, strong child.

But how much longer these juvenile squabbles would be a problem for the community was anyone's guess. Like Trevor, Gordon had no visitors this week and he was making no secret of his disgust with the project. 'Nothing has changed,' he said, shaking his head wearily from side to side. 'It's the same old things. After a while you just think, Forget it, I've had enough of this nonsense. I just want to get away from here, as far and as quickly as I can.'

'But things have improved since Ron's gone?'

'No. It is pretty much the same. As I told you before, if I had known what it would be like before I came, I wouldn't have come. It's nothing like I thought it would be.'

'Is it the TV programme?'

'It's because of the people. The people they have here, they make it so painful to be here, I just want to go.'

Cassie, however, still wanted to stick it out. She had tried to persuade him to stay, but he had made up his mind. 'So I suppose the best thing for me is just to stay on my own,' Cassie sighed.

And Beans

Hilary had been noticeably much more in her element, with her gaggle of husband, children, and friends from Scarborough around her. Now, she told me, she was thinking of going. It was something she had been pondering for a while now, but seeing her family again had just made her wonder whether it was worth it. 'I've always been really enthusiastic, right from the start,' she told me, 'but it just seemed to become ridiculous, all the contraband and then agreeing to have rules and people not sticking by them. I just thought: Am I part of a farce?'

All this made her miss 'them at home' more. 'But I couldn't say anything,' she explained. 'I wouldn't write it, because they'd think I was unhappy and then they'd be unhappy.' So she had waited to discuss it till her husband Paul and the children had come to the island. She'd been planning to go back with them. But Paul (a short, genial, bearded carpentry teacher with a fondness for feeble jokes), it seemed, was quite happy for her to stay.

His major problem, he told me, when she'd first been gone in January had been cooking – he wasn't very good at it. But he'd had a lot of help from friends and the ladies in the school where he worked, and now he had a range of special meals that he could prepare, so that was OK. So now, although it was obviously Hilary's choice, he'd told her to give it a bit longer. 'Because she's put such a lot of effort into what she's done so far. And she is very good across the community. She will gel with anybody. And coming home, once you leave that's it.' He didn't want her coming home, then saying, 'Yeah, maybe I should have stuck it a bit longer.' So, on his advice, she was going to take it as it came and see how she felt in a month's time.

So what did he think of his wife's media profile, I asked. Paul didn't disappoint me by missing the joke. 'Lots of people said to me at first, "Hey, your wife spoke!" Somebody had just cooked a meal, Ray, I think, and he said, "I've done this and I've done that, and Hilary said, "And beans." And that's all she said,' he laughed. 'Everyone at home said, "Oh, she'll be getting the one-liners soon." '

Surprise, Surprise

That afternoon Roger was taking Oliver up to the Dun Loch to play on the raft they had built, so I abandoned my visitor interviews and joined them. Again, it was my first summertime visit to the loch, its dark waters set invitingly in the surrounding heathery bowl of mountain. Inviting to look at, but freezing to actually dive into, not that diving was really an option on these slimy, slippery brown rocks. Even with both arms out at right angles, it was hard to balance. Instead, I paddled Oliver's little raft out to the middle and swam from there, wondering, as I emerged breathless forty-five seconds later, whether I had just put an end to my own chances of having children and taking part in such a charmingly bucolic scene as this.

That evening the breeze strengthened and there were white tops on the waves in Taransay Strait. Was it going to be too rough for the boat? Roger thought so. I lay waiting on a mattress in the schoolhouse, my packed bag beside me. Philiy appeared, with a couple of cameras. Something special was going to happen, she told me, but she wasn't allowed to say what. All right then, it was Gordon's mother. Gordon had no visitors for Visitors' Week, so the BBC were flying in his mother. She was over here from St Kitts anyway for an eye operation.

'We nearly thought,' wrote Julie Lowe, 'we'd changed over from BBC 1 to ITV when Lion TV sprang a "Surprise Surprise" on Gordon. The Careys had chosen to keep a pretty low profile over Visitors' Week, as was their custom. But they were lured down to the beach by Gordon's fishing buddies, Colin and Pat, on the pretext that they were going to need help unloading a new oven. Cassie and the kids had also come down to watch, Cassie being a a keen cook and so having a vested interest. Colin passed the binoculars to Gordon, saying he thought he recognised someone on the boat. Gordon, not particularly interested, but to humour Colin, had a quick casual look, and then lowered the binoculars to peer in puzzlement at the boat. It was wonderful. You could almost see the cogs whirr and the connections being made. Gordon snatched the binoculars back up to his eyes and shouted out incredulously, "That's my sister!" and then a moment later, "That's my mum. It's my mum and my sister!" In great excitement he rushed down onto the boat, followed by a frantic film crew. I'd never seen him move so fast or look so happy. Would this shore him up sufficiently, emotionally, to make him retract his resignation? I wondered.

'His mother, aged 89, wearing a blindingly white Panama and trainers with her summer dress, refused to be carried off the boat despite not being that steady on her legs. It had been a windy crossing and the boat had rocked from side to side alarmingly, and as she described her journey, she too rocked from side to side alarmingly, playing up to the cameras for all she was worth and enjoying herself thoroughly.'

Despite being fantastically cheesy, it was a genuinely moving occasion. To see the despondent Gordon's face light up was a treat, and even though the presence of the cameras made things, as so often, desperately self-conscious, and the carpenter repeated 'Oh my life! I don't *believe* it!' perhaps one time too many to be entirely convincing, the TV pros on hand kept it all from falling apart. That was another thing I'd noticed, as I'd watched the crew following the castaways and their visitors around: just how natural and easy the castaways were with the cameras these days, while their guests were still as bashful as anything, with all the symptoms of the first-time filmed, not sure where to look, what to do with your hands, whether you should occasionally sneak meaningful aside-style glances at the lens and so on. So now, as Gordy's elderly mum stumbled up off the boat, Ben and Padraig, tanned and handsome, were there to greet her. 'Welcome to Taransay,' said Ben, with effortless superiority, bang in the middle of the scene as ever. I began to wonder whether Mike's endless grumbles about Ben deliberately hogging the limelight were true. He was certainly a master of giving the impression that he just happened to be there. Even if he didn't know what it meant, 'vacuous' was not the word for Ben. You had to hand it to him, he was a TV natural.

Back over the water in the Harris Hotel I found Julie's mother waiting for me, insisting generously on buying me a post-prandial pint of Velvet. We were joined eventually by Chris the producer (and his mobile), his wife Maggie (and their baby alarm), psychologist Cynthia and the skinny blonde press officer from BBC Scotland, who had been enjoying the full works in the hotel dining room. And we were perhaps not as discreet as we should have been about the castaways in front of Julie's mother.

Somewhere Else

Another person who had been on the receiving end of an unusually large helping of TV generosity was Tammy Huff, who had also been preparing to spend the week without visitors. But on the first Saturday of Visitors' Week she had found herself slipping into festal mode and making illicit use of a mobile phone that was on the island. 'I ummed and aahed about using it,' she told me, 'then I thought, Why not. Everyone's got people here for a couple of days, what's a five minute phone call?' But calling from her pod she found her dad unusually guarded. Then after a couple of minutes he told her the news he – and Lion – had been keeping from her: her mother was back in hospital and iller than ever.

Lion offered her a twenty-four-hour trip home, and after a night's thought, she accepted. With Elaine and a camera accompanying her, she flew down to Luton, drove home to Sandy and surprised her sick mother in hospital. 'You're not meant to be here,' her mother kept repeating, when confronted with her radiant daughter. 'That's all she could get out to begin with,' says Tammy. 'She was just shocked and hung onto me as if I was going to disappear into thin air.'

When she had left, after another visit a day later, her mother had been disappointed, but that was no longer something Tammy could worry about. 'I knew she would be,' she told the camera. 'That was part of my torment about coming. But she was happy, so it achieved what it was meant to achieve, so let her be angry as well as happy 'cos it doesn't bother me.'

Tammy had come a long way since the days when she had described her relationship with her mother, with her usual tact and concern, as, 'I didn't know where my mother started and I ended.' (Sandy, to whom she had said this, had remarked that it summed it up.) 'I'd been at home all this time,' Tammy went on, 'and she has got her illness. So really this is my first time away from home. No fault of hers, no fault of mine. But Mark,' she'd added then, 'I don't mind you writing about this, but I don't want it to come out wrong. My mother is a lovely person.'

Now, as she left the hospital and her beloved mother, Tammy told the camera she was glad she had made the trip. 'My mind's at rest, I've seen Mum, I've hugged her, and now I can't wait to get back to the island, can't wait to get back home to Paible.' She had confused her dad a few times, she added, by saying, 'This year Paible is my home.' But her room in Sandy was now full of junk and though she wasn't sure where she would be next year, 'it's going to be somewhere else'.

On her return, she was ready to come out to camera about her relationship with Toby. Stepping off the boat, she embraced her boyfriend on the rocks, a heartfelt clinch that became, five weeks later, HUG THAT SHOWS ISLAND CASTAWAY HAS DESERTED HER OLD FLAME. 'It was just a case of people know now,' she told me. 'We're happy with it. We know it's something strong, so let's do it.'

A New Dimension

Back on the island the week had three more days to run. As they prepared to leave, the numerous visitors were encouraged to register their opinions in the video diary room. Toby's mum Hazel was impressed, and quite convinced they weren't putting on a front for visitors. 'They seem quite relaxed, busily getting on as a community. I think there's a great atmosphere here and they've a lot to teach us townies.' Padraig's sister Maureen thought it was all really well organised and they seemed really comfortable and happy. And as for the food! 'Absolutely wonderful meals that you'd expect today in restaurants.' Mike's sister Ashley was sad to go, but happy to see Mike looking really well. Policeman Steve was impressed with the low crime rate – 'no traffic offences, if you want a community beat officer, I'll put my name down.'

It was generally agreed that people weren't at all the way they'd been seen on TV. 'When you watch television you quickly start judging people,' said Jessie Jowers, 'and start putting them into categories as if they're characters in fiction and yet when you come you see everyone's a real person and it's not a soap opera and they're not just two-dimensional.'

By and large the influx seemed to have done the castaways good, too. For Ben, seeing all the families and friends had just added a new dimension to everyone. 'It gives other people a whole new perspective,' agreed Jessie Jowers (who seemed to be rather enjoying her time in the video diary room), 'on who these people are and where they're coming from and maybe change their opinions about them.' At the party on the last night, she said, she'd been talking to one of Gwyneth's daughters. Because they had arrived not knowing what had been going on, it meant they had no preconceptions about anyone.

'And for the first time I think for maybe six weeks, since she'd had a falling out with Peter, Gwyn grabbed Peter by the hand and pulled him over and said, "Look at those two beautiful girls together." It's probably taken us coming and meeting her and her family and her seeing where Peter's coming from, that he's got a family that loves him, to see that he's not an ogre. Still, it must have taken quite a lot of guts to do that.'

It had been a good session in the steading on the last night, Julie Lowe reported. Coloured tissue paper covered the lights and a rug was stolen out of the schoolhouse to cover the grubby hardboard floor. The castaways and their guests brought out the last stash of alcohol and partied into the night, dressed up in their best gear. 'Big Mike and his policeman friend,' she continued, 'who had done big, tough-guy stuff all week (camping without tents, mountain climbing, diving and braving the jellyfish etc), completely blew this macho image by attending the party in full drag, complete with wigs and make-up. They appeared to be very comfortable in their rig-outs, Mike looking surprisingly feminine and showing a startling facial resemblance to Jamie Lee Curtis, while his friend was much more along the lines of Boy George. Mike's mum, while clearly shocked by this, was a very good sport about it, but looked relieved when an hour and a half later, the boys went to change back into their normal attire.' Mike had only agreed to become 'Tallulah' for the night because so many people had asked him whether he would. It wasn't quite a habit, yet, but the Action Man did seem to enjoy the makeover.

As at all the best parties, wild rumours circulated about who had got up to what with whom, but the influx of guests certainly provided some variety for the islanders. For the first, and possibly the last time in the year, the island's notional heart-throb had female company in his tiny pod, sleeping, he assured me with a smile, on seperate bunks.

In the morning, the weather had worsened and there was some uncertainty about the boat getting across. But by noon the last of the invaders had gone, leaving the castaways, wrote Julie, exhausted and emotionally wrung out. 'We straggled back to the steading in the fine drizzle and looked around stupidly and in some bewilderment at the few of us that were left. It felt like the aftermath of a Christmas, when friends and more distant relations had finally left, leaving just the close family to kick off their shoes, collapse into an armchair and go "Thank God". This sounds horribly ungrateful to everyone who slogged all the way up here, spending more money than they would on a two-week package to a Greek island, but that is absolutely not the intention.'

Julie felt very strongly, she went on, that it was vitally important for the castaways to regroup after the rigours of the week; so she took the initiative of preparing a special End of Visitors' Week supper. Rosemary and Sheila came to join her in the kitchen. Then: 'Willing hands helped to tidy the steading and make it ours again. We put out candles on the tables to make it more ceremonial and then lingered over supper, enjoying the relative peace and quiet and the feeling that we were at last, our own family. Not everyone came. Some had lapsed into unconsciousness and others needed to be quiet on their own, but eighty-five per cent or thereabouts joined in and it was lovely.'

The word 'family', first mentioned in the aftermath of the Harris show, was now repeated across the video diaries. Not that everyone, of course, wanted to buy into the increasingly cosy scene.

Chapter 20

Self Sufficiency

As if to underline the fact that the holiday was over, a week of howling wind and rain now swept in over Taransay. 'We have not seen weather like this for many months,' wrote Mike on Wednesday 9 August, 'and I guess it will serve to remind some people just how harsh this place can be.'

The Action Man's main current concern was that Peter didn't muscle in on the big, overnight fuel-gathering party planned for the following Monday. 'Pete has now said that he wants to come along,' he wrote in his diary, 'which will not please most of those who intend going. Our greatest fear is that he will try to take over this project when the credit deserves to go to Roger. Our plan therefore, is to leave camp at 8 am on Monday (weather permitting) as Pete does not get up early ...' As it turned out, Mike needn't have concerned himself. Sad events in the real world were to overtake his island worries.

Roger Stephenson, meanwhile, was ecstatic over the success of his Big Idea. 'We have just come back,' he wrote on 15 August, 'from an amazing two-day trip to Black Pipe Beach. Patrick, Mike (1 day), Padraig, Trevor, Toby, Tammy, Tanya, Philiy, Dez, Ben, Rosemary (1 day), Oliver, young Mike and me. For me, this expedition was the very essence of the castaway idea: community, teamwork and self-sufficiency, all in the most stunning setting on the edge of our kingdom.

'Fuel acquisition – such a vital task for any community, any castaway, any Hebridean, was the force which took us there and produced such a vibrant atmosphere,' he went on. 'The happy coincidence of a decent peat-bank, a beach full of huge timbers and a landing point all in close proximity to each other, was the essential starting point. And its distance from home – inevitable given the hundreds of years of occupation – only served to heighten the sense of connection with our environment. Our evening meal round the camp fire felt ultimately castaway. This "full range of British [and Irish] society" sat side by side in a unique way, barely imaginable anywhere else, unified, with a single common aim.'

For the first half of the year, the doctor explained, the community had got through 15.5 tonnes of wood, 40 bags of peat, 200 bags of coal – all imported at a cost of £3000. As a result of this project they had now ordered just 150 bags of coal for the rest of the year. '£1000 at very most.'

Not everyone had seen the expedition in such a euphoric light. The weather was so bad – 'pissing it down' – that Mike hoped the trip would be postponed. Personally, he thought it madness to work in such weather. Nonetheless when the others left, he was at the front, and joined in eagerly with the chopping and splitting. But by 4 pm, the Action Man had had enough. He sloped off and left them all to it. Plodding back, he thought of a hot shower and dry clothes every step of the way.

When he got back Dez and Liz told Mike Pete and Sheila's sad news. Pete's sister-in-law had died of cancer. 'It was not wholly unexpected,' Mike wrote later, 'but very sad all the same.' The couple left the island the next day for the funeral. In their absence they were to miss the biggest, and potentially most controversial, departure of the year.

A Chicken Issue

For a long while now, Gordon Carey had been unhappy with life on the island. He had formally given in his notice to Lion during Visitors' Week. Cassie was his only reason for staying. If it hadn't been for her, he said on camera, he would have left long ago. His complaints remained the same: devious people, double standards – though as he rarely gave names or examples, even in interview, it was hard to fathom precisely what cheesed him off so mightily.

Bearing in mind the splenetic exchange of words they had had back in January, it was heartening that Mike was one of the Careys' best allies now, calling round regularly to visit and chat. On Tuesday 8 August he had found them packing. The following Monday, after a post-fuel-gathering shower, the Action Man called round to the Careys' pod again. 'We chatted about all sorts of stuff but mainly their intentions to leave and some of the recent tensions which have sealed matters for them. Cassie was the linchpin. When Gordy had been very down she had convinced him to hang in there. Now that she has felt attacked they are quitting. I cannot see anything that can be done to make them stay now. They are really down and just looking for a way out.'

Their main argument, he explained, was about the chickens, and how they were kept and cleaned. 'Gordy, Cassie and Trish look after one set of chickens, but they say that others are always checking up and criticising the way they do things. I suspect they were referring to Sheila and Hilary.'

The chicken group had been, since the outset of the project, the most famously dysfunctional of the castaways' work teams, perhaps because it had always attracted some who, in the eyes of many castaways, saw it as an easy option. Ron had been a founding member; Warren and Peter likewise. Julie Lowe had joined when Ron left in early July. Now, determined that she really wanted to try to become a Mills and Boon author, under the pseudonym Tara Cast, Julie had decided to concentrate her energies on cows and teaching and resign from the chicken group. 'I was only ever going to help out for the summer holidays,' she wrote, 'but it seemed that now was as good a time as any to bow out. The whole of the chicken arrangements were in a pickle, so as I left, I called a chicken group meeting so that everyone could be together to rearrange the rota.' While moving the cow food, she had also noticed there was only minimal chicken feed left. 'So I told Gordon that there would be a chicken meeting and asked him if he could come with an estimate of how much food the cocks got through in a week so that we could work out how much to order. He didn't come. At the meeting, the remaining chicken people did a much-needed reorganisation of feeding/cleaning/ordering/killing and eating arrangements. When Gordon heard that things had been changed in his absence, he apparently threw a wobbly and then said that he'd never eat chicken or have anything to do with chickens, ever again.'

'The Carey family and chickens,' she continued combatively, 'have been a bit of an issue throughout, and their having more chicken than anyone else on the island was beginning to cause unrest. The next thing we heard was that the Careys were reconstructing their crates and packing up to leave asap. It looked as if they were going to have to work out their notice, and then all of a sudden, they were going the following day ...'

The last straw that had ended Cassie's determination to stay – even if her husband left – is hard to pinpoint precisely: the only certainty is that it had to do with chickens. In long farewell interviews with both Tanya and Paul, Cassie touched, tearfully, on the Careys' numerous other frustrations: the dislike of the community food; the inadequate schooling for Yoneh; the hypocrisy of people who were polite to your face and rude behind your back; the drinking; the swearing in front of the children; the never feeling part of the community. But in the end it came back, as always, to chickens. Gordon had refused to let Cassie prepare a chicken for Sheila and Peter; the community had badmouthed her and Gordon during the meeting about chickens which they hadn't attended; Julia had then had a face-to-face row with Cassie over their attitudes to helping themselves to chicken from the cold store. All this had contributed to the moment where Cassie had found herself in tears in the steading: 'I sat down there and I cried. I thought, I'm arguing about a piece of chicken, which to me is ridiculous. I mean what's a piece of chicken? It's nothing.' Nothing, and then again, everything. Having initially said that they must stay two weeks, the powers that be had decided to let the Careys go off immediately, on the fortnightly supply boat of Thursday 17 September.

Ben, for one, was very sorry to see them go. 'It happened so quickly,' he reported. 'We found out about six o'clock on the Wednesday evening that the production company had allowed them to leave. The next day they were on the boat.

'We all gathered down by the rocks,' he said, describing their departure. 'The landing craft came and they were very, sort of, stiff-upper-lipped, I suppose – until suddenly I think the realisation just sunk in – that this was it. And they were very upset. A few people commented, Why is Gordon so upset? He's been wanting to leave since the day he arrived here. Well, of course he's going to be upset! My God! What an investment we've all made for this year – an emotional, mental investment. You can't belittle eight months on the island together – and Gordon was on the Advance Party as well. I'd say for everyone who's come here, this was a dream we wanted to realise. And to leave here with the realisation that you hadn't fulfilled that dream is really sad. Which is why I'm doing my utmost now to forget the fact that this isn't the dream I expected. I'm just going to make it into a different dream.'

As the boat drew away, the gathered castaways broke into song. 'Gordon's fishing, Gordon's fishing. Caught no fish, caught no fish. Try again tomorrow, try again tomorrow ...' It was one of the rounds that the choir had been practising. The words, Roger told me later, had come spontaneously from one of the kids. Now Dez's voice started it up, and the others followed, a motley group of white people saying goodbye to their only black family, and with it, perhaps, their dreams of being thought of as a totally successful contemporary community. First the gay man, then the black family ... it didn't, on the face of things, look great.

'I feel it was the biggest opportunity ever,' Gwyneth said to camera on the beach, 'with so many different people, from different walks of life, different religions, different colours – and why the hell couldn't we have made a go of it? I feel quite ashamed, I really do.'

The ever-thoughtful Padraig had already been pondering these issues on the video diary: first, why – *au fond* – the Careys had left: 'Gordon's never been happy here,' he said, 'and I'm just trying to work out what he expected of the place and how he expected it to work. He's a nice guy in many ways, I like him a lot, but he can be standoffish, uncooperative, rude to some people. He never has to me but to others he certainly has been, he just refuses to acknowledge their presence sometimes. They've rarely attended meetings: they say they feel they're not part of the community, but I don't think they've bothered to get involved in it that much. I mean, we've had plenty of instances of social occasions where they could have come along without having to breach any of their religious tenets, without having to drink or be in the company of those who drink, but even then nothing much has happened.' It was a pity, he continued, because they were nice people and they obviously did get on well with some of the community. 'So I don't know what we were meant to do to make them feel included.'

The Irishman now moved on to the more vexed angle of how this departure would be seen by the castaways' public. 'I'm just worried that outside perceptions of us will be unfair, because Ray, the uncouth, uneducated, old-fashioned builder type, left; Ron, another minority, the gay man, also left; and now the Careys, the only black people on the island, are leaving. I'm worried that people will think the majority in the middle has forced out the minorities and I don't think that's the case at all. The Careys being black has nothing to do with their reasons for leaving, just as Ron's being gay had very little to do with his. So I hope people don't think we've been deliberately isolating and excluding the minorities here because we haven't. I mean, I'm in a minority one way, being Irish, but that doesn't matter a damn to me or anyone else as far as I can see. So don't think we're all a crowd of domineering, dominating bastards 'cos we're not, we're just trying to function together as a community and that's not always easy.'

Fortunately for the community's good name, the potentially controversial story of the Careys leaving was dwarfed in the press by another ejection: that of the villain of the latest 'reality TV' programme to grab the nation's imagination – *Big Brother*'s Nasty Nick. Nonetheless, an exclusive story followed. For Gordon, with credit card troubles and a desire to relocate to the Caribbean, the lure of the journalist's cheque book was too much. WE WERE THE TOKEN BLACKS CAUGHT UP IN A MIDDLE CLASS GAME ... AT TIMES I FELT LIKE A SLAVE AS OUR POOR CHILDREN WERE HUMILIATED screamed the banner headline in the *Sunday Mirror*. In the ensuing exclusive, Padraig's worst fears were realised. The Careys, the rag reported, were now 'disillusioned and bitter at their treatment among TV's castaways'. Their children had endured 'racist humiliation', as 'the children of some of the other castaways refused to play with them – because they were black'. 'It was the last place we expected to encounter racial hatred, especially aimed at the children,' Cassie is reported as saying. 'We were deceived into taking part in the programme,' said Gordon. 'They told me I was wanted for my skills. Really, the producers just wanted some token blacks ... it was just some middle class game, and we were the black people who were going to be part of the fun ...' Eventually, he continued, he had found out that people were talking about them in racist terms behind their backs. 'They would call us black b******s. There were times I felt like tugging my forelock and saying "Yes, massa", like some slave boy. We were never accepted by the rest ... most of all, I believe, because we're black.'

Oh dear, oh dear. The man who had so admirably refused to play the race card earlier in the year had certainly done so – or been persuaded into doing so – now. 'Apparently,' wrote Peter to his mother, 'some article appeared recently in the *Daily Mirror* alluding to our racism – utter nonsense.' The other castaways, by and large, agreed with this analysis. Though, as mixed-race Warren Latore pointed out to me on my next visit: 'Other people have been interviewed as to whether there's racism here – I have not been asked once. It seems to be more important whether the people who would be the perpetrators of racism think there is racism here than the victims.' So *did* he think there was racism on the island? He wasn't going to answer that, he told me. So did he think there was any shadow of truth in what Gordon said in the paper? 'Yeah, there is.' He didn't want to talk about it. 'But it's all ignorance driven.'

The issue of colour, combined with that of an unusual culture, further confused by people's natural desire not to believe they were in any way prejudiced (to the point of making exceptions and allowances) meant that the truth of this story would never be simple. Back on the island the day after their departure, Mike's report on the post-Carey fallout was about as frank as it got on the record. Dez had a low opinion of Gordon because they had a bust-up. Hilary was one of the more honest people in her own way and kind with it. She and Gordon had not got on so she and he kept out of each other's way. She didn't dislike him, though, and did get on OK with Cassie. She said goodbye to both of them, but didn't make a song and dance about it.'

Tammy Huff has the last word. 'There was a slight rumour,' she told the video diary, 'when the Careys left that we had let down the minority groups here. I felt very strongly and angry about that because we didn't let them down, that's wrong. It wasn't the minority groups, it was the individuals that were picked to represent them; and they were off-the-wall, really hard, exceptional, trying people. Even if they were whites and middle class we still would not have got on with them and they still would have probably left.'

Saddle Restuffing Costs

Even as the Careys had been packing their bags for their sudden departure, another island issue was reaching a crunch turning point, with a head-to-head over the budget between Roger and production director Shahana Meer, who had flown up from London to address the issues raised in a letter Roger had written on the castaways' behalf, expressing their concern about their ever-dwindling resources. It didn't go well. 'Roger got very angry,' reported Julie Lowe, 'and walked out when he saw that despite his best efforts, we weren't going to get any more money. Sometimes he really is his own worst enemy. He's made himself look inflexible and unreasonable again, and it's all on film. He has his principles, and so important are they to him, that he's not prepared to compromise. Because his concerns are of little importance to others of us, we end up getting impatient and irritable with his vehemence. This contrasted sharply with the filming of the choir rehearsal the night before, which was hilarious and wonderful.'

At issue were, in Roger's words, 'all sorts of minor things that we've been ripped off for. We thought our budget was this and suddenly it's this.' The horse gear, for example. Because the horse had been a) inappropriate and b) pregnant, the castaways felt entitled to complete reimbursement for all the horse gear. Then there was the bill for the water pipe: an infrastructure issue that shouldn't have been part of the budget at all. 'There were several other things as well,' Roger told me, 'which added up to a good few thousand pounds.' He had actually walked out, not over any specific issue, but because he felt the camera was inappropriate. 'When you are negotiating with your paymaster you don't want to be on camera because we know how they use footage of us negotiating with Lion. They use just us and not Lion.'

'I felt very sorry for Becci and Shahana,' wrote Mike. 'Of course we need to voice our opinions and fight our corner and they have to take the hard line business approach. In the end we have been told that we may be able to resell any unused waterpipe if they can find a secondhand buyer for it. The argument that it should have been in the Set-Up and not the Capital budget failed. On the horse front they also stood their ground. We are only getting back £400 for part of the collar and saddle restuffing costs. But what can we do? The budget currently stands at about £7500 and we shall lose £2000 of that because the Careys have gone. An argument was put forward that we should not lose £30 per person per week, but that was knocked back too.'

In the end there was a resolution. Though not giving her ground on the contested issues, Meer suddenly offered the option of money in lieu of a boat that been promised to the community by Chris Kelly if they managed to stick to the Rules and police themselves. 'She remained completely inflexible,' said Roger, 'then suddenly out of the hat, offered us this boat money. My interpretation of that is, "We're in charge. We're not giving you what you asked for, but we'll give you this as a little sweetener, because we realise the feeling is quite strong."'

The castaways took the cash. It was getting a little late in the year for a boat, and in any case they already had one. Dez had reconstructed a dinghy that he'd seen buried in the sand on Pig Beach in January. In early summer he'd dug it up and repaired it, pretending that the fibreglass he was ordering from Lion was for schoolhouse art projects. It was now watertight, they had found an old mast for it in the roof of the steading and it would soon be ready to launch.

Ouch!

The weather had now changed for the better and – budget worries aside – life was happy and tranquil for most of the castaways. Philiy and Padraig were back together again; Mike had been allowed to move to the altogether more spacious surroundings of the Careys' old pod; and Colin and Warren had finally managed to catch a fish, albeit from Angus's boat in the middle of the strait. 'How ironic,' observed Mike, 'that it happened the day after Gordy left.'

'Looking through my diary,' says Roger, 'the words "perfection", "fair" and "calm" seem to reoccur a lot in July and August.' Julie Lowe's circular letter expressed the general mood. 'On days that I can shut myself away and write, it's really good,' she wrote. 'On days that I have to get out and shovel muck, it's really good. On days that I can shear sheep, milk cows and bake bread, it's really good. On wet days when I can sit in the steading arguing the merits of a dodgy word in a furious game of Scrabble, it's good too. At this moment, I am sitting on a rock on the beach, the computer on my lap, looking at the sun sparkling on the sea. Floozie is at my feet, asleep on the sand, tired out after a hectic morning "fishing" and chasing the seagulls. I am very content and happy to be here these days, and feel that the year at last is "coming good".'

The old community fault lines had not vanished, but were now perhaps accepted to the point of almost being forgotten. On Tuesday 22 August Mike hosted a pod-warming for his new abode and in inviting his guests found he had 'totally forgotten about the politics'. Gwyn and Pat had found out that Pete was coming and asked if they could come another night. 'It turned out to be a good evening. In the end it was just Pete and myself and we actually had quite a good chat about this and that.'

Everyone turned up to celebrate Tanya's birthday on the following Friday, even though the venue was a good walk away at the bothy. The filmmaker had already been well impressed by the presents she received, 'which show', she said, 'the creativity that is on the island'. Dez had made a wooden fish; Philiy a beautiful embroidered purse; Wee Mike a wooden model of a camera, 'which I think is incredibly ingenious and pretty impressive for a lad his age'. Sheila had painted a picture of the Evil Camerawoman's favourite view. 'She actually asked around and found out where it was, and then Peter made this beautiful driftwood frame.

'It goes without saying,' she concluded, 'that my birthday here was unlike any other that I've had, or am going to have, in my life. It was just a real community event. I got woken up in the morning by the kids rushing in to give presents. And Felix and Ciara followed me around the whole day, they were so enthralled by the idea of it being somebody's birthday. There's been this debate about me, whether I'm a real castaway because I'm here to do the filmmaking and the position that puts me in. But if there was any proof to the contrary, that I am really a part of the community, I think my birthday and its celebrations provided that.'

The food for the party was carried up to the bothy by willing hands from the kitchen team. Ben got into organising mode and laid it all out on a table in tupperware containers; then fifty night lights were set into the cracks in the walls. When Tanya arrived, a bit late, at seven o'clock, everyone sang 'Happy Birthday' to her. There was then a beautiful sunset. 'Absolutely incredible,' said Tanya, 'the quality of light, the orange glow that spread across the hills was wonderful.' As darkness fell the little dwelling was transformed. 'Never had the bothy looked so nice,' wrote Mike. 'The fire was roaring, the candles glowing, tummies full of food and everyone with a full glass and a smile on their face.' 'A magical, magical evening,' agreed Tanya.

A bit too magical for some. Many of the castaways were drinking newly brewed nettle-wine, which they had nicknamed Ouch! on account of its capacity to make people both drunk and ill. 'Clearly Tanya wanted to bump me off,' joked Julia Corrigan on the video diary later, 'because she gave me some wine to drink that she called Ouch! I thought it was called Ouch! because it's made of nettles, but oh no, it's called Ouch! because the next morning you feel as if somebody's beaten you over the head, repeatedly, with a baseball bat. I had one tin mug full of Ouch! – which is a horrible, ghastly yellow colour, it looks like monkey vomit – and after I'd drunk it, my speech got very slurred, my eyes began to cross and I suddenly started to say, loudly, "I'm going to be sick!" So I was dragged outside – I certainly had no control over my legs – and I promptly threw up what felt like eight hundred times, in the nettles funnily enough, which seems like poetic justice to me.' 'I wouldn't touch it with a barge pole,' wrote Peter, who had arrived late with Sheila. 'Julia got utterly lathered, completely out of it.' Poor Julie Lowe was so inebriated she couldn't find her way back to her tarpaulined camp, then managed to lose the bothy as well. 'I kept slipping on the wet grass and whenever I tripped, my head torch would bounce and whack me on the nose, which hurt.' She was saved from further bruising and a wet night on the heather by Toby, who had seen her light bobbing about hopelessly in the distance and had nobly gone into the rain to investigate.

Part of the Good People

At last the community had reached the kind of concord that its creators could only have dreamt (or even had nightmares) about. So it was fortunate, that on a side-dash from the Edinburgh TV festival, they were able to see it in such a condition. The party of 'bigwigs' visiting the island on 28 August comprised Chris Kelly, Jeremy Mills, Colin Cameron and Peter Salmon, Controller of BBC 1, in whose office the whole audacious idea had been dreamed up. 'They had a great day and went all round the site,' wrote Mike. 'Philiy was taking pictures of them at their request. Tanya was filming etc. It went well and they were happy with what they had spent millions on.' Mike hadn't believed they had come just to look. 'I must confess I thought they were over here with some sort of agenda or ulterior motive.' Like installing a *Big Brother* style web-cam, he thought, or reinforcing the contract after Gordon had become the third ex-castaway to sell his story. 'I went on to discuss this with Jeremy over dinner and he was actually very hurt that some of us doubt Lion's motives so much.'

Ever resourceful, three of the castaways had produced something more than polytunnels and fanks for the top brass to be impressed by. Dez, Colin and Warren appeared from the raft with a substantial load of fresh fish. 'It was nice,' reported Mike, 'that the BBC guys and Jeremy were here to see something so major. It was the first decent haul from the raft. That is what we were led to believe anyway.' In fact the catch had been a set-up. Dez and the two other castaway rogues had caught the whole lot from Angus's rib, way out in the middle of the Sound, then transferred themselves and their booty onto the raft.

Colin Cameron was certainly impressed, enthusing about the incident in an upbeat description of his Taransay visit in the BBC's house magazine *Ariel*. 'The sun sparkled off an indigo sea,' he wrote, 'the sand was bleached tropical.

Bronzed and fit, castaways Ben, Des and Warren, buoyed up by their latest haul of mackerel, waved happily from their makeshift pontoon tethered deep into the Sound as we roared past in an inflatable craft ...'

The Action Man was actually leaving with the producers. A painful problem with his teeth had necessitated a trip to Glasgow. Having packed, he went to talk to the woman who had now become probably his closest friend on the island – Hilary. 'She said once again that she was thinking about leaving. It was not anything to do with issues or the project but the fact that she was missing her family far too much.'

Three days later, on the last day of August, while Mike was still away, the Scarborough Mum finally headed home. She had given it the extra month she had promised her husband during Visitors' Week, and her mind was now made up to go. 'Since Visitors' Week,' she told the camera, 'I just think about home.' Asked about other reasons for leaving, she replied. 'Some of it wasn't as I expected – but I'm not really bothered about that any more. I just want to go home.' Her dazzling relaxed smile as she headed down over the grass to the boat said it all. 'Three cheers for Hilary!' shouted Ben. 'Hip hip hooray!' joined in the other castaways, using a phrase that surely hadn't been heard on television since the 1960s. But it was the quietest and least controversial of the departures yet. As she had come and been, so she had left: straightforward, discreet, nice and normal.

Her departure was a blow for those closest to her. 'Our best friend and neighbour is leaving today,' wrote Peter. 'For about two months her heart has not been in it and she has hummed and hawed, but the day before yesterday she went for a long walk with Sheila, then made up her mind. Last night we all had a very moving evening, the whole community genuinely *sad*. The others were meant to go. Hilary was part of the good people but missed her family. It will leave a huge hole in our lives. So a very strange air of ending around us. All our neighbours gone – we now have three rooms to play with.'

'We're now down to twenty-nine from the original thirty-six,' a 'sad' Sandy told her video diary. 'That's nearly a fifth no longer here. I went for a walk this morning – ten minutes or so along the beach – and was suddenly aware of a sense of urgency at having to do what I wanna do. There are things that I haven't done yet and for the first time I was aware that time's running out. The fact that Hilary's gone – it's almost as if things are beginning to draw to an end. I suppose in some ways they are. We're two-thirds of the way through this year. That leaves a third left, I know, but four months suddenly doesn't seem very long.'

The island's granny wasn't alone with such thoughts. 'I'm starting to think,' said Ben, 'Oh my gosh! In just four months time I'm going to be over there as well and this will all be over. It's really got me thinking, imagining I was in her shoes leaving tomorrow and going back to London, back to my job at *Tatler*. How would I feel? Would I have done everything I'd wanted to do, learned everything I'd wanted to learn, experienced the sort of island experience that I wanted? I couldn't answer that, actually. Certainly if I left tomorrow I'd feel really sad, because I absolutely love it up here.' But adding it up, he'd learned to bake bread, he'd sheared a sheep, he'd put up fencing, he'd done water piping, he'd turfed, he'd fly-fished. Short of learning to knit, which he seriously was contemplating, 'much to everyone's amusement', there wasn't so much left to do.

Loneliness and Lost Years

Perhaps the person most seriously affected by this latest departure was Mike. 'I think it is obvious to those here that I am out of sorts at the moment,' he wrote on Sunday 3 September, only a day after he'd returned from his dental session in Glasgow. 'It's not really to do with the fact that I was on the mainland. In the main it is that Hilary has left, as she was a great friend and a person that I spent a lot of time with. I shall miss her a great deal.' In the absence of a girlfriend or other platonic mate on the island he had bonded closely with the kindly Scarborough mum. Now, suddenly, he found himself more alone than ever.

Serious events in the outside world had also claimed Trevor for a few days. His father was close to death in intensive care. He had left with Mike and the producers and was now back home in the Wirral realising – between visits to the hospital – quite what a rat race he'd left behind. 'So I'm going to treat the next four months when I get back with a lot more passion,' he told the minicam he'd taken with him. 'I'm certainly going to play more of an active part in what's happening, and not be complacent about it.'

For things were not going to be the same for Trev when he finished his island year. He now described his time as brickie and driving instructor as 'the lost years, the years all you did was work, work, work.' To underline his commitment to a new life post-Taransay, on Tuesday he sold his house and his car to one of his extended family as they sat round his dad's bed. Just coming away had made him realise how much he missed and loved his closest mates on the island. 'You think you know your family really well,' he told the minicam, 'but when you come off the island and you've got people like Toby and Trish there, you realise that you don't know your family that well at all. Everybody's so busy doing their lives, doing their jobs, you might see them once a week, chat for a few hours on a superficial level and go. My mum or dad or me brother and sister don't know anything about me really, compared to Toby and Trish. It's something that's unravelled over the eight months and it's only coming back that you find that contrast. The next four months I'm going to try and get as much interaction with the community as possible. It's a fantastic, once in a lifetime opportunity.'

In unexpected ways, were the ambitions that Jeremy Mills had declared for the project way back at the outset at last beginning to come true?

The Next Booker Prize Winner

Back on the island, as August gave way to September, Taransay life rolled along peacefully enough. The night of 2 September saw Colin and Pat's joint birthday party, with a bar in the steading and the birthday boys dressed as the Blues brothers. On Monday 4 September the community woke to find a partition had been erected overnight in the steading to recreate the snug area for the colder months ahead. 'It had not been done at midnight and it was there by 6.30 am,' wrote Mike. 'Everyone was trying to figure out who had done it but no one would say and whoever had done it was not saying. The finger was pointed at me by several people but it wasn't me.' The most likely candidates, he thought, were Colin and Warren.

He had noticed another development in the community. 'Peter seems to be making massive efforts to get on with people and it has certainly been noticed. He's a good chap at heart. It's cynical to say, but he may now be feeling the absence of Hilary, who was one of his great supporters, allies and friends. The group now seems small and it is important now more than ever for us all to get on with each other. I hope that we can be supportive of each other until the year end and that things remain calm.'

Having largely got rid of destabilising elements, the community was indeed starting to pull together and 'perform'. The next day saw the culmination of Roger's fuel project, when the gathered turfs and chopped wood was brought back by boat from Black Pipe Beach to Paible Central. Angus had agreed to swap a morning's use of his landing craft for Philiy's blue-eyed favourite – Taran the calf.

Roger was nervous. The weather had been poor and the sea was still rough. As he tried, first thing, to confirm with Angus on the VHF that the trip was still on, 'at the crucial moment the hardware let us down'. The jumpy doctor had to resort to use of the 'emergency' satellite phone. Even when he got the final green light at 9.30 and mobilised the masses for the hike across the island, he was still anxious. 'There was quite a swell running and I did wonder, for a while, whether Angus had miscalculated.'

But all was well. The Hebridean knew his waters, and once at Black Pipe the loading was 'an incredibly slick operation', with four to five tons of wood and 120-odd bags of peat carried down the 'fairly dodgy' rocky slope in short order. 'The attractive climate,' wrote Roger, 'the stunning setting and, dare I say it, the community spirit all conspired to effect the loading in exactly one hour.' 'The only two men who did not go across,' grumbled Mike, 'were Warren and Pete. No surprises there and it certainly didn't earn them any brownie points. They could have both done it and Warren could still have made it back in time to do the filming at this end.'

After a brief ten-minute sandwich break, the team hiked back to base to perform the same operation in reverse, 'but with many extra fresh hands to help'. After another hour, 'it was deeply gratifying,' wrote Roger, 'to sit atop this huge pile of wood and peat', even if 'these huge chunks of timber still have to be sawn up before they will bring warmth to our chilly wintry toes.

'For me,' he mused, 'this job had another meaning, though. There has been added urgency to all our expeditions out and about this stunning island recently. We have been driven by a sense that it is all coming to an end soon – the days of summer are passing. So this transport of our winter fuel heralds a major contraction in our lives – from enormous, expansive, lazy hikes; from sleepy rafting sessions across the Dun Loch; from long, late evenings round a fire on the beach, deep into the night; from all that to six hours of daylight, relentless stormy winds and rain, and, I suspect, a desperate craving for home.'

The endless upsets of the spring and summer months had undoubtedly given way to a new calmer, even duller mood. After lunch on Thursday 7 September Mike found himself having an unusually early drink with Colin and agreeing that 'the project, despite being calm and level at the moment, has lost a whole lot of its sparkle. Early afternoon drinking is surely a sign of boredom setting in.' 'This month has been relatively quiet,' wrote Julie Lowe. 'School has gone back and a semblance of normality has settled onto the community. The children have been happy to go back, I think. School gives their days a pattern and a focus, and now the weather means they can't play on the beach all day, I think they're quite pleased to have something to do.

'It's a very different classroom for me this term. Ciara and Felix, both coming from educationally pro-active homes, have been beautifully prepared for formal learning, are at around the same kind of level and are very easy to teach. They are being really stretched now, and unsurprisingly, are loving it. They positively adore coming to school, and are extremely proud of their success in "carrying" sums. I'm very proud of their success in "carrying" sums too!'

As for Wee Mike, his educational progress had made the pages of the *Sunday Times*, in an ill-researched article headlined TV'S CASTAWAY LEARNS TO LOVE BOOKS. 'He was a child of his time,' readers were told. 'Michael Prater loved Playstation and watching television but seldom picked up a book. His head teacher had considered putting him on a special reading programme.' But nine months on the island away from the twenty-first century's 'couch potato culture' had transformed him, apparently. 'Now the nine-year-old devours books. His mother recently found him engrossed in *Angela's Ashes*.'

It was a heart-warming story, an encouragement for traditionalists and sentimentalists of all ages. The only drawback was that it wasn't strictly, or even vaguely, true. 'Little Mike,' Julie Lowe's letter continued, 'despite what the papers say about his reading progress is not quite the next Booker Prize Winner they are making him out to be. He has made huge progress, and I think he will have a good chance of keeping up with his class when he returns to mainstream schooling next year. He's missing Hilary a lot. She gave him a lot of time and attention, and he adored her.'

Monica was angrier about the misrepresentation, which she thought could be actively damaging. The whole story had come, she told me when I visited at the end of the month, from a comment that Trish had made to Peter Salmon on the bigwigs' day out. 'She was raving on about how Mikey has improved and she said, "The other day I caught him reading *Angela's Ashes* in my pod." Peter Salmon just saw the light when he heard that and thought, Oh wow! He was talking to Jeremy about it. Success story, success story. That's where it all came from. But it wasn't true that he was reading *Angela's Ashes*. Mikey couldn't read *Angela's Ashes*. He had obviously picked it up, as a child may do, and looked through it, saying "What's this, Mum?" or something. But I, as his teacher, was absolutely fuming about this article in the *Sunday Times* about the education on the island. None of the teachers were consulted or interviewed. It was inaccurate and exaggerated and it made me really angry.'

Meanwhile, the long-running stand-off between Peter and Gwyneth had achieved some sort of resolution. 'Yesterday was a funny one,' wrote Pete on Wednesday 13 September. 'I was out pulling up onions and loading barrows. It was still, overcast and very quiet. Gwyneth was out picking some beans. Then she charges over to tell me how angry I had made her over some comments I made about how we should leave this place when we've finished. I'm very keen that we tidy up, leave it all shipshape, and expressed some cynicism about what happens about tools – they are scattered to the wind. Anyway we proceeded to talk for about two hours. After a lot of initial hostility on her part – she caught me on a day when I was feeling very happy and at peace with the world – she seemed to calm down. So after saying she would never apologise for coffee incident etc blah blah, we ended up going into a great deal of depth about why we had acted in certain ways. She is not very articulate so I never can really plumb the depths of what upsets her about my "style", but at least we begged to differ, shook hands and are now on speaking terms. There's much general relief all round for others – we hadn't spoken since late June. For a place as small and intimate as this that's quite a feat. I suppose we are both stubborn.'

The underlying reason for the initial fight was not mentioned, indeed seemed to have been forgotten. Since Ron had left, the community's carefully constructed justice system had not been used once. Visitors' Week had seen plenty of illicit alcohol and gifts come onto the island, but perhaps that had been generally regarded as a saturnalian exception to the Rules. In the past month, though, many of the community members had gone quietly back to their old ways and nobody had turned a hair. On Friday 8 September Pat and Colin had been helicoptered to Stornoway for treatment to, respectively, an abscessed tooth and a suspected broken finger, and the chance of loading up with contraband had not gone untaken. 'It was as much a military operation as it usually is,' wrote Mike. 'Bits of paper were finding their way to the guys along with money for things that people wanted.' When the helicopter returned the smugglers persuaded the pilot to land behind the MacKay House, Mike wrote, 'because they had so much stuff and didn't want to ruffle the feathers of those who had not ordered anything. Colin, Pat, Warren, Sandy, Tammy and myself had all got stuff. There were others, too, and the benefits of it will be sampled by many more.' Mike now had seven bottles of whisky in his pod.

Then, on 16 September, another of the Rules was broken as Jules received visitors. 'Dad, sister, brother-in-law, brother, aunt etc,' wrote Mike. 'They are all so like Jules: grinning, laughing, loud and cheerful. All definitely Jolly Hockey Sticks types. It was nice for Jules and it was nice seeing them.'

The presents they had brought with them were, wrote Jules, 'astounding'. 'Sally brought the most enormous cake I have ever seen. It's a Christmas cake for thirty castaways, complete with base, marzipan, icing and tartan bow. Aunt Patricia and Uncle Donald sent an absolutely massive wedge of Cheshire Cheese. I also got a whole case of wine, chocolate, Earl Grey teabags, lovely soap and talc and best of all, new undies. Lion TV are very keen that I be taken to court over the illicit visit, so I'm planning on using the cake and chocolate as bribes to ensure a lenient sentence.'

Sitting Ducks

On 28 September the Lion boat arrived carrying Becci White, Cynth the psychologist, Padraig Nallen, who had been off the island for an unexpected funeral, and myself. I was experiencing my usual culture shock, arriving on the beach after an early flight from London, to be reminded just what a gloriously precarious project this was. We were supposed to be taking food supplies and mail across with us, but the tide was up too high, so the landing craft couldn't load from the beach. Reliable Angus wasn't around; instead we had two boatmen I'd not seen before. One was at the helm waving and gesturing in incomprehensible fashion, the other had disembarked into a tiny rubber dinghy and was making erratic progress towards the headland at the edge of the bay. Meanwhile Angus's brother Norman (in a hurry to get off for lunch) shouted at us from the grassy cliff top that we should head out across the rocks towards the headland, he would pass the cargo down ...

To cut the ensuing sit-com episode short, we eventually all made it, with damp suitcases and one dry sack of mail. It had taken four individual trips crouched above the swilling water at the bottom of the rubber dinghy with the man whose accent was so thick even Cynth couldn't understand it. I was now in my underpants and Cynth was soaked through, having taken a tumble on some seaweed and fallen arse-first into a rock pool (putting her mobile out of action). But we were there! We were exhilarated! The beautiful island loomed ever closer across the heaving swell!

The castaways were in a new mood, it struck me immediately. Without provocative Ron and the Careys the atmosphere was tangibly more relaxed. Heading round the pods, which were noticeably more settled and lived-in than ever, there seemed, now, to be just one major issue that people were discussing openly, and two that people was talking about behind their hands. Compared to the high drama days of spring, the gossip anemometer was measuring Force Two rather than Force Nine.

Discreet Issue One was Mike. 'He's very up and down,' said Monica, frank and open as ever. 'Has highs and lows. Doesn't really want to be on this island, but will feel a failure if he leaves, so he's trying to force himself to stay.' Did I know about him dressing up as a woman? Well, yes, I'd read his diary, up to the middle of September, knew he'd done it a couple of times at parties. 'It's moved on from there,' said Mon. The previous Thursday he had come to a meeting in full drag and introduced himself as 'Tallulah'. It had been difficult to know whether he was serious or not. 'That was what was so strange. He put it on the agenda. I was chairing the meeting. I had to go over to Mike and say, "OK. Item

number two on the agenda. Mike, I believe you've got something to say to us."
Switch camera onto Mike in this blonde wig and skirt. And he's going, "Well, I
just want to say, have any of you got a problem with this?" It was all really
weird. We don't know whether it was an attention-seeking thing or whether he
was confused about his sexuality or whether he is a heterosexual but into cross-
dressing. There's a multitude of possibilities. But there was something worrying
about the way it was. It wasn't natural.'

Colin the butcher was worried about the Action Man, too. He had 'lost the
plot' the other day while helping with a pig-drop in the slaughterhouse. 'He
won't be involved in killing any more animals because he just lost it.' Colin had
sent Mike up to talk to Roger about his symptoms, which he had described as a
tingling in his head which moved down to his body and caused him to 'lose the
plot'. There was a feeling, he added, that Mike could lose it more generally.

In his new, larger pod, though, Mike seemed fine – frank and constructive
about his recent depression. He'd had a long session with Cynth, which had
made him feel a whole lot better and more confident. As for the Tallulah thing,
that was just a bit of fun; he'd been amused when Toby and Trev had taken him
aside for a serious chat, 'concerned,' he smiled broadly 'that I really am a
tranny'. They had also wanted to talk about the implications of his cross-
dressing re 'the press, hate mail, his family etc.' Gwyneth had had a rather more
practical reaction: she had given Mike a couple of dresses.

Issue Two was more difficult: Trish, Trevor and Trish's kids. Although both
Trev and Trish denied point blank that they were an item, the word still was that
they were. 'It's so obvious,' said Monica. 'You see them going off for walks arm
in arm. You see them at parties and social events after they've had a drink –
Trevor will have his arm around her. I've no interest in causing her any distress
or upset, it's only when the kids are concerned that I think it's bad, because
basically Trish is spending all her time writing a book or something with Trevor
– God knows what they're doing. Jodene has been virtually fostered by the
Corrigans.

'It's something that needs to be spoken about,' Julia Corrigan agreed. 'If this
wasn't a television programme and if we really were living here and people
couldn't just stump off in a huff if they didn't like what you said, I'd have plenty
to say on the issue. Instead, I'm really cagey about the whole thing. But it's
common knowledge that Trish and Trevor spend all their time in their pod.
They go and get meals brought to their pod. Jodene lives here with me now,
which is a wonderful arrangement as far as I'm concerned. Wee Mike hangs
around with Dez and Liz, who get his meals on weekends. But I think Jodene's

probably quite lonely for her mum. I'm not really on friendly enough terms with Trish to be able to go and have a go at her and say, "Look, what are you doing?" She's writing her *Peggy Peg* books and he's writing his script and they think they're going to make their fame and fortune. Maybe they will. It'll be great if they do. But the trouble is they've got two kids.'

It was with some trepidation that I approached Trish to tackle her about all this. But she was her usual forthright self, bringing up the issue before I did. 'I've been podbound,' she told me. 'Haven't you heard? There's been rumours.' She had been helping Trev with his script, she went on. It had started with him showing her bits and her making suggestions and now they were working on it together – full-time. 'Honest to God, Mark, we've been on it from eight o'clock in the morning till half-twelve at night.' People had been gossiping about it, she agreed. 'But the thing is, they've got nothing else to do. They try and slag off anybody that's got an ounce of get-up-and-go in them and make it sound sordid.' And what about Jodene and Mike? 'The only thing that happened there was I wasn't giving my kids my time. But they knew where I was. They could come and check.' But the thing was, the computer was limited, so when she and Trev got to it they went hell for leather. 'This is a once in a lifetime chance to have these conditions.' Anyway, she had asked Jodene to come home. 'But she's not coming home.' So as soon as the script was finished, in two days' time, Trish was going to spend a couple of nights a week over at her pod, helping her with *her* book on Taransay fairies. And as for Michael, Dez and he were fantastic together. 'Michael's the only one who'll play football with Dez,' Trish laughed, in her attractive inclusive way.

Issue Three, being about the project as a whole, was out in the open. Increasingly, it seemed, many members of the community felt like 'sitting ducks' in 'a TV La La Land', 'a giant media game' over which they felt they had little control. Everyone who had left the island – bar Hilary – had now sold their story, and for substantial amounts. £30,000, it was rumoured, for Ron; £10, 000 for Ray; £8000 for the Careys. Ron had now sold his story again – twice. They didn't want to be mercenary about it, the whole idea of the project had been to get away from such considerations, but if this is what it had become, why shouldn't they benefit, too? Why should they meekly accept the £2500 end of project fee for behaving themselves, when they could just walk off the island and make enough to put down a deposit on a house?

The key protest seemed to be that they had no right of reply. There was Ron, slagging them off as 'vacuous' and 'disgusting', as 'neurotics' and 'nasties', and betraying confidences made in private before the project even started, and what was their redress? The only thing they felt they could do was withdraw their co-operation, which is what Liz and Julie Lowe were going to do the following week, when the press arrived again, to do interviews for 'long-lead' magazine titles.

They were sitting ducks in another way, too, recipients of letters they could well do without. Roger and Rosemary were still getting random hate mail, and since the recent bunch of programmes, the community had also been getting communications of the kind that get passed on to the police. It got worse, with death threats against both adults and (appallingly) children. The tawdry scrap of A4 was passed around in the steading with nervous laughter, but there was no doubting the concern, as mothers discussed the possibility of such a sick fantasy being made real. Would there be a boatman to take such a character? Could they get across the strait at night? And I, too, as I followed my wavering torch beam back to bed across the new-moon darkness of the steading field, found myself scanning the black outline of the dunes beyond the snoring cows. Out here, it wasn't a TV programme, it was wind and rain and isolation, it was flesh and blood.

A Great Experience

But in the morning the sun rose through spectacular swathes of pink and orange into a clear blue sky. It was, it turned out, the last perfect day of summer. Mike was soon out in his wetsuit, Ben and Toby off to the raft, Dez to play with his newly launched boat. Tammy was posing on her pod steps for photos for *Marie Claire*, taken by castaway photographer Philiy. Julie was in the steading kitchen getting an impromptu supper ready for the ceilidh she'd organised for that evening.

The bad news, I reflected, as I sat under the maypole having a coffee in the sunshine, was what the castaways had always talked about first. But once the fears and grumbles were out of the way, my instincts on arrival had been right; there was plenty of unsensational good news, too. After Roger's end-of-August bust-up with Shahana, the budget issue had finally been sorted. A group of women – Rosemary, Monica, Sandy and Julia – had taken over, and actually sat down and worked out what the castaways needed and could now afford. By placing one big order they had removed the crippling haulage costs of earlier in the year. Now, with their field, polytunnels, animals and a few extra dry goods that would be arriving shortly, they were self-sufficient till the New Year. Indeed, they had a vegetable surplus, and the pile of veggies that I could see being sorted and stacked in the kitchen was to sell at a market stall in Stornoway over the weekend (fetching £190, it transpired).

And it wasn't just Julie and Ben who had found happiness on this island they now all called 'home'. 'You'd be hard pushed to find anyone here who say they regret coming,' Warren had told me – high praise from this most critical of Castaways. 'Not quite what I expected,' his partner Monica agreed. 'But a great experience. I love people-watching.' 'I hear everyone saying,' said Toby, 'that if they could do the year again they would.' 'It's human nature not to dwell on the good things,' Liz pointed out. 'We're not bitching all the time, we do have a lot of fun and laughter as well.' 'There's a good sense of camaraderie round here,' added Padraig, 'which was one of the things I'd been hoping for.' As for the kids: everyone agreed they had had a whale of a time, able to play freely and safely, build dens, make toys out of old matchsticks, find exciting stuff washed up on the beaches. 'Like rope,' said Wee Mike. It somehow seemed no surprise that the book he was now on was – no, not *Angela's Ashes* – but Enid Blyton's *Secret Seven*. For a year, the youngsters had returned to the joys of an old-fashioned childhood.

The projects the adults had come with, too, had by and large paid off. Rosemary judged the Home Education experiment 'a great success'; so much so that they were going to take Oliver and Felix out of school next year. Philiy Page's photography had gone from strength to strength. With her pictures of Castaways published – she grinned under her nose-rings – now in all the national newspapers, plus a swathe of magazines, she had a portfolio the hardest-networking recent graduate in London would envy. Sheila had painted and drawn more than she had since she'd been a student at the Slade, images that were now to be a part of this book. Trevor had, with a bit of professional help from Lion, finished a screenplay – *On The Pull* – that he was proud of and thought had a good chance.

And though Padraig hadn't, as it happened, found time for his serious writing and Sandy was only now finally getting round to her christening gown, many others had been surprised by the new things they'd learned. Dez could tile; Ben could knit; Tammy Huff *had* learned to juggle. Action Man Mike had enjoyed being more involved with children than he'd ever been, and had started painting (rather well) in watercolour, while butcher Colin had rediscovered an old talent for oils. Little Ciara had been taught piano by the doctor, while Liz had loved discovering about growing and Alternative Technology. The management consultant had found the time to complete an Open University course in the latter subject and had now become, she laughed, 'a bit of a greenie.'

There were plenty of lessons of a deeper kind, too. 'I've had the time and space to develop self-awareness,' Tanya told me; the profound experience of her year had made her more decisive, more uncompromising about getting what she wanted out of her life. Trevor had, by his own admission, changed from a Jack-the-Lad loner 'to a lot more respecting women'. Anyone in particular? 'Just Trish.' While the care assistant herself had got her eating under control, was a lot calmer inside and knew what direction she was going in now. 'My confidence is up tenfold.' Peter was slower to express opinions than he had been, had learnt, he said, to hold off till he could see the more complex picture. Tammy Huff was definitely coming off the island a different person – 'a lot stronger', while Ben was going to go back, 'I hope, even more tolerant.' As for the psychological assault course earlier in the year. 'That's gone into my little book of life. Now I know people like that exist, my way of dealing with it has been honed, if you like.' For Pat and Gwyn, something they already knew had been confirmed. 'The simple things in life are the best. You can get by on so little. It's all such a race to do with money and possessions back there – but if you're happy in life, that's what matters.' Julia Corrigan agreed. Back home she'd felt out of control of her life. Every day had been a mad dash just to get things done. On Taransay she'd had the chance to be contemplative, wander on beaches, feed chickens, pat cows.' Husband Colin too had been liberated from the tyranny of the clock. 'Time means nothing here. At home, our lives are regimented by time.'

They had all been changed, they reckoned; few were planning to go back to their old lives. Julia and Colin were going to travel for a year, then look for a community to join; Dez and Liz were planning to leave the city and set up a smallholding; Tammy was leaving home; Pat and Gwyn were moving to Harris; Julie Lowe was never going to live with people again.

At teatime I followed Roger, Rosemary, their kids and psychologist Cynth up to the Dun Loch, arriving, sadly, just as they were leaving, but not too late for a freezing sunset swim. A week later a letter arrived from Roger, describing the scene I'd missed: 'There was an awesome sense of finality with our "last day of summer" while you were here. Our trip to Oliver's raft held inescapable pangs of nostalgia. It was as calm and sunny as those balmy days in July and August, but this time the sun was low, casting completely new shadows across the loch. I pottered out to the buoy, way out in the middle, which marked our anchor point and had held so much potential as a distant oasis of peace, and realised that it had never quite lived up to that potential. It was Oliver's dream to drift out there, tie up and just sit, or fish, or forget the world. But whenever he got near, the distance from shore, and the increasing depth of water beneath, raised anxieties which he hadn't expected. An allegory for *Castaway 2000*?'

Whether it was or not, you had to look on the bright side: even the reluctant doctor was at last happy on Taransay.

He had a second bit of news, too. 'Have you guessed? Rosemary's pregnant. We're very excited by another little life, another great adventure beginning.'

The steading